Central
Statistical
Office

"Our mission is to improve
stimulate research and infor
government and the wider
providing a quality statistica

Regional Trends 30

1995 edition
30th year of Regional Statistics

Editor: JENNY CHURCH

Associate Editor: ALISON HOLDING

Production team: JANE DARNBROUGH
MAX BONINI
ANDY LEACH
JAN KIERNAN
DAVE BARAN
KRYSIA MACDONALD
CARLTON BROWN
CERI DAVIES
STEVE WHYMAN

London: HMSO

Introduction

This latest edition of *Regional Trends* updates and expands the unique description of the regions of the United Kingdom. In 15 chapters it covers a wide range of demographic, social, industrial and economic statistics, taking a look at most aspects of life. To make it easy to understand the differences between regions, information is given in simple and clear tables, maps and charts.

Regional Trends provides essential statistics for a wide range of people: for example, policy-makers and planners in both the public and private sectors; marketing professionals; market researchers; students; and anyone with general regional interests. The book brings together data from diverse sources and, for many topics, is the only place where data for the whole of the United Kingdom are available in one table.

How to use *Regional Trends*

The contents of *Regional Trends* falls broadly into five sections.

Regional Profiles: these are contained in Chapter 1. For each of the 11 standard regions of the United Kingdom there is a double page spread *Profile* in which major regional trends are highlighted with simple text and a few key charts comparing the region to the United Kingdom as a whole.

European Community: Chapter 2 is devoted to regional statistics for the whole of the *European Community*. Each member country is divided into regions which are approximately the same size as the 11 planning regions of the United Kingdom according to a European Commission Nomenclature described as NUTS I.

Topic areas: the third section comprises Chapters 3 to 13. Each chapter takes a *social or economic topic area* such as labour market, housing and transport and presents data, mainly in table form, which allows the 11 regions of the United Kingdom to be compared.

Counties: Sub-regions, that is *counties* for England and Wales and similar geographical areas for Scotland and Northern Ireland, are compared in Chapter 14.

Districts: Chapter 15 contains information on all *districts* within the United Kingdom, of which there are about 500. This is the lowest level of disaggregation in the book.

Coverage and definitions

It is not always possible to give data for more than one year in any table or chart. However, many items are published each year, and trends can be analysed by referring to earlier editions. Due to variations in coverage and definitions, some care may be needed when comparing data from more than one source. Readers should consult the

Appendix as well as reading the footnotes relevant to each table and chart for help in analysing trends or comparing different sources.

Regional boundaries

Standard regions are used as far as is possible throughout the book. Although data for Greater London are given wherever possible, it is not a standard region in its own right, but part of the South East region. Definitions of both the standard and non-standard regions along with explanatory notes are given in the Appendix. Maps of standard regions and counties are given in Chapters 1 and 14. The United Kingdom comprises Great Britain and Northern Ireland; Great Britain consists of England, Wales and Scotland. The Isle of Man and the Channel Isles are not part of the United Kingdom. The Scilly Isles are included as part of Cornwall throughout except Chapter 15 where they are shown separately.

Sources

The source of the data is given at the foot of each table and chart. Much of the information included in the Population and Households and the Labour market Chapters of *Regional Trends* can be found on the National Online Manpower Information System (NOMIS) which is an online database run by Durham University under contract to the Employment Department. It contains government statistics down to the smallest available geographic area which may be unpublished elsewhere. The Central Statistical Office publication *Social Trends (HMSO)* contains further details on many of the topics covered in this book, generally at national level only.

Availability on diskette

The data contained in the tables, maps and charts in *Regional Trends 30* are available on diskette, price £25.00. An order form is enclosed.

Contributors

The Editor and Associate Editor wish to thank all their colleagues in the Government Statistical Service and contributors in other organisations without whose help this publication would not be possible. Thanks also go to the CSO Graphic Design Unit.

Regional Statistics Section
Central Statistical Office
PO Box 1333
Millbank Tower
Millbank
London
SW1P 4QQ   *Telephone number for enquiries: 0171 217 4238/4372*

Contents

Living standards 8

Crime and Justice 9

10 Transport

11 Environment

12 Regional accounts

13 Industry and Agriculture

14 Sub-regional

15 Districts

1 Regional profiles

Standard regions of the United Kingdom

North

Population density (persons per sq. km.)

- 1,000 or over
- 600 – 999
- 300 – 599
- 150 – 299
- Under 149

Former Metropolitan counties

Northumberland

Tyne & Wear

Durham

Cleveland

Cumbria

Population
Population density varies widely in the North: Northumberland and Cumbria are the two most sparsely populated counties in England, while Tyne and Wear is one of the most densely populated.

(Table 15.1)

Education
In 1992/93, the North had one of the lowest proportions of pupils who achieved GCSE grades A-C in all core subjects in their last year of compulsory schooling, but the highest participation rate of three and four year olds in education.

(Tables 4.4 and 4.8)

Labour market
In Spring 1994, around one in 75 employees in the North had been made redundant in the previous three months, a higher proportion than in any other region of Great Britain.

(Table 5.19)

The North had the second highest claimant unemployment rate of any region in 1994, at 11.3 per cent.

(Table 5.21)

Housing
More than a quarter of dwellings in the North are occupied by council tenants, the highest proportion of all the regions in England and Wales.

(Table 6.2)

Health
Men in the North have given up smoking cigarettes at a much faster rate than women, so that a higher proportion of women than men now smoke them.

(Table 7.13)

Living standards
One in six households in the North had a weekly income of less than £80 in 1993, a higher proportion than in any other region.

(Table 8.2)

Households in the North are most likely to have central heating, but least likely to own a dishwasher.

(Table 8.14)

Crime and Justice
Recorded crime in the North fell by 5 per cent between 1992 and 1993.

(Table 9.1)

Transport
Households in the North, together with those in Scotland, are least likely to own a car.

(Table 10.2)

Industry
The North had the second highest level of gross value added per employee in manufacturing in 1992, after the South East.

(Table 13.4)

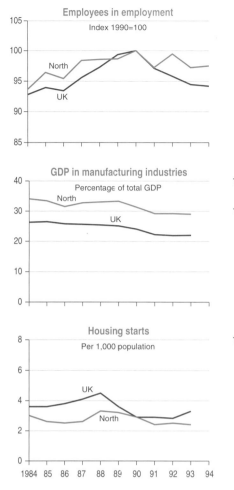

Employees in employment
Index 1990=100

Average claimant unemployment rate
Percentages

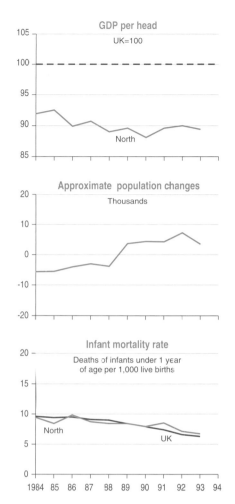

GDP per head
UK=100

GDP in manufacturing industries
Percentage of total GDP
North
UK

Average gross weekly earnings (full-time)
GB=100
(for males and females separately)
Females
Males

Approximate population changes
Thousands

Housing starts
Per 1,000 population
UK
North

Average dwelling price
Mid year, UK=100
North

Infant mortality rate
Deaths of infants under 1 year
of age per 1,000 live births
North
UK

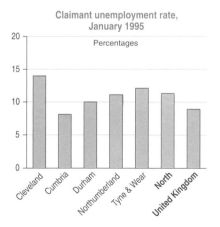

Claimant unemployment rate,
January 1995
Percentages

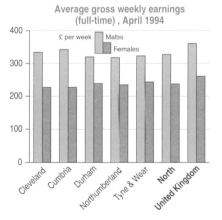

Average gross weekly earnings
(full-time) , April 1994
£ per week   Males
              Females

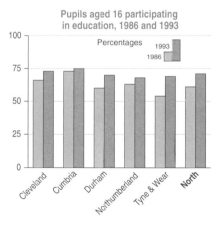

Pupils aged 16 participating
in education, 1986 and 1993
Percentages   1993
               1986

Yorkshire & Humberside

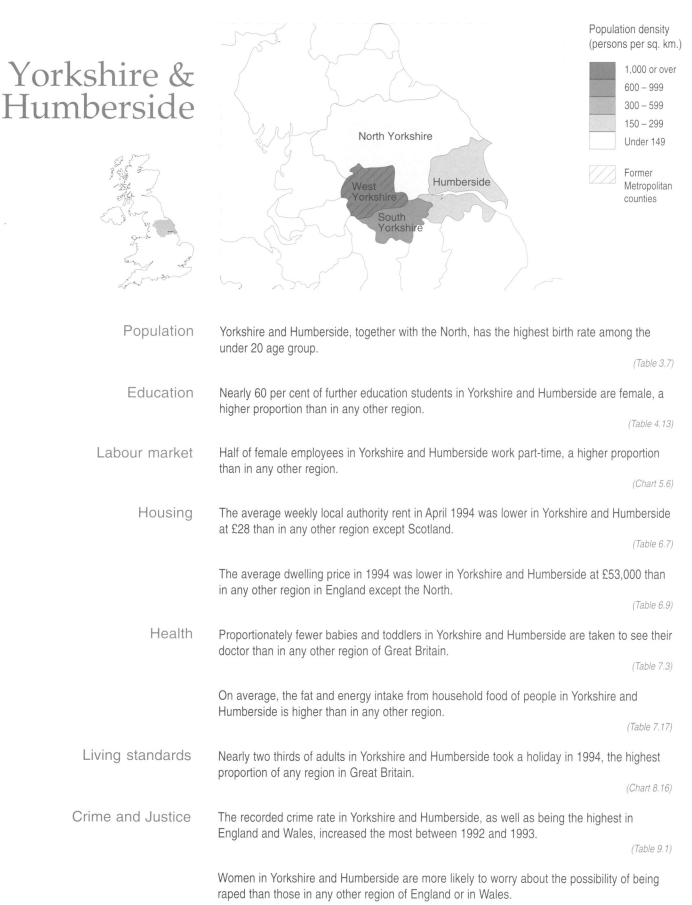

Population density
(persons per sq. km.)

	1,000 or over
	600 – 999
	300 – 599
	150 – 299
	Under 149
	Former Metropolitan counties

North Yorkshire

West Yorkshire

Humberside

South Yorkshire

Population

Yorkshire and Humberside, together with the North, has the highest birth rate among the under 20 age group.

(Table 3.7)

Education

Nearly 60 per cent of further education students in Yorkshire and Humberside are female, a higher proportion than in any other region.

(Table 4.13)

Labour market

Half of female employees in Yorkshire and Humberside work part-time, a higher proportion than in any other region.

(Chart 5.6)

Housing

The average weekly local authority rent in April 1994 was lower in Yorkshire and Humberside at £28 than in any other region except Scotland.

(Table 6.7)

The average dwelling price in 1994 was lower in Yorkshire and Humberside at £53,000 than in any other region in England except the North.

(Table 6.9)

Health

Proportionately fewer babies and toddlers in Yorkshire and Humberside are taken to see their doctor than in any other region of Great Britain.

(Table 7.3)

On average, the fat and energy intake from household food of people in Yorkshire and Humberside is higher than in any other region.

(Table 7.17)

Living standards

Nearly two thirds of adults in Yorkshire and Humberside took a holiday in 1994, the highest proportion of any region in Great Britain.

(Chart 8.16)

Crime and Justice

The recorded crime rate in Yorkshire and Humberside, as well as being the highest in England and Wales, increased the most between 1992 and 1993.

(Table 9.1)

Women in Yorkshire and Humberside are more likely to worry about the possibility of being raped than those in any other region of England or in Wales.

(Table 9.15)

Industry

Output of coal in the Selby area in 1992-93 was almost 11 tonnes per manshift, almost twice the amount of any other production area.

(Table 13.13)

Employees in employment

Index 1990=100

UK

Yorkshire & Humberside

Average claimant unemployment rate

Percentages

Yorkshire & Humberside

UK

GDP per head

UK=100

Yorkshire & Humberside

GDP in manufacturing industries

Percentage of total GDP

Yorkshire & Humberside

UK

Average gross weekly earnings (full-time)

GB=100
(for males and females separately)

Males

Females

Approximate population changes

Thousands

Housing starts

Per 1,000 population

UK

Yorkshire & Humberside

Average dwelling price

Mid year, UK=100

Yorkshire & Humberside

Infant mortality rate

Deaths of infants under 1 year
of age per 1,000 live births

Yorkshire & Humberside

UK

1984 85 86 87 88 89 90 91 92 93 94

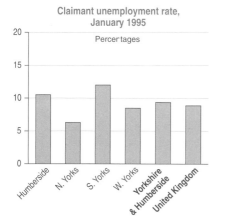

Claimant unemployment rate, January 1995

Percentages

Humberside · N. Yorks · S. Yorks · W. Yorks · **Yorkshire & Humberside** · **United Kingdom**

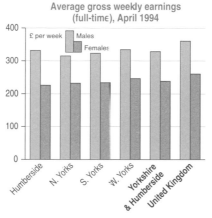

Average gross weekly earnings (full-time), April 1994

£ per week — Males / Females

Humberside · N. Yorks · S. Yorks · W. Yorks · **Yorkshire & Humberside** · **United Kingdom**

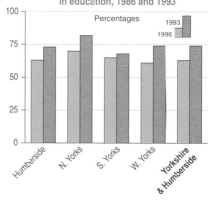

Pupils aged 16 participating in education, 1986 and 1993

Percentages

1993 / 1986

Humberside · N. Yorks · S. Yorks · W. Yorks · **Yorkshire & Humberside**

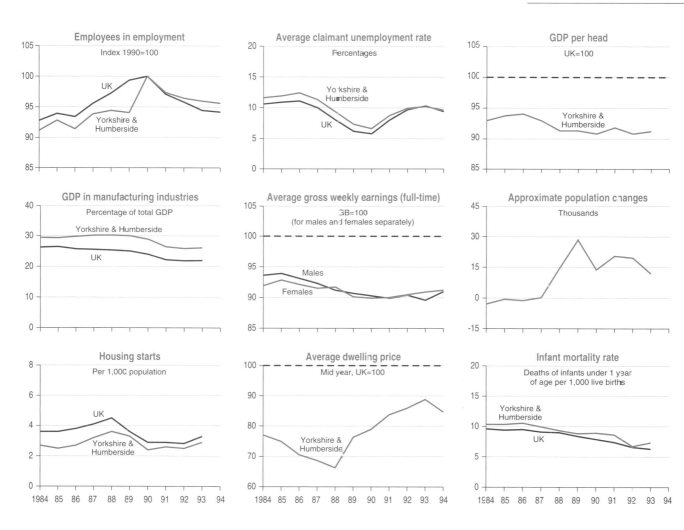

East Midlands

Population density
(persons per sq. km.)

1,000 or over
600 – 999
300 – 599
150 – 299
Under 149

Derbyshire
Lincolnshire
Nottinghamshire
Leicestershire
Northamptonshire

Population

The East Midlands, together with Northern Ireland, has the third fastest growing population, after East Anglia and the South West.

(Table 3.1)

One person in every 20 in the East Midlands belongs to an ethnic minority group; the proportion is only higher in the South East and the West Midlands.

(Table 3.14)

Education

The average size of secondary classes is smaller in the East Midlands than in any other English region.

(Table 4.2)

Labour market

On average, women in the East Midlands work the longest hours for the lowest pay.

(Table 5.14)

The East Midlands had the lowest recorded incidence rate for working days lost due to labour disputes in Spring 1994 at five days lost per 1,000 employees.

(Table 5.17)

Housing

Seven out of ten dwellings in the East Midlands are owner-occupied; only the South West and Wales have higher proportions.

(Table 6.2)

Health

About a quarter of adults in the East Midlands smoked cigarettes in 1992, the lowest proportion of all the regions.

(Table 7.13)

Living standards

Households in the East Midlands are more likely to own a tumble drier and (together with those in the North) a washing machine than those in any other region.

(Table 8.14)

Crime and Justice

The East Midlands had the highest recorded crime rate of violence against the person of all the regions in England and in Wales in 1993.

(Table 9.1)

Drink-driving offences in the East Midlands were more likely than in other regions to attract a prison sentence in 1993, but the average length of sentence was the shortest.

(Table 9.12)

Industry

Manufacturing accounted for a higher proportion of gross domestic product in the East Midlands in 1993 than in any other region.

(Table 12.3)

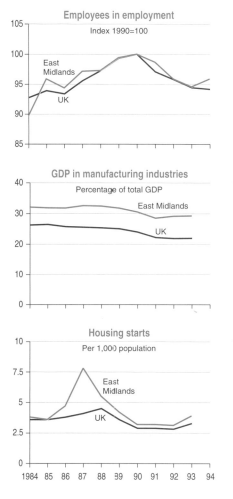

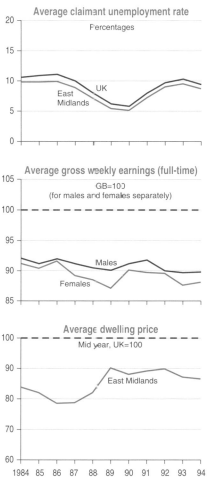

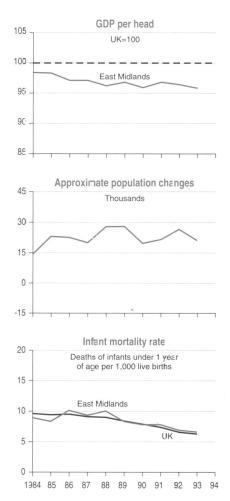

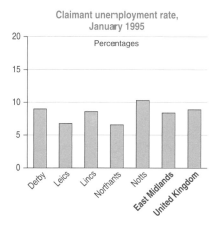

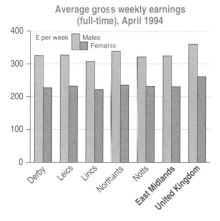

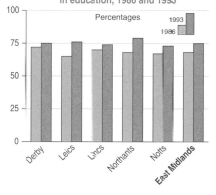

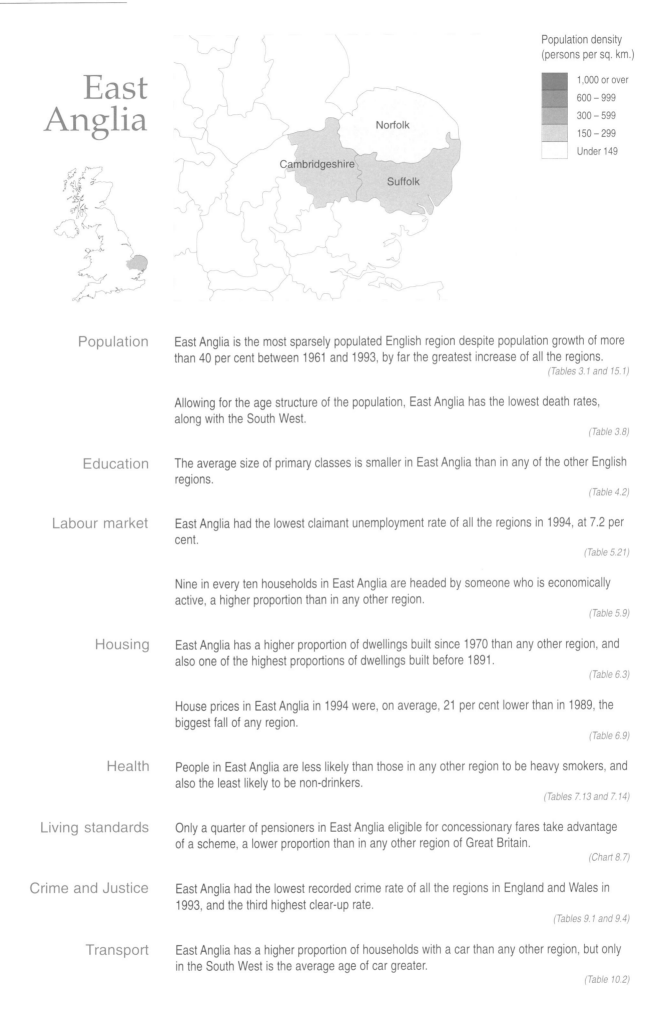

East Anglia

Population density
(persons per sq. km.)

1,000 or over
600 – 999
300 – 599
150 – 299
Under 149

Norfolk

Cambridgeshire

Suffolk

Population

East Anglia is the most sparsely populated English region despite population growth of more than 40 per cent between 1961 and 1993, by far the greatest increase of all the regions.

(Tables 3.1 and 15.1)

Allowing for the age structure of the population, East Anglia has the lowest death rates, along with the South West.

(Table 3.8)

Education

The average size of primary classes is smaller in East Anglia than in any of the other English regions.

(Table 4.2)

Labour market

East Anglia had the lowest claimant unemployment rate of all the regions in 1994, at 7.2 per cent.

(Table 5.21)

Nine in every ten households in East Anglia are headed by someone who is economically active, a higher proportion than in any other region.

(Table 5.9)

Housing

East Anglia has a higher proportion of dwellings built since 1970 than any other region, and also one of the highest proportions of dwellings built before 1891.

(Table 6.3)

House prices in East Anglia in 1994 were, on average, 21 per cent lower than in 1989, the biggest fall of any region.

(Table 6.9)

Health

People in East Anglia are less likely than those in any other region to be heavy smokers, and also the least likely to be non-drinkers.

(Tables 7.13 and 7.14)

Living standards

Only a quarter of pensioners in East Anglia eligible for concessionary fares take advantage of a scheme, a lower proportion than in any other region of Great Britain.

(Chart 8.7)

Crime and Justice

East Anglia had the lowest recorded crime rate of all the regions in England and Wales in 1993, and the third highest clear-up rate.

(Tables 9.1 and 9.4)

Transport

East Anglia has a higher proportion of households with a car than any other region, but only in the South West is the average age of car greater.

(Table 10.2)

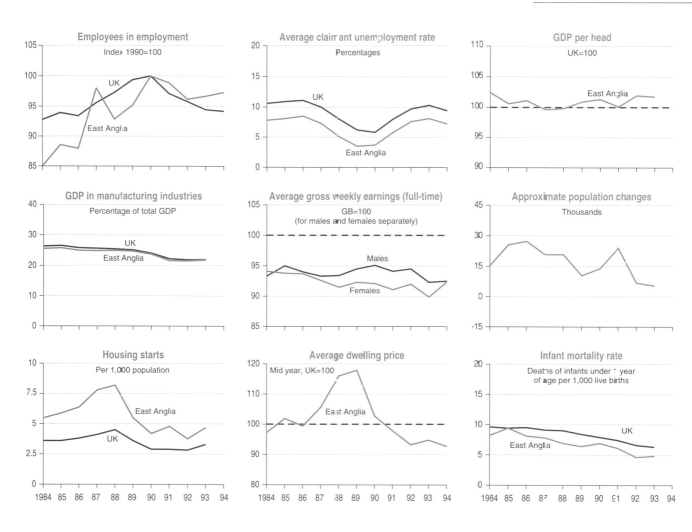

Employees in employment
Index 1990=100

UK

East Anglia

Average claimant unemployment rate
Percentages

UK

East Anglia

GDP per head
UK=100

East Anglia

GDP in manufacturing industries
Percentage of total GDP

UK

East Anglia

Average gross weekly earnings (full-time)
GB=100
(for males and females separately)

Males

Females

Approximate population changes
Thousands

Housing starts
Per 1,000 population

East Anglia

UK

Average dwelling price
Mid year, UK=100

East Anglia

Infant mortality rate
Deaths of infants under 1 year
of age per 1,000 live births

UK

East Anglia

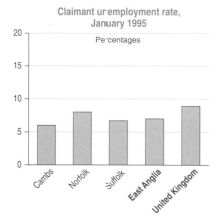

Claimant unemployment rate, January 1995
Percentages

Cambs · Norfolk · Suffolk · **East Anglia** · **United Kingdom**

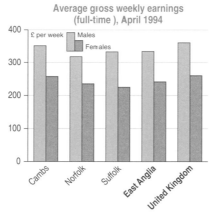

Average gross weekly earnings (full-time), April 1994
£ per week · Males · Females

Cambs · Norfolk · Suffolk · **East Anglia** · **United Kingdom**

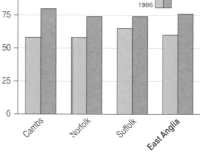

Pupils aged 16 participating in education, 1986 and 1993
Percentages · 1993 · 1986

Cambs · Norfolk · Suffolk · **East Anglia**

South East

Population density
(persons per sq. km.)

1,000 or over

600 – 999

300 – 599

150 – 299

Under 149

Former
Metropolitan
counties

Bedfordshire

Bucks   Herts   Essex

Oxfordshire

Greater
London

Berkshire

Surrey   Kent

Hampshire

West
Sussex   East
Sussex

Isle of Wight

Population

One in ten people in the South East belongs to an ethnic minority group, the largest proportion of all the regions in Great Britain; this rises to more than one in five in Greater London.

(Table 3.14)

Education

Over half the 18 year olds in the South East outside of Greater London achieved two or more 'A' level passes in schools in 1992/93, compared with less than a fifth in Greater London.

(Table 4.7)

Labour market

Over a sixth of employees in the South East work in the financial services sector, the greatest proportion of any region.

(Table 5.5)

The South East has the highest economic activity rates of all the regions.

(Table 5.8)

Greater London had a claimant unemployment rate of 10.7 per cent in 1994, compared with 7.8 per cent in the rest of the South East.

(Table 5.21)

Housing

Fewer than three in five dwellings in Greater London are owner-occupied, compared with nearly three in four in the rest of the South East.

(Table 6.2)

Health

The proportion of non-drinkers in Greater London is about double that in the rest of the South East, and significantly higher than in any other region in Great Britain.

(Table 7.14)

Living standards

One in five households in the South East had a gross weekly income of £650 or more in 1993.

(Table 8.2)

Although households in the South East are most likely to own a deep freezer, a compact disc player, a video and a home computer, they are least likely to own a washing machine.

(Table 8.14)

Crime and Justice

Greater London's recorded crime rate is 40 per cent higher than in the rest of the South East, but it fell by 4 per cent between 1992 and 1993, double the fall in the rest of the region.

(Table 9.1)

Environment

Nearly a quarter of the land in the South East is designated as an Area of Outstanding Natural Beauty.

(Chart 11.10)

Employees in employment

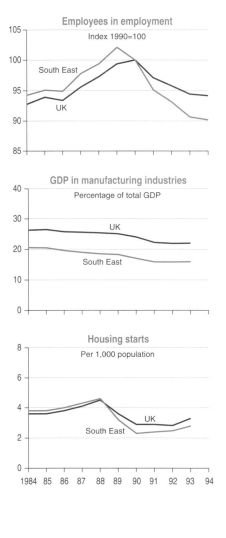

Index 1990=100

South East

UK

Average claimant unemployment rate

Percentages

UK

South East

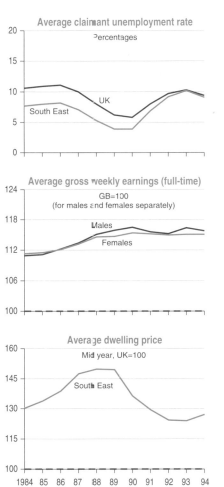

GDP per head

UK=100

South East

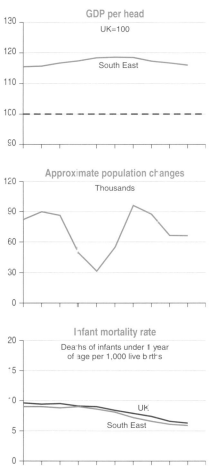

GDP in manufacturing industries

Percentage of total GDP

UK

South East

Average gross weekly earnings (full-time)

GB=100
(for males and females separately)

Males

Females

Approximate population changes

Thousands

Housing starts

Per 1,000 population

UK

South East

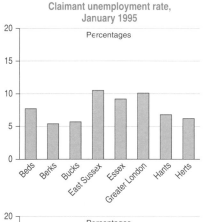

Average dwelling price

Mid year, UK=100

South East

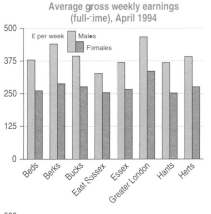

Infant mortality rate

Deaths of infants under 1 year
of age per 1,000 live births

UK

South East

Claimant unemployment rate, January 1995

Percentages

Beds | Berks | Bucks | East Sussex | Essex | Greater London | Hants | Herts

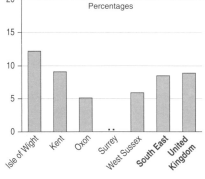

Percentages

Isle of Wight | Kent | Oxon | Surrey | .. | West Sussex | **South East** | **United Kingdom**

Average gross weekly earnings (full-time), April 1994

£ per week | Males | Females

Beds | Berks | Bucks | East Sussex | Essex | Greater London | Hants | Herts

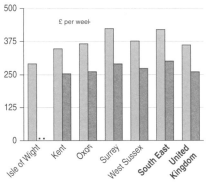

£ per week

Isle of Wight | .. | Kent | Oxon | Surrey | West Sussex | **South East** | **United Kingdom**

Pupils aged 16 participating in education, 1986 and 1993

Percentages | 1993 | 1986

Beds | Berks | Bucks | East Sussex | Essex | Greater London | Hants | Herts

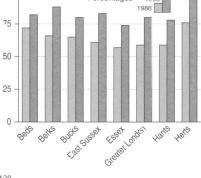

Percentages

Isle of Wight | Kent | Oxon | Surrey | West Sussex | **South East** | **United Kingdom**

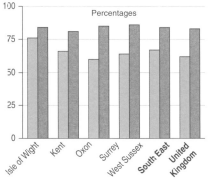

South West

Population density
(persons per sq. km.)

1,000 or over
600 – 999
300 – 599
150 – 299
Under 149

Gloucestershire

Avon

Wiltshire

Somerset

Devon

Dorset

Cornwall

Population

The South West has the oldest population: more than one person in every five is a pensioner, with one in 20 aged 80 or over.

(Table 3.3)

Education

In 1992/93, the South West had the highest proportion of pupils in England and Wales who achieved at least one graded exam result in their last year of compulsory schooling.

(Table 4.7)

Labour market

The South West had the lowest claimant unemployment rate after East Anglia in 1994, at 8.3 per cent, and also had the largest fall in claimant unemployment of all the regions.

(Table 5.21)

Housing

The South West, together with Wales, has the highest proportion of dwellings which are owner-occupied of all the regions.

(Table 6.2)

On average, rents are higher in the South West than in any other region except the South East.

(Table 6.7)

Health

Proportionately fewer elderly people in the South West have a limiting long-standing illness than in any other region.

(Table 7.3)

Living standards

Households in the South West are more likely to have gilts or unit trusts, or stocks and shares, than those elsewhere in Great Britain.

(Table 8.3)

Crime and Justice

Although the South West has one of the lowest recorded crime rates for robbery, it increased the most between 1992 and 1993.

(Table 9.1)

Police forces in the South West are more likely than those in any other region of England or in Wales to give a formal oral caution for an indictable offence.

(Table 9.7)

Transport

Although households in the South West are more likely than those elsewhere except for East Anglia to own a car, on average their cars are oldest.

(Table 10.2)

Environment

The South Western region accounts for nearly two fifths of the bathing waters around the United Kingdom and has one of the best records for the cleanness of them.

(Table 11.4)

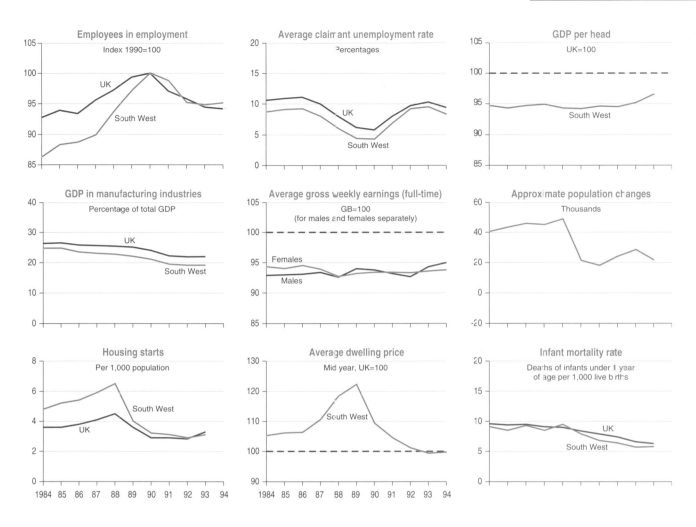

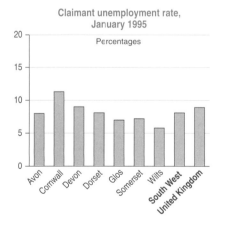
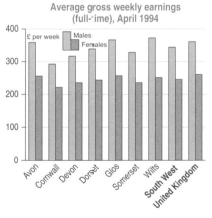
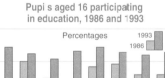
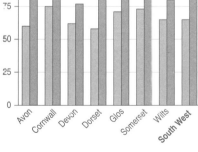

West Midlands

Population density
(persons per sq. km.)

1,000 or over

600 – 999

300 – 599

150 – 299

Under 149

Former
Metropolitan
counties

Staffordshire

Shropshire

West
Midlands

Warwickshire

Hereford &
Worcester

Population

The West Midlands Metropolitan County is the second most densely populated county, after Greater London, with nearly 3,000 people per square kilometre.

(Table 15.1)

One in 12 people in the West Midlands belongs to an ethnic minority group, a proportion second only to the South East.

(Table 3.14)

Education

The average size of secondary classes is bigger in the West Midlands, together with the North, than in any other region of Great Britain.

(Table 4.2)

Labour market

Together with the South East, the West Midlands saw the second largest fall in claimant unemployment in 1994 of all the regions.

(Table 5.21)

Almost a quarter of the labour force of the West Midlands are employed in manufacturing, a higher proportion than in any other region.

(Table 5.1)

Housing

On average, dwellings in the West Midlands, together with those in the North West, are smaller than those in the other regions of England.

(Table 6.4)

Health

Proportionately more elderly people in the West Midlands, together with those in Scotland, visit the doctor than in any other region.

(Table 7.3)

Of the regions of Great Britain, the West Midlands has one of the highest proportions of non-drinkers and one of the lowest proportions of people drinking more than the recommended sensible levels.

(Table 7.14)

Living standards

Average gross weekly household income was lower in the West Midlands in 1993, at £301, than in any other region except the North.

(Table 8.1)

Crime and Justice

The West Midlands has the highest proportions of women police officers and of officers from the ethnic minorities.

(Table 9.14)

Industry

The West Midlands had the lowest level per person employed of gross value added in manufacturing in 1992 of any of the English regions at £22,000.

(Table 13.4)

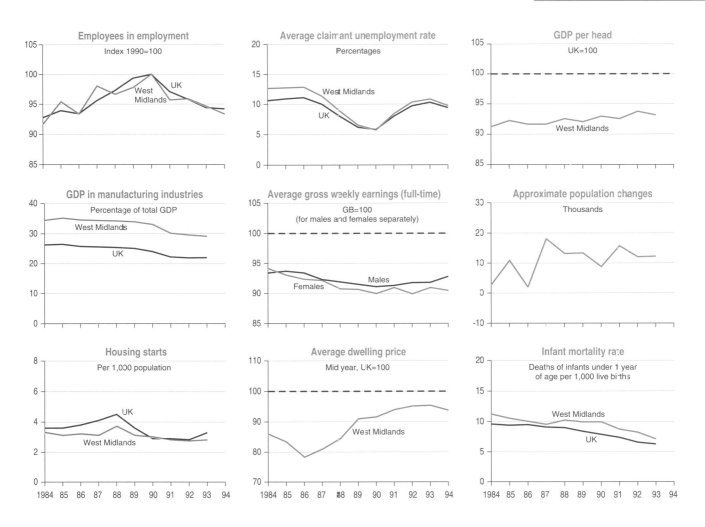

Employees in employment
Index 1990=100

Average claimant unemployment rate
Percentages

GDP per head
UK=100

GDP in manufacturing industries
Percentage of total GDP

Average gross weekly earnings (full-time)
GB=100
(for males and females separately)

Approximate population changes
Thousands

Housing starts
Per 1,000 population

Average dwelling price
Mid year, UK=100

Infant mortality rate
Deaths of infants under 1 year
of age per 1,000 live births

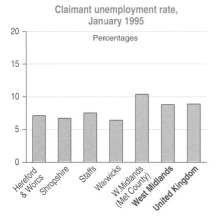

Claimant unemployment rate, January 1995
Percentages

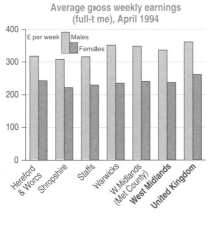

Average gross weekly earnings (full-time), April 1994
£ per week Males Females

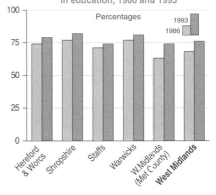

Pupils aged 16 participating in education, 1986 and 1993
Percentages
1993
1986

North West

Population density
(persons per sq. km.)

1,000 or over

600 – 999

300 – 599

150 – 299

Under 149

Former
Metropolitan
counties

Lancashire

Merseyside

Gtr
Manchester

Cheshire

Population

The population of the North West fell by an average of 0.1 per cent per year between 1981 and 1993.

(Table 3.1)

Nearly two in every five births in the North West are outside marriage, the highest proportion of any region.

(Table 3.15)

Education

The average size of primary classes is larger in the North West than in any other region of Great Britain.

(Table 4.2)

Labour market

Male average earnings in the North West in April 1994 were second only to those in the South East, at £ 344 per week.

(Table 5.13)

The North West has the highest proportion of young people among its unemployed, with nearly half of claimants in the region in January 1995 aged under 30.

(Table 5.24)

Housing

In April 1994, private sector fair rents were, on average, lower in the North West at £27 per week than in any other region of England or in Wales.

(Table 6.7)

Health

Nearly half the elderly people in the North West have a limiting long-standing illness, a higher proportion than in any other region.

(Table 7.3)

Living standards

Three quarters of pensioners in the North West take advantage of a concessionary fare scheme, a higher proportion than in any other region of Great Britain.

(Chart 8.7)

Crime and Justice

Recorded crime in the North West fell by 5 per cent between 1992 and 1993, and the region had the highest clear-up rate in England in 1993.

(Tables 9.1 and 9.4)

Environment

Overall, the North West has the poorest record for the cleanness of its bathing waters.

(Table 11.4)

Industry

The fall in the number of businesses registered for VAT during 1993 was proportionately higher in the North West than in any other region.

(Table 13.11)

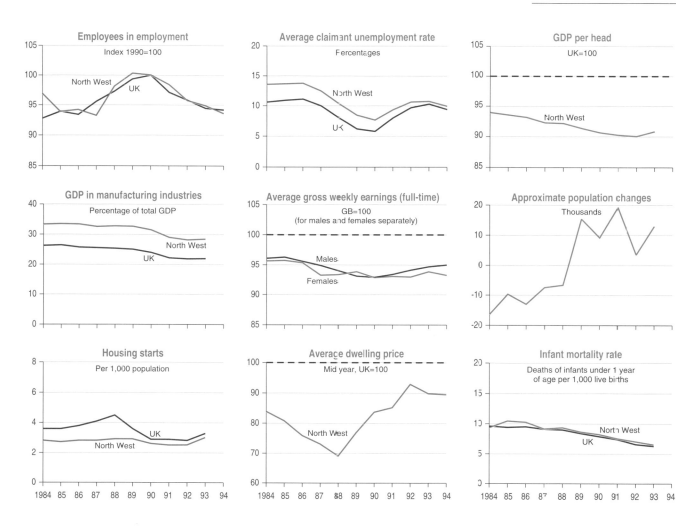

Employees in employment
Index 1990=100

North West
UK

Average claimant unemployment rate
Percentages

North West
UK

GDP per head
UK=100

North West

GDP in manufacturing industries
Percentage of total GDP

North West
UK

Average gross weekly earnings (full-time)
GB=100
(for males and females separately)

Males
Females

Approximate population changes
Thousands

Housing starts
Per 1,000 population

UK
North West

Average dwelling price
Mid year, UK=100

North West

Infant mortality rate
Deaths of infants under 1 year
of age per 1,000 live births

North West
UK

1984 85 86 87 88 89 90 91 92 93 94

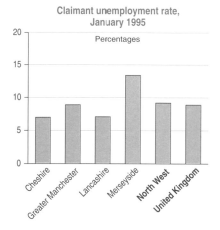

**Claimant unemployment rate,
January 1995**
Percentages

Cheshire
Greater Manchester
Lancashire
Merseyside
North West
United Kingdom

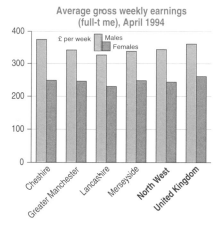

**Average gross weekly earnings
(full-time), April 1994**

£ per week   Males
             Females

Cheshire
Greater Manchester
Lancashire
Merseyside
North West
United Kingdom

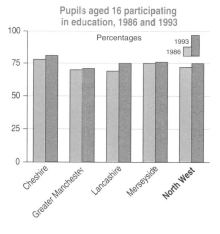

**Pupils aged 16 participating
in education, 1986 and 1993**
Percentages

1993
1986

Cheshire
Greater Manchester
Lancashire
Merseyside
North West

Wales

Population density
(persons per sq. km.)

▨	1,000 or over
▨	600 – 999
▨	300 – 599
▨	150 – 299
▢	Under 149

Clwyd

Gwynedd

Powys

Dyfed

Gwent

West Glamorgan
Mid Glamorgan
South Glamorgan

Population

Old age pensioners make up a fifth of the population in Wales, a proportion second only to the South West.

(Table 3.3)

Education

Wales has the highest percentage of three and four year olds in education apart from the North.

(Table 4.4)

Labour market

Wales is the only region where the proportion of males employees in manufacturing has not fallen since 1981.

(Table 5.5)

Average earnings for men in April 1994 were lower in Wales than in any other region except Northern Ireland.

(Table 5.13)

A higher proportion of employees in Wales than in any other region belong to a trade union.

(Table 5.26)

Housing

Wales, together with the South West, has the highest proportion of dwellings which are owner-occupied of all the regions.

(Table 6.2)

Housing associations are building more new homes in Wales per head of population than in any other region.

(Table 6.6)

Health

The infant mortality rate has declined more rapidly in Wales since 1981 than in any other region.

(Table 7.2)

Living standards

Proportionately fewer adults in Wales took a holiday in 1994 than in any other region of Great Britain.

(Chart 8.16)

Crime and Justice

Within England and Wales, police in Wales, together with those in the North West, had the highest clear-up rate for recorded crime in 1993; Dyfed-Powys police were the most successful of all the forces.

(Chart 9.3 and Table 9.4)

Industry

At £25,500, Wales had the third highest level of gross value added per employee in manufacturing in 1992, after the South East and the North.

(Table 13.4)

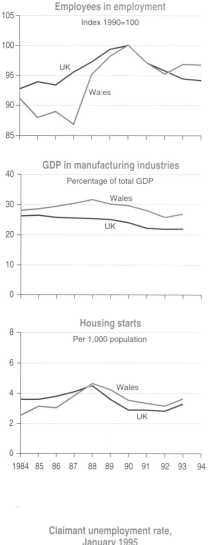

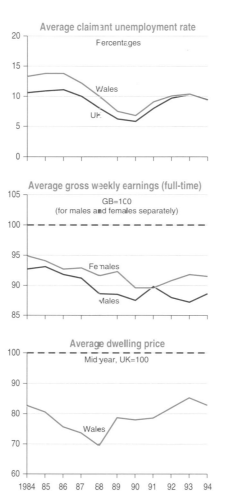

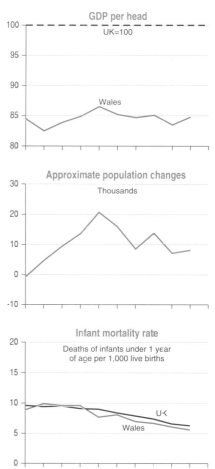

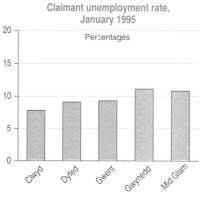

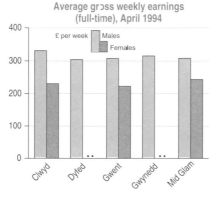

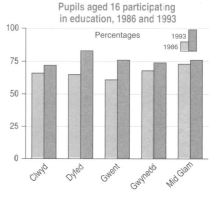

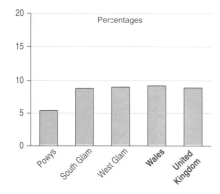

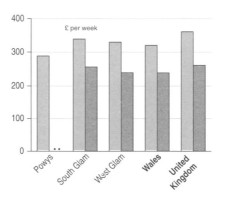

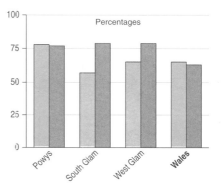

Scotland

Population

Scotland is the most sparsely populated region in the United Kingdom.

(Table 15.1)

Education

Nearly a quarter of boys and over a third of girls in their last year of compulsory schooling in 1992/93 achieved grades A-C in all core subjects of the National Curriculum in their SCE standard exams, a better record than in any region of England or in Wales.

(Table 4.8)

Labour market

Employees in Scotland have, on average, a more generous paid holiday entitlement than those in any other region.

(Table 5.12)

Housing

House prices rose by 31 per cent in Scotland between 1989 and 1994, the biggest rise of any region.

(Table 6.9)

Nearly 60 per cent of dwellings in Scotland have been built since the Second World War, the highest proportion after East Anglia and Northern Ireland.

(Table 6.3)

Health

Elderly people in Scotland (and also in the West Midlands) are more likely than those in any other region to consult a GP.

(Table 7.3)

Living standards

A greater proportion of household income in Scotland in 1993 came from wages and salaries, and a smaller proportion from self employment, than in any other region.

(Table 8.1)

Crime and Justice

Recorded crime in Scotland fell by 8 per cent between 1992 and 1993.

(Table 9.1)

Around 90 per cent of prison sentences for adults in Scotland are for one year or less.

(Table 9.13)

Transport

Although households in Scotland, together with those in the North, are the least likely to have a car, on average their cars are newer than elsewhere except in Northern Ireland.

(Table 10.2)

Regional Trends 30, © Crown copyright 1995

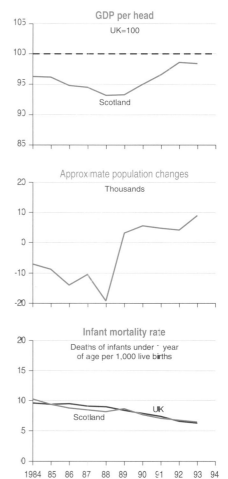

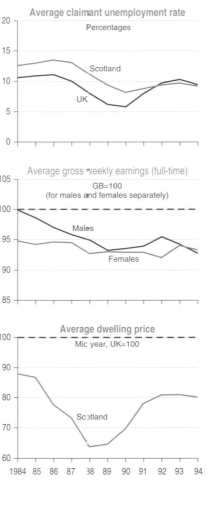

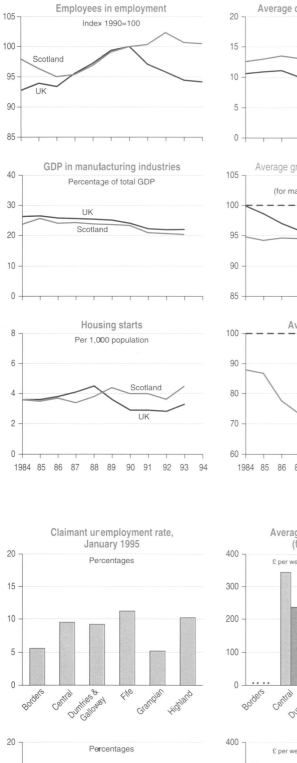

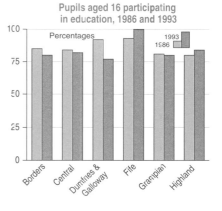

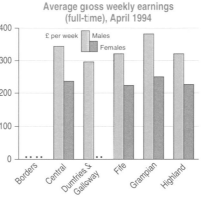

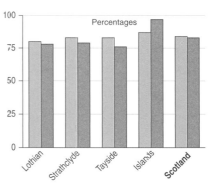

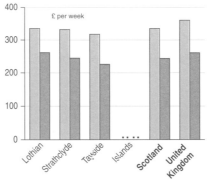

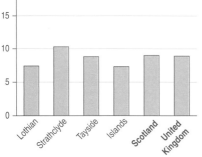

Northern Ireland

Population density
(persons per sq. km.)

1,000 or over
600 – 999
300 – 599
150 – 299
Under 149

North
Eastern

Belfast

Western

South
Eastern

Southern

Population

Northern Ireland has the youngest population, with proportionately more children and fewer pensioners than any other region.

(Table 3.3)

Education

Nearly a quarter of secondary schools in Northern Ireland have 400 pupils or fewer, while only just over a tenth have over 1,000 pupils, the highest and lowest proportions respectively.

(Table 4.3)

Labour market

Over half of female and almost a third of male employees in employment in Northern Ireland work in public administration and other services.

(Table 5.5)

Northern Ireland has the lowest proportion of employees working part-time of any region.

(Chart 5.6)

Male average earnings in April 1994 were lower in Northern Ireland than in any other region.

(Table 5.13)

Housing

The stock of dwellings in Northern Ireland rose by nearly 18 per cent between 1981 and 1993, the second fastest rate of increase of any region, after East Anglia.

(Table 6.1)

Health

One in six men in Northern Ireland is a heavy smoker, together with Scotland the highest proportion of all the regions.

(Table 7.13)

Living standards

A fifth of household income in Northern Ireland in 1993 came from social security benefits.

(Table 8.1)

Crime and Justice

Northern Ireland's known drug problem is very small compared with Great Britain's.

(Table 9.11)

Environment

Overall, Northern Ireland has the best record for the cleanness of its bathing waters.

(Table 11.4)

Agriculture

Small farms are, relatively, both more numerous and account for proportionately more output in Northern Ireland than is the case elsewhere in the United Kingdom.

(Table 13.17)

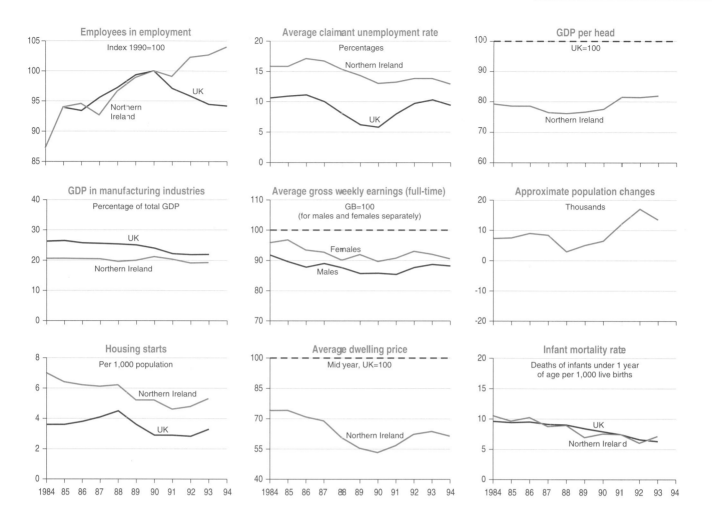

Employees in employment
Index 1990=100

UK

Northern Ireland

Average claimant unemployment rate
Percentages

Northern Ireland

UK

GDP per head
UK=100

Northern Ireland

GDP in manufacturing industries
Percentage of total GDP

UK

Northern Ireland

Average gross weekly earnings (full-time)
GB=100
(for males and females separately)

Females

Males

Approximate population changes
Thousands

Housing starts
Per 1,000 population

Northern Ireland

UK

Average dwelling price
Mid year, UK=100

Northern Ireland

Infant mortality rate
Deaths of infants under 1 year
of age per 1,000 live births

UK

Northern Ireland

1984 85 86 87 88 89 90 91 92 93 94

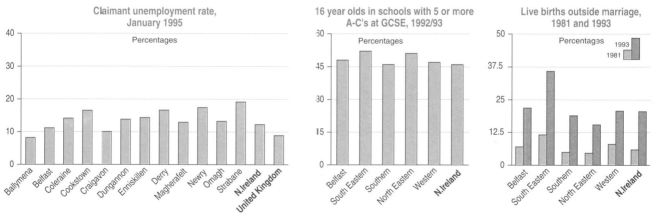

Claimant unemployment rate, January 1995
Percentages

Ballymena, Belfast, Coleraine, Cookstown, Craigavon, Dungannon, Enniskillen, Derry, Magherafelt, Newry, Omagh, Strabane, **N.Ireland**, **United Kingdom**

16 year olds in schools with 5 or more A-C's at GCSE, 1992/93
Percentages

Belfast, South Eastern, Southern, North Eastern, Western, **N.Ireland**

Live births outside marriage, 1981 and 1993
Percentages

1993
1981

Belfast, South Eastern, Southern, North Eastern, Western, **N.Ireland**

2 European Communities Regional Statistics

Population

Scotland is one of the largest regions in the EC with an area similar to the combined areas of the Benelux countries; it is also one of the most sparsely populated regions.

Excluding the city regions in Germany and Belgium, the North West with 872 persons per square kilometre is the third most densely populated region in the EC, after Attiki (Greece) and Ile de France.

The South West with 18.6 per cent has, along with the Nord-Ovest region of Italy, the third largest proportion of people aged 65 or over; only Emilia-Romagna and the Centro regions of Italy have larger proportions.

Births

Northern Ireland has the highest birth rate of any EC region with 15.9 births per thousand population in 1992, three times the rate in Brandenburg (Germany).

Deaths

At 12.0 deaths per thousand population in 1992, the North has one of the highest death rates in the EC; only five regions in Germany have higher rates.

East Anglia and Bremen (Germany) had the lowest infant mortality rates of all the EC regions in 1992 with 4.6 and 4.7 deaths of infants under the age of one per thousand live births respectively.

The North, North West, Wales and Scotland have some of the highest death rates from circulatory causes; only some German regions have higher rates.

The South East has, together with West-Nederland (Netherlands), the lowest death rate from road accidents of all the EC regions, while six other UK regions have the second lowest rate.

Transport

The North, Scotland and Northern Ireland have some of the lowest rates of car ownership in the EC.

Labour market

Only Bassin-Parisien (France) and West-Nederland (Netherlands) have higher proportions of their workforce in the service sector than the South East.

Only East Anglia, the East Midlands and the South West had a lower unemployment rate than the EC average in 1992.

Gross domestic product

The South East and East Anglia are the only regions in the United Kingdom where GDP is above the EC average.

Regional Trends 30, © Crown copyright 1995

European Community regions

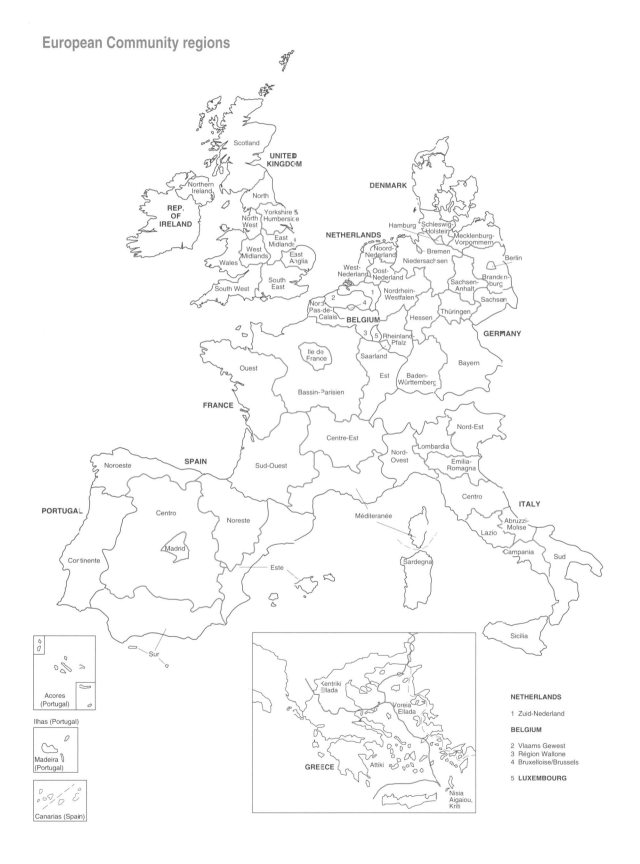

NETHERLANDS

1 Zuid-Nederland

BELGIUM

2 Vlaams Gewest
3 Région Wallone
4 Bruxelloise/Brussels

5 LUXEMBOURG

2.1 European Communities comparisons

	Area (sq km) 1992	Population[1] (thousands) 1992	Persons per sq km 1992	Percentage of population		Births (per 1,000 pop.) 1992	Deaths (per 1,000 pop.) 1992	Infant mortality (per 1,000 births) 1992
				Aged under 15 1992	Aged 65 or over 1992			
EUR 12	**2,358,804**	**346,453.7**	**146.9**	*18.0*	*14.8*	**11.4**	**9.9**	**7.0**
Belgium	**30,518**	**10,045.2**	**329.2**	*18.2*	*15.2*	**12.4**	**10.3**	**6.9**
Vlaams Gewest	13,512	5,809.7	430.0	*18.0*	*14.7*	12.1	9.7	6.7
Region Wallonne	16,844	3,284.6	195.0	*18.7*	*15.5*	12.5	11.1	7.3
Bruxelles-Brussels	161	950.8	5,890.8	*17.5*	*17.5*	13.6	11.6	7.0
Denmark	**43,080**	**5,171.4**	**120.0**	*16.9*	*15.6*	**13.1**	**11.8**	**6.6**
Germany[2]	**356,959**	**80,614.6**	**225.8**	*16.3*	*15.0*	**10.0**	**11.0**	**6.2**
Baden-Wuerttemberg	35,751	10,075.3	281.8	*16.4*	*14.3*	11.7	9.5	5.1
Bayern	70,554	11,683.1	165.6	*16.0*	*15.1*	11.5	10.3	5.3
Berlin	889	3,455.9	3,886.9	*15.9*	*14.0*	8.6	12.2	6.3
Brandenburg	29,477	2,543.8	86.3	*20.1*	*12.3*	5.3	11.5	7.5
Bremen	404	684.5	1,694.0	*13.4*	*17.4*	9.9	12.1	4.7
Hamburg	755	1,678.8	2,222.6	*12.9*	*17.4*	9.8	12.2	6.5
Hessen	21,114	5,878.2	278.5	*15.0*	*15.5*	10.4	10.8	5.8
Mecklenburg-Vorpommern	23,421	1,873.1	80.2	*21.5*	*11.1*	5.8	10.8	7.8
Niedersachsen	47,349	7,526.7	159.0	*15.6*	*15.8*	11.1	11.1	6.1
Norcrhein-Westfalin	34,072	17,594.5	516.4	*15.7*	*15.1*	11.2	10.7	7.0
Rheinland-Pfalz	19,846	3,851.1	194.1	*16.0*	*15.9*	11.1	11.1	6.7
Saarland	2,570	1,080.4	420.4	*14.9*	*15.8*	10.1	11.6	7.7
Sachsen	18,408	4,664.0	253.1	*18.2*	*15.9*	5.4	13.2	6.6
Sachsen-Anhalt	20,443	2,809.1	137.5	*18.6*	*14.3*	5.8	12.7	7.9
Schleswig-Holstein	15,731	2,664.1	169.3	*15.0*	*15.9*	10.8	11.4	5.7
Thueringen	16,176	2,552.1	158.2	*19.2*	*13.9*	5.7	11.8	7.8
Greece	**131,957**	**10,313.7**	**78.2**	*18.1*	*14.3*	**10.1**	**9.5**	**8.4**
Voreia Ellade	56,792	3,323.6	58.5	*17.9*	*12.3*	10.1	9.3	8.0
Kentriki Ellade	53,899	2,446.6	45.4	*17.4*	*17.8*	9.1	10.5	7.9
Attik	3,808	3,539.9	929.6	*18.5*	*12.9*	10.6	8.9	9.6
Nisia Aigaiou, Kriti	17,458	1,003.6	57.5	*19.8*	*17.5*	11.0	10.3	6.5
Spain	**504,790**	**39,085.1**	**77.4**	*18.7*	*13.8*	**10.0**	**8.4**	**7.4**
Norceste	45,297	4,437.8	98.0	*16.5*	*16.1*	7.4	9.7	7.2
Noreste	70,366	4,118.8	58.5	*16.4*	*14.6*	8.1	8.5	8.0
Madrid	7,995	4,910.2	614.2	*18.9*	*12.3*	10.2	7.1	8.5
Centro	215,025	5,466.1	25.4	*17.5*	*16.7*	9.0	9.0	5.5
Este	60,249	10,501.5	174.3	*18.1*	*14.1*	10.0	8.9	6.6
Sur	98,616	8,149.0	82.6	*22.1*	*11.7*	12.5	7.9	8.8
Canarias	7,242	1,501.7	207.4	*21.6*	*9.6*	11.6	6.8	5.2
France	**543,965**	**57,372.1**	**105.5**	*20.0*	*14.3*	**13.0**	**9.1**	**6.8**
Ile de France	12,012	10,861.6	904.2	*20.3*	*10.9*	15.3	7.2	7.1
Bassin-Parisien	145,645	10,369.0	71.2	*20.8*	*14.5*	12.7	9.4	7.2
Norc-Pas-de-Calais	12,414	3,978.7	320.5	*23.4*	*12.2*	14.3	9.1	7.1
Est	48,030	5,048.3	105.1	*20.6*	*12.9*	13.1	8.7	6.8
Ouest	85,099	7,542.1	88.6	*20.0*	*15.7*	11.8	9.5	6.3
Sud-Ouest	103,599	6,014.3	58.1	*17.2*	*18.0*	10.6	10.6	6.6
Centre-Est	69,711	6,777.7	97.2	*20.0*	*14.1*	12.8	8.7	6.1
Mediterranee	67,455	6,780.4	100.5	*18.5*	*17.2*	12.1	10.1	6.3
Ireland	**68,895**	**3,549.1**	**51.5**	*26.3*	*11.4*	**14.5**	**8.7**	**6.7**
Italy	**301,303**	**56,858.8**	**188.7**	*15.8*	*15.4*	**10.1**	**9.6**	**8.0**
Norc-Ovest	34,079	6,089.2	178.7	*12.1*	*18.6*	7.6	11.8	9.0
Lomoardia	23,859	8,867.9	371.7	*13.8*	*14.6*	8.7	9.4	6.3
Norc-Est	39,816	6,477.1	162.7	*14.0*	*16.0*	9.0	9.9	5.6
Emila-Romagna	22,124	3,913.5	176.9	*11.4*	*19.6*	7.2	10.9	6.6
Centro	41,142	5,772.3	140.3	*12.9*	*19.3*	7.8	11.0	7.6
Lazio	17,227	5,151.9	299.1	*15.3*	*14.2*	10.0	8.9	9.7
Campania	13,595	5,648.6	415.5	*21.5*	*11.2*	14.6	7.8	9.6
Abruzzi-Molise	15,231	1,583.5	104.0	*16.5*	*17.1*	10.1	10.1	8.8
Sud	44,430	6,723.5	151.3	*20.3*	*12.9*	12.6	8.0	7.7
Sicilia	25,707	4,981.9	193.8	*20.0*	*13.8*	13.8	9.2	9.8
Sarcegna	24,090	1,649.3	68.5	*18.3*	*12.6*	9.8	8.1	6.3
Luxembourg	**2,586**	**392.5**	**151.8**	*17.7*	*13.5*	**13.1**	**10.2**	**8.6**
Netherlands[3]	**41,029**	**15,182.3**	**370.0**	*18.3*	*13.0*	**13.0**	**8.6**	**6.3**
Noord-Nederland	11,388	1,605.2	140.9	*18.3*	*14.1*	11.9	9.2	6.5
Oost-Nederland	10,494	3,108.2	296.2	*19.4*	*12.5*	13.3	8.4	6.3
West-Nederland	11,854	7,116.8	600.4	*17.9*	*13.5*	13.2	8.8	6.3
Zuid-Nederland	7,291	3,352.1	459.7	*18.0*	*11.7*	12.6	7.9	6.2
Portugal	**91,971**	**9,862.4**	**107.2**	*19.4*	*13.9*	**11.7**	**10.3**	**9.3**
Continente	88,927	9,371.1	105.3	*19.1*	*14.0*	11.5	10.2	8.9
Acores	2,248	237.8	105.7	*25.9*	*12.5*	15.5	11.0	16.3
Madeira	796	253.6	318.5	*23.6*	*11.7*	13.4	10.1	11.2
United Kingdom	**241,752**	**58,006.5**	**239.9**	*19.2*	*15.7*	**13.5**	**11.0**	**6.6**
North	15,415	3,098.9	201.0	*19.3*	*15.9*	12.9	12.0	7.1
Yorkshire & Humberside	15,411	5,002.3	324.6	*19.3*	*15.9*	13.4	11.1	6.7
East Midlands	15,627	4,061.9	259.9	*19.2*	*15.7*	13.1	10.7	6.9
East Anglia	12,570	2,088.6	166.2	*18.7*	*17.0*	12.5	10.6	4.6
South East	27,224	17,703.4	650.3	*18.8*	*15.2*	14.0	10.1	6.1
South West	23,829	4,746.3	199.2	*18.0*	*18.6*	12.1	11.6	5.7
West Midlands	13,004	5,277.5	405.8	*19.7*	*15.3*	13.6	10.6	8.2
North West	7,342	6,399.6	871.6	*20.0*	*15.7*	13.7	11.7	7.0
Wales	20,766	2,898.5	139.6	*19.4*	*17.2*	12.9	11.7	5.9
Scotland	77,080	5,111.2	66.3	*18.9*	*15.1*	12.9	11.9	6.8
Northern Ireland	13,483	1,618.4	120.0	*24.3*	*12.7*	15.8	9.3	6.0

Please see the Appendix for the footnotes to this table.

Source: Statistical Office of the European Communities

2.1 *(continued)*

	Dependency rate 1991	Proportion of 16-18 year olds in education or training[4] (per cent)	Causes of death 1992[5] (rate per 100,000 population)				Transport, 1992	
			Circulatory system	Cancer (all neoplasms)	All accidents	Road traffic accidents	Length of motorways (km) per 1000 sq km[6]	Private cars per 1,000 population[7]
EUR 12	1.2	..	..	..	..	..	15.0	..
Belgium	1.5	90	413	275	41	18	53.4	400
Vlaams Gewest	1.4	82	395	267	36	17	62.2	406
Region Wallonne	1.6	93	439	279	47	22	46.2	379
Bruxelles-Brussels	1.5	130	431	302	50	11	80.5	438
Denmark	0.8	81	505	293	45	12	15.2	310
Germany[2]	1.0	94	570	263	37	14	30.9	..
Baden-Wuerttemberg	1.0	93	452	238	32	11	28.2	512
Bayern	0.9	91	529	250	37	16	30.1	512
Berlin	0.9	91	616	262	33	12	68.6	229
Brandenburg	0.9	..	655	207	52	26	26.0	..
Bremen	1.1	88	597	313	35	10	113.8	416
Hamburg	1.0	100	528	320	46	8	107.2	418
Hessen	1.1	93	529	278	43	12	44.1	524
Mecklenburg-Vorpommern	0.9	..	560	221	71	30	10.1	..
Niedersachsen	1.1	92	563	269	30	15	26.7	494
Nordrhein-Westfalin	1.2	99	539	282	29	8	62.9	479
Rheinland-Pfalz	1.1	89	620	276	28	12	40.8	515
Saarland	1.3	95	642	275	24	9	87.9	516
Sachsen	1.0	..	801	267	55	19	21.9	..
Sachsen-Anhalt	1.0	..	703	262	58	22	10.8	..
Schleswig-Holstein	1.0	91	592	280	36	12	28.3	491
Thueringen	1.0	..	706	228	40	19	15.6	..
Greece	1.5	60	471	198	34	22	1.7	174
Voreia Ellade	1.4	..	471	206	33	23	0.8	140
Kentriki Ellade	1.4	..	518	188	34	22	2.6	94
Attiki	1.6	..	426	201	37	21	9.7	277
Nisia Aigaiou, Kriti	1.4	..	514	190	33	20	0.0	121
Spain	1.6	68	352	202	39	20	5.2	321
Noroeste	1.5	73	410	228	46	26	4.8	296
Noreste	1.5	79	324	217	39	20	..	299
Madrid	1.6	75	268	177	32	12	..	391
Centro	1.7	68	401	214	39	20	..	261
Este	1.4	63	369	216	42	22	..	374
Sur	1.7	63	341	173	31	17	1.9	271
Canarias	1.5	65	262	163	31	11	19.2	351
France	1.3	89	308	244	57	16	13.0	410
Ile de France	1.1	91	219	203	41	10	39.2	360
Bassin-Parisien	1.3	85	314	255	60	19	12.0	421
Nord-Pas-de-Calais	1.6	91	310	252	47	10	37.0	343
Est	1.3	87	309	242	53	15	16.9	401
Ouest	1.3	91	322	254	61	18	6.9	436
Sud-Ouest	1.3	89	391	265	63	19	6.8	462
Centre-Est	1.2	90	297	234	61	17	17.3	432
Mediterranee	1.4	86	349	263	66	20	16.4	420
Ireland	1.6	77	394	211	28	11	0.5	242
Italy	1.5	69	424	260	41	16	20.9	475
Nord-Ovest	1.3	70	537	326	53	17	35.0	543
Lombardia	1.2	66	387	302	41	19	21.7	542
Nord-Est	1.3	72	414	298	49	22	21.1	506
Emilia-Romagna	1.2	76	496	334	51	24	28.5	573
Centro	1.3	74	518	320	49	17	15.1	549
Lazio	1.4	73	378	247	40	16	28.4	542
Campania	1.8	67	372	182	25	9	31.9	336
Abruzzi-Molise	1.5	77	473	220	43	14	24.4	429
Sud	1.8	64	362	175	33	14	13.6	339
Sicilia	1.9	58	403	178	28	10	23.3	396
Sardegna	1.6	70	336	201	44	18	0.0	404
Luxembourg	1.3	65	430	254	47	19	36.7	511
Netherlands[3]	1.1	92	340	237	24	9	51.6	373
Noord-Nederland	1.2	92	374	255	25	12	23.5	364
Oost-Nederland	1.2	90	341	228	26	10	55.5	376
West-Nederland	1.1	93	343	243	24	7	61.5	360
Zuid-Nederland	1.1	90	313	221	21	9	74.1	401
Portugal	1.1	49	447	190	44	27	5.1	..
Continente	1.1	..	446	191	44	28	5.2	325
Acores	1.5	..	530	200	39	17	0.0	..
Maderia	1.1	..	380	159	52	30	0.0	..
United Kingdom	1.0	66	501	280	21	8	13.5	365
North	1.1	65	558	311	21	8	10.9	306
Yorkshire & Humberside	1.0	68	514	279	20	8	20.5	334
East Midlands	1.0	62	495	273	21	9	11.8	358
East Anglia	1.0	61	483	275	24	11	1.8	419
South East	0.9	67	444	264	18	7	34.0	395
South West	1.0	65	540	303	20	8	12.5	419
West Midlands	1.0	69	486	278	22	8	29.1	399
North West	1.1	65	546	295	22	8	63.5	341
Wales	1.2	61	547	301	23	8	5.8	352
Scotland	1.0	68	571	296	31	10	3.5	311
Northern Ireland	1.3	70	442	221	23	12	8.4	305

Please see the Appendix for the footnotes to this table.

Source: Statistical Office of the European Communities

2.1 (continued)

	Persons in employment[1] (thousands) 1992	Employment[1,8], 1992 percentage in			Unemployment rate[1] (per cent) 1992	Long-term unemployed[1] as a percentage of the unemployed, 1991
		Agriculture	Industry	Services		
EUR 12	140,175.7	5.8	32.6	61.2	9.2	..
Belgium	3,770.3	2.9	30.9	66.2	6.7	61.0
Vlaams Gewest	2,298.6	3.1	34.2	62.6	4.9	58.0
Reçion Wallonn	1,140.6	3.2	27.6	69.1	9.5	62.2
Bruxelles-Brussels	331.1	0.2	18.5	81.3	9.0	67.1
Denmark	2,636.6	5.2	27.1	67.5	9.1	32.4
Germany[2]	36,528.3	3.7	39.1	57.2	6.4	..
Baden-Wuerttemberg	4,834.2	3.3	46.1	50.6	2.8	43.6
Bayern	5,809.3	6.0	40.7	53.4	2.9	34.9
Berlin	1,641.0	0.7	28.5	70.8	9.9	..
Brandenburg	1,122.5	6.4	33.6	60.0	12.7	..
Bremen	295.0	0.8	31.0	68.2	7.6	34.6
Hamburg	775.0	1.1	25.3	73.5	5.3	50.1
Hessen	2,715.3	2.4	36.3	61.3	3.6	46.0
Mecklenburg-Vorpommern	804.6	8.5	27.5	64.0	16.2	..
Niedersachsen	3,370.7	4.9	37.1	58.1	5.3	42.7
Nordrhein-Westfalin	7,508.1	2.2	41.4	56.4	5.5	46.5
Rheinland-Pfalz	1,725.6	3.5	39.7	56.8	3.6	44.9
Saarland	436.1	1.0	40.0	59.1	6.0	54.2
Sachsen	1,980.5	3.2	42.7	54.1	12.4	..
Sachsen-Anhalt	1,202.7	5.4	40.3	54.3	14.1	..
Schleswig-Holstein	1,225.6	4.8	28.5	66.7	4.5	55.5
Thueringen	1,082.1	4.8	41.0	54.2	13.8	..
Greece	3,680.0	21.9	25.4	52.8	7.8	46.5
Voreia Ellade	1,215.2	30.5	26.5	43.0	6.7	47.2
Kertriki Ellade	767.7	40.0	20.3	39.8	8.0	42.1
Attiki	1,350.1	1.3	29.2	69.5	9.7	42.2
Nisia Aigaiou, Kriti	347.0	31.5	17.6	50.9	3.6	53.8
Spain	12,457.7	10.1	32.7	57.2	17.8	48.7
Noroeste	1,482.1	23.6	28.9	47.6	16.6	57.2
Noreste	1,388.8	6.5	40.1	53.4	15.3	57.3
Madrid	1,660.4	0.6	29.1	70.2	12.5	52.2
Centro	1,638.1	17.3	30.9	51.8	18.4	46.8
Este	3,658.4	4.8	39.5	55.6	14.9	47.9
Sur	2,184.5	14.0	26.3	59.7	25.9	43.5
Canarias	445.3	9.2	17.7	73.1	24.7	47.3
France	22,021.4	5.9	29.5	64.4	10.0	38.9
Ile de France	4,889.0	0.4	25.0	74.4	8.2	31.6
Bassin-Parisien	3,936.8	8.2	32.7	59.0	10.1	41.7
Nord-Pas-de-Calais	1,307.7	2.9	36.8	60.4	12.9	57.6
Est	1,957.0	4.0	37.4	58.1	7.7	40.1
Ouest	2,850.6	11.0	29.0	59.9	10.1	37.7
Sud-Ouest	2,334.7	11.9	25.3	62.7	10.3	35.8
Centre-Est	2,551.4	5.5	34.2	60.3	9.7	29.8
Mediterranee	2,194.2	4.9	22.2	72.7	13.2	43.7
Ireland	1,148.8	13.7	28.0	58.1	15.3	59.7
Italy	21,015.4	7.9	33.1	59.0	8.5	66.7
Nord-Ovest	2,393.7	5.8	36.8	57.3	6.5	61.4
Lombardia	3,719.3	2.7	43.7	53.6	3.4	55.0
Nord-Est	2,658.3	6.5	37.7	55.8	3.7	44.4
Emilia-Romagna	1,703.2	8.9	35.6	55.5	3.6	35.7
Centro	2,285.2	5.8	35.5	58.7	6.0	59.0
Lazio	1,933.8	4.6	21.8	73.6	8.3	69.5
Campania	1,689.0	10.7	25.6	63.8	17.2	79.8
Abruzzi-Molise	578.8	10.9	30.9	58.2	9.9	65.1
Sud	2,076.4	16.6	26.2	57.1	13.3	65.8
Sicilia	1,456.5	14.9	21.9	63.2	17.5	73.9
Sardegna	521.2	12.4	26.6	61.0	15.0	66.3
Luxembourg	164.6	3.5	28.9	67.6	2.1	27.4
Netherlands[3]	6,613.8	4.4	25.6	70.1	5.6	43.1
Noord-Nederland	646.7	5.0	27.0	68.0	7.6	37.3
Oost-Nederland	1,314.8	6.1	28.0	65.8	5.3	42.9
West-Nederland	3,200.2	3.3	20.6	76.0	5.4	43.6
Zuid-Nederland	1,452.1	4.7	33.6	61.7	5.2	45.9
Portugal	4,509.1	11.5	32.6	56.0	3.8	42.0
Continente	4,307.0	11.3	32.7	56.0	3.8	41.9
Accres	88.6	18.3	24.3	57.5	3.2	43.8
Maderia	113.5	13.3	35.2	51.5	3.2	45.2
United Kingdom	25,629.6	2.2	30.1	67.3	9.8	27.1
North	1,285.3	1.9	33.3	64.0	10.9	33.8
Yorkshire & Humberside	2,179.8	1.8	34.0	63.9	9.8	27.1
East Midlands	1,876.2	2.4	37.8	59.2	8.6	25.4
East Anglia	977.2	4.0	30.1	65.5	7.6	21.7
South East	8,065.9	1.3	24.5	73.8	9.5	21.0
South West	2,128.8	3.6	28.2	67.9	9.0	24.8
West Midlands	2,309.5	2.1	37.4	60.1	10.3	31.8
North West	2,726.8	1.3	32.1	66.2	10.5	29.7
Wales	1,203.9	4.0	29.8	65.9	9.5	25.2
Scotland	2,271.2	3.4	30.7	65.4	9.9	31.7
Northern Ireland	604.9	5.3	27.9	66.2	15.4	39.3

Please see the Appendix for the footnotes to this table.

Source: Statistical Office of the European Communities

2.1 *(continued)*

| | Gross domestic product per head EUR 12=100 1992 | Percentage of GDP in 1992 derived from | | | Agricultural holdings | | |
		Agriculture	Industry	Services	Economic value of farms (SGM) EUR 12=100 1988-1991	Wheat 100kg/ha 1991	Barley 100kg/ha 1991
EUR 12	100	..	..	..	100	..	..
Belgium	110	..	..	..	248	..	..
Vlaams Gewest	111	..	..	..	237	..	..
Region Wallonn	88	..	..	..	269	..	..
Bruxelles-Brussels	175	..	..	..	..	..	..
Denmark	108	3.9	26.4	69.6	328	72	54
Germany[2]	108	1.3	38.6	60.2	167	68	57
Baden-Wuerttemberg	132	1.1	44.6	54.3	111	67	55
Bayern	127	1.5	38.7	59.8	130	66	56
Berlin	96	0.2	41.0	58.8	..	..	..
Brandenburg	44	..	..	..	..	52	51
Bremen	156	0.3	34.2	65.5	..	..	..
Hamburg	198	0.2	25.6	74.2	..	79	67
Hessen	150	0.7	31.0	68.4	137	66	58
Mecklenburg-Vorpommern	41	..	..	..	..	65	55
Niedersachsen	106	3.3	36.8	59.9	241	77	59
Nordrhein-Westfalin	114	0.9	40.5	58.6	202	80	63
Rheinland-Pfalz	103	1.8	42.0	56.2	182	58	49
Saarland	110	0.3	40.0	59.7	142	55	44
Sachsen	42	..	..	..	..	59	56
Sachsen-Anhalt	44	..	..	..	..	60	60
Schleswig-Holstein	105	2.8	32.3	65.0	330	81	71
Thueringen	38	..	..	..	..	58	57
Greece	50	16.3	27.4	56.3	37	31	27
Voreia Ellade	47	24.7	30.9	44.4	39	32	32
Kentriki Ellade	48	28.3	30.3	41.4	38	29	31
Attiki	56	2.0	26.5	71.5	29	23	16
Nisia Aigaiou, Kriti	44	24.3	20.0	55.7	30	13	14
Spain	78	4.0	33.5	62.5	49	25	21
Noroeste	64	6.3	35.4	58.2	35	20	18
Noreste	89	3.5	41.8	54.7	59	28	25
Madrid	98	0.2	27.1	72.8	46	17	20
Centro	63	7.5	35.3	57.1	54	20	20
Este	90	2.1	35.7	62.2	48	38	30
Sur	61	8.1	30.0	61.9	49	31	16
Canarias	75	3.3	21.0	75.7	48	15	16
France	113	3.2	29.8	67.0	208	67	61
Ile de France	170	0.3	27.2	72.5	544	81	72
Bassin-Parisien	103	5.9	34.1	60.0	290	72	67
Nord-Pas-de-Calais	90	1.8	32.8	65.4	273	74	71
Est	104	2.9	36.9	60.2	181	63	60
Ouest	94	6.2	28.2	65.7	208	61	56
Sud-Ouest	97	4.9	26.8	68.3	158	52	47
Centre-Est	107	2.7	35.1	62.2	135	52	45
Mediterranee	97	3.7	22.2	74.1	186	36	34
Ireland	77	10.5	35.5	54.0	102	81	57
Italy	106	3.9	30.3	65.8	66	26	36
Nord-Ovest	120	2.5	34.2	63.3	78	51	52
Lombardia	135	1.7	39.0	59.3	156	57	56
Nord-Est	120	4.0	34.3	61.8	80	58	53
Emilia-Romagna	129	5.0	33.6	61.5	149	44	47
Centro	109	3.3	32.4	64.3	69	33	33
Lazio	121	2.1	19.8	78.1	53	26	33
Campania	73	4.9	21.8	73.4	44	28	28
Abruzzi-Molise	92	5.9	28.8	65.3	45	23	23
Sud	72	8.3	21.0	70.7	49	13	15
Sicilia	73	7.9	19.8	72.3	46	13	12
Sardegna	80	5.2	25.3	69.5	50	5	8
Luxembourg	131	1.4	32.9	65.7	201	47	33
Netherlands[3]	103	4.1	30.1	65.7	453	77	57
Noord-Nederland	104	5.5	43.2	51.3	445	73	59
Oost-Nederland	90	5.2	28.7	66.1	359	79	57
West-Nederland	110	3.4	24.5	72.1	567	79	55
Zuid-Nederland	98	4.5	34.7	60.8	453	75	54
Portugal	67	5.8	37.0	57.2	34	15	9
Continente	69	5.8	37.0	57.2	35	..	..
Acores	41	..	..	..	33	..	..
Maderia	44	..	..	..	16	..	..
United Kingdom	99	1.8	32.3	65.9	311	73	55
North	88	1.8	40.6	57.5	302	76	58
Yorkshire & Humberside	91	1.9	37.8	60.3	509	77	60
East Midlands	93	2.7	39.7	57.6	480	76	58
East Anglia	101	4.9	31.4	63.7	622	74	58
South East	116	0.7	23.7	75.6	396	67	58
South West	94	3.5	30.0	66.6	278	67	53
West Midlands	91	2.0	39.3	58.6	316	74	51
North West	89	0.9	36.9	62.2	330	67	55
Wales	84	2.2	39.1	58.7	194	62	47
Scotland	97	2.7	32.7	64.6	296	75	51
Northern Ireland	80	4.0	29.7	66.3	123	69	46

Please see the Appendix for the footnotes to this table.

Source: Statistical Office of the European Communities

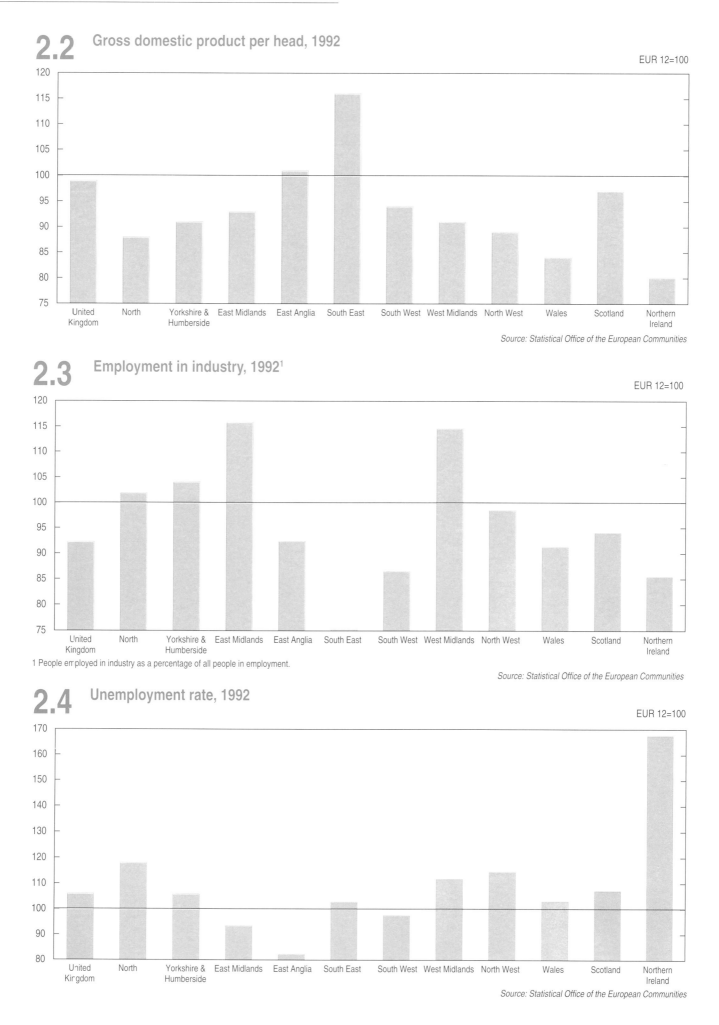

2.2 Gross domestic product per head, 1992

EUR 12=100

Source: Statistical Office of the European Communities

2.3 Employment in industry, 1992[1]

EUR 12=100

1 People employed in industry as a percentage of all people in employment.

Source: Statistical Office of the European Communities

2.4 Unemployment rate, 1992

EUR 12=100

Source: Statistical Office of the European Communities

3 Population and Households

Population change   East Anglia and the South West have had the fastest growing populations since 1981, while the populations in the North, the North West and Scotland have all fallen slightly.

(Table 3.1)

Between mid-1992 and mid-1993, the South West had the smallest net natural change with births exceeding deaths by less than one thousand; however, it had by far the largest net inward migration of any region.

(Table 3.12)

Age   Northern Ireland has the youngest population, with the highest proportion of children and the lowest proportion of pensioners of any region, while the South West has the oldest population.

(Table 3.3)

Births   Northern Ireland has the highest birth rate and Scotland the lowest among all women of childbearing age.

(Table 3.7)

In 1993, over 90 per cent of births in the North to girls under the age of 20 were outside marriage, compared with 80 per cent of births in the South East, the highest and lowest proportions.

(Table 3.15)

Deaths   Allowing for the age structure of the population, Scotland has the highest death rates and the South West and East Anglia the lowest.

(Table 3.8)

Social class   The South East has the highest proportion of economically active people in skilled non-manual occupations, while the West Midlands and Yorkshire and Humberside have the highest proportions in skilled manual occupations.

(Table 3.13)

Ethnic minorities   Only about one in 100 people in the North, South West, Wales and Scotland classify themselves as belonging to an ethnic minority population, compared with one in ten in the South East.

(Table 3.14)

Cohabitation   The proportion of adults who are cohabiting is lowest in Scotland and Northern Ireland and highest in East Anglia and the South East.

(Chart 3.17)

Households   Scotland has a higher proportion of one-person households and the South West a lower proportion than any other region in Great Britain.

(Table 3.18)

Families   One in eight families in the North consists of a lone parent with dependent children, compared with one in 14 in East Anglia and the South West.

(Table 3.19)

Introduction

A full population census is held every 10 years; the most recent was conducted in 1991. Between the Censuses the population figures are rolled forward using annual estimates of the components of population change (births, deaths and net migration - both inter-regional and international). As each decade proceeds, errors creep into the rolled forward figures, mainly because of the difficulty of estimating migration. The decennial census is used as a base for both revising previous years' data and deriving estimates for the following decade. Inter-regional migration has more effect than international migration on local population levels.

The main source of information on migration between the United Kingdom and other countries is the International Passenger Survey (IPS). However this survey excludes migration between the United Kingdom and the Irish Republic and also movements of the Armed Forces and diplomatic personnel. It also does not count as migrants those seeking asylum after entering the United Kingdom, and others who enter as visitors but subsequently are granted an extension of stay for a year or more ('visitor switchers'). The effect of this latter group is partly balanced by visitor switchers leaving the country. IPS results, shown in Table 3.11, appear to indicate a net outflow from the United Kingdom in 1993. However, if allowance is made for asylum seekers, visitor switchers, and movements to and from the Irish Republic, there was net civilian inward migration of about 37 thousand.

All the items in this chapter give data either for the standard regions or for counties. However, the Office of Population Censuses and Surveys (OPCS) has also produced population statistics for Great Britain by type of area. This area classification is based on data for local authority districts drawn from the 1991 Census. A number of variables from each of the following fields are taken into account: demographic structure, household composition, housing, socio-economic character and employment. The comparison of the different variables across local authority districts resulted in the classification of six types - or families - of area: Rural areas, Prospering areas, Maturer areas, Urban centres, Mining and Industrial areas, and finally Inner London as a separate area because the dominant characteristics of the Inner London boroughs are not matched elsewhere.

The 'Rural areas' family accounted for 10.1 million people in 1991 - about 18 per cent of the population of Great Britain. Not surprisingly, it comprises large parts of the South West, East Anglia, Wales and Scotland and significant parts of the North, Yorkshire and Humberside and both the East and West Midlands. About 12.2 million people - 22 per cent of the GB population - lived in 'Prospering areas'. These

"A full population census

Regional Trends 30, © Crown copyright 1995

areas are characterised by low unemployment, high availability of cars, high proportions of people with higher educational qualifications, and high proportions of people in Social Classes I and II. 'Prospering areas' are heavily concentrated in the South East outside London, but there are also significant pockets in the South West, the East and West Midlands, East Anglia, the North West and in the Grampian region of Scotland. The 'Maturer areas', accounting for 6.6 million people or 11 per cent of the GB population, are characterised by above average proportions of pensioners and indications of relative prosperity. University towns, traditional seaside towns - notably on the south and east coasts - and Outer London boroughs dominate this type of area.

The 'Urban centres' share characteristics such as above average proportions of households without cars and people who travel to work by public transport. Within the 'family', there are two distinct groupings: mixed economies which are characterised by service centres or new and expanding towns; and manufacturing districts, characterised by above average proportions of not only manufacturing work, but also of people in ethnic minority groups. Around 11.2 million people (just over 20 per cent of the GB population) lived in 'Urban centres' in 1991, which are mostly concentrated in the Central, Strathclyde and Lothian regions of Scotland, Lancashire, Greater Manchester, West Yorkshire, West Midlands Metropolitan County, and in Essex and Kent along the Thames estuary. Smaller pockets are dotted around England.

'Mining and Industrial areas' are characterised by a tradition of mining and industry, by de-industrialisation, and by above national averages in 'deprivation' variables such as limiting long-term illness. The districts which comprise this family type are heavily concentrated in South Wales, South Yorkshire, Merseyside, Tyne and Wear, Cleveland and Strathclyde. Altogether, 11.8 million people, or 22 per cent of the GB population, lived in such areas in 1991.

The Inner London grouping is very distinctive, sharing well above average proportions of people in ethnic minority groups, one-person households, and people who travel to work by public transport. All but five districts in the very heart of London have well above average values in the 'deprivation' variables. This family is the smallest of the six with a population of 3.4 million (just over 6 per cent of the GB population). An article giving a detailed description of the area classification can be found in OPCS' publication *Population Trends, Number 79, Spring 1995*.

is held every 10 years...."

3.1 Resident population[1]: by gender

Thousands and percentages

	Population (thousands)					Annual growth rate (percentages)	
	1961	1971	1981	1991	1993	1961-81	1981-93
Males							
United Kingdom	25,528	27,167.3	27,409.2	28,245.6	28,473.6	0.4	0.3
North	1,506	1,533.2	1,516.8	1,506.5	1,513.6	-	-
Yorkshire & Humberside	2,262	2,384.9	2,395.0	2,441.7	2,460.6	0.3	0.2
East Midlands	1,611	1,797.8	1,894.8	1,989.6	2,014.9	0.8	0.5
East Anglia	720	838.6	932.1	1,027.4	1,032.1	1.3	0.9
South East	7,774	8,288.5	8,259.7	8,621.3	8,698.9	0.3	0.4
Greater London	..	3,611.4	3,277.6	3,352.0	3,383.2	..	0.3
Rest of South East	..	4,677.1	4,982.1	5,269.3	5,315.7	..	0.5
South West	1,796	1,989.9	2,117.2	2,295.6	2,324.4	0.8	0.8
West Midlands	2,304	2,542.4	2,555.6	2,596.3	2,610.1	0.5	0.2
North West	3,099	3,193.2	3,124.0	3,109.7	3,127.0	-	-
England	21,072	22,568.5	22,795.0	23,588.1	23,781.7	0.4	0.4
Wales	1,275	1,328.5	1,365.1	1,407.0	1,416.6	0.3	0.3
Scotland	2,485	2,515.7	2,494.9	2,469.5	2,478.5	-	-0.1
Northern Ireland	696	754.6	754.2	780.9	796.7	0.4	0.5
Females							
United Kingdom	27,279	28,760.7	28,943.0	29,562.3	29,717.6	0.3	0.2
North	1,607	1,618.9	1,600.6	1,585.2	1,588.7	-	-0.1
Yorkshire & Humberside	2,415	2,517.4	2,523.5	2,541.1	2,553.4	0.2	0.1
East Midlands	1,719	1,854.1	1,958.0	2,045.8	2,068.0	0.7	0.5
East Anglia	769	849.5	961.8	1,054.5	1,061.8	1.1	0.8
South East	8,297	8,836.8	8,751.5	9,015.5	9,070.5	0.3	0.3
Greater London	..	3,918.0	3,528.0	3,538.0	3,549.8	..	0.1
Rest of South East	..	4,918.8	5,223.6	5,477.6	5,520.7	..	0.5
South West	1,916	2,121.9	2,264.1	2,422.1	2,443.6	0.8	0.6
West Midlands	2,458	2,603.6	2,631.1	2,669.1	2,679.6	0.3	0.2
North West	3,308	3,441.0	3,335.2	3,286.5	3,285.4	-	-0.1
England	22,489	23,843.2	24,025.8	24,619.9	24,751.0	0.3	0.2
Wales	1,360	1,411.8	1,448.4	1,484.5	1,489.8	0.3	0.2
Scotland	2,699	2,719.9	2,685.3	2,637.5	2,641.7	-	-0.1
Northern Ireland	731	785.8	783.5	820.4	835.1	0.3	0.5
All persons							
United Kingdom	52,807	55,928.0	56,352.2	57,807.9	58,191.2	0.3	0.3
North	3,113	3,152.1	3,117.4	3,091.7	3,102.3	-	-
Yorkshire & Humberside	4,677	4,902.3	4,918.4	4,982.8	5,014.1	0.3	0.2
East Midlands	3,330	3,651.9	3,852.8	4,035.4	4,082.9	0.7	0.5
East Anglia	1,489	1,688.1	1,893.9	2,081.9	2,093.9	1.2	0.8
South East	16,071	17,125.3	17,011.2	17,636.8	17,769.4	0.3	0.4
Greater London	7,977	7,529.4	6,805.6	6,889.9	6,933.0	-0.8	0.2
Rest of South East	8,094	9,595.9	10,205.6	10,746.9	10,836.4	1.2	0.5
South West	3,712	4,111.8	4,381.4	4,717.8	4,768.0	0.8	0.7
West Midlands	4,762	5,146.0	5,186.6	5,265.5	5,289.7	0.4	0.2
North West	6,407	6,634.2	6,459.1	6,396.1	6,412.4	-	-0.1
England	43,561	46,411.7	46,820.8	48,208.1	48,532.7	0.4	0.3
Wales	2,635	2,740.3	2,813.5	2,891.5	2,906.5	0.3	0.3
Scotland	5,184	5,235.6	5,180.2	5,107.0	5,120.2	-	-0.1
Northern Ireland	1,427	1,540.4	1,537.7	1,601.4	1,631.8	0.4	0.5

1 See Appendix notes.

Source: Office of Population Censuses and Surveys; General Register Offices for Scotland and Northern Ireland

3.2 Population growth, mid 1981-1992 and projected growth[1] 1993-2003

Population growth mid 1981-1993

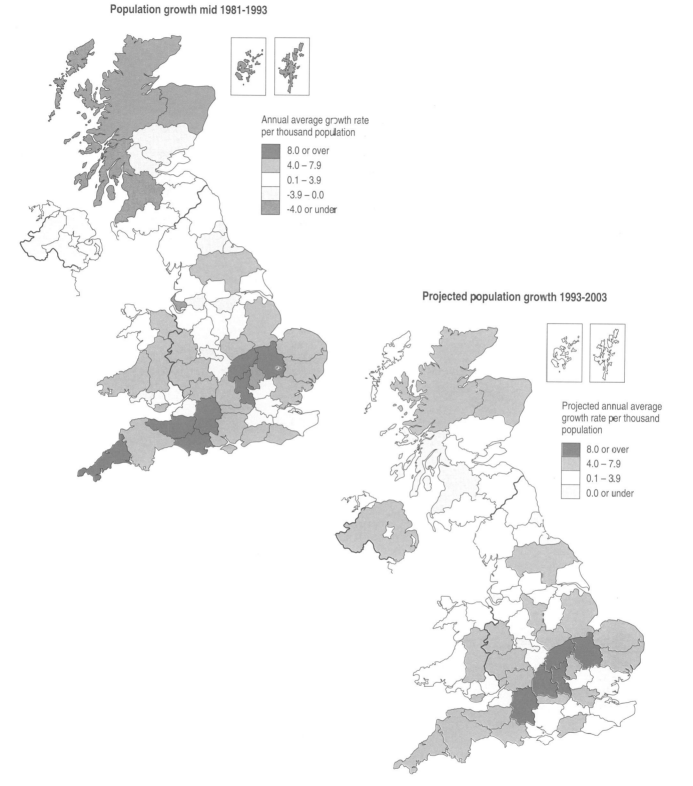

Annual average growth rate per thousand population

- 8.0 or over
- 4.0 – 7.9
- 0.1 – 3.9
- -3.9 – 0.0
- -4.0 or under

Projected population growth 1993-2003

Projected annual average growth rate per thousand population

- 8.0 or over
- 4.0 – 7.9
- 0.1 – 3.9
- 0.0 or under

1 Mid-1993 population estimates and 1992-based national and sub-national population projections.

Source: Office of Population Censuses and Surveys; Welsh Office; General Register Offices for Scotland and Northern Ireland

3.3 Resident population[1]: by age and gender, 1993

Thousands and percentages

	0-4	5-15	16-44	Males 45-64 Females 45-59	Males 65-79 Females 60-79	80 and over	All ages
Males (thousands)							
United Kingdom	1,991.9	4,147.8	12,252.2	6,390.2	3,008.4	683.1	28,473.6
North	103.1	225.1	637.2	348.5	167.3	32.2	1,513.6
Yorkshire & Humberside	172.7	358.3	1,061.8	547.5	262.8	57.5	2,460.6
East Midlands	138.3	291.1	854.6	462.4	220.9	47.5	2,014.9
East Anglia	67.7	144.9	431.3	237.5	120.6	30.0	1,032.1
South East	617.9	1,222.4	3,876.0	1,905.5	861.2	215.9	8,698.9
Greater London	252.9	458.6	1,609.2	682.9	303.9	75.6	3,383.2
Rest of South East	365.1	763.7	2,266.8	1,222.6	557.3	140.3	5,315.7
South West	150.0	323.1	952.1	539.5	285.5	74.1	2,324.4
West Midlands	185.5	386.8	1,103.3	600.9	277.5	56.2	2,610.1
North West	227.5	474.2	1,326.0	705.2	324.8	69.3	3,127.0
England	1,662.8	3,425.9	10,242.5	5,347.1	2,520.6	582.8	23,781.7
Wales	96.7	211.9	575.8	329.5	167.6	35.2	1,416.6
Scotland	165.9	362.3	1,090.6	557.3	250.9	51.5	2,478.5
Northern Ireland	66.5	147.7	343.3	156.3	69.2	13.6	796.7
Females (thousands)							
United Kingdom	1,896.1	3,929.6	11,892.6	5,053.8	5,353.9	1,591.6	29,717.6
North	97.7	213.2	624.4	271.7	302.1	79.6	1,588.7
Yorkshire & Humberside	164.3	339.3	1,013.9	432.8	465.5	137.6	2,553.4
East Midlands	131.0	275.0	825.8	358.3	371.9	105.9	2,068.0
East Anglia	65.7	137.0	412.5	184.5	200.9	61.0	1,061.8
South East	589.1	1,157.7	3,773.6	1,520.5	1,533.7	495.9	9,070.5
Greater London	242.1	437.6	1,591.1	551.6	548.7	178.8	3,549.8
Rest of South East	347.0	720.1	2,182.5	969.0	985.0	317.2	5,520.7
South West	141.8	305.0	915.3	424.7	494.2	162.6	2,443.6
West Midlands	176.3	365.2	1,059.1	463.8	484.0	131.1	2,679.6
North West	215.7	449.9	1,293.8	556.1	594.5	175.4	3,285.4
England	1,581.7	3,242.5	9,918.4	4,212.5	4,446.8	1,349.1	24,751.0
Wales	92.4	200.7	561.2	258.1	293.3	84.1	1,489.8
Scotland	158.7	345.4	1,073.8	454.5	482.8	126.5	2,641.7
Northern Ireland	63.3	141.0	339.2	128.8	131.0	31.9	835.1
All persons (percentages)							
United Kingdom	6.7	13.9	41.5	19.7	14.4	3.9	100.0
North	6.5	14.1	40.7	20.0	15.1	3.6	100.0
Yorkshire & Humberside	6.7	13.9	41.4	19.5	14.5	3.9	100.0
East Midlands	6.6	13.9	41.2	20.1	14.5	3.8	100.0
East Anglia	6.4	13.5	40.3	20.2	15.4	4.3	100.0
South East	6.8	13.4	43.0	19.3	13.5	4.0	100.0
Greater London	7.1	12.9	46.2	17.8	12.3	3.7	100.0
Rest of South East	6.6	13.7	41.1	20.2	14.2	4.2	100.0
South West	6.1	13.2	39.2	20.2	16.4	5.0	100.0
West Midlands	6.8	14.2	40.9	20.1	14.4	3.5	100.0
North West	6.9	14.4	40.9	19.7	14.3	3.8	100.0
England	6.7	13.7	41.5	19.7	14.4	4.0	100.0
Wales	6.5	14.2	39.1	20.2	15.9	4.1	100.0
Scotland	6.3	13.8	42.3	19.8	14.3	3.5	100.0
Northern Ireland	8.0	17.7	41.8	17.5	12.3	2.8	100.0

1 See Appendix notes.

Source: Office of Population Censuses and Surveys; General Register Offices for Scotland and Northern Ireland

3.4 Population density, 1993[1]

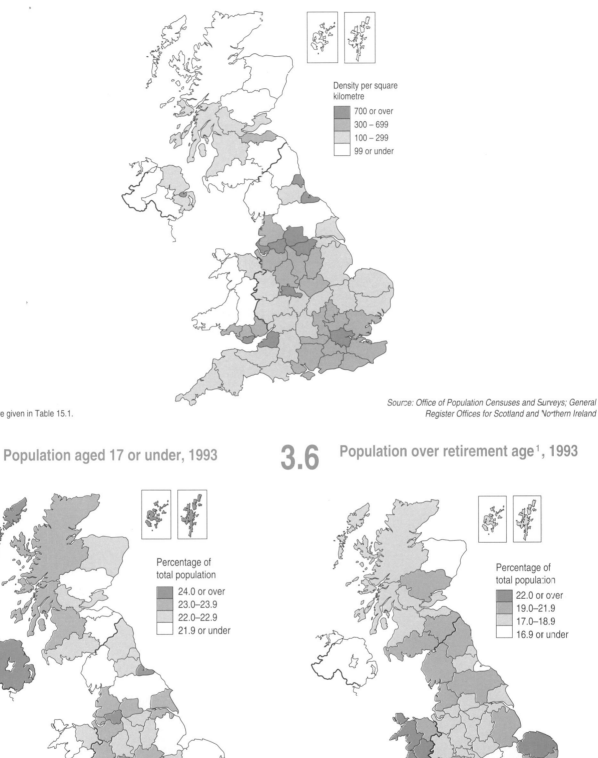

Density per square kilometre

- 700 or over
- 300 – 699
- 100 – 299
- 99 or under

1 Actual data are given in Table 15.1.

Source: Office of Population Censuses and Surveys; General Register Offices for Scotland and Northern Ireland

3.5 Population aged 17 or under, 1993

Percentage of total population

- 24.0 or over
- 23.0–23.9
- 22.0–22.9
- 21.9 or under

Source: Office of Population Censuses and Surveys; General Register Offices for Scotland and Northern Ireland

3.6 Population over retirement age[1], 1993

Percentage of total population

- 22.0 or over
- 19.0–21.9
- 17.0–18.9
- 16.9 or under

1 Males aged 65 or over, females aged 60 or over.

Source: Office of Population Censuses and Surveys; General Register Offices for Scotland and Northern Ireland

3.7 Age specific birth rates

Rates

	Live births per 1,000 women in age groups[1]							
	Under 20	20-24	25-29	30-34	35-39	40 and over	All ages	TPFR[2]
1971								
United Kingdom	50	154	155	79	34	9	84	2.41
North	53	175	165	79	34	9	88	2.57
Yorkshire & Humberside	58	166	155	75	33	9	87	2.48
East Midlands	53	156	145	70	30	8	82	2.31
East Anglia	50	162	152	72	29	8	84	2.36
South East	43	135	150	78	32	8	79	2.23
Greater London	45	115	134	79	35	9	75	2.09
Rest of South East	42	154	164	78	30	7	83	2.37
South West	45	150	144	67	26	6	77	2.19
West Midlands	55	163	160	82	37	11	89	2.54
North West	59	169	160	83	37	10	90	2.59
England	50	152	153	77	33	9	83	2.37
Wales	57	164	154	74	31	8	85	2.44
Scotland	48	163	164	85	36	10	86	2.53
Northern Ireland	43	158	206	136	64	20	107	3.13
1981								
United Kingdom	28	107	130	70	22	5	62	1.81
North	33	118	123	60	19	4	62	1.78
Yorkshire & Humberside	31	117	128	59	18	6	62	1.80
East Midlands	30	113	127	63	19	4	61	1.79
East Anglia	24	115	135	64	17	5	61	1.79
South East	24	92	128	76	25	5	61	1.75
Greater London	29	83	114	80	31	6	62	1.71
Rest of South East	21	100	138	73	22	4	60	1.79
South West	24	103	132	63	18	3	57	1.71
West Midlands	32	109	133	69	20	7	62	1.84
North West	33	111	132	68	23	5	64	1.86
England	28	104	129	69	22	5	61	1.78
Wales	30	121	127	67	21	6	63	1.86
Scotland	31	112	132	66	21	4	63	1.83
Northern Ireland	27	135	173	118	52	13	86	2.59
1993								
United Kingdom	31	82	114	87	34	6	62	1.76
North	39	89	115	75	26	4	60	1.74
Yorkshire & Humberside	39	92	115	78	28	5	63	1.79
East Midlands	32	86	119	81	28	5	61	1.75
East Anglia	25	82	122	84	31	5	60	1.74
South East	24	71	108	96	42	8	63	1.75
Greater London	29	69	94	94	48	10	64	1.72
Rest of South East	22	73	120	98	37	6	62	1.78
South West	24	78	119	89	33	6	60	1.74
West Midlands	35	93	118	83	32	6	64	1.83
North West	38	91	115	82	31	5	64	1.81
England	31	82	114	87	34	6	63	1.76
Wales	37	96	122	79	30	5	63	1.84
Scotland	31	72	110	80	28	4	57	1.62
Northern Ireland	28	83	134	105	44	9	71	2.01

1 The rates for women aged under 20, 40 and over and all ages are based upon the population of women aged 15-19, 40-44 and 15-44 respectively.
2 The Total Period Fertility Rate (TPFR) measures the average number of children which would be born if women were to experience the age-specific fertility rates of the year in question throughout their child-bearing life.

Source: Office of Population Censuses and Surveys; General Register Offices for Scotland and Northern Ireland

3.8 Age-specific death rates: by gender, 1993

Rates and Standardised Mortality Ratios

| | Deaths per 1,000 population for specific age groups | | | | | | | | | | | SMR[1] (UK = 100) |
	Under 1	0-4	5-14	15-24	25-34	35-44	45-54	55-64	65-74	75-84	85 and over	
Males												
United Kingdom	7.0	1.7	0.2	0.7	0.9	1.7	4.4	13.6	38.5	94.4	204.3	100
North	7.4	1.7	0.2	0.7	0.9	1.8	5.1	15.9	44.2	103.1	205.7	111
Yorkshire & Humberside	7.9	1.8	0.2	0.7	0.7	1.5	4.5	14.1	39.7	96.8	207.6	102
East Midlands	7.6	1.7	0.2	0.8	0.8	1.5	4.0	13.2	38.1	95.0	204.8	99
East Anglia	5.8	1.4	0.1	0.7	0.9	1.3	3.5	11.0	32.5	85.6	201.8	89
South East	6.5	1.6	0.1	0.6	0.9	1.7	4.0	11.6	34.9	88.8	197.3	93
Greater London	7.1	1.7	0.2	0.6	1.1	2.2	4.7	13.1	36.8	90.5	196.8	98
Rest of South East	6.1	1.4	0.1	0.6	0.8	1.4	3.6	10.7	33.8	87.9	197.5	90
South West	6.0	1.4	0.2	0.6	0.8	1.3	3.6	11.5	32.5	85.7	196.0	89
West Midlands	8.1	1.9	0.2	0.7	0.8	1.6	4.2	13.8	39.5	96.5	207.3	102
North West	7.1	1.7	0.2	0.8	1.0	1.7	4.8	15.9	43.7	102.1	214.3	110
England	7.0	1.6	0.2	0.7	0.9	1.6	4.2	13.1	37.6	92.9	202.3	98
Wales	6.5	1.6	0.2	0.8	1.0	1.8	4.5	14.5	40.1	97.8	198.5	103
Scotland	7.3	1.7	0.2	0.9	1.2	2.1	6.0	17.2	45.8	107.3	226.6	118
Northern Ireland	7.8	1.8	0.3	1.1	1.1	1.6	4.5	14.8	41.7	100.6	228.1	109
Females												
United Kingdom	5.6	1.3	0.1	0.3	0.5	1.1	2.8	8.0	22.4	60.3	158.8	100
North	5.9	1.4	0.1	0.2	0.5	1.1	3.1	9.4	27.0	66.2	164.9	110
Yorkshire & Humberside	6.6	1.6	0.2	0.3	0.4	1.0	2.7	8.0	23.4	60.7	155.9	100
East Midlands	5.3	1.2	0.2	0.3	0.4	1.0	2.6	8.0	21.8	60.0	160.4	99
East Anglia	3.8	0.9	0.1	0.3	0.4	0.9	2.4	6.6	19.1	54.8	154.8	91
South East	5.3	1.3	0.1	0.3	0.4	1.0	2.6	7.2	20.2	56.4	153.5	94
Greater London	6.0	1.5	0.1	0.3	0.5	1.0	2.8	8.0	21.4	57.0	150.6	96
Rest of South East	4.8	1.1	0.1	0.3	0.4	0.9	2.4	6.8	19.5	56.0	155.2	93
South West	5.6	1.3	0.1	0.3	0.4	1.1	2.6	6.7	18.0	54.1	149.5	90
West Midlands	6.0	1.3	0.2	0.2	0.4	1.1	2.6	7.7	22.8	61.5	159.2	101
North West	5.9	1.4	0.1	0.3	0.5	1.2	3.2	9.0	25.5	66.2	161.4	108
England	5.6	1.3	0.1	0.3	0.4	1.0	2.7	7.7	21.8	59.2	156.1	98
Wales	4.5	1.0	0.1	0.3	0.4	1.1	2.8	8.7	22.8	60.7	160.9	101
Scotland	5.5	1.4	0.2	0.3	0.6	1.3	3.5	10.0	27.3	70.5	184.3	119
Northern Ireland	6.3	1.5	0.2	0.3	0.5	1.2	3.0	9.0	23.3	61.3	174.3	106
All persons												
United Kingdom	6.3	1.5	0.2	0.5	0.7	1.4	3.6	10.7	29.7	72.9	170.0	100
North	6.7	1.6	0.2	0.5	0.7	1.4	4.1	12.6	34.8	79.5	174.5	111
Yorkshire & Humberside	7.3	1.7	0.2	0.5	0.6	1.3	3.6	10.9	30.8	73.9	168.2	101
East Midlands	6.5	1.5	0.2	0.6	0.6	1.3	3.3	10.6	29.3	73.4	171.7	99
East Anglia	4.8	1.2	0.1	0.5	0.6	1.1	3.0	8.8	25.3	67.0	167.8	90
South East	5.9	1.4	0.1	0.5	0.7	1.3	3.2	9.4	26.8	68.4	164.4	93
Greater London	6.5	1.6	0.2	0.5	0.8	1.6	3.7	10.5	28.4	69.2	161.8	97
Rest of South East	5.5	1.3	0.1	0.5	0.6	1.2	3.0	8.8	25.9	68.0	165.9	91
South West	5.8	1.4	0.1	0.5	0.6	1.2	3.1	9.0	24.5	66.2	161.6	89
West Midlands	7.1	1.6	0.2	0.5	0.6	1.3	3.4	10.8	30.4	74.5	170.9	101
North West	6.5	1.5	0.2	0.5	0.7	1.5	4.0	12.4	33.6	78.9	173.4	109
England	6.3	1.5	0.2	0.5	0.7	1.3	3.4	10.4	29.0	71.7	167.5	98
Wales	5.5	1.3	0.2	0.6	0.7	1.4	3.7	11.5	30.6	74.3	169.9	102
Scotland	6.4	1.6	0.2	0.6	0.9	1.7	4.7	13.4	35.4	83.6	194.3	119
Northern Ireland	7.0	1.7	0.2	0.7	0.8	1.4	3.7	11.8	31.4	75.6	187.4	107

1 Standardised Mortality Ratio, ie adjusted for the age structure of the population. See Appendix notes.

Source: Office of Population Censuses and Surveys; General Register Offices for Scotland and Northern Ireland

3.9 Live births[1], deaths and natural increase in population

Thousands and rates

	Thousands					Rate per 1,000 population				
	1961	1971	1981	1991	1993	1961	1971	1981	1991	1993
Live births										
United Kingdom	944.4	901.6	730.8	792.5	761.7	17.9	16.1	13.0	13.7	13.1
North	60.1	52.7	39.8	41.1	38.6	18.7	16.7	12.8	13.3	12.4
Yorkshire & Humberside	82.8	80.2	62.6	68.6	65.4	17.8	16.4	12.7	13.8	13.0
East Midlands	53.9	56.7	49.2	54.0	51.7	17.6	15.5	12.8	13.4	12.7
East Anglia	24.6	26.7	23.7	26.3	25.6	16.5	15.8	12.5	12.6	12.2
South East	279.5	266.4	220.3	247.7	244.3	16.6	15.4	13.0	14.0	13.7
Greater London	96.8	113.1	92.4	105.8	104.4	17.0	15.2	13.5	15.4	15.1
Rest of South East	182.6	153.3	127.9	141.9	139.9	15.6	14.9	12.6	13.2	12.9
South West	56.2	57.2	50.4	57.6	56.5	16.3	13.9	11.5	12.2	11.9
West Midlands	88.7	88.3	67.5	74.2	69.8	18.6	17.2	13.0	14.1	13.2
North West	120.5	112.0	84.7	91.2	84.5	18.3	16.9	13.1	14.3	13.2
England	766.4	740.1	598.2	660.8	636.5	17.6	15.9	12.8	13.7	13.1
Wales	44.9	43.1	35.8	38.1	36.6	17.0	15.8	12.7	13.2	12.6
Scotland	101.2	86.7	69.1	67.0	63.3	19.5	16.6	13.3	13.1	12.4
Northern Ireland	31.9	31.8	27.3	26.3	24.9	22.4	20.7	17.8	16.6	15.3
Deaths										
United Kingdom[2]	631.8	645.1	658.0	646.2	657.9	12.0	11.5	11.6	11.2	11.3
North	38.1	39.1	38.2	38.0	38.0	11.9	11.9	12.3	12.3	12.2
Yorkshire & Humberside	57.9	57.7	59.1	57.3	57.3	12.5	12.0	12.0	11.5	11.4
East Midlands	34.5	37.3	42.8	43.9	45.3	11.2	11.0	11.2	10.9	11.1
East Anglia	17.3	18.9	21.0	22.7	23.1	11.6	11.2	11.1	10.9	11.1
South East	187.4	194.0	188.6	182.5	184.4	11.9	11.2	11.1	10.3	10.4
Greater London	62.0	85.0	77.6	68.9	68.5	11.4	11.5	11.3	10.0	9.9
Rest of South East	125.4	109.0	111.0	113.6	115.9	13.4	12.9	10.9	10.6	10.7
South West	43.1	47.3	54.4	56.2	56.9	12.4	12.3	12.5	11.9	11.9
West Midlands	51.8	53.4	56.4	57.0	58.0	10.9	10.4	10.9	10.8	11.0
North West	88.0	84.7	80.4	76.4	77.5	13.3	12.4	12.4	12.0	12.1
England	518.0	532.4	541.0	534.0	540.6	11.9	11.5	11.6	11.1	11.1
Wales	33.7	34.8	35.0	34.1	35.9	12.8	12.7	12.4	11.8	12.3
Scotland	63.9	61.6	63.8	61.0	64.0	12.3	11.8	12.4	12.0	12.5
Northern Ireland	16.1	16.2	16.3	15.1	15.6	11.3	10.6	10.6	9.5	9.6
Natural increase										
United Kingdom	312.6	256.5	72.8	146.3	103.9	5.9	4.6	1.4	2.5	1.8
North	21.9	13.6	1.6	3.1	0.6	6.8	4.1	0.5	1.0	0.2
Yorkshire & Humberside	24.9	22.5	3.5	11.3	8.1	5.3	4.7	0.7	2.3	1.6
East Midlands	19.5	19.4	6.4	10.1	6.4	6.4	5.7	1.6	2.5	1.6
East Anglia	7.3	7.8	2.7	3.6	2.4	4.9	4.7	1.4	1.7	1.2
South East	92.1	72.3	31.7	65.2	59.9	4.7	4.2	1.9	3.7	3.4
Greater London	34.8	28.1	14.8	36.9	35.9	5.6	3.7	2.2	5.4	5.2
Rest of South East	57.2	44.3	16.9	28.3	24.0	2.2	2.0	1.7	2.6	2.2
South West	13.1	9.9	-4.0	1.4	-0.4	3.9	2.8	-1.0	0.3	-0.1
West Midlands	36.9	34.9	11.1	17.2	11.9	7.7	6.8	2.1	3.3	2.2
North West	32.6	27.2	4.3	14.8	7.1	5.0	4.2	0.7	2.3	1.1
England	248.3	207.7	57.2	126.8	95.9	5.7	4.6	1.2	2.6	2.0
Wales	11.2	8.3	0.8	4.0	0.7	4.2	3.1	0.3	1.4	0.2
Scotland	37.3	25.1	5.3	6.0	-0.7	7.2	4.8	0.9	1.2	-0.1
Northern Ireland	15.8	15.6	11.0	11.2	9.3	11.1	10.1	6.9	7.1	5.7

1 Births data for all countries and regions are based on the mother's usual area of residence. However 1961 and 1971 births registered in England and Wales to mothers usually resident outside England and Wales are assigned to region of occurrence; from 1972 such births are not included in the regional figures but in the UK totals only. Annual births data are given for year of occurrence in England and Wales, and for year of registration in Scotland and Northern Ireland. See Appendix notes.
2 From 1981 onwards, UK death figures include deaths occurring in England and Wales to non-residents of England and Wales. These numbers are excluded from the data for England and Wales and the standard regions.

Source: Office of Population Censuses and Surveys; General Register Offices for Scotland and Northern Ireland

3.10 Inter-regional movements[1], 1993

Thousands

		Region of origin										
	United Kingdom	North	Yorkshire & Humberside	East Midlands	East Anglia	South East	South West	West Midlands	North West	Wales	Scotland	Northern Ireland
Region of destination												
United Kingdom	.	50	87	83	49	252	101	92	101	48	47	12
North	47	.	9	3	2	12	3	3	8	1	5	1
Yorkshire & Humberside	88	11	.	14	4	24	6	8	5	3	4	1
East Midlands	93	4	16	.	7	30	7	13	9	3	3	1
East Anglia	57	2	4	7	.	31	4	3	3	1	2	-
South East	224	12	22	26	23	.	51	28	27	14	17	3
South West	121	3	6	7	4	64	.	14	9	9	4	1
West Midlands	83	3	7	11	3	26	11	.	1	7	3	1
North West	92	8	14	8	3	26	7	11	.	8	6	2
Wales	52	1	3	3	1	16	8	8	9	.	2	-
Scotland	54	6	5	3	2	19	4	3	7	2	.	2
Northern Ireland	11	-	1	-	-	5	1	1	1	-	1	.

1 Based on patients re-registering with NHS doctors in other parts of the United Kingdom. See Appendix notes.

Source: Office of Population Censuses and Surveys; General Register Offices for Scotland and Northern Ireland

3.11 International migration[1,2]

Thousands

	Inflow					Outflow				
	1981	1986	1991	1992	1993	1981	1986	1991	1992	1993
United Kingdom	153	250	267	216	209	233	213	239	227	213
North	6	11	7	5	5	15	8	4	6	5
Yorkshire & Humberside	9	13	20	9	16	14	14	14	14	11
East Midlands	5	10	13	12	10	10	5	7	11	9
East Anglia	4	8	14	11	10	5	12	15	11	12
South East	81	129	134	114	108	103	103	112	105	115
Greater London	50	78	79	62	60	56	51	68	56	61
Rest of South East	31	51	55	53	47	47	52	45	49	54
South West	10	18	18	16	15	13	16	19	17	12
West Midlands	11	11	14	8	14	13	8	18	13	12
North West	13	24	14	20	12	23	16	19	17	13
England	138	224	234	196	188	196	182	207	194	189
Wales	3	8	8	5	6	11	6	6	7	7
Scotland	10	16	22	13	15	21	21	24	23	15
Northern Ireland	2	2	3	1	-	5	4	2	3	1

1 Subject to relatively large sampling errors where estimates are based on small numbers of contacts. See Appendix notes.
2 Excludes migration to and from the Irish Republic, Channel Isles and Isle of Man. Adjustment of the figures shown are required for persons who are granted extensions of stay in the United Kingdom or abroad. See Appendix notes.

Source: International Passenger Survey, Office of Population Censuses and Surveys

3.12 Components of population change, mid-1992 to mid-1993

Thousands

	Resident population mid-1992	Births	Deaths	Net natural change	Net civilian migration and other changes	Total change	Resident population mid-1993
United Kingdom	58,006.5	764.2	634.6	129.6	55.1	184.7	58,191.2
North	3,098.9	39.2	37.2	2.0	1.4	3.4	3,102.3
Yorkshire & Humberside	5,002.3	65.9	55.7	10.2	1.5	11.7	5,014.1
East Midlands	4,061.9	52.2	43.6	8.6	12.4	21.0	4,082.9
East Anglia	2,088.6	25.5	22.2	3.3	2.0	5.3	2,093.9
South East	17,703.2	243.1	178.7	64.4	1.8	66.2	17,769.4
Greater London	6,904.6	104.1	66.6	37.5	-9.1	28.4	6,933.0
Rest of South East	10,798.7	139.0	112.1	26.9	10.8	37.7	10,836.4
South West	4,746.3	56.2	55.3	0.9	20.9	21.7	4,768.0
West Midlands	5,277.5	70.5	56.2	14.3	-2.1	12.2	5,289.7
North West	6,399.5	85.7	74.9	10.8	2.1	12.9	6,412.4
England	48,378.3	638.3	523.9	114.4	40.0	154.4	48,532.7
Wales	2,898.5	36.7	33.8	3.0	5.0	8.0	2,906.5
Scotland	5,111.2	64.3	61.9	2.4	6.6	9.0	5,120.2
Northern Ireland	1,618.4	24.9	15.1	9.9	3.6	13.4	1,631.8

Source: Office of Population Censuses and Surveys; General Register Offices for Scotland and Northern Ireland

3.13 Social class[1] of economically active population, Spring 1994

Percentages and thousands

	Social class						Total	
	Professional occupations (I)	Managerial and technical (II)	Skilled occupations non - manual (IIIN)	Skilled occupations manual (IIIM)	Partly skilled occupations (IV)	Unskilled occupations (V)	Other[2]	economically active population (= 100%) (thousands)
United Kingdom	5.3	28.3	21.8	20.8	14.8	5.7	3.3	28,239
North	4.3	25.3	22.0	22.0	16.0	7.0	3.5	1,417
Yorkshire & Humberside	3.7	26.4	20.8	23.7	16.1	6.1	3.2	2,394
East Midlands	4.3	27.5	20.8	22.9	16.3	5.3	3.0	2,020
East Anglia	5.0	26.4	20.8	21.2	17.2	6.2	3.1	1,098
South East	6.9	32.2	23.4	17.3	12.3	4.8	3.1	8,943
Greater London	7.7	33.6	23.3	15.7	11.1	4.6	3.9	3,370
Rest of South East	6.4	31.4	23.4	18.2	13.0	5.0	2.6	5,573
South West	5.1	29.1	20.6	20.1	15.8	5.7	3.5	2,360
West Midlands	4.1	24.9	20.1	23.8	17.6	6.4	3.2	2,585
North West	4.8	27.0	21.7	22.0	15.5	5.8	3.1	2,971
England	5.4	28.8	21.9	20.5	14.8	5.6	3.2	23,789
Wales	4.8	26.3	20.5	23.0	16.0	6.1	3.3	1,297
Scotland	5.4	25.8	22.0	22.2	14.3	6.8	3.5	2,471
Northern Ireland	4.3	24.5	20.9	23.1	15.7	6.1	5.4	683

1 Based on occupation. See Appendix notes.
2 Includes members of the armed forces, those who did not state their social class, and for the unemployed those whose previous occupation was more than eight years ago, or those who never had a job.

Source: Labour Force Survey, Employment Department; Department of Economic Development, Northern Ireland

3.14 Resident population: by ethnic group[1], Summer 1994

Percentages and thousands

	White	Black	Indian	Pakistani/ Bangladeshi	Mixed/ other	All persons (= 100%) (thousands)
Great Britain	94.2	1.5	1.6	1.3	1.3	55,893
North	98.6	..	..	0.4	0.6	3,052
Yorkshire & Humberside	95.4	0.6	1.1	2.2	0.7	4,948
East Midlands	95.1	0.8	2.8	0.4	0.8	4,066
East Anglia	98.2	0.5	..	..	0.8	2,125
South East	89.5	3.6	2.5	1.8	2.6	17,524
Greater London	77.8	8.3	5.1	3.4	5.3	6,753
Rest of South East	96.8	0.6	0.9	0.7	0.9	10,771
South West	98.8	0.3	0.2	..	0.5	4,740
West Midlands	91.6	1.4	3.3	2.7	1.0	5,239
North West	95.4	0.7	1.1	1.7	1.2	6,322
England	93.5	1.7	1.8	1.5	1.5	48,017
Wales	98.8	..	..	0.4	0.4	2,888
Scotland	99.0	..	..	0.4	0.3	4,988

1 For some ethnic origins in some regions, sample sizes are too small to provide a reliable estimate. See Appendix notes to Labour market chapter.

Source: Labour Force Survey, Employment Department

3.15 Live births outside marriage[1]: by age of mother, 1981[2] and 1993

Percentages and numbers

	Under 20	20-24	25-29	30-34	35-39	40 or over	All ages	Number of live births outside marriage (=100%)
1981								
United Kingdom	45.5	14.5	6.5	6.1	7.8	11.8	12.5	91,330
North	50.0	13.2	6.2	5.7	5.1	12.6	13.2	5,270
Yorkshire & Humberside	45.8	14.5	6.4	6.9	10.2	11.2	13.5	8,430
East Midlands	44.0	14.1	6.1	5.6	12.3	14.4	12.6	6,180
East Anglia	34.2	11.6	4.5	7.2	2.7	17.0	9.5	2,250
South East	48.4	16.3	7.2	6.3	7.5	13.2	12.6	27,780
Greater London	57.3	23.4	0.6	7.9	9.0	14.3	17.2	15,890
Rest of South East	40.7	11.3	4.9	5.1	6.2	12.1	9.3	11,890
South West	41.7	11.2	5.5	5.0	6.8	17.0	10.3	5,210
West Midlands	45.9	13.8	6.6	5.8	9.4	8.4	12.8	8,640
North West	52.3	18.1	7.8	6.7	7.3	11.2	15.5	13,160
England	47.2	15.0	6.7	6.2	7.9	12.3	12.9	76,920
Wales	40.1	11.8	5.0	6.7	8.0	13.7	11.2	4,020
Scotland	39.1	13.7	6.5	6.0	8.9	12.4	12.2	8,447
Northern Ireland	33.1	8.0	3.9	3.2	3.4	3.9	7.0	1,902
1993								
United Kingdom	85.2	49.1	23.8	17.9	19.7	22.8	31.7	241,862
North	91.5	54.7	25.9	19.0	21.9	27.1	37.2	14,372
Yorkshire & Humberside	84.3	48.9	23.4	18.6	21.4	23.0	34.0	22,238
East Midlands	87.0	49.2	22.5	17.1	20.0	23.6	32.1	16,612
East Anglia	81.4	42.4	19.4	15.3	17.3	25.2	27.4	7,007
South East	80.1	47.1	24.7	18.4	19.9	22.8	29.3	71,592
Greater London	76.2	48.4	30.5	22.7	23.9	24.9	32.9	34,385
Rest of South East	83.0	46.2	20.6	15.2	16.5	20.9	26.6	37,207
South West	85.4	46.0	21.5	16.3	20.1	24.9	28.9	16,344
West Midlands	82.3	47.5	24.8	18.5	19.5	22.0	33.1	23,141
North West	88.5	57.3	29.3	20.4	21.1	25.1	38.2	32,275
England	84.4	49.3	24.4	18.3	20.2	23.5	32.0	203,581
Wales	89.7	50.8	23.9	19.2	21.8	24.8	35.2	12,893
Scotland	88.4	50.4	21.4	16.2	19.0	20.6	31.3	19,855
Northern Ireland	88.3	39.2	13.2	9.1	9.0	10.3	21.9	5,459

1 Births in England and Wales are assigned to areas according to usual residence of mother at date of birth, as stated at registration. If the address of usual residence is outside England and Wales, the birth is included in the UK total, but excluded from regional and national totals. In 1993 there were 74 such live births outside marriage.
2 Live births for 1981 for England and Wales are based on a 10 per cent sample.

Source: Office of Population Censuses and Surveys; General Register Offices for Scotland and Northern Ireland

3.16 Marriage

Thousands and percentages

	Total marriages (thousands)			Remarriages[1] as a percentage of all marriages					
				Males			Females		
	1971	1981	1992	1971	1981	1992	1971	1981	1992
United Kingdom	459.4	397.8	356.0	*14.3*	*25.2*	*27.4*	*13.4*	*24.0*	*26.9*
North	26.9	23.1	17.9	*11.1*	*22.9*	*27.3*	*11.3*	*22.4*	*27.4*
Yorkshire & Humberside	39.9	35.7	30.5	*15.0*	*26.0*	*29.9*	*14.7*	*25.7*	*29.8*
East Midlands	27.8	26.7	24.8	*14.8*	*26.2*	*29.6*	*14.4*	*25.4*	*29.7*
East Anglia	13.2	13.1	13.4	*14.5*	*28.7*	*30.6*	*14.1*	*27.9*	*30.8*
South East	145.9	120.9	110.8	*16.7*	*27.5*	*26.5*	*14.9*	*25.4*	*25.5*
Greater London	69.2	50.5	44.6	*15.9*	*25.2*	*22.7*	*13.6*	*22.3*	*20.9*
Rest of South East	76.6	70.4	66.3	*17.4*	*29.1*	*29.0*	*16.1*	*27.7*	*28.5*
South West	29.7	30.9	29.8	*16.1*	*29.3*	*30.8*	*15.0*	*28.1*	*30.5*
West Midlands	42.4	36.0	30.7	*13.7*	*24.5*	*26.9*	*13.2*	*23.6*	*26.9*
North West	56.5	45.7	36.9	*14.7*	*25.8*	*28.4*	*14.0*	*24.7*	*27.9*
England	382.3	332.2	295.0	*15.2*	*26.5*	*28.0*	*14.3*	*25.3*	*27.6*
Wales	22.4	19.8	16.6	*12.9*	*23.6*	*28.2*	*12.6*	*23.2*	*27.7*
Scotland	42.5	36.2	35.1	*9.3*	*18.3*	*25.5*	*9.1*	*16.9*	*25.1*
Northern Ireland	12.2	9.6	9.4	*3.4*	*8.0*	*11.5*	*2.9*	*7.8*	*10.9*

1 Marriages in which at least one of the partners had been married previously.

Source: Office of Population and Censuses Surveys; General Register Offices for Scotland and Northern Ireland

3.17 Cohabitation amongst people aged 16-59, 1991-1993[1]

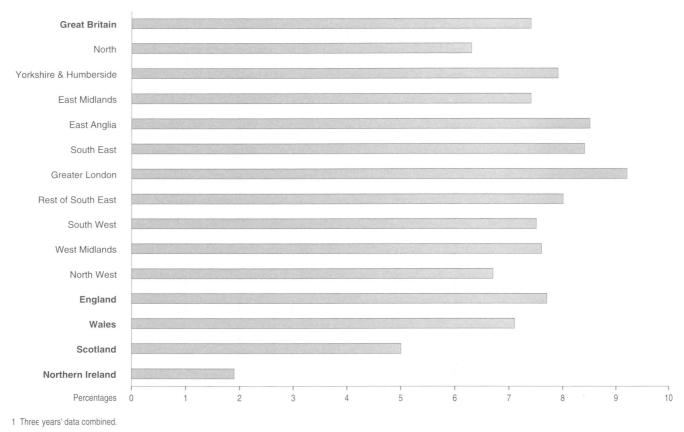

1 Three years' data combined.

Source: General Household Survey; Northern Ireland, Continuous Household Survey

3.18 Household size, 1993-94[1]

Percentages

	Percentage of households with the following number of persons						
	1	2	3	4	5	6	7 or more
Great Britain	28	35	15	15	5	1	1
North	29	32	16	15	6	1	1
Yorkshire & Humberside	29	36	16	14	4	1	1
East Midlands	27	37	16	15	4	1	-
East Anglia	27	38	13	15	6	1	1
South East	28	35	15	15	5	2	1
Greater London	32	33	14	14	6	2	1
Rest of South East	26	37	15	15	5	2	1
South West	26	37	16	15	5	1	-
West Midlands	27	34	15	16	5	2	1
North West	29	33	16	15	5	2	1
England	28	35	15	15	5	2	1
Wales	28	34	18	13	5	2	1
Scotland	31	31	16	15	5	1	-

1 See Appendix notes.

Source: Family Resources Survey, Department of Social Security

3.19 Families: by type, 1988-1989[1] and 1992-1993[1]

Percentages

	1988-1989					1992-1993				
	Families with dependent children		Families with non-dependent children only		Couple families with no children	Families with dependent children		Families with non-dependent children only		Couple families with no children
	Couple	Lone parent	Couple	Lone parent		Couple	Lone parent	Couple	Lone parent	
Great Britain	36	7	12	5	39	35	10	11	5	40
North	33	10	15	6	37	34	12	13	4	37
Yorkshire & Humberside	36	8	12	5	39	34	8	12	4	41
East Midlands	36	6	12	4	42	35	8	9	6	42
East Anglia	34	7	11	5	44	33	7	10	3	46
South East	36	6	11	5	42	36	10	10	5	40
Greater London	33	9	10	7	41	34	14	9	5	38
Rest of South East	37	5	11	4	43	36	7	10	4	42
South West	37	6	10	4	43	34	7	8	4	46
West Midlands	39	8	13	5	35	35	10	12	5	38
North West	37	9	13	6	36	35	11	11	6	37
England	36	7	12	5	40	35	9	11	5	40
Wales	36	7	14	6	38	37	9	10	5	39
Scotland	40	7	12	7	34	33	11	12	5	39
Northern Ireland	46	10	12	7	25	..	..	..	..	..

1 Two years data combined.

Source: General Household Survey; Northern Ireland, Continuous Household Survey

3.20 Economic activity of married and lone mothers with dependent children[1], Spring 1994[2]

Percentages

	Married mothers[3]					Lone mothers				
	Economically active				Econ-	Economically active				Econ-
	Employed full-time	Employed part-time	Total in emp- loyment[4]	ILO unemp- loyed	omically inactive	Employed full-time	Employed part-time	Total in emp- loyment[4]	ILO unemp- loyed	omically inactive
United Kingdom	19.2	35.6	61.7	4.7	33.5	15.4	20.6	39.1	8.6	52.3
North	19.0	36.1	59.9	5.8	34.3	14.1	23.1	38.0	..	53.6
Yorkshire & Humberside	17.3	40.0	62.5	4.5	32.9	14.3	22.9	39.0	10.4	50.6
East Midlands	18.8	36.5	62.3	5.1	32.6	..	30.4	45.9	..	48.4
East Anglia	14.5	41.5	63.9	4.8	31.3	..	..	43.9	..	42.6
South East	19.0	32.4	59.5	4.3	36.2	17.8	17.7	39.4	8.2	52.4
Greater London	21.7	23.6	53.2	4.7	42.1	16.7	13.4	33.3	8.7	58.0
Rest of South East	17.4	37.5	63.2	4.1	32.8	19.1	22.5	46.3	7.6	46.1
South West	15.8	39.1	64.5	4.6	30.8	12.6	26.3	45.2	..	48.8
West Midlands	19.0	38.0	63.4	5.2	31.5	14.6	19.1	37.1	9.6	53.3
North West	23.6	36.8	65.6	3.8	30.6	14.5	18.2	34.4	7.9	57.6
England	18.9	36.0	62.0	4.6	33.4	15.4	20.6	39.3	8.3	52.3
Wales	16.3	35.7	59.5	6.7	33.8	16.4	23.4	42.6	..	49.8
Scotland	21.7	35.2	62.7	5.6	31.7	14.8	21.0	37.5	12.3	50.2
Northern Ireland	24.4	25.7	55.3	..	41.0	..	..	34.1	..	61.0

1 Aged under 16.
2 In some cases, sample sizes are too small to provide a reliable estimate.
3 Includes those cohabiting.
4 Includes the self employed, those on Government Employment and Training Programmes, and unpaid family workers.

Source: Labour Force Survey, Employment Department; Department of Economic Development, Northern Ireland

4 Education and Training

Class sizes

The smallest class sizes in both primary and secondary schools are in Scotland.

(Table 4.2)

School sizes

One in three secondary schools in Wales and in the South West has more than a thousand pupils, compared with just over one in ten in Northern Ireland.

(Table 4.3)

Under fives

Three quarters of three and four year olds in the North and in Wales attended a maintained school in 1993/94.

(Table 4.4)

Education after age 16

Within Great Britain, 16 year olds in Scotland are the most likely to remain in education while those in Wales and the North are least likely.

(Table 4.6)

Exam results

Pupils in Scotland are more likely than those in any other region of Great Britain to achieve at least one graded exam result in their last year of compulsory schooling.

(Table 4.7)

Among the English regions, pupils in the South West are the most likely to achieve GCSE grades A-C in all the core subjects of the National Curriculum in their last year of compulsory schooling.

(Table 4.8)

Further education

There are more females than males in further education in every region except Scotland.

(Table 4.14)

Expenditure

In Great Britain in 1992/93, local government expenditure per head of population aged 5-21 ranged from £1,960 in East Anglia to £2,280 in Wales.

(Chart 4.15)

Capital expenditure accounted for more than 7 per cent of total local government expenditure on education in Northern Ireland in 1992/93, three times the proportion in the West Midlands.

(Table 4.16)

Training

More than 11 in every 20 Youth Training participants in the South West in 1993-94 gained a qualification, the highest proportion of any region.

(Table 4.18)

Employees in Yorkshire and Humberside, the South East and Wales were the most likely to receive some off-the-job training in 1994, while those in Northern Ireland were least likely.

(Table 4.19)

Introduction

There are five stages of education: nursery, primary, secondary, further and higher education. Primary and secondary education are compulsory for all children between the ages of five and 16 years, and the transition is normally at age 11 in England, Wales and Northern Ireland and 12 in Scotland. However, some local education authorities in England operate a system of middle schools which cater for pupils on either side of this age, and these are deemed either primary or secondary according to the age range of the pupils. Post-compulsory secondary education usually lasts for two years. No fees are payable at any primary or secondary school wholly maintained by the local education authority, but it is open to parents, if they choose, to pay for their children to attend other schools. In Northern Ireland, children who attain the age of 4 on or before 1 July are required to commence primary school the following September.

On reaching the minimum school-leaving age, pupils have a variety of options. They may leave or continue at school, or they may continue full-time, part-time or evening study at other institutions - usually a college of further education. Rates of 16-year-olds participating in education are given in Table 4.6. Those who stay on at school or continue study at FE establishments may, after further study, seek admission to higher education courses at higher education institutions (such as universities, including the former polytechnics) or colleges of higher education. The choice depends, amongst other things, on what examination results have been achieved.

In general, the education services of the United Kingdom are not subject to detailed central control. Some central control is, however, exercised over the curriculum taught during compulsory schooling. In particular, the *Education Reform Act 1988* introduced the National Curriculum in England and Wales, which includes the core subjects of English, mathematics and science (Welsh in Welsh-speaking schools in Wales) and seven (eight in Wales) other foundation subjects.

The 1988 Act also provided for local authorities to delegate the management of school budgets to the schools themselves, and for schools to seek withdrawal from LEA control and become self-governing. At January 1994, there were 260 grant maintained primary and 554 grant maintained secondary schools in England, and a further five grant maintained primary and ten grant maintained secondary schools in Wales. The numbers of pupils and teachers in grant maintained schools are shown in Table 4.1.

"There are five

In previous editions, *Regional Trends* has included tables on school leavers' qualifications and destinations drawn from surveys conducted by the Department for Education, the Welsh Office, the Scottish Office and the Department for Education Northern Ireland. Whilst surveys of destinations of school leavers are still conducted in Scotland and Northern Ireland, the surveys by the DFE and the Welsh Office are no longer undertaken. As a result, information on examination achievements in Great Britain is presented in a new format in Tables 4.7 and 4.8. For GCSEs, the data reflect all achievements at any time by pupils aged 16 at the end of the school year (Year 4 pupils' SCE Standard Grades in Scotland). Within England and Wales, the figures relating to GCE 'A' levels reflect the achievements in school - as opposed to other institutions such as Colleges of Further Education - of pupils aged between 17 and 19 at the end of the school year as a percentage of the 18 year old population. This age spread takes account of those pupils sitting the exams a year early or resitting them. In Scotland, pupils mostly sit their Highers a year earlier, in Year S5, although they can resit them or take additional subjects in S6. However, the data for Scotland relates only to S5 pupils' exam results.

Data on examination achievements by pupils in Northern Ireland are not included in these tables, as they are not available by gender. In 1992/93, 48 per cent of Year 12 pupils achieved 5 or more GCSEs at grades A - C and 85 per cent of those taking 'A' levels achieved at least two passes.

Table 4.16 shows the proportions of young people meeting two of the National Targets for Education and Training. 'Foundation targets' are required for young people entering the labour market who need to have a firm basis on which to develop their skills. People then need to keep on learning and developing their skills, in particular to keep up with technological changes and new markets, and so 'Lifetime learning targets' have also been developed. The targets have been set using the new competence-based National Vocational Qualifications (NVQs), Scottish Vocational Qualifications (SVQs), or their academic equivalents. Details of the targets are in the Appendix.

It should be noted that the data in Table 4.16 relate to the region in which the person is resident, and not where they obtained the qualifications. This can lead to some distortion of the regional picture of educational standards; this is particularly relevant in Northern Ireland, where many qualified young people leave the Province to enter higher education or seek employment in mainland Britain.

stages of education...."

4.1 Pupils and teachers: by type of school, January 1994[1]

Thousands and numbers

| | Public sector schools | | | | Non-maintained schools | All special schools | All schools | |
	Nursery schools	Primary schools	Secondary schools Total	Of which compre-hensive[2]			Total	Of which grant maintained[3]
Pupils[4] (thousands)								
United Kingdom	61.6	4,997.7	3,587.5	3,023.9	637.5	114.2	9,398.5	565.0
North	3.4	275.2	206.7	183.1	18.4	6.4	510.1	10.4
Yorkshire & Humberside	2.6	439.5	328.2	286.4	31.7	8.7	810.8	15.5
East Midlands	1.6	345.0	264.0	227.9	32.9	6.3	649.8	57.2
East Anglia	0.6	162.7	130.0	113.9	21.9	2.7	317.9	28.6
South East	10.4	1,410.9	998.3	813.7	281.2	36.6	2,737.4	319.1
Greater London	5.5	561.9	358.5	328.6	109.9	12.6	1,048.4	109.2
Rest of South East	4.9	849.0	639.9	485.2	171.3	24.0	1,689.0	209.9
South West	1.6	368.7	279.5	239.4	59.9	8.6	718.3	51.6
West Midlands	4.7	483.1	336.6	298.8	90.7	12.5	927.6	46.7
North West	5.9	608.6	390.3	363.4	54.7	15.7	1,075.2	26.5
England	30.8	4,093.5	2,933.6	2,526.7	591.5	97.6	7,747.0	555.5
Wales	2.3	275.7	194.4	185.9	10.7	3.6	486.6	9.5
Scotland	24.5	438.4	311.3	311.3	34.4	8.6	817.1	.
Northern Ireland	4.1	190.1	148.3	.	0.9	4.4	347.7	.
Teachers[4] (thousands)								
United Kingdom	2.8	224.1	225.1	191.3	60.0	19.0	531.1	33.5
North	0.2	12.0	12.4	11.2	1.6	0.9	27.1	0.6
Yorkshire & Humberside	0.1	19.1	19.9	17.6	2.8	1.4	43.3	0.9
East Midlands	0.1	15.1	16.5	14.3	3.2	1.1	36.0	3.4
East Anglia	-	7.3	8.0	7.1	2.3	0.4	18.0	1.7
South East	0.6	63.9	61.1	50.2	27.8	6.0	159.4	18.9
Greater London	0.3	26.3	22.5	20.7	10.0	2.4	61.5	6.6
Rest of South East	0.3	37.6	38.6	29.6	17.8	3.6	97.9	12.3
South West	0.1	16.1	16.7	14.4	6.3	1.3	40.3	3.0
West Midlands	0.2	20.9	20.4	18.3	7.2	1.9	50.6	2.8
North West	0.3	26.2	24.0	22.3	4.4	2.8	57.7	1.6
England	1.6	180.6	178.8	155.3	55.5	15.9	432.3	32.9
Wales	0.1	12.4	12.2	11.7	1.1	0.6	26.4	0.6
Scotland	0.9	22.5	24.3	24.3	3.3	1.9	52.8	.
Northern Ireland	0.2	8.8	9.8	.	0.1	0.6	19.5	.
Pupils per teacher[4] (thousands)								
United Kingdom	22.0	22.3	15.9	15.8	10.6	6.0	17.7	16.9
North	21.0	23.0	16.7	16.4	11.4	6.9	18.9	16.2
Yorkshire & Humberside	19.1	23.0	16.5	16.3	11.4	6.0	18.7	16.9
East Midlands	18.9	22.9	16.0	15.9	10.1	5.6	18.1	16.7
East Anglia	19.3	22.3	16.3	16.1	9.7	6.7	17.7	17.3
South East	17.5	22.1	16.3	16.2	10.1	6.1	17.2	16.9
Greater London	16.8	21.3	15.9	15.9	11.0	5.3	17.0	16.5
Rest of South East	18.4	22.6	16.6	16.4	9.6	6.6	17.3	17.1
South West	20.4	23.0	16.8	16.7	9.6	6.8	17.8	17.3
West Midlands	23.5	23.1	16.5	16.4	12.6	6.5	18.3	16.7
North West	20.3	23.2	16.3	16.3	12.4	5.7	18.6	16.6
England	19.5	22.7	16.4	16.3	10.6	6.1	17.9	16.9
Wales	20.6	22.3	15.9	15.9	9.6	6.4	18.4	16.9
Scotland	25.9	19.5	12.8	12.8	10.5	4.5	15.5	.
Northern Ireland	24.7	21.7	15.1	.	10.0	6.8	17.8	.

1 See Appendix notes.
2 Great Britain only.
3 England and Wales only.
4 Full-time equivalents.

Source: Department For Education; Welsh Office; The Scottish Office Education Department; Department of Education, Northern Ireland

4.2 Average class sizes[1], 1981 and 1994

Numbers

| | One teacher classes | | | | All classes | | | |
| | Primary | | Secondary | | Primary | | Secondary | |
	1981	1994	1981	1994	1981	1994	1981	1994
Great Britain	..	..	..	..	..	26.8	..	21.4
North	24.1	26.6	20.5	21.5	24.7	26.9	21.2	22.0
Yorkshire & Humberside	24.7	27.0	21.3	21.6	25.1	27.4	21.9	21.9
East Midlands	26.0	26.6	21.2	20.9	26.3	27.0	22.0	21.3
East Anglia	24.5	25.8	21.0	21.0	24.9	26.2	22.2	21.6
South East	25.0	26.8	20.5	21.4	25.3	27.0	21.1	21.7
Greater London	23.1	26.7	19.6	21.7	23.5	27.0	20.2	22.1
Rest of South East	26.2	26.8	21.1	21.3	26.6	27.0	21.8	21.6
South West	26.1	26.9	21.7	21.5	26.4	27.1	22.2	21.8
West Midlands	25.1	27.0	20.8	21.7	25.4	27.4	21.3	22.0
North West	26.0	27.5	20.7	21.5	26.2	27.9	21.4	21.8
England	25.2	26.9	20.8	21.4	25.5	27.2	21.5	21.8
Wales	..	..	..	..	..	25.6	..	20.1
Scotland	..	..	..	..	23.8	24.7	19.9	19.4

1 Maintained schools only.

Source: Department For Education; Welsh Office; The Scottish Office Education Department

4.3 Primary and secondary schools in the public sector: by size, 1993/94[1]

Percentages and numbers

| | Primary schools | | | | | Secondary schools | | | | |
| | Number of pupils on the register | | | | Total schools (=100%) (numbers) | Number of pupils on the register | | | | Total schools (= 100%) (numbers) |
	50 or under	51-100	101-200	Over 200		400 or under	401-800	801-1,000	Over 1,000	
United Kingdom	8.2	12.8	30.2	48.7	23,698	11.7	40.5	21.2	26.6	4,495
North	8.3	12.0	35.1	44.7	1,332	20.2	36.8	18.1	24.9	277
Yorkshire & Humberside	6.2	11.7	33.8	48.2	2,022	21.9	34.4	16.5	27.3	425
East Midlands	8.6	16.8	33.1	41.6	1,766	13.2	46.0	16.7	24.1	348
East Anglia	11.3	20.9	30.2	37.6	914	15.6	48.0	13.3	23.1	173
South East	3.0	8.6	31.4	56.9	5,998	6.4	41.0	24.0	28.6	1,191
Greater London	-	1.0	23.0	76.0	1,968	2.2	37.5	25.2	35.1	405
Rest of South East	4.4	12.4	35.6	47.6	4,030	8.5	42.7	23.4	25.3	786
South West	9.2	21.8	30.5	38.4	2,038	10.1	38.7	19.9	31.3	336
West Midlands	5.1	10.5	27.2	57.1	2,065	9.8	43.9	22.2	24.1	428
North West	2.7	5.3	31.3	60.8	2,548	3.1	39.6	28.9	28.4	450
England	5.5	11.8	31.5	51.2	18,683	10.7	40.7	21.5	27.2	3,628
Wales	15.6	16.0	32.9	35.5	1,698	4.4	43.6	18.5	33.5	227
Scotland	21.2	13.7	21.6	43.5	2,341	17.4	33.8	22.3	26.5	408
Northern Ireland	16.0	25.9	23.0	35.1	976	23.7	47.4	17.2	11.6	232

1 See Appendix notes.

Source: Department For Education; Welsh Office; The Scottish Office Education Department; Department of Education, Northern Ireland

4.4 Education of children under five, 1993/94

Thousands and percentages

	Under fives in maintained schools[1]	
	Total (thousands)	Percentage of the 3 and 4 year old population
United Kingdom	810.7	52
North	61.2	76
Yorkshire & Humberside	88.7	66
East Midlands	55.5	50
East Anglia	19.9	36
South East	206.1	43
South West	43.9	37
West Midlands	85.6	58
North West	113.8	64
England	674.7	52
Wales	55.9	73
Scotland	56.7	44
Northern Ireland	23.3	45

1 Maintained nursery and primary schools; grant aided in Northern Ireland.

Source: Department For Education; Welsh Office;
The Scottish Office Education Department;
Department of Education, Northern Ireland

4.5 Day care of children under five[1]: by type of day care, March 1993

Thousands and numbers

	Local authority provided and registered[2] day-care places[3]			
	Day nurseries (thousands)	Child-minders[1] (thousands)	Play-groups (thousands)	Total per 100 pop. aged under 5 years[1]
United Kingdom	153.5	352.0	478.3	25.2
North	5.3	29.7	15.5	24.9
Yorkshire & Humberside	10.8	54.0	32.9	28.8
East Midlands	9.2	13.2	32.4	20.3
East Anglia	3.7	4.9	20.3	21.5
South East	54.8	65.8	171.3	24.2
South West	10.1	9.0	49.5	23.3
West Midlands	15.7	27.4	36.1	21.7
North West	22.8	96.7	37.7	35.0
England	132.4	300.7	395.8	25.4
Wales	5.2	11.6	24.9	21.8
Scotland	13.8	26.2	43.0	25.6
Northern Ireland	2.1	13.5	14.6	23.1

1 For England, Wales and Scotland, places with childminders are for children aged under eight. See Appendix notes.
2 A small number of places provided by facilities exempt from registration are excluded.
3 Figures for a few authorities in England have been estimated using the latest available data. Day-care figures for Northern Ireland are the average number of available places during year ending 31 March 1993.

Source: Department of Health; Welsh Office; The ScottishOffice;
Department of Health and Social Services, Northern Ireland

4.6 16 year-olds participating in school or further education, 1985/86 and 1993/94[1]

Thousands and percentages

	1985/86[2]				1993/94			
		In further education[3] (thousands)		Participation rate[4] (percentages)		In further education[3] (thousands)		Participation rate[4] (percentages)
	At school (thousands)	Full-time	Part-time		At school (thousands)	Full-time	Part-time	
United Kingdom	253.8	180.3	165.1	67	251.6	216.9	54.7	80
North	9.3	10.5	8.9	61	9.6	11.7	3.4	71
Yorkshire & Humberside	18.9	15.3	15.8	63	17.9	18.4	6.5	77
East Midlands	14.0	13.7	13.5	68	17.2	14.6	3.3	76
East Anglia	7.2	5.8	5.0	60	9.6	7.7	1.6	80
South East	78.2	53.5	33.2	62	79.2	71.3	9.9	84
Greater London	32.6	15.1	11.2	59	28.4	25.1	3.4	82
Rest of South East	45.6	38.4	22.0	64	50.8	46.2	6.5	84
South West	18.4	16.2	10.9	65	21.1	18.4	3.5	83
West Midlands	18.4	21.0	17.5	68	19.6	22.3	4.8	78
North West	20.0	26.3	25.3	72	17.9	30.1	6.5	75
England	184.5	162.5	130.0	65	192.0	194.4	39.4	79
Wales	13.5	8.2	7.3	65	9.0	10.6	3.2	68
Scotland	47.9	5.7	22.4	87	39.5	4.7	7.4	87
Northern Ireland	8.0	3.9	5.3	60	11.1	7.2	4.8	99

1 See Appendix notes.
2 1984/85 data for Scotland.
3 Includes pupils in sixth form colleges (in England only in 1985/86).
4 16 year olds expressed as a percentage of the 16 year old population. The Northern Ireland figure is not comparable as it is based on enrolments as opposed to head counts and therefore includes some element of double counting.

Source: Department For Education; Welsh Office; The Scottish Office Education Department; Department of Education, Northern Ireland

4.7 Examination achievements of pupils in schools: by gender, 1992/93[1]

Percentages and thousands

	Percentage of 16 year olds[2] achieving GCSEs or SCE Standard Grade				All 16 year olds[2] in schools (=100%) (thousands)	17-19 year olds[3] achieving 2 or more A levels/ 3 or more SCE Highers (percentages)
	5 or more grades A-C	5 or more grades A-G	1 or more grade A-G	No graded results		
Males						
Great Britain	36.6	81.2	89.2	10.8	314.8	20.8
North	32.4	78.9	87.3	12.7	17.3	12.6
Yorkshire & Humberside	31.6	78.3	87.6	12.4	28.1	14.3
East Midlands	34.9	83.1	90.4	9.6	23.3	18.3
East Anglia	38.0	85.2	91.3	8.7	11.7	18.8
South East	38.6	82.1	88.8	11.2	94.6	32.1
Greater London	33.4	76.6	85.9	14.1	32.8	17.6
Rest of South East	41.3	85.0	90.4	9.6	61.8	50.5
South West	40.3	85.4	91.7	8.3	26.3	20.6
West Midlands	32.8	79.9	88.4	11.6	30.6	15.4
North West	36.0	76.8	87.2	12.8	36.1	13.1
England	36.2	81.3	88.9	11.1	268.1	20.0
Wales	31.8	72.2	86.5	13.5	16.6	26.0
Scotland	42.8	84.6	93.6	6.4	30.1	24.1
Females						
Great Britain	45.8	86.3	92.1	7.9	298.7	23.0
North	40.8	83.9	90.7	9.3	16.6	14.8
Yorkshire & Humberside	40.1	83.6	90.6	9.4	26.4	15.5
East Midlands	43.4	87.4	93.1	6.9	21.7	20.0
East Anglia	49.7	90.1	93.5	6.5	11.2	22.4
South East	47.3	86.9	91.6	8.4	90.4	33.3
Greater London	41.8	82.3	88.7	11.3	32.2	18.7
Rest of South East	50.4	89.5	93.3	6.7	58.2	52.8
South West	50.5	90.1	94.0	6.0	25.0	23.6
West Midlands	41.9	85.8	91.9	8.1	28.6	16.5
North West	44.1	83.9	90.5	9.5	34.4	13.5
England	45.2	86.3	91.8	8.2	254.3	21.6
Wales	41.5	80.1	91.5	8.5	15.5	33.5
Scotland	54.1	89.7	95.4	4.6	28.8	28.6

1 See Appendix notes.
2 Aged 16 at the end of the school year.
3 Aged 17-19 at the end of the school year in England and Wales as a percentage of the 18 year old population. The figures for Scotland are not strictly comparable with those for England and Wales; pupils in Scotland mostly sit Highers one year earlier and the figures relate to the results of pupils in Year S5 as a percentage of the 17 year old population.

Source: Department For Education; Welsh Office; The Scottish Office Education Department

4.8 Pupils[1] achieving GCSE grades A-C[2]: by selected subjects and gender, 1992/93[3]

Percentages

	English	Mathe-matics	Any science[4]	Biology	Chem-istry	Physics	Any modern langu-age[5]	French	Geo-graphy	History	Craft Design Techno-logy	All core sub-jects[6]
Males												
Great Britain	43.9	39.5	40.5	7.3	9.4	10.8	..	19.6	22.4	17.0	18.9	..
North	37.8	36.0	34.6	6.5	8.1	8.4	19.3	14.9	21.3	16.3	17.5	15.8
Yorkshire & Humberside	37.6	34.9	34.5	6.1	7.8	8.4	21.8	16.5	21.5	15.3	16.9	16.6
East Midlands	41.8	37.1	38.6	5.0	5.1	6.4	21.9	17.8	21.9	15.2	17.2	17.2
East Anglia	42.6	41.3	43.4	3.4	3.6	4.1	23.7	19.2	25.3	19.0	21.6	18.6
South East	46.5	42.2	40.6	7.9	8.1	8.6	27.4	21.9	22.7	19.4	17.4	21.1
Greater London	42.9	36.7	34.1	6.9	7.6	8.3	24.7	17.7	17.7	17.3	15.3	17.5
Rest of South East	48.4	45.1	44.1	8.5	8.3	8.8	28.8	24.1	25.4	20.5	18.5	23.1
South West	47.4	45.2	44.6	8.6	9.0	10.0	27.6	23.4	25.0	18.8	22.4	22.1
West Midlands	40.5	34.2	36.4	5.4	5.5	6.2	21.8	17.2	20.9	16.0	14.3	16.7
North West	42.7	37.4	38.8	7.4	8.6	9.7	23.0	18.0	21.4	17.4	17.3	18.5
England	43.3	39.3	39.2	6.9	7.5	8.2	24.4	19.5	22.4	17.7	17.6	19.1
Wales	34.3	35.7	37.6	4.4	5.2	5.3	..	15.0	23.1	14.0	17.8	..
Scotland	54.1	43.4	54.0	12.2	29.3	37.1	29.2	22.8	21.9	13.0	31.1	23.8
Females												
Great Britain	60.7	40.4	41.3	9.0	7.4	5.7	..	31.4	20.0	22.4	9.2	..
North	54.8	37.4	34.8	8.2	7.1	5.7	34.0	27.8	18.0	21.3	5.2	23.7
Yorkshire & Humberside	55.3	35.9	34.8	7.2	6.4	5.0	35.8	27.6	17.9	21.1	6.7	23.5
East Midlands	59.3	36.9	38.0	5.9	4.0	3.5	34.3	28.5	19.9	20.4	9.3	23.6
East Anglia	63.6	42.4	43.9	3.9	2.8	2.5	39.7	33.3	23.6	26.5	10.3	27.5
South East	61.9	43.0	41.4	5.4	4.3	3.7	40.2	32.4	21.2	23.8	6.5	27.9
Greater London	56.8	37.5	35.5	4.3	3.4	2.9	36.8	27.7	17.5	22.0	7.5	23.1
Rest of South East	64.7	46.0	44.7	6.0	4.8	4.1	42.1	35.1	23.3	24.7	6.0	30.5
South West	64.4	45.4	45.2	9.4	7.0	5.8	43.0	36.9	23.5	23.2	10.1	30.6
West Midlands	58.2	35.2	36.9	4.7	3.5	3.2	34.6	27.4	18.7	21.8	6.2	23.2
North West	58.7	38.1	38.7	8.4	6.5	5.6	36.7	29.6	17.4	22.2	5.5	26.1
England	60.0	40.0	39.6	6.5	5.1	4.3	38.0	30.8	20.1	22.7	7.0	26.3
Wales	51.9	37.0	38.0	4.5	4.2	3.2	..	28.3	17.8	20.5	12.7	..
Scotland	71.8	45.0	58.0	34.2	30.0	19.1	47.2	38.0	19.9	21.1	26.3	34.5

1 Pupils in their last year of compulsory schooling.
2 SCE standard grades in Scotland.
3 See Appendix notes.
4 Including biology, chemistry and physics as separate subjects.
5 Including French.
6 English, mathematics, a science and a modern language.

Source: Department For Education; Welsh Office;
The Scottish Office Education Department

Regional Trends 30, © Crown copyright 1995

4.9 Enrolments on adult education courses in LEA maintained centres: by age[1] and gender, 1993/94

Thousands

	Part-time day				Evening only[2]				
	Persons aged 16-18		Persons aged 19 or over		Persons aged 16-18		Persons aged 19 or over		
	Males	Females	Males	Females	Males	Females	Males	Females	Total
North	0.2	0.1	3.4	12.3	1.0	1.7	11.0	30.6	60.3
Yorkshire & Humberside	0.1	0.2	4.6	19.5	0.7	1.7	8.4	22.2	57.4
East Midlands	3.0	3.1	7.6	30.2	3.3	5.2	20.5	47.1	120.0
East Anglia	1.3	2.0	3.0	12.8	1.3	1.9	10.3	25.1	57.6
South East	3.1	4.7	45.2	165.7	2.8	5.7	87.5	188.4	503.1
Greater London	1.2	1.9	21.7	72.4	0.8	1.7	31.9	64.5	196.1
Rest of South East	1.9	2.8	23.5	93.3	2.0	4.0	55.6	123.9	307.0
South West	0.6	1.1	6.6	27.6	0.7	1.7	15.9	40.3	94.5
West Midlands	1.0	1.1	8.6	29.3	2.7	3.9	18.7	39.4	104.7
North West	0.4	0.7	8.8	32.8	2.2	3.0	15.7	35.9	99.6
England	9.6	13.0	87.8	330.2	14.8	24.8	188.1	429.1	1,097.3
Wales	0.3	0.5	3.6	14.2	0.5	0.7	8.9	22.3	50.9

1 Age at 31 August 1993.
2 Includes open and distance learning.

Source: Department For Education; Welsh Office

4.10 New student awards made by local education authorities: by region of domicile, 1992/93

Thousands and rates

	Mandatory awards					Discretionary awards			
	First degrees	Teacher training	Other higher education	Total	Rates[1]	Higher education	Further education	Total	Rates[1]
United Kingdom	226.5	35.2	56.1	317.8	4,480	..	..	..	..
North	9.8	1.9	2.3	14.1	3,736	2.2	5.4	7.5	1,996
Yorkshire & Humberside	15.7	3.0	3.7	22.4	3,694	0.9	17.2	18.1	2,990
East Midlands	14.6	2.5	2.9	20.0	4,000	1.2	17.0	18.2	3,652
East Anglia	7.1	1.1	1.4	9.6	3,787	0.3	3.2	3.5	1,380
South East	78.5	10.0	12.9	101.3	4,925	4.1	29.3	33.4	1,623
Greater London	32.7	4.0	5.3	42.0	5,740	1.8	6.0	7.8	1,060
Rest of South East	45.8	5.9	7.6	59.3	4,476	2.3	23.3	25.6	1,934
South West	18.2	3.2	3.5	24.9	4,358	3.0	13.7	16.7	2,927
West Midlands	19.5	3.2	3.8	26.4	4,003	1.9	5.9	7.8	1,187
North West	25.6	4.0	5.5	35.1	4,401	1.3	21.2	22.5	2,823
England	188.9	28.9	36.0	253.8	4,359	14.9	112.9	127.9	2,196
Wales	11.1	3.0	2.8	16.9	4,600	0.6	10.3	10.9	2,966
Scotland	18.5	2.4	15.1	36.0	5,602	..	..	..	..
Northern Ireland	8.0	0.9	2.1	11.1	4,250	0.9	1.1	2.0	804

1 Rate per 10,000 population aged 17 at August 1992.

Source: Department For Education; The Scottish Office Education Department; Department of Education, Northern Ireland

4.11 Undergraduate students: by region of study and domicile, 1992/93

Percentages

Region of domicile	North	Yorkshire & Humberside	East Midlands	East Anglia	Greater London	Rest of South East	South West	West Midlands	North West	England	Wales	Scotland[1]	Northern Ireland
Region of study													
North	58	11	4	1	4	4	1	3	9	95	1	3	..
Yorkshire & Humberside	7	56	7	1	4	4	2	5	10	97	1	2	..
East Midlands	4	14	42	2	8	7	3	9	8	97	2	1	..
East Anglia	2	6	8	10	41	18	5	4	4	99	1	1	..
South East	2	4	4	2	29	39	6	4	5	96	3	2	..
Greater London	2	4	4	2	49	21	7	4	5	97	2	1	..
Rest of South East	2	5	4	2	14	53	5	5	4	95	4	2	..
South West	2	4	4	1	14	12	44	6	4	93	6	1	..
West Midlands	2	7	7	1	6	6	5	52	8	95	4	1	..
North West	6	12	5	1	4	4	2	6	58	96	2	2	..
England	6	12	8	2	17	18	8	10	14	95	3	2	..
Wales	1	4	4	1	7	6	7	5	8	41	58	1	..
Scotland	1	1	..	..	1	1	..	..	1	4	..	95	..
Northern Ireland	3	2	2	1	3	3	1	2	6	22	1	10	67

1 Information on region of domicile is not held for English non-university students studying in Scotland, hence these are only included in the England and United Kingdom totals.

Source: Department For Education; Welsh Office; The Scottish Office Education Department; Department of Education, Northern Ireland

4.12 Average size of student loans, 1993/94

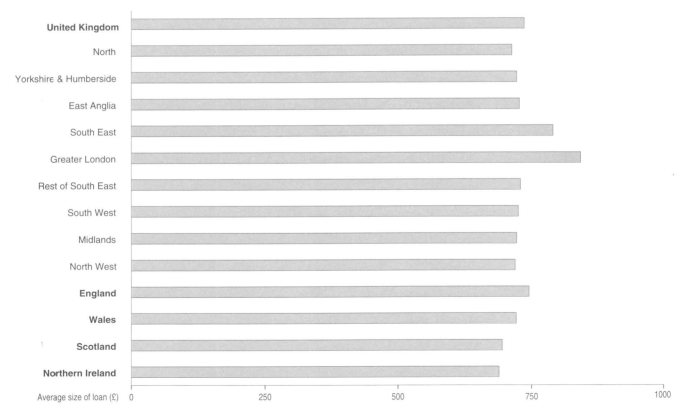

Source: Department for Education; Welsh Office; The Scottish Office Education Department; Department of Education, Northern Ireland

4.13 Home students in further education[1]: by gender and region of domicile, 1993/94

Thousands

Region of domicile	Full-time/ sandwich students		Part-time day students		Evening only students		All students		
	Males	Females	Males	Females	Males	Females	Males	Females	Total
United Kingdom	362.8	378.8	339.9	423.8	279.7	462.9	982.5	1,265.6	2,248.1
North	17.1	19.4	18.6	19.3	13.9	21.8	49.6	60.5	110.1
Yorkshire & Humberside	29.0	30.6	34.9	50.5	29.4	51.3	93.4	132.4	225.8
East Midlands	24.2	26.8	22.2	30.3	21.2	34.3	67.6	91.4	159.0
East Anglia	11.1	11.6	9.4	11.3	9.2	15.8	29.8	38.7	68.4
South East	117.3	118.2	82.1	121.7	86.0	135.1	285.3	375.0	660.3
Greater London	49.9	49.9	36.3	60.1	38.2	57.1	124.4	167.1	291.5
Rest of South East	67.4	68.3	45.8	61.5	47.7	78.1	160.9	207.9	368.8
South West	28.5	28.9	24.6	31.8	23.4	39.3	76.5	100.1	176.6
West Midlands	36.4	40.7	34.0	38.8	29.8	46.2	100.2	125.7	225.9
North West	45.9	51.7	41.6	55.5	33.9	58.9	121.4	166.2	287.6
England[2]	309.9	328.0	267.9	359.5	246.9	402.7	824.7	1,090.2	1,914.9
Wales	17.4	18.4	12.7	12.1	12.0	21.5	42.1	52.0	94.1
Scotland	25.4	21.8	47.2	38.5	11.8	19.1	84.5	79.5	163.9
Northern Ireland	10.1	10.5	12.0	13.7	9.0	19.6	31.1	43.8	74.9
Other United Kingdom[3]	0.1	0.1	..	..	..	..	0.1	0.1	0.2

1 See Appendix notes. Excludes students in adult education centres and private institutions.
2 Figures include English students studying in Scotland, for whom no region of domicile is held.
3 Includes Channel Islands, Isle of Man, and home students whose region of domicile was unknown or unclassified.

Source: Department For Education; Welsh Office; The Scottish Office Education Department;
Department of Education, Northern Ireland

4.14 Education expenditure by local government, 1992-93[1]

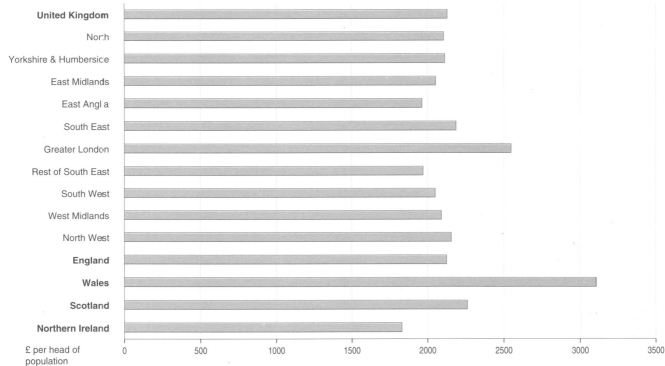

£ per head of population aged 5-21[2]

1 Total net recurrent and capital expenditure on, or related to, education. Includes central government expenditure on Grant Maintained schools and also voluntary grammer schools in Northern Ireland. Care should be taken in comparing expenditure between territories as methods of service delivery and local authority responsibilities vary between them.
2 Population aged 4-21 for Northern Ireland.

Source: Department For Education; Welsh Office; The Scottish Office Education Department; Department of Education, Northern Ireland

4.15 Local education authority expenditure, 1992-93

Percentages and £ million

	Pre-primary and primary schools	Second-ary schools	Special schools	Continuing education	Admini-stration & inspec-tion[1]	Other educa-tional services[1]	School catering services[1]	Capital expend-iture	Total (= 100%) (£ million)
United Kingdom	32.2	33.3	5.8	22.3	1.5	1.0	0.5	3.4	26,743.9
North	33.1	36.0	5.2	21.4	0.7	0.4	0.2	2.9	1,431.7
Yorkshire & Humberside	32.4	35.2	4.4	23.6	0.3	0.4	0.1	3.6	2,317.0
East Midlands	31.1	35.9	5.6	23.3	1.0	0.1	0.1	2.9	1,816.3
East Anglia	32.1	35.3	4.8	22.3	0.5	0.3	0.1	4.6	880.7
South East	32.0	31.8	6.8	25.2	1.1	0.1	-	2.9	8,054.1
Greater London	33.6	28.6	7.2	26.5	1.2	0.2	-	2.6	3,519.9
Rest of South East	30.8	34.3	6.5	24.1	1.0	-	-	3.2	4,534.2
South West	30.0	32.5	5.6	26.4	0.7	-	0.1	4.6	2,008.8
West Midlands	33.6	33.8	6.0	23.0	0.9	0.2	0.1	2.4	2,449.6
North West	32.5	32.6	6.6	24.0	0.8	0.2	0.1	3.2	3,072.3
England	32.1	33.3	6.1	24.2	0.9	0.2	0.1	3.2	22,030.5
Wales	30.6	31.7	3.2	21.9	4.1	1.9	2.7	3.8	1,441.7
Scotland	32.9	34.9	5.3	9.1	4.4	7.1	2.5	3.9	2,544.0
Northern Ireland	35.9	31.1	4.1	10.5	4.8	2.7	3.5	7.3	727.7

1 Expenditure on most central services under these headings in England and Wales has been recharged to columns 1-4.

Source: Department For Education; Welsh Office; The Scottish Office Education Department; Department of Education, Northern Ireland

4.16 Young people meeting National Targets for Education and Training[1]

Percentages[2]

	Young people qualified to at least NVQ level 2[3]					Young people qualified to at least NVQ level 3[4]				
	1986	1991	1992	1993	1994	1986	1991	1992	1993	1994
United Kingdom	45.2	54.3	58.4	61.5	64.1	25.7	30.2	34.0	36.9	39.4
North	41.8	49.6	53.8	57.9	62.6	20.4	28.9	27.9	32.7	36.3
Yorkshire & Humberside	42.0	49.8	55.1	62.6	62.3	19.8	24.2	31.2	35.1	37.7
East Midlands	40.1	50.3	56.7	59.3	62.2	23.5	30.1	28.5	36.9	37.3
East Anglia	45.7	51.4	53.7	63.2	61.7	26.3	27.5	28.8	35.5	35.4
South East	48.2	55.8	59.8	62.8	66.7	29.5	32.4	36.5	37.7	40.3
Greater London	49.8	57.2	58.6	61.1	67.5	33.3	36.9	41.6	42.1	45.2
Rest of South East	47.0	54.9	60.6	63.9	66.2	26.9	28.8	32.8	34.5	36.8
South West	43.9	55.8	60.8	63.0	65.7	23.9	30.3	31.2	37.7	40.3
West Midlands	42.9	52.8	56.1	56.4	58.1	23.0	25.1	30.6	35.4	37.9
North West	42.0	51.6	54.4	58.8	62.3	23.8	26.8	29.7	34.3	36.3
England	44.5	53.2	57.3	60.9	63.7	25.3	29.2	32.4	36.3	38.5
Wales	38.5	52.0	55.6	57.9	60.2	19.8	24.0	29.5	30.6	36.4
Scotland	55.7	65.3	70.2	69.4	69.3	32.6	42.2	51.0	49.1	49.3
Northern Ireland	44.8	52.7	56.9	61.3	66.8	25.2	29.8	32.1	31.4	39.2

1 See Appendix notes.
2 As a percentage of all young people in the age group. Figures for NVQ level 2 relate to 19-21 year olds and those for NVQ level 3 to 21-23 year olds.
3 Or academic equivalent of 5 CGSE grades A-C.
4 Or academic equivalent of 2 A levels. Figures for 1993 onwards are not comparable with earlier years because of changes in the LFS qualifications questions.

Source: Labour Force Survey, Employment Department; Department of Economic Development, Northern Ireland

4.17 Training for Work and Youth Training Schemes[1]: trainees on programmes, March 1994

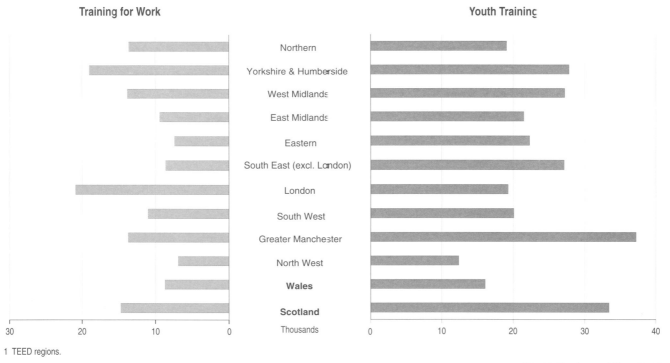

1 TEED regions.

Source: Employment Department

4.18 Training for Work and Youth Training leavers[1], 1993-94

Percentages and thousands

	Training for Work						Youth Training					
	Status six months after leaving (percentages)						Status six months after leaving (percentages)					
	In employ-ment	In further educ-ation or training	Unemp-loyed	Other	Gained qualifi-cation[2] (percent-ages)	All leavers (thou-sands)	In employ-ment	In further educ-ation or training	Unem-loyed	Other	Gained qualifi-cation[2] (percent-ages)	All leavers (thou-sands)
Great Britain	37	8	49	5	..	147.8	53	17	25	6	..	283.6
Northern	31	8	56	5	40	13.6	47	18	30	5	50	19.1
Yorkshire & Humberside	38	8	49	5	40	19.0	53	17	25	5	50	27.8
West Midlands	40	8	48	5	45	13.8	53	16	25	5	49	27.2
East Midlands	44	6	43	6	35	9.4	57	16	22	5	50	21.5
Eastern	35	6	52	7	47	7.4	57	15	23	5	49	22.3
South East (excl. London)	37	7	50	6	49	8.6	60	13	21	6	52	27.1
London	33	8	52	7	38	20.9	43	21	30	5	46	19.3
South West	37	7	49	7	43	11.0	59	15	21	5	56	20.1
Greater Manchester	39	5	51	5	36	13.7	55	15	24	5	50	37.2
North West	37	8	50	5	42	6.9	54	17	24	5	50	12.4
England	37	7	50	6	39	124.4	54	16	25	5	49	234.0
Wales	40	9	48	4	41	8.7	48	17	28	6	44	16.1
Scotland	32	14	46	8	..	14.7	49	17	26	7	..	33.4

1 TEED regions. See Appendix notes.
2 Those who gained a qualification or a credit towards one.

Source: Employment Department

4.19 Employees of working age[1] receiving job-related training[2]

Percentages[3]

	1986		1991		1993		1994	
	Received some on-the-job training	Received some off-the-job training	Received some on-the-job training	Received some off-the-job training	Received some on-the-job training	Received some off-the-job training	Received some on-the-job training	Received some off-the-job training
United Kingdom	4.8	7.5	6.6	10.5	6.1	10.4	6.7	10.8
North	4.9	8.3	7.5	10.0	5.8	10.5	7.8	11.1
Yorkshire & Humberside	4.2	7.4	6.7	9.9	6.8	9.8	7.5	11.5
East Midlands	4.4	8.4	5.5	9.7	5.7	8.9	5.6	9.6
East Anglia	5.2	8.8	6.8	11.4	5.5	10.1	6.7	9.4
South East	5.5	8.1	7.0	11.6	6.4	11.6	7.1	11.4
Greater London	5.5	8.0	6.8	11.2	6.5	12.2	7.0	11.4
Rest of South East	5.5	8.1	7.1	11.8	6.4	11.2	7.1	11.4
South West	4.8	7.9	6.7	10.7	6.1	10.6	6.2	11.0
West Midlands	5.0	7.0	6.4	9.6	6.1	9.7	5.7	10.1
North West	3.9	7.2	6.5	11.0	5.8	10.2	6.7	11.1
England	4.9	7.8	6.7	10.8	6.2	10.6	6.8	10.9
Wales	5.1	6.6	6.5	9.3	6.0	11.0	6.0	11.4
Scot and	3.6	5.0	6.0	8.6	6.0	9.4	6.7	9.3
Northern Ireland	3.5	6.1	4.6	8.6	3.9	9.2	5.3	8.9

1 Working age is defined as men aged 16 - 64 and women aged 16 - 59. See Appendix notes.
2 Spring quarter of each year. Those employees receiving both on and off-the-job training are counted in both columns.
3 As a percentage of all employees of working age.

Source: Labour Force Survey, Employment Department; Department of Economic Development, Northern Ireland

5 Labour market

Labour force

Service industries account for 60 per cent of the labour force in the South East compared with 50 per cent in the East and West Midlands.

(Table 5.1)

Over 15 per cent of the labour force in the South West was self employed in Spring 1994, compared with 9 per cent in the North and Scotland.

(Table 5.1)

Almost two in five male employees who are employed in the East Midlands and the West Midlands in 1994 worked in manufacturing.

(Table 5.5)

In Scotland, one in nine male employees in 1994 was in the construction industry, double the proportion in both the South East and the South West.

(Table 5.5)

Qualifications

Scotland and the South East have the highest qualified workforce: two fifths are qualified to at least 'A' level standard or equivalent and less than a sixth have no qualifications.

(Table 5.10)

Holidays

Paid holiday entitlements are most generous in Scotland and the North and least generous in the East Midlands.

(Table 5.12)

Wages and hours

On average, men in the South East work the shortest hours yet earn the most - £100 per week more in April 1994 than those in Northern Ireland, where earnings were lowest.

(Table 5.13)

Labour disputes

The North West lost 19 days per 1,000 employees due to labour disputes in 1994, nearly four times the rate in the East Midlands.

(Table 5.17)

Redundancies

In Spring 1994, redundancies were highest in the North, where 13 in every 1,000 employees lost their job; in the South West and the North West fewer than nine in every 1,000 did so.

(Table 5.19)

Claimant unemployment

More than one in five unemployed men and one in ten unemployed women in Northern Ireland have been unemployed for over five years.

(Table 5.20)

The level of unemployment fell in all regions between 1993 and 1994, but the fall was greatest in the South West.

(Table 5.21)

Introduction

Many of the items in this chapter present data from the Employment Department's Labour Force Survey (LFS). There are problems in drawing together data on the same subject from different sources. For example, the question in the LFS as to whether the respondent is employed produces a 'people' measure of employment, whereas a question addressed to employers asking the number of people they employ, as in the biennial Census of Employment, produces a 'jobs' measure. Thus if someone has a second job they will be included twice in the 'job' count. Similarly, the number of people who are classified by the LFS as unemployed (which corresponds to the International Labour Organisation (ILO) definition of unemployment) differs from the number of people claiming unemployment benefits and satisfying the conditions for the receipt of benefit ('claimant unemployed'). Time series of these two measures of unemployment appear as Tables 5.21 and 5.22; however, as the time period over which measurement was made is not the same for both, comparison should not be made other than of the trends shown.

The structure of the workforce has changed over the last 20 years. One of the most striking changes has been the significant rise in self-employment. Between 1976 and 1991, the self-employed as a percentage of the UK civilian workforce increased by half; over the subsequent two years it fell off slightly, but in 1994 it was almost back at its 1991 level, with around one in eight of the workforce self-employed (Table 5.4). The proportion of the workforce that were self-employed remained lower than its 1991 level in Yorkshire and Humberside, the East Midlands, the North West and the South West, but in the North, the South East and Wales the self-employed accounted for a higher proportion of the workforce than in 1991. Only in Northern Ireland has the rate of self-employment remained constant since 1976 at around one in ten people.

A significant proportion of the self-employed work at home. In addition, about one employer in ten employs homeworkers of some kind or another, that is people who either work mainly at home or live at their place of work. The Census of Population indicates that some 1.2 million people in Great Britain, about 5 per cent of the working population, were homeworkers in 1991. There was little variation in the overall percentages for England, Wales and Scotland, but not surprisingly, rural and some tourist areas recorded the highest percentages of homeworkers, with almost half of agricultural workers classified as homeworkers.

"....significant rise in self-employment...."

Glossary of terms

Employees (Labour Force Survey)	A count, obtained from household surveys, of persons aged 16 and over who regard themselves as paid employees. People with two or more jobs are counted only once.
Employees in employment (employer survey based measure)	A count, obtained from surveys of employers, of jobs held by civilians who are paid by an employer who runs a PAYE tax scheme. People with two or more jobs are counted in each job.
The self-employed	A count, mainly obtained from household surveys, of persons aged 16 and over who regard themselves as self-employed, ie who in their main employment work on their own account, whether or not they have employees, and are responsible for payment of their own income tax and National Insurance contributions.
Government employment and training programme participants	A count, obtained from household surveys, of those who said they were participants on Youth Training, Employment Training (Training for Work after April 1993), Employment Action or Community Industry programmes, or a programme organised by a TEC/LEC.
Work-related government training programme participants	A count, obtained from administrative returns, of all participants who receive some form of work experience in the course of their placement, but who do not have a contract of employment and are not self-employed.
The labour force in employment	A count, obtained from household surveys and censuses, of employees in employment, self-employed persons, participants in government employment and training programmes, and persons doing unpaid family work.
The workforce in employment	A count of employees in employment (obtained from employer-based surveys), self-employed persons, all HM Forces, and participants on work-related government training schemes.
The claimant unemployed	A measure, known as the claimant count, and derived from administrative sources, which counts as unemployed those people who are claiming unemployment related benefits at Employment Service local offices (formerly Unemployment Benefit Offices).
The ILO unemployed	An International Labour Organisation (ILO) recommended measure, used in household surveys such as the Labour Force Survey, which counts as unemployed those aged 16 or over who are without a job, are available to start work in the next two weeks and who have been seeking a job in the last four weeks, or are waiting to start a job already obtained.
The workforce	The **workforce in employment** *plus* the **claimant unemployed**.
The economically active	The **labour force in employment** *plus* the **ILO unemployed**.
The civilian labour force	The **labour force in employment** *plus* the **ILO unemployed** *less* **HM Forces**.
Claimant unemployment rate	The percentage of the **workforce** who are **claimant unemployed**.
ILO unemployment rate	The percentage of the **economically active** who are **ILO unemployed**.
The economically inactive	Persons who are neither part of the labour force in employment nor ILO unemployed. For example, all people under 16, those retired or looking after a home, or those permanently unable to work.
The population of working age	Males aged 16 to 64 years and females aged 16 to 59 years.
Civilian economic activity rate	The percentage of the population in a given age group which is in the **civilian labour force**.

Some of these terms are covered in more detail in the Appendix notes.

5.1 The labour force[1], Spring 1994

Percentages and thousands

	Manufacturing employees	Construction employees	Service employees	Other employees	Self employed	On GETP[2]	ILO unemployed	Total labour force[3] (=100%) (thousands)
United Kingdom	16.0	3.6	55.4	2.0	11.7	1.2	9.5	28,239
North	16.4	4.6	53.7	2.2	8.9	2.1	11.7	1,417
Yorkshire & Humberside	18.6	4.3	53.8	2.0	9.6	1.3	9.8	2,394
East Midlands	22.0	3.6	50.4	3.1	11.0	0.9	8.3	2,020
East Anglia	18.2	3.3	53.6	3.4	13.0	..	7.4	1,098
South East	11.6	2.9	59.8	1.3	13.1	0.9	9.6	8,943
Greater London	7.9	2.7	61.3	0.7	12.9	1.0	13.0	3,370
Rest of South East	13.9	3.1	58.9	1.7	13.3	0.8	7.6	5,573
South West	14.3	2.8	55.8	2.4	15.3	1.2	7.5	2,360
West Midlands	23.6	3.3	49.2	1.8	10.2	1.4	9.9	2,585
North West	19.0	3.7	54.8	1.3	9.6	1.0	10.2	2,971
England	16.3	3.4	55.6	1.8	11.8	1.1	9.5	23,789
Wales	16.2	3.9	51.9	2.2	13.9	1.5	9.4	1,297
Scotland	14.3	5.7	55.6	3.3	9.0	1.5	9.9	2,471
Northern Ireland	12.3	3.5	53.9	2.3	12.4	3.0	11.5	683

1 Based on SIC 92. See Appendix notes.
2 Government employment and training programmes.
3 Includes unpaid family workers.

Source: Labour Force Survey, Employment Department; Department of Economic Development, Northern Ireland

5.2 Civilian labour force[1]: by age, 1994 and 2001

Percentages and thousands

	1994[2]					2001[2]				
	Percentages aged				All ages (= 100%) (thou-sands)	Percentages aged				All ages (= 100%) (thou-sands)
	16-24	25-44	Females 45-59 Males 45-64	Females 60+ Males 65+		16-24	25-44	Females 45-59 Males 45-64	Females 60+ Males 65+	
United Kingdom	17.8	49.5	30.1	2.6	28,851	16.4	49.7	31.4	2.6	29,577
North	17.0	51.8	29.3	1.9	1,445	15.7	51.7	30.7	1.9	1,444
Yorkshire & Humberside	17.9	49.9	30.2	2.0	2,446	16.3	49.8	32.0	1.9	2,495
East Midlands	16.7	50.3	30.7	2.3	2,098	15.0	50.5	32.2	2.3	2,182
East Anglia	17.3	48.4	31.2	3.1	1,066	15.9	48.8	32.4	2.9	1,138
South East	17.6	48.9	30.2	3.3	9,117	16.3	49.3	31.3	3.1	9,398
Greater London	17.6	50.7	29.0	2.8	3,444	16.2	51.5	29.8	2.6	3,499
Rest of South East	17.7	47.8	31.0	3.5	5,673	16.4	48.1	32.1	3.4	5,899
South West	17.6	48.4	30.9	3.1	2,394	16.1	48.7	32.2	3.0	2,534
West Midlands	18.0	48.6	31.1	2.4	2,646	16.6	48.6	32.5	2.3	2,671
North West	17.9	50.2	29.6	2.2	3,121	16.6	49.8	31.3	2.2	3,139
England	17.6	49.3	30.3	2.7	24,332	16.2	49.5	31.7	2.6	25,001
Wales	18.6	50.3	28.9	2.1	1,351	17.1	51.0	29.8	2.1	1,393
Scotland	18.7	50.0	28.9	2.4	2,468	16.8	50.0	30.7	2.4	2,454
Northern Ireland	20.2	50.5	27.1	2.1	699	18.7	51.5	27.9	2.0	730

1 See Appendix notes.
2 Projections from 1991 estimates.

Source: Labour Force Survey, Employment Department; Department of Economic Development, Northern Ireland

5.3 Civilian labour force[1]: by gender

Thousands

	Estimates						Projections[2]			
	1971	1981	1984[3]	1984[3]	1990	1991	1992	1993	1994	2001
Males										
United Kingdom	15,965	16,038	15,866	15,929	16,374	16,300	16,300	16,288	16,279	16,420
North	894	893	848	850	841	826	823	818	815	798
Yorkshire & Humberside	1,401	1,399	1,364	1,368	1,400	1,396	1,394	1,391	1,389	1,391
East Midlands	1,070	1,125	1,115	1,125	1,169	1,185	1,188	1,191	1,193	1,221
East Anglia	479	529	544	545	589	585	589	593	596	628
South East	4,982	4,957	4,996	5,011	5,133	5,109	5,110	5,110	5,112	5,188
Greater London	..	2,008	1,956	1,986	1,990	1,933	1,930	1,926	1,922	1,921
Rest of South East	..	2,949	3,040	3,026	3,143	3,176	3,180	3,184	3,190	3,267
South West	1,118	1,189	1,191	1,199	1,291	1,309	1,315	1,320	1,326	1,382
West Midlands	1,546	1,512	1,471	1,476	1,550	1,537	1,533	1,529	1,524	1,513
North West	1,881	1,825	1,773	1,776	1,803	1,784	1,779	1,771	1,765	1,743
England	13,371	13,429	13,302	13,351	13,776	13,731	13,731	13,724	13,720	13,865
Wales	766	766	743	746	767	763	766	765	764	775
Scotland	1,426	1,449	1,433	1,441	1,424	1,402	1,399	1,394	1,388	1,361
Northern Ireland	402	395	388	391	407	404	404	406	407	420
Females										
United Kingdom	9,534	10,845	11,202	11,320	12,526	12,472	12,471	12,519	12,572	13,157
North	500	584	592	597	629	632	629	629	630	645
Yorkshire & Humberside	813	947	961	969	1,050	1,050	1,049	1,052	1,056	1,103
East Midlands	615	740	784	785	903	889	892	898	905	961
East Anglia	258	351	368	373	475	457	460	465	470	510
South East	3,156	3,414	3,621	3,662	3,987	3,971	3,971	3,988	4,006	4,210
Greater London	..	1,437	1,453	1,473	1,538	1,519	1,516	1,519	1,522	1,578
Rest of South East	..	1,977	2,167	2,189	2,449	2,453	2,455	2,469	2,484	2,632
South West	634	800	866	880	1,023	1,045	1,049	1,058	1,068	1,152
West Midlands	906	1,000	999	1,014	1,130	1,119	1,117	1,119	1,122	1,158
North West	1,176	1,281	1,255	1,271	1,355	1,356	1,352	1,354	1,356	1,396
England	8,059	9,117	9,446	9,551	10,553	10,520	10,520	10,564	10,612	11,136
Wales	396	483	510	511	585	580	582	584	587	618
Scotland	877	998	994	1,004	1,103	1,086	1,082	1,081	1,081	1,093
Northern Ireland	202	247	251	255	285	286	287	290	292	309
All persons										
United Kingdom	25,499	26,883	27,068	27,249	28,900	28,772	28,771	28,807	28,851	29,577
North	1,394	1,477	1,440	1,447	1,469	1,458	1,452	1,448	1,445	1,444
Yorkshire & Humberside	2,214	2,346	2,325	2,338	2,450	2,446	2,443	2,444	2,445	2,495
East Midlands	1,685	1,865	1,900	1,909	2,072	2,074	2,080	2,089	2,093	2,182
East Anglia	737	880	913	918	1,064	1,043	1,049	1,057	1,063	1,138
South East	8,138	8,371	8,617	8,673	9,120	9,080	9,082	9,098	9,117	9,398
Greater London	..	3,445	3,410	3,459	3,528	3,452	3,446	3,445	3,444	3,499
Rest of South East	..	4,926	5,207	5,214	5,592	5,629	5,635	5,653	5,673	5,899
South West	1,752	1,989	2,057	2,079	2,314	2,354	2,364	2,379	2,394	2,534
West Midlands	2,452	2,512	2,470	2,490	2,680	2,656	2,650	2,648	2,646	2,671
North West	3,058	3,105	3,028	3,047	3,158	3,141	3,131	3,125	3,121	3,139
England	21,430	22,546	22,748	22,902	24,329	24,251	24,251	24,287	24,332	25,001
Wales	1,162	1,248	1,253	1,257	1,352	1,343	1,347	1,349	1,351	1,393
Scotland	2,303	2,447	2,428	2,445	2,527	2,488	2,481	2,475	2,468	2,454
Northern Ireland	603	642	640	646	693	690	692	696	699	730

1 Aged 16 or over. See Appendix notes.
2 Projected from 1991 estimates.
3 GB labour force definitions up to 1984, ILO definitions from 1984.

Source: Labour Force Survey, Employment Department; Department of Economic Development, Northern Ireland

5.4 Employment structure of the civilian workforce[1]: by gender

Thousands

	1976	1981	1986	1991	1992	1993	1994
United Kingdom							
Civilian workforce	25,895	26,685	27,644	28,264	28,155	27,986	27,736
Males	16,040	16,212	16,198	16,042	15,928	15,754	15,549
Females	9,856	10,473	11,446	12,221	12,227	12,232	12,187
Employees in employment	22,557	21,892	21,387	22,262	21,937	21,626	21,562
Males	13,401	12,562	11,744	11,530	11,239	10,978	10,911
Females	9,156	9,331	9,644	10,731	10,698	10,648	10,651
Self-employed (with or without employees)	2,073	2,272	2,802	3,408	3,215	· 3,184	3,290
Claimant unemployed (males and females)	1,266	2,521	3,229	2,241	2,678	2,865	2,586
WRGTP[2]	.	.	226	353	325	311	298
North							
Civilian workforce	1,450	1,407	1,424	1,383	1,407	1,401	1,393
Males	918	865	844	785	801	799	791
Females	533	541	580	598	606	602	602
Employees in employment	1,255	1,122	1,061	1,089	1,106	1,081	1,084
Males	769	654	585	567	574	553	553
Females	486	468	476	522	531	527	531
Self-employed (with or without employees)	96	92	111	118	119	124	126
Claimant unemployed (males and females)	100	192	232	141	151	167	156
WRGTP[2]	.	.	20	35	31	29	27
Yorkshire & Humberside							
Civilian workforce	2,244	2,258	2,320	2,365	2,361	2,363	2,326
Males	1,407	1,389	1,368	1,336	1,325	1,326	1,296
Females	837	868	951	1,029	1,036	1,037	1,030
Employees in employment	1,967	1,852	1,762	1,866	1,859	1,850	1,843
Males	1,190	1,083	970	962	945	938	928
Females	777	768	792	904	914	912	915
Self-employed (with or without employees)	167	169	223	258	240	240	230
Claimant unemployed (males and females)	109	237	312	203	227	240	221
WRGTP[2]	.	.	22	38	35	34	31
East Midlands							
Civilian workforce	1,696	1,774	1,888	1,940	1,916	1,899	1,919
Males	1,054	1,083	1,112	1,096	1,091	1,059	1,074
Females	642	691	776	844	825	841	845
Employees in employment	1,497	1,467	1,490	1,535	1,514	1,493	1,514
Males	900	855	831	796	786	755	766
Females	597	613	659	739	729	739	748
Self-employed (with or without employees)	128	152	181	245	214	207	222
Claimant unemployed (males and females)	71	155	199	139	169	180	166
WRGTP[2]	.	.	17	22	20	20	17
East Anglia							
Civilian workforce	780	833	915	999	1,008	1,021	1,016
Males	493	521	543	572	579	578	567
Females	286	312	371	427	429	442	450
Employees in employment	669	681	717	795	784	788	793
Males	404	400	402	417	412	405	403
Females	265	281	314	377	372	383	390
Self-employed (with or without employees)	78	91	109	139	143	142	142
Claimant unemployed (males and females)	32	61	81	57	74	82	72
WRGTP[2]	.	.	7	8	8	9	8
South East							
Civilian workforce	8,224	8,573	9,049	9,172	9,118	9,016	8,949
Males	5,027	5,158	5,232	5,195	5,134	5,085	5,025
Females	3,196	3,414	3,817	3,977	3,984	3,930	3,925
Employees in employment	7,246	7,263	7,255	7,316	7,119	6,929	6,892
Males	4,243	4,135	3,968	3,791	3,649	3,540	3,504
Females	3,003	3,128	3,287	3,525	3,470	3,389	3,389
Self-employed (with or without employees)	687	762	986	1,173	1,115	1,105	1,175
Claimant unemployed (males and females)	290	548	772	628	826	919	818
WRGTP[2]	.	.	36	56	58	63	64
South West							
Civilian workforce	1,812	1,972	2,098	2,305	2,243	2,264	2,261
Males	1,133	1,209	1,228	1,302	1,261	1,270	1,256
Females	679	763	870	1,004	982	994	1,004
Employees in employment	1,513	1,541	1,579	1,731	1,694	1,687	1,693
Males	894	883	862	881	849	842	840
Females	619	658	717	850	845	845	853
Self-employed (with or without employees)	204	275	307	399	330	346	362
Claimant unemployed (males and females)	94	156	196	153	197	210	185
WRGTP[2]	.	.	17	23	21	21	21

5.4 *(continued)*

Thousands

	1976	1981	1986	1991	1992	1993	1994
West Midlands							
Civilian workforce	2,472	2,519	2,537	2,577	2,581	2,564	2,493
Males	1,552	1,551	1,518	1,487	1,495	1,468	1,417
Females	921	967	1,019	1,089	1,086	1,096	1,077
Employees in employment	2,186	2,051	1,961	2,051	2,014	1,987	1,960
Males	1,325	1,199	1,110	1,094	1,064	1,033	1,017
Females	861	852	852	957	950	954	943
Self-employed (with or without employees)	166	176	204	273	273	268	263
Claimant unemployed (males and females)	120	291	342	216	263	278	242
WRGTP[2]	.	.	30	37	32	30	28
North West							
Civilian workforce	3,046	3,051	3,055	3,040	3,004	2,974	2,888
Males	1,857	1,829	1,772	1,715	1,682	1,657	1,603
Females	1,189	1,221	1,284	1,325	1,322	1,317	1,284
Employees in employment	2,637	2,466	2,295	2,383	2,332	2,311	2,279
Males	1,543	1,391	1,234	1,221	1,171	1,151	1,139
Females	1,094	1,075	1,061	1,163	1,160	1,160	1,140
Self-employed (with or without employees)	220	230	286	329	316	305	286
Claimant unemployed (males and females)	188	355	444	281	314	319	286
WRGTP[2]	.	.	31	46	42	40	37
England							
Civilian workforce	21,732	22,385	23,286	23,781	23,637	23,503	23,245
Males	13,445	13,608	13,618	13,492	13,368	13,243	13,029
Females	8,286	8,777	9,668	10,290	10,270	10,260	10,217
Employees in employment	18,982	18,444	18,120	18,766	18,421	18,125	18,060
Males	11,275	10,600	9,962	9,733	9,450	9,217	9,151
Females	7,706	7,844	8,158	9,034	8,971	8,909	8,909
Self-employed (with or without employees)	1,745	1,946	2,408	2,932	2,749	2,737	2,805
Claimant unemployed (males and females)	1,005	1,994	2,578	1,818	2,222	2,395	2,146
WRGTP[2]	.	.	180	266	246	245	234
Wales							
Civilian workforce	1,193	1,205	1,217	1,248	1,258	1,259	1,278
Males	769	753	736	713	716	712	732
Females	424	452	481	535	541	547	546
Employees in employment	995	939	887	956	950	966	965
Males	612	551	494	490	479	488	487
Females	383	389	393	466	471	478	478
Self-employed (with or without employees)	127	119	143	161	168	150	180
Claimant unemployed (males and females)	71	146	174	110	121	126	117
WRGTP[2]	.	.	13	21	20	17	16
Scotland							
Civilian workforce	2,347	2,421	2,430	2,482	2,512	2,480	2,467
Males	1,429	1,437	1,417	1,395	1,408	1,365	1,356
Females	918	983	1,014	1,087	1,104	1,115	1,111
Employees in employment	2,071	2,002	1,879	1,997	2,024	1,991	1,987
Males	1,210	1,128	1,021	1,030	1,036	1,000	996
Females	861	874	858	967	988	992	990
Self-employed (with or without employees)	138	136	176	223	215	216	222
Claimant unemployed (males and females)	139	283	351	216	232	241	226
WRGTP[2]	.	.	24	46	41	33	32
Northern Ireland							
Civilian workforce	624	675	711	753	749	744	745
Males	396	413	427	443	437	433	433
Females	228	262	284	310	312	310	312
Employees in employment	509	507	501	542	542	544	551
Males	304	283	267	277	275	274	276
Females	205	224	235	265	268	270	274
Self-employed (with or without employees)	64	70	76	92	83	81	82
Claimant unemployed (males and females)	51	98	126	98	104	103	96
WRGTP[2]	.	.	8	20	19	16	16

1 See Appendix notes.
2 Work Related Government Training Programmes.

Source: Employment Department

5.5 Employees in employment: by Standard Industrial Classification and gender, 1981 and 1994[1]

Percentages and thousands

	Agriculture, forestry, fishing (0)	Energy and water supply (1)	Metals, minerals and chemicals (2)	Metal goods, engineering and vehicles industries (3)	Other manufacturing (4)	Total manufacturing (2)-(4)
1981 Males						
United Kingdom	2.2	4.9	5.9	18.4	10.9	35.2
North	1.8	9.6	10.8	19.0	8.7	38.6
Yorkshire & Humberside	2.0	9.9	9.9	15.4	12.6	38.0
East Midlands	2.8	10.0	5.6	20.6	14.8	41.0
East Anglia	6.7	2.5	3.7	15.7	13.3	32.7
South East	1.2	2.4	3.2	16.2	9.5	28.9
South West	4.1	2.7	3.8	18.6	11.2	33.6
West Midlands	1.7	3.9	8.3	32.4	9.1	49.8
North West	0.9	3.9	7.5	19.8	14.1	41.4
England	1.9	4.6	5.8	19.2	11.0	36.0
Wales	3.3	10.1	11.3	13.6	7.2	32.1
Scotland	3.4	5.7	5.0	15.5	11.1	31.6
Northern Ireland	5.6	3.1	3.9	11.3	13.6	28.9
1981 Females						
United Kingdom	1.0	1.0	2.1	6.5	10.6	19.2
North	0.4	1.3	2.4	6.0	10.1	18.6
Yorkshire & Humberside	0.9	1.2	2.7	4.8	14.8	22.3
East Midlands	1.5	1.1	2.6	5.9	21.1	29.6
East Anglia	3.9	0.6	1.2	5.6	12.7	19.5
South East	0.8	0.9	1.8	6.6	7.2	15.6
South West	1.5	0.9	1.3	5.5	8.5	15.3
West Midlands	1.0	1.0	4.0	13.3	8.5	25.7
North West	0.4	1.0	2.6	6.2	13.0	21.8
England	1.0	1.0	2.3	6.9	10.5	19.6
Wales	1.1	1.4	2.2	6.1	8.0	16.3
Scotland	0.7	1.0	1.2	4.6	11.9	17.7
Northern Ireland	1.5	0.6	0.6	3.4	14.4	18.4
1994 Males						
United Kingdom	1.8	2.2	4.0	13.4	10.3	27.7
North	1.6	3.3	7.1	14.2	10.8	32.1
Yorkshire & Humberside	1.8	2.3	6.7	12.7	13.4	32.8
East Midlands	2.2	2.1	4.6	17.0	16.4	38.1
East Anglia	4.1	2.5	2.7	12.7	12.9	28.2
South East	0.9	1.8	2.1	10.0	7.6	19.7
Greater London	-	1.5	1.0	5.2	7.3	13.6
Rest of South East	1.7	2.0	3.0	14.1	7.8	24.9
South West	3.2	1.8	3.0	13.9	9.8	26.7
West Midlands	1.6	1.6	6.0	23.6	9.7	39.2
North West	0.9	2.0	4.8	15.2	12.4	32.4
England	1.6	2.0	4.0	13.7	10.4	28.1
Wales	2.9	2.7	8.2	13.0	10.9	32.0
Scotland	2.2	4.1	2.4	12.0	9.2	23.7
Northern Ireland	5.9	1.9	3.1	8.5	12.6	24.2
1994 Females						
United Kingdom	0.6	0.7	1.4	3.6	7.2	12.2
North	0.3	0.9	1.5	3.4	8.5	13.4
Yorkshire & Humberside	0.5	0.6	1.7	2.8	9.3	13.7
East Midlands	0.8	0.5	1.8	3.7	14.7	20.2
East Anglia	1.9	0.7	0.7	3.6	8.0	12.3
South East	0.5	0.7	1.2	3.1	4.8	9.2
Greater London	-	0.7	0.6	1.7	5.0	7.3
Rest of South East	0.9	0.6	1.6	4.2	4.7	10.6
South West	1.0	0.7	0.7	3.3	5.1	9.0
West Midlands	0.7	0.6	2.2	7.1	6.7	16.0
North West	0.4	0.7	1.8	3.4	7.8	13.0
England	0.6	0.7	1.4	3.7	7.1	12.2
Wales	0.7	0.8	1.4	4.9	7.4	13.7
Scotland	0.4	0.8	1.1	3.4	7.5	12.0
Northern Ireland	0.8	0.3	0.6	2.1	9.8	12.5

5.5 *(continued)*

Percentages and thousands

	Construction (5)	Distribution, hotels and catering, repairs (6)	Transport and communication (7)	Banking, finance, insurance, business services & leasing (8)	Public administration and other services (9)	All industries and services (= 100%) thousands
1981 Males						
United Kingdom	8.1	15.2	9.1	7.2	18.1	12,562
North	9.8	11.7	7.8	4.4	16.3	654
Yorkshire & Humberside	8.2	13.9	8.0	4.8	15.2	1,083
East Midlands	6.8	13.9	6.7	4.5	14.3	855
East Anglia	8.7	16.8	9.1	5.8	17.8	400
South East	7.3	17.3	11.6	10.9	20.5	4,135
South West	8.2	17.7	8.0	6.4	19.3	883
West Midlands	6.8	13.0	5.8	5.1	13.9	1,199
North West	8.0	14.1	9.2	6.0	16.5	1,391
England	7.6	15.4	9.2	7.5	17.7	10,600
Wales	9.1	12.6	8.2	4.8	19.9	551
Scotland	11.4	13.9	9.4	5.7	18.8	1,128
Northern Ireland	9.3	14.3	5.9	4.8	28.0	283
1981 Females						
United Kingdom	1.2	24.3	3.0	9.0	41.3	9,331
North	1.1	28.4	2.2	6.3	41.7	468
Yorkshire & Humberside	1.2	25.6	2.3	6.9	39.6	768
East Midlands	1.0	22.2	2.7	6.2	35.8	613
East Anglia	1.2	24.7	2.7	7.9	39.5	281
South East	1.4	23.1	4.1	12.5	41.6	3,128
South West	1.2	28.8	2.4	8.6	41.3	658
West Midlands	1.2	22.9	2.3	7.4	38.5	852
North West	1.1	24.5	2.5	7.8	40.9	1,075
England	1.2	24.3	3.1	9.4	40.4	7,845
Wales	1.1	24.8	2.2	6.0	47.3	389
Scotland	1.4	26.1	2.6	7.4	43.1	874
Northern Ireland	0.9	17.3	1.7	5.8	53.9	224
1994 Males						
United Kingdom	6.8	19.4	8.5	12.3	21.1	10,911
North	8.6	16.5	7.6	8.6	21.7	553
Yorkshire & Humberside	8.1	19.0	8.0	9.1	18.8	928
East Midlands	6.8	18.9	6.7	7.6	17.6	766
East Anglia	6.6	19.5	9.2	10.4	19.5	403
South East	5.5	20.7	10.5	18.5	22.5	3,504
Greater London	4.7	19.9	12.7	23.4	24.1	1,622
Rest of South East	6.1	21.3	8.7	14.2	21.2	1,882
South West	5.1	22.2	6.8	12.2	22.0	840
West Midlands	6.7	18.6	6.7	9.1	16.5	1,017
North West	6.8	19.1	8.7	10.1	20.1	1,139
England	6.4	19.8	8.7	13.0	20.5	9,151
Wales	7.1	17.1	7.1	8.3	22.6	487
Scotland	11.1	17.9	8.3	9.5	23.1	996
Northern Ireland	6.9	17.6	5.9	7.1	30.5	276
1994 Females						
United Kingdom	1.3	23.9	2.8	12.8	45.7	10,651
North	1.2	25.3	2.0	8.2	48.6	531
Yorkshire & Humberside	1.5	25.4	2.3	10.4	45.6	915
East Midlands	1.3	23.9	2.2	9.0	42.2	748
East Anglia	1.2	25.0	2.2	11.6	44.1	390
South East	1.4	22.1	3.8	17.8	44.5	3,389
Greater London	1.4	20.2	4.8	22.3	43.2	1,469
Rest of South East	1.4	23.6	3.1	14.4	45.4	1,919
South West	1.2	27.4	2.1	13.4	45.2	853
West Midlands	1.4	23.5	2.5	10.7	44.5	943
North West	1.2	25.0	2.8	10.6	46.3	1,140
England	1.3	24.0	2.9	13.4	44.9	8,909
Wales	1.1	24.3	1.9	8.4	49.2	478
Scotland	1.4	24.0	2.4	11.1	48.0	990
Northern Ireland	0.8	20.9	1.6	7.7	55.3	274

1 At June. Figures are based on SIC 80. See Appendix notes.

Source: Employment Department

5.6 Part-time employees[1]: by gender, Spring 1994

1 As a percentage of all employees.

Source: *Labour Force Survey, Employment Department; Department of Economic Development, Northern Ireland*

5.7 Self employment: by broad industry group[1]

Percentages

	1991[2]				1993				1994			
	Agri-culture & related	Manu-facturing	Constr-uction	Serv-ices	Agri-culture & related	Manu-facturing	Constr-uction	Serv-ices	Agri-culture & related	Manu-facturing	Constr-uction	Serv-ices
United Kingdom	9.6	10.8	22.2	57.0	8.7	11.2	21.0	58.9	8.4	8.1	24.1	59.4
North	10.1	11.2	15.7	62.7	10.6	11.5	16.1	61.9	13.0	..	20.3	60.3
Yorkshire & Humberside	12.9	11.9	18.1	56.9	6.7	14.8	19.1	59.4	7.1	8.0	24.8	60.1
East Midlands	9.7	14.5	21.2	54.5	10.2	14.2	23.2	52.2	9.5	9.3	26.7	54.4
East Anglia	9.8	10.6	23.5	55.8	10.8	10.7	24.8	53.5	10.6	8.1	24.2	56.8
South East	4.3	10.1	24.4	60.6	4.3	9.8	21.7	64.0	2.8	7.9	24.2	65.1
Greater London	..	9.9	20.3	67.4	..	9.5	16.6	72.1	..	6.9	18.6	74.1
Rest of South East	5.9	10.3	26.8	56.5	6.0	10.0	24.8	59.2	4.3	8.5	27.4	59.8
South West	15.9	8.5	25.3	50.0	13.4	11.2	24.5	50.8	12.6	7.9	25.7	53.7
West Midlands	10.9	13.9	22.8	51.7	7.1	11.5	22.3	59.0	8.4	10.6	26.0	54.7
North West	5.9	12.4	20.5	61.0	4.7	12.2	18.5	64.6	..	9.0	24.5	63.3
England	8.4	11.1	22.7	57.4	7.0	11.3	21.6	60.0	6.3	8.3	24.6	60.6
Wales	15.8	7.7	21.9	54.3	20.7	7.8	18.4	53.2	21.2	7.5	24.3	47.1
Scotland	15.7	10.3	16.2	57.7	15.6	13.6	16.6	54.1	16.0	7.0	17.9	59.1
Northern Ireland	23.3	..	20.2	47.7	26.7	..	19.9	44.2	27.2	..	20.6	46.3

1 Based on SIC 92. Spring quarter of each year. In some cases, sample sizes are too small to provide a reliable estimate. See Appendix notes.
2 The small number of respondents who did not give their economic status was excluded from the analysis.

Source: *Labour Force Survey, Employment Department; Department of Economic Development, Northern Ireland*

5.8 Economic activity rates[1]: by gender

Percentages

	Estimates								Projections[2]			
	1981	1984[3]	1984[3]	1986	1988	1989	1990	1991	1992	1993	1994	2001
Males												
United Kingdom	76.5	74.2	74.5	73.8	74.0	74.3	74.3	73.8	73.7	73.6	73.4	72.6
North	76.9	72.4	72.5	71.9	72.1	71.7	71.0	70.1	70.0	69.8	69.7	68.7
Yorkshire & Humberside	76.6	73.6	73.8	72.9	72.4	73.0	73.6	73.3	73.2	73.1	73.0	72.1
East Midlands	77.8	75.2	75.9	75.4	74.4	75.7	74.7	75.3	75.2	75.1	75.0	74.2
East Anglia	73.8	73.0	73.2	71.5	72.5	72.8	73.9	72.6	72.5	72.4	72.3	71.8
South East	77.3	76.3	76.6	75.7	76.6	76.4	76.2	75.7	75.6	75.6	75.5	75.0
Greater London	77.6	75.4	76.6	75.8	75.8	76.1	76.3	74.4	74.5	74.6	74.6	74.7
Rest of South East	77.2	76.9	76.6	75.6	77.1	76.5	76.1	76.5	76.4	76.2	76.1	75.2
South West	72.2	69.9	70.4	71.0	71.1	72.1	71.8	71.9	71.8	71.7	71.6	71.0
West Midlands	78.0	74.5	74.7	75.0	75.5	75.8	76.4	75.7	75.5	75.3	75.1	73.8
North West	77.0	74.1	74.2	73.9	73.7	74.0	74.1	73.5	73.4	73.3	73.1	72.0
England	76.7	74.4	74.7	74.2	74.5	74.7	74.7	74.3	74.2	74.1	73.9	73.2
Wales	73.3	70.3	70.6	69.0	68.9	70.1	69.9	69.0	69.0	68.8	68.7	67.7
Scotland	76.9	74.8	75.2	73.0	73.1	73.2	73.3	72.6	72.4	72.3	72.1	70.9
Northern Ireland	76.5	73.2	73.8	73.5	72.6	73.2	72.1	71.3	71.0	71.1	71.1	70.7
Females												
United Kingdom	47.5	48.3	48.8	49.5	50.8	52.4	52.8	52.5	52.5	52.7	52.9	54.9
North	46.3	46.6	47.0	47.4	49.2	50.4	49.3	49.7	49.7	49.8	50.0	51.7
Yorkshire & Humberside	47.7	47.9	48.2	49.2	49.4	50.5	51.3	51.4	51.3	51.6	51.8	53.9
East Midlands	48.4	50.1	50.1	51.5	51.9	54.9	54.9	53.8	53.7	53.9	54.1	55.8
East Anglia	46.3	46.7	47.3	49.0	54.0	54.1	56.0	53.4	53.3	53.5	53.7	55.6
South East	48.8	50.9	51.5	51.4	52.9	54.4	55.0	54.7	54.7	55.0	55.3	57.6
Greater London	50.1	50.9	51.6	50.7	51.8	53.7	54.3	53.9	54.0	54.4	54.9	57.9
Rest of South East	47.9	51.0	51.5	51.8	53.6	54.9	55.5	55.3	55.2	55.4	55.5	57.4
South West	44.0	46.1	46.8	47.4	50.4	52.0	51.6	52.2	52.2	52.4	52.6	54.7
West Midlands	48.8	48.1	48.8	50.7	50.9	52.7	53.3	52.7	52.6	52.8	53.0	54.5
North West	48.9	47.8	48.4	49.3	51.2	52.0	51.5	51.7	51.7	51.9	52.1	54.1
England	47.9	48.9	49.4	50.0	51.6	53.0	53.3	53.1	53.0	53.3	53.5	55.5
Wales	42.2	44.0	44.1	45.1	44.5	48.2	48.7	48.1	48.5	48.7	48.9	50.8
Scotland	47.4	46.8	47.3	47.7	49.3	50.8	51.6	51.2	51.1	51.2	51.4	52.6
Northern Ireland	43.5	43.3	43.8	44.9	44.7	46.0	47.4	47.4	47.5	47.7	48.0	49.6

1 Percentage of the home population aged 16 or over who are in the civilian labour force. See Appendix notes.
2 Projected from 1991 estimates.
3 GB labour force definitions up to 1984, ILO definitions from 1984.

Source: Labour Force Survey, Employment Department; Department of Economic Development, Northern Ireland

5.9 Households: by economic activity of head of household[1], Spring 1994

Percentages and thousands

	Economically active									Number of house-holds (= 100%) (thou-sands)
	In employment									
	Employees									
	Full-time[2]	Part-time[2]	All em-ployees[3]	Self employed	On GETP[4]	All in employ-ment	ILO unem-ployed	All econ-omically active	Econ-omically inactive	
United Kingdom	57.5	4.1	61.6	13.1	0.6	75.4	8.7	84.0	16.0	16,766
North	52.8	4.3	57.1	9.2	..	67.4	10.9	78.4	21.6	888
Yorkshire & Humberside	58.1	4.6	62.7	10.8	..	74.3	8.8	83.1	16.9	1,427
East Midlands	61.2	3.9	65.2	12.5	..	78.4	7.3	85.7	14.3	1,186
East Anglia	62.5	5.0	67.5	14.9	..	82.9	6.7	89.6	10.4	617
South East	58.2	3.7	62.0	14.8	0.5	77.4	9.1	86.5	13.5	5,311
Greater London	52.9	3.9	56.9	13.7	0.6	71.3	11.7	83.1	16.9	2,146
Rest of South East	61.8	3.6	65.4	15.5	0.4	81.5	7.3	88.8	11.2	3,165
South West	57.5	4.7	62.2	17.6	..	80.3	7.1	87.4	12.6	1,345
West Midlands	58.8	3.9	62.7	11.7	..	75.1	9.3	84.4	15.6	1,464
North West	54.7	4.4	59.1	11.2	..	70.9	9.1	80.0	20.0	1,804
England	57.8	4.1	62.0	13.3	0.5	76.0	8.8	84.7	15.3	14,042
Wales	51.8	4.6	56.4	13.8	..	71.1	6.8	77.9	22.1	805
Scotland	59.6	4.0	63.6	9.7	0.7	74.1	8.4	82.6	17.4	1,511
Northern Ireland	48.6	2.9	51.5	14.9	..	67.6	10.5	78.1	21.9	409

1 Of working age: male heads aged 16-64, female heads aged 16-59. See Appendix notes.
2 Respondents' self-assessment.
3 Includes those not stating whether full-time or part-time.
4 Government employment and training programmes. For some regions, sample sizes are too small to provide a reliable estimate.

Source: Labour Force Survey, Employment Department; Department of Economic Development, Northern Ireland

5.10 Economically active of working age[1]: by highest qualification[2], Spring 1994

Percentages and thousands

	Degree or equiva-lent	Higher education below degree	GCE A level or equiva-lent	Appren-ticeship	GCE O level or equiva-lent	CSE below grade 1	Other qualifi-cations[3]	No qualif-ications	Total[4] (= 100%) (thou-sands)
United Kingdom	12.4	9.1	15.4	11.9	17.7	5.2	9.5	18.5	27,434
North	8.6	9.6	13.1	15.1	18.4	6.9	8.7	19.3	1,382
Yorkshire & Humberside	10.0	8.6	14.7	13.5	17.7	5.9	9.6	19.6	2,332
East Midlands	10.0	9.9	15.3	12.6	17.3	6.2	7.8	20.7	1,971
East Anglia	10.2	8.6	15.4	11.8	18.0	6.7	10.8	18.5	1,065
South East	16.1	8.7	15.9	9.6	18.5	4.6	10.5	15.9	8,650
Greater London	20.3	7.9	15.0	7.7	15.7	3.4	14.2	15.4	3,265
Rest of South East	13.6	9.1	16.4	10.7	20.1	5.3	8.3	16.1	5,386
South West	11.4	9.1	16.4	11.4	18.8	6.5	8.2	17.9	2,288
West Midlands	10.0	8.8	14.3	10.8	16.5	5.8	10.0	23.3	2,515
North West	11.1	9.5	13.5	13.8	17.9	5.7	8.9	19.6	2,905
England	12.5	9.0	15.1	11.5	18.0	5.6	9.6	18.4	23,109
Wales	10.9	9.6	13.1	12.9	19.3	5.4	8.9	19.7	1,251
Scotland	12.1	10.8	20.4	14.5	14.9	1.8	9.4	15.9	2,408
Northern Ireland	11.3	7.8	12.7	15.7	14.5	2.7	5.6	28.9	666

1 Men aged 16-64 and women aged 16-59.
2 See Appendix notes.
3 Includes YTS certificate.
4 Includes those who did not state their qualifications.

Source: Labour Force Survey, Employment Department; Department of Economic Developments, Northern Ireland

5.11 Population aged 16 and over: by occupational grouping[1], Spring 1994

Percentages and thousands

| | In employment | | | | | | | | | | | | Number of persons (=100%) (thousands) |
| | Employees | | | | | | | | | | | | |
	Managerial & administrators	Professional, associate professional & technical	Clerical & secretarial	Craft & related	Personal & protective services	Sales	Plant & machine operative	Other	Self-employed	All in employment[2]	ILO unemployed	Economically inactive	
United Kingdom	7.0	9.3	8.1	5.1	5.3	4.0	4.7	4.4	7.3	56.3	5.9	37.8	45,393
North	5.7	7.8	7.0	5.1	5.6	4.4	5.1	4.6	5.2	51.9	6.9	41.2	2,409
Yorkshire & Humberside	6.5	8.3	7.4	6.0	5.6	4.3	5.7	4.5	5.9	55.3	6.0	38.7	3,904
East Midlands	7.2	8.8	8.0	6.8	4.8	4.0	5.7	4.2	6.9	57.5	5.2	37.2	3,219
East Anglia	6.8	8.7	7.9	5.2	6.1	4.4	6.1	5.5	8.4	60.0	4.8	35.2	1,695
South East	9.0	10.8	9.0	3.7	5.1	4.0	3.2	3.8	8.5	58.2	6.2	35.5	13,874
Greater London	8.9	11.3	8.9	2.9	4.5	3.4	2.3	3.7	8.1	54.9	8.2	36.9	5,336
Rest of South East	9.1	10.6	9.1	4.2	5.6	4.5	3.8	3.9	8.7	60.3	5.0	34.7	8,538
South West	6.6	8.8	7.5	4.7	6.2	4.1	4.4	4.6	9.5	57.4	4.7	37.9	3,802
West Midlands	6.2	8.2	7.8	6.4	4.9	3.8	6.8	4.7	6.4	56.7	6.2	37.1	4,111
North West	6.3	8.9	8.0	5.5	5.3	4.1	5.1	4.0	5.8	53.9	6.1	39.9	4,947
England	7.4	9.4	8.2	5.0	5.3	4.1	4.7	4.2	7.4	56.7	5.9	37.3	37,961
Wales	4.3	8.1	6.8	4.8	5.0	3.6	4.9	4.6	7.9	51.5	5.3	43.1	2,280
Scotland	5.2	10.0	8.0	6.1	5.6	4.1	4.8	5.4	5.6	56.2	6.2	37.7	3,964
Northern Ireland	4.3	7.3	7.2	5.2	5.0	3.9	4.1	4.3	7.1	50.8	6.6	42.5	1,188

1 See Appendix notes.
2 Includes those on government employment or training programmes, unpaid family workers, and occupation not stated/inadequately described.

Source: Labour Force Survey, Employment Department; Department of Economic Development, Northern Ireland

5.12 Employees' paid annual holiday entitlement, Autumn 1994[1]

Percentages

	10 days or less	11-15 days	16-20 days	21-25 days	26-30 days	31-35 days	More than 35 days
Great Britain	6.8	7.3	23.5	37.9	16.1	3.1	5.4
North	6.6	6.5	22.5	37.3	17.6	3.2	6.2
Yorkshire & Humberside	6.7	7.9	23.8	37.8	15.1	3.0	5.7
East Midlands	7.4	9.2	23.9	37.8	14.3	2.9	4.5
East Anglia	7.8	6.3	22.3	40.1	16.2	2.5	4.9
South East	6.5	6.5	23.2	39.0	17.0	2.9	4.9
Greater London	7.3	6.5	23.8	37.6	16.6	3.5	4.7
Rest of South East	6.0	6.6	22.9	39.9	17.2	2.5	5.0
South West	7.2	6.8	24.3	40.1	13.7	2.1	5.8
West Midlands	6.6	9.1	23.6	36.8	14.9	4.1	4.9
North West	7.1	7.6	23.2	36.2	16.7	3.9	5.4
England	6.8	7.3	23.4	38.2	16.0	3.1	5.2
Wales	8.2	8.3	21.6	36.7	15.4	3.4	6.4
Scotland	6.1	6.7	24.9	34.9	17.3	3.6	6.5

1 Full-time employees. Excluding public holidays. See Appendix notes.

Source: Labour Force Survey, Employment Department

5.13 Average weekly earnings and hours for men[1], April 1994

	Average gross weekly earnings							Percentage of employees who received overtime pay	Average weekly hours	
		of which								
	Total (£)	Overtime pay (£)	PBR etc pay[2] (£)	Shift etc premium pay (£)	Percentage earning under				Total including overtime (hours)	Overtime (hours)
					£220	£300	£400			
All full-time male employees										
United Kingdom	361.0	25.3	14.5	6.1	21.7	46.4	70.4	35.2	41.6	3.3
North	327.8	27.4	13.7	8.6	25.0	51.9	76.6	37.3	42.0	3.7
Yorkshire & Humberside	329.5	27.7	14.5	6.3	24.9	51.1	76.2	39.0	42.3	3.9
East Midlands	325.0	27.3	15.3	6.2	24.7	52.1	78.5	38.5	42.3	3.8
East Anglia	334.8	25.6	12.4	5.7	23.2	52.0	74.7	37.8	42.1	3.6
South East	419.4	22.8	16.6	5.1	15.2	36.8	59.9	30.5	40.9	2.8
Greater London	467.3	21.3	19.1	5.4	11.5	31.1	52.8	27.2	40.1	2.4
Rest of South East	380.0	24.1	14.5	4.9	18.3	41.4	65.7	33.3	41.6	3.1
South West	343.9	24.3	12.6	5.8	23.6	48.8	72.1	35.9	41.4	3.3
West Midlands	336.2	26.9	14.9	5.7	23.8	51.0	75.8	38.1	42.2	3.8
North West	343.9	25.8	13.4	7.0	23.5	48.3	73.6	35.6	41.6	3.4
England	367.0	25.1	14.9	5.9	20.7	45.3	69.5	34.8	41.6	3.3
Wales	320.9	25.9	13.4	7.8	27.4	54.1	77.7	37.8	41.9	3.5
Scotland	335.6	25.0	11.9	6.3	24.8	51.2	74.8	36.7	41.4	3.3
Northern Ireland	319.2	31.9	9.2	4.9	32.8	55.1	74.4	38.8	41.9	3.8
Full-time manual male employees										
United Kingdom	279.7	40.2	13.7	9.7	31.6	65.1	88.3	53.5	44.7	5.6
North	278.5	38.4	16.7	12.2	32.6	65.3	87.9	49.8	44.4	5.4
Yorkshire & Humberside	277.0	42.2	17.7	9.6	32.8	65.8	89.3	56.9	45.0	5.9
East Midlands	273.3	41.1	17.3	9.7	32.4	65.8	90.6	55.5	44.9	5.8
East Anglia	273.5	39.8	12.0	9.1	32.3	69.0	89.7	56.1	44.9	5.6
South East	299.2	41.6	10.7	8.9	25.1	58.5	83.8	52.6	44.8	5.4
Greater London	314.0	41.7	11.5	10.1	21.5	53.8	79.7	49.2	44.5	5.3
Rest of South East	290.0	41.6	10.2	8.2	27.4	61.4	86.3	54.7	45.0	5.5
South West	271.1	40.2	11.2	9.3	34.8	69.6	90.1	54.9	44.8	5.7
West Midlands	274.2	41.5	16.2	9.2	32.1	66.2	90.6	54.9	44.8	5.8
North West	279.4	39.7	12.4	11.7	31.8	64.6	89.3	52.8	44.4	5.4
England	282.6	40.9	13.7	9.8	30.4	64.0	87.9	53.9	44.8	5.6
Wales	272.3	38.9	16.6	12.1	35.7	68.6	88.6	52.8	44.5	5.5
Scotland	269.5	37.0	13.2	8.9	34.3	69.9	90.5	51.4	44.3	5.2
Northern Ireland	241.7	34.2	11.4	7.7	48.5	77.6	93.9	48.0	44.0	5.0
Full-time non-manual male employees										
United Kingdom	427.3	13.1	15.1	3.0	13.7	31.2	55.7	20.3	38.9	1.4
North	385.2	14.4	10.2	4.4	16.1	36.3	63.4	22.7	39.1	1.5
Yorkshire & Humberside	384.8	12.5	11.1	2.8	16.6	35.6	62.5	20.2	39.1	1.5
East Midlands	379.5	12.6	13.3	2.6	16.5	37.7	65.6	20.5	39.4	1.5
East Anglia	397.6	10.9	12.9	2.2	13.9	34.6	59.3	19.1	39.0	1.3
South East	483.2	12.8	19.7	3.1	9.9	25.2	47.2	18.8	38.7	1.3
Greater London	531.5	12.8	22.2	3.4	7.3	21.6	41.6	18.0	38.1	1.2
Rest of South East	437.5	12.9	17.3	2.8	12.5	28.6	52.5	19.6	39.2	1.4
South West	400.0	12.0	13.8	3.2	15.0	32.7	58.3	21.2	38.7	1.3
West Midlands	399.9	12.0	13.6	2.1	15.2	35.4	60.5	20.8	39.4	1.6
North West	402.1	13.3	14.2	2.8	16.0	33.6	59.4	20.0	38.9	1.4
England	433.1	12.7	15.9	2.9	13.2	30.7	55.0	19.8	38.9	1.4
Wales	375.6	11.2	9.8	2.9	18.0	37.7	65.5	20.9	38.6	1.2
Scotland	400.6	13.2	10.7	3.8	15.6	32.7	59.3	22.2	38.6	1.4
Northern Ireland	388.7	29.8	7.2	2.4	18.7	35.0	56.9	30.5	40.0	2.8

1 Data relate to full-time male employees on adult rates whose pay for the survey pay-period was not affected by absence. See Appendix notes.
2 PBR etc pay is payments-by-results, bonuses, commission and other incentive payments.

Source: New Earnings Survey, Employment Department; Department of Economic Development, Northern Ireland

5.14 Average weekly earnings and hours for women[1], April 1994

| | Average gross weekly earnings | | | | | | | Percentage of employees who received overtime pay | Average weekly hours | |
| | | of which | | | Percentage earning under | | | | | |
	Total (£)	Overtime pay (£)	PBR etc pay[2] (£)	Shift etc premium pay (£)	£170	£220	£300		Total including overtime (hours)	Overtime (hours)
All full-time female employees										
United Kingdom	260.8	6.4	5.5	2.9	23.3	46.9	71.0	19.0	37.6	0.9
North	237.0	5.8	3.4	3.4	28.3	55.5	77.5	18.1	37.7	0.9
Yorkshire & Humberside	238.4	6.5	4.2	2.9	30.3	55.3	76.8	20.2	37.7	1.0
East Midlands	230.5	6.5	6.4	2.4	33.1	58.4	79.7	21.4	38.0	1.0
East Anglia	241.6	6.2	3.8	2.9	26.5	53.4	77.0	19.6	37.5	0.8
South East	301.1	7.1	6.8	2.5	13.2	31.6	59.6	18.9	37.5	0.9
Greater London	336.5	7.5	7.6	2.6	8.0	20.3	48.3	18.2	37.1	0.8
Rest of South East	268.0	6.7	6.1	2.5	18.0	42.1	70.1	19.6	38.0	1.0
South West	245.4	5.4	4.1	2.6	25.3	52.9	75.5	19.6	37.5	0.8
West Midlands	236.5	5.5	7.2	2.8	29.0	55.7	78.9	18.6	37.8	0.9
North West	243.6	6.0	5.2	3.1	26.2	53.0	76.6	18.9	37.5	0.9
England	264.6	6.4	5.8	2.7	22.1	45.3	70.1	19.2	37.6	0.9
Wales	239.0	5.2	4.4	4.1	28.3	54.6	76.9	17.3	37.4	0.8
Scotland	244.1	6.6	3.3	3.8	27.1	54.2	75.1	19.8	37.3	0.9
Northern Ireland	236.7	5.1	4.6	4.3	36.0	56.7	74.6	12.9	37.4	0.6
Full-time manual female employees										
United Kingdom	180.9	11.5	9.7	5.4	53.4	78.2	94.0	29.6	40.1	2.1
North	172.9	9.8	7.2	7.3	57.7	80.8	94.9	23.1	39.7	1.7
Yorkshire & Humberside	172.7	13.0	8.6	5.6	58.1	83.5	96.3	36.0	40.2	2.3
East Midlands	169.7	11.7	15.5	3.5	62.2	84.7	96.2	31.4	40.0	2.1
East Anglia	172.5	11.1	6.9	4.9	58.2	83.7	96.2	31.6	39.8	1.8
South East	204.4	13.6	5.5	5.1	41.1	67.8	88.2	31.4	40.5	2.4
Greater London	221.8	13.1	4.8	5.6	33.8	60.0	84.1	32.2	40.4	2.4
Rest of South East	193.2	13.9	6.0	4.9	45.7	72.9	90.9	30.8	40.5	2.4
South West	173.4	9.6	7.8	5.3	53.4	82.6	97.2	30.2	39.9	1.8
West Midlands	175.4	11.6	17.7	5.0	56.1	79.2	95.7	29.7	40.4	2.3
North West	175.7	11.1	11.1	4.6	55.9	78.2	95.9	29.5	39.8	1.9
England	183.1	12.0	9.8	5.0	52.3	77.2	93.6	30.8	40.1	2.2
Wales	175.7	11.8	9.9	7.0	54.8	79.5	95.8	30.6	40.2	2.0
Scotland	176.9	9.4	6.9	7.2	53.6	80.2	94.9	25.1	39.7	1.5
Northern Ireland	155.5	6.0	15.6	4.3	73.9	91.3	97.1	17.4	38.9	1.2
Full-time non-manual female employees										
United Kingdom	277.9	5.3	4.5	2.5	16.8	40.1	66.1	16.8	37.0	0.6
North	251.9	4.9	2.5	2.5	21.5	49.6	73.4	16.9	37.2	0.7
Yorkshire & Humberside	253.9	5.0	3.1	2.2	23.7	48.5	72.2	16.4	37.1	0.6
East Midlands	252.2	4.6	3.2	2.0	22.6	49.0	73.8	17.8	37.3	0.6
East Anglia	256.9	5.2	3.1	2.4	19.5	46.8	72.7	17.0	37.0	0.6
South East	315.5	6.2	7.0	2.1	9.0	26.2	55.4	17.1	37.1	0.7
Greater London	349.9	6.9	7.9	2.2	5.0	15.7	44.2	16.5	36.7	0.7
Rest of South East	281.4	5.5	6.1	2.1	13.0	36.6	66.4	17.6	37.5	0.7
South West	259.3	4.6	3.3	2.1	19.9	47.2	71.4	17.5	37.0	0.6
West Midlands	253.8	3.8	4.3	2.2	21.4	49.0	74.1	15.4	37.1	0.5
North West	258.3	4.9	3.9	2.7	19.8	47.5	72.4	16.5	37.0	0.6
England	281.3	5.3	5.0	2.2	16.0	38.7	65.3	16.9	37.1	0.6
Wales	257.4	3.3	2.8	3.2	20.7	47.4	71.4	13.4	36.7	0.5
Scotland	261.8	5.9	2.4	2.9	20.2	47.4	69.9	18.4	36.7	0.7
Northern Ireland	259.9	4.9	1.5	4.3	25.1	46.8	68.1	11.6	37.0	0.5

1 Data relate to full-time female employees on adult rates whose pay for the survey pay-period was not affected by absence. See Appendix notes.
2 PBR etc pay is payments-by-results, bonuses, commission and other incentive payments.

Source: New Earnings Survey, Employment Department; Department of Economic Development, Northern Ireland

5.15 Average weekly earnings[1]: by Standard Industrial Classification[2] and gender, April 1994

£ per week

	All industries and services (Divisions 0 to 9)		Agriculture, forestry & fishing (Division 0)		Energy & water supply industries (Division 1)		All manufacturing industries (Divisions 2 to 4)	
	Males	Females	Males	Females	Males	Females	Males	Females
United Kingdom	361.0	260.8	240.1	195.6	457.0	303.5	349.4	225.2
North	327.8	237.0	..	..	429.4	..	334.2	214.6
Yorkshire & Humberside	329.5	238.4	235.0	..	413.3	262.3	326.5	199.4
East Midlands	325.0	230.5	252.8	..	388.5	..	322.3	195.0
East Anglia	334.8	241.6	248.6	..	377.2	..	342.0	221.1
South East	419.4	301.1	251.2	..	510.6	350.5	409.6	280.5
Greater London	467.3	336.5	..	..	..	407.5	445.3	318.4
Rest of South East	380.0	268.0	252.4	..	458.8	307.8	395.1	261.5
South West	343.9	245.4	233.2	..	498.0	..	341.5	220.8
West Midlands	336.2	236.5	226.7	..	415.4	289.2	328.2	203.6
North West	343.9	243.6	..	..	473.5	..	340.5	214.0
England	367.0	264.6	242.8	197.2	456.3	306.1	353.5	230.2
Wales	320.9	239.0	..	..	424.5	..	327.5	206.7
Scotland	335.6	244.1	240.3	..	490.1	303.8	335.2	204.4
Northern Ireland	319.2	236.7	146.4	..	373.0	..	282.8	174.9

	Manufacture of metals, mineral products & chemicals (Division 2)		Metal goods, engineering & vehicle industries (Division 3)		Other manufacturing industries (Division 4)		Construction (Division 5)	
	Males	Females	Males	Females	Males	Females	Males	Females
United Kingdom	367.3	247.9	353.2	229.7	335.7	216.6	327.1	227.7
North	368.3	..	331.1	212.3	313.4	207.9	292.6	..
Yorkshire & Humberside	354.4	227.5	317.1	201.2	319.0	192.0	304.6	..
East Midlands	356.7	221.3	329.8	209.9	301.5	186.1	318.4	..
East Anglia	353.7	..	346.8	205.5	333.5	223.8	308.5	..
South East	433.8	293.6	403.3	267.7	409.9	286.2	390.1	257.2
Greater London	..	307.9	409.2	292.5	466.4	330.5	414.2	273.1
Rest of South East	417.6	288.4	401.7	260.8	372.8	250.3	373.7	247.0
South West	338.7	..	354.0	229.7	323.9	216.7	320.4	..
West Midlands	329.4	199.9	333.0	212.5	315.0	194.7	313.1	216.0
North West	373.8	258.8	346.0	217.5	314.6	200.3	318.9	..
England	370.5	249.4	355.8	232.3	342.1	223.4	335.5	231.9
Wales	355.9	..	325.7	207.2	305.4	193.3	284.4	..
Scotland	353.8	..	344.6	219.2	319.0	195.3	306.9	..
Northern Ireland	308.5	222.3	320.4	208.9	249.3	161.7	285.9	..

	Distribution, hotels & catering, repairs (Division 6)		Transport & communication (Division 7)		Banking, finance, insurance, business services & leasing (Division 8)		Other services (Division 9)	
	Males	Females	Males	Females	Males	Females	Males	Females
United Kingdom	292.5	201.1	351.0	281.8	459.6	280.9	373.4	284.5
North	269.0	174.2	297.2	222.4	359.8	219.8	348.4	265.8
Yorkshire & Humberside	276.0	187.8	316.8	245.1	376.8	229.9	359.1	276.4
East Midlands	288.1	185.8	311.8	225.3	371.2	234.6	349.3	274.2
East Anglia	273.0	186.4	349.3	237.7	381.3	230.7	356.9	280.5
South East	325.4	236.3	404.6	322.4	544.1	332.3	399.2	309.5
Greater London	330.9	259.5	422.5	347.4	618.5	377.4	425.2	334.4
Rest of South East	321.4	217.3	385.7	295.4	424.8	271.2	371.7	285.3
South West	271.8	183.3	311.1	246.6	416.0	246.5	363.0	271.9
West Midlands	291.2	183.2	320.3	266.6	397.1	233.8	368.3	274.2
North West	291.0	190.6	321.0	244.3	384.3	242.3	365.2	273.1
England	299.6	205.9	357.6	286.5	472.4	286.9	376.2	287.3
Wales	245.6	170.9	298.6	..	342.7	217.6	349.3	270.2
Scotland	254.1	178.5	319.5	248.9	373.5	242.5	357.0	275.1
Northern Ireland	236.4	166.4	298.8	262.0	336.2	246.5	393.0	271.0

1 Average gross weekly earnings; data relate to full-time employees on adult rates whose pay for the survey pay-period was not affected by absence. See Appendix notes.
2 Classification is based on SIC 80.

Source: New Earnings Survey, Employment Department; Department of Economic Development, Northern Ireland

5.16 Main method of travel to work, Autumn 1994[1]

Percentages

	British Rail train[2]	Other rail[2]	Bus	Car	Motor cycle[2]	Bicycle	Foot	Other[2]	Not stated[3]
Region of domicile									
Great Britain	2.8	1.9	7.4	57.1	1.0	3.1	10.4	0.4	16.0
North	..	1.3	10.2	58.8	..	1.9	11.7	.	14.7
Yorkshire & Humberside	1.0	..	11.2	59.4	1.0	3.3	10.4	.	13.4
East Midlands	0.7	..	6.0	60.2	1.4	4.1	11.8	.	15.4
East Anglia	1.0	-	3.0	58.8	1.9	8.4	9.1	.	17.4
South East	6.6	5.6	5.7	52.0	1.1	3.0	8.7	0.3	17.2
Greater London	8.9	14.3	9.6	37.5	1.0	2.0	8.3	0.4	18.0
Rest of South East	5.2	0.4	3.3	60.5	1.2	3.6	8.9	0.3	16.6
South West	0.6	-	4.2	58.0	1.7	4.2	12.0	..	19.0
West Midlands	0.9	..	8.5	61.4	0.7	2.5	10.2	..	15.7
North West	1.1	0.2	8.8	61.4	0.7	2.6	11.2	0.6	13.5
England	3.0	2.2	6.9	56.9	1.1	3.3	10.1	0.4	16.1
Wales	..	..	5.3	60.9	..	1.6	11.3	..	19.3
Scotland	..	..	12.6	56.6	..	1.5	12.2	0.9	13.9

1 See Appendix notes.
2 For some regions, sample sizes are too small to provide a reliable estimate.
3 Includes people who work at home.

Source: Labour Force Survey, Employment Department

5.17 Working days lost due to labour disputes[1]

Rates[2]

	1981	1991	1993	1994
United Kingdom	195	34	30	13
North	301	75	20	8
Yorkshire & Humberside	242	29	13	10
East Midlands	79	11	2	5
East Anglia	117	50	4	9
South East	116	19	15	8
South West	111	6	3	12
West Midlands	299	8	11	15
North West	281	104	5	19
England	179	32	11	11
Wales	311	20	21	14
Scotland	299	62	57	8
Northern Ireland	136	32	29	9

1 Regional rates are based on data for stoppages that exclude widespread disputes that cannot be allocated to a specific region. These are included in the United Kingdom strike rate only. See Appendix notes.
2 Days lost per 1,000 employees.

Source: Employment Department

5.18 Employees absent due to sickness[1]

Percentages

	1986	1991	1993	1994
United Kingdom	4.5	4.8	4.8	4.4
North	4.7	5.3	4.7	3.9
Yorkshire & Humberside	4.0	4.5	5.2	4.6
East Midlands	4.6	4.8	4.0	4.5
East Anglia	4.4	3.7	3.6	4.0
South East	4.6	4.4	4.7	4.3
Greater London	4.7	4.7	5.0	5.2
Rest of South East	4.6	4.2	4.6	3.8
South West	4.5	4.8	4.9	3.7
West Midlands	4.3	5.2	5.0	4.7
North West	4.3	5.0	4.8	4.7
England	4.5	4.7	4.7	4.4
Wales	4.2	5.5	4.9	4.4
Scotland	4.2	5.3	5.0	4.7
Northern Ireland	4.2	5.0	5.7	5.7

1 Spring of each year. Percentages of employees absent from work due to illness or injury for at least one day in the week before interview. See Appendix notes.

Source: Labour Force Survey, Employment Department; Department of Economic Development, Northern Ireland

5.19 Redundancies[1]

Thousands and rates

	Thousands					Rate per 1,000 employees				
	1990[2]	1991	1992	1993[2]	1994[2]	1990[2]	1991	1992	1993[2]	1994[2]
Great Britain	181	388	322	262	205	8.1	17.8	15.1	12.4	9.7
North	..	21	19	18	14	..	18.4	16.6	16.5	13.0
Yorkshire & Humberside	20	30	31	25	21	10.1	15.5	16.2	13.0	10.8
East Midlands	17	32	32	23	16	10.3	19.4	19.9	13.9	10.0
East Anglia	..	12	15	..	..	..	14.1	17.8	..	..
South East	61	126	101	77	63	8.5	17.8	14.8	11.3	9.3
Greater London	26	53	37	29	23	9.5	20.0	14.7	11.4	9.3
Rest of South East	35	74	64	48	40	7.9	16.5	14.8	11.2	9.3
South West	11	26	25	22	15	6.0	14.7	14.3	12.5	8.7
West Midlands	17	44	32	27	21	8.1	21.2	16.1	13.9	10.5
North West	18	43	32	28	20	7.4	17.7	13.6	12.3	8.7
England	157	332	286	228	177	8.2	17.6	15.6	12.5	9.6
Wales	11	27	17	11	10	10.4	26.3	16.6	11.4	10.6
Scotland	12	28	19	22	18	6.1	14.4	9.7	11.5	9.4

1 Refers to those made redundant in the three months prior to each Spring survey. See Appendix notes.
2 For some regions, sample sizes are too small to provide a reliable estimate.

Source: Labour Force Survey, Employment Department

5.20 Unemployed claimants[1]: by duration and gender, January 1995

Percentages and numbers

	2 weeks or less	Over 2 and up to 8 weeks	Over 8 and up to 13 weeks	Over 13 and up to 26 weeks	Over 26 weeks up to 1 year	Over 1 and up to 2 years	Over 2 and up to 3 years	Over 3 and up to 5 years	Over 5 years	Total (= 100%) (numbers)
Males										
United Kingdom	5.6	12.1	8.7	15.9	17.8	16.1	8.1	10.3	5.5	1,918,221
North	4.7	12.9	9.4	17.1	17.2	15.5	7.4	9.6	6.2	128,076
Yorkshire & Humberside	5.9	13.6	9.4	16.6	17.4	14.6	6.8	9.8	6.0	173,249
East Midlands	6.3	13.4	8.9	15.7	17.5	15.4	7.7	10.1	5.0	123,995
East Anglia	7.0	15.3	10.4	17.1	16.6	14.9	7.2	8.6	2.9	53,521
South East	5.6	10.5	8.0	15.9	18.7	17.8	9.5	11.0	3.2	578,233
Greater London	4.4	8.6	6.9	15.4	19.3	19.3	10.3	11.8	4.0	303,413
Rest of South East	6.8	12.5	9.2	16.5	18.0	16.1	8.6	10.0	2.3	274,820
South West	6.4	13.4	9.9	17.2	18.0	15.1	7.4	9.4	3.3	137,609
West Midlands	5.3	10.9	7.6	14.6	17.7	16.1	8.9	12.8	6.1	172,814
North West	6.0	12.7	8.9	15.9	17.6	15.5	7.2	9.5	6.6	214,995
England	5.7	12.0	8.7	16.1	17.9	16.2	8.2	10.4	4.7	1,582,492
Wales	5.6	13.5	9.6	17.1	17.1	15.6	7.3	9.8	4.7	90,065
Scotland	5.4	14.1	9.7	16.5	18.4	15.2	6.6	8.1	6.1	173,340
Northern Ireland	3.3	7.2	5.3	10.6	12.9	15.3	10.1	12.9	22.3	72,324
Females										
United Kingdom	8.7	13.7	10.3	19.8	20.0	13.8	5.3	5.2	3.1	585,132
North	8.9	14.3	10.9	20.0	19.3	13.1	4.8	5.0	3.7	31,603
Yorkshire & Humberside	9.0	14.7	10.4	19.6	20.0	12.8	4.4	5.4	3.9	49,239
East Midlands	9.6	14.4	10.2	19.6	19.9	13.0	5.0	5.1	3.2	38,120
East Anglia	10.6	15.5	11.5	20.1	18.7	12.6	4.8	4.4	1.8	18,345
South East	8.1	12.3	9.6	20.2	20.9	15.4	6.2	5.5	1.9	190,238
Greater London	6.6	10.9	8.9	20.4	21.4	17.0	6.8	6.0	2.1	104,054
Rest of South East	9.9	14.1	10.4	20.1	20.2	13.5	5.5	4.8	1.6	86,184
South West	10.2	14.5	11.8	20.5	19.0	12.6	4.6	4.7	2.2	46,581
West Midlands	7.9	12.3	9.0	19.0	20.9	14.7	6.0	6.6	3.6	54,268
North West	9.4	15.1	10.3	19.7	19.4	13.0	4.8	4.6	3.6	61,027
England	8.8	13.5	10.1	19.9	20.2	14.0	5.4	5.3	2.7	489,421
Wales	9.5	15.3	11.0	21.3	19.1	12.3	4.5	4.5	2.5	25,760
Scotland	8.9	16.4	12.5	19.1	19.6	11.7	3.9	4.3	3.6	50,392
Northern Ireland	6.0	10.4	7.3	17.5	17.9	14.7	7.7	7.4	11.1	19,559

1 Not seasonally adjusted. See Appendix notes.

Source: Employment Department

5.21 Claimant unemployment rates[1]

Percentages

	Seasonally adjusted annual averages									
	1981	1986	1987	1938	1989	1990	1991	1992	1993	1994
United Kingdom	8.1	11.1	10.0	8.0	6.2	5.8	8.0	9.7	10.3	9.4
North	11.7	15.2	13.9	11.8	9.8	8.7	10.3	11.1	11.9	11.3
Yorkshire & Humberside	8.8	12.4	11.3	9.3	7.3	6.6	8.7	9.9	10.2	9.6
East Midlands	7.4	9.9	8.9	7.1	5.4	5.1	7.2	9.0	9.5	8.7
East Anglia	6.2	8.5	7.3	5.1	3.5	3.7	5.8	7.6	8.1	7.2
South East	5.4	8.2	7.1	5.3	3.9	3.9	6.9	9.2	10.2	9.1
Greater London	5.4	9.1	8.2	6.6	5.1	5.0	8.0	10.5	11.6	10.7
Rest of South East	5.4	7.4	6.1	4.2	2.9	3.1	5.9	8.2	9.0	7.8
South West	6.6	9.2	8.0	6.0	4.4	4.3	6.9	9.2	9.5	8.3
West Midlands	10.0	12.8	11.3	8.8	6.5	5.7	8.4	10.3	10.8	9.7
North West	10.2	13.7	12.4	10.3	8.4	7.6	9.3	10.6	10.7	9.9
England	7.6	10.5	9.3	7.3	5.6	5.3	7.7	9.6	10.2	9.3
Wales	10.4	13.7	12.1	9.9	7.4	6.7	9.0	10.0	10.3	9.3
Scotland	10.0	13.5	13.1	11.2	9.4	8.2	8.8	9.4	9.7	9.2
Northern Ireland	12.6	17.1	16.7	15.3	14.3	13.0	13.2	13.8	13.8	12.9

1 See Appendix notes.

Source: Employment Department

5.22 ILO unemployment rates[1]

Percentages

	Spring quarter of each year								
	1986	1987	1988	1989	1990	1991	1992	1993	1994
United Kingdom	11.2	10.7	8.8	7.2	6.8	8.3	9.6	10.2	9.5
North	14.6	13.4	13.4	11.1	10.3	10.8	11.2	11.2	11.7
Yorkshire & Humberside	12.3	11.6	10.9	8.6	7.4	8.3	9.9	9.8	9.8
East Midlands	10.3	10.4	7.7	6.8	6.6	7.3	8.7	9.0	8.3
East Anglia	8.6	8.6	5.6	4.2	4.8	6.3	7.1	8.3	7.4
South East	8.5	7.7	6.1	4.9	5.2	7.3	9.4	10.3	9.6
Greater London	10.3	9.3	8.0	6.7	6.7	9.1	11.9	13.2	13.0
Rest of South East	7.3	6.7	4.9	3.8	4.2	6.1	7.9	8.5	7.6
South West	8.9	8.6	6.2	5.3	5.0	7.5	9.1	9.2	7.5
West Midlands	12.5	12.8	8.9	7.5	6.7	9.4	10.7	11.6	9.9
North West	13.9	12.9	11.5	9.4	7.9	9.6	10.1	10.9	10.2
England	10.5	10.0	8.2	6.7	6.3	8.1	9.6	10.2	9.5
Wales	14.3	13.3	11.4	9.1	8.1	9.3	8.9	9.5	9.4
Scotland	13.7	14.8	12.0	9.8	9.3	9.2	9.5	10.1	9.9
Northern Ireland	15.7	15.2	13.9	12.5	11.6	12.0	12.1	12.5	11.5

1 See Appendix notes.

Source: Labour Force Survey, Employment Department; Department of Economic Development, Northern Ireland

5.23 Claimant unemployment: by county[1], January 1995

Unemployment rate[2], January 1995

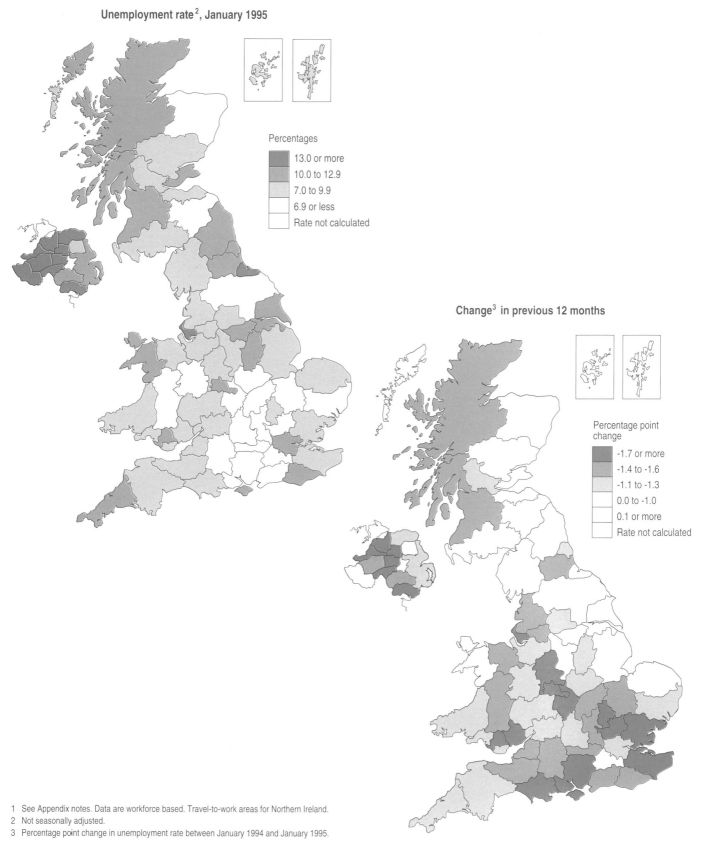

Percentages

- 13.0 or more
- 10.0 to 12.9
- 7.0 to 9.9
- 6.9 or less
- Rate not calculated

Change[3] in previous 12 months

Percentage point change

- -1.7 or more
- -1.4 to -1.6
- -1.1 to -1.3
- 0.0 to -1.0
- 0.1 or more
- Rate not calculated

1 See Appendix notes. Data are workforce based. Travel-to-work areas for Northern Ireland.
2 Not seasonally adjusted.
3 Percentage point change in unemployment rate between January 1994 and January 1995.

Source: Employment Department

5.24 Unemployed claimants[1]: by age and gender, January 1995

Percentages and numbers

	Percentage aged						Total (= 100%) numbers
	Under 20	20-29	30-39	40-49	50-59	60 or over	
Males							
United Kingdom	6.5	35.9	24.9	16.8	14.4	1.4	1,918,221
North	7.1	35.8	25.0	16.8	14.3	1.1	128,076
Yorkshire & Humberside	7.1	37.2	23.8	16.1	14.5	1.3	173,249
East Midlands	6.7	36.0	23.4	16.8	15.4	1.8	123,995
East Anglia	6.9	34.1	22.6	17.8	16.4	2.2	53,521
South East	5.4	34.9	26.6	17.1	14.3	1.7	578,233
Greater London	4.9	36.4	28.6	16.2	12.6	1.3	303,413
Rest of South East	5.9	33.2	24.4	18.2	16.1	2.1	274,820
South West	6.2	34.1	23.3	17.9	16.7	1.8	137,609
West Midlands	6.8	36.0	24.0	16.5	15.2	1.6	172,814
North West	7.6	38.8	24.3	15.5	12.8	1.0	214,995
England	6.4	35.9	24.9	16.8	14.6	1.5	1,582,492
Wales	7.8	38.2	24.0	16.3	12.8	1.0	90,065
Scotland	7.4	36.4	24.4	16.6	14.1	1.2	173,340
Northern Ireland	5.2	33.1	27.3	19.1	14.2	1.1	72,324
Females							
United Kingdom	12.4	38.6	17.3	16.5	15.2	0.1	585,132
North	15.8	36.9	16.5	16.5	14.2	-	31,603
Yorkshire & Humberside	14.1	39.3	15.9	15.9	14.7	-	49,239
East Midlands	12.6	38.0	16.4	17.4	15.6	-	38,120
East Anglia	12.7	36.2	15.7	19.3	16.0	-	18,345
South East	10.0	39.6	18.6	16.3	15.3	0.1	190,238
Greater London	9.3	42.6	19.8	14.7	13.6	0.1	104,054
Rest of South East	11.0	36.1	17.2	18.3	17.3	0.1	86,184
South West	11.5	37.1	16.8	17.9	16.6	-	46,581
West Midlands	13.0	38.0	16.0	16.5	16.4	0.1	54,268
North West	14.7	40.2	16.6	15.0	13.4	-	61,027
England	12.2	38.8	17.2	16.5	15.2	0.1	489,421
Wales	14.5	38.2	16.6	16.7	14.0	-	25,760
Scotland	13.6	37.7	17.5	16.1	15.0	-	50,392
Northern Ireland	11.6	37.1	18.8	15.9	16.5	0.1	19,559
All persons							
United Kingdom	7.9	36.6	23.1	16.7	14.6	1.1	2,503,353
North	8.8	36.0	23.3	16.7	14.3	0.9	159,679
Yorkshire & Humberside	8.7	37.7	22.0	16.1	14.5	1.0	222,488
East Midlands	8.1	36.5	21.7	16.9	15.4	1.4	162,115
East Anglia	8.4	34.7	20.9	18.1	16.3	1.6	71,866
South East	6.5	36.1	24.6	16.9	14.5	1.3	768,471
Greater London	6.0	38.0	26.4	15.8	12.8	1.0	407,467
Rest of South East	7.2	33.9	22.7	18.2	16.4	1.6	361,004
South West	7.6	34.9	21.7	17.9	16.6	1.4	184,190
West Midlands	8.3	36.5	22.1	16.5	15.5	1.2	227,082
North West	9.2	39.1	22.6	15.4	13.0	0.8	276,022
England	7.8	36.6	23.1	16.7	14.7	1.2	2,071,913
Wales	9.3	38.2	22.3	16.4	13.1	0.7	115,825
Scotland	8.8	36.7	22.9	16.5	14.3	0.9	223,732
Northern Ireland	6.6	33.9	25.5	18.4	14.7	0.9	91,883

1 Not seasonally adjusted. See Appendix notes.

Source: Employment Department

5.25 Vacancies[1] at jobcentres

Thousands

	1981	1986	1988	1989	1990	1991	1992	1993	1994
United Kingdom	91.1	188.8	248.6	219.5	173.6	117.9	117.1	127.9	158.0
North	4.0	9.8	11.4	10.7	10.7	6.6	6.0	6.1	6.8
Yorkshire & Humberside	5.3	11.3	15.5	13.3	11.7	7.9	7.9	9.9	11.8
East Midlands	5.4	10.3	13.8	12.9	10.5	7.1	7.3	8.7	10.9
East Anglia	3.5	6.2	9.7	8.3	5.4	3.2	3.5	4.2	5.4
South East	34.0	70.8	95.1	71.7	47.6	28.8	29.2	31.4	41.5
Greater London	16.2	30.0	32.2	23.6	14.8	8.2	8.3	10.0	13.2
Rest of South East	17.8	40.8	62.9	48.1	32.8	20.6	20.9	21.4	28.2
South West	7.7	18.1	20.4	18.5	13.9	9.9	9.0	9.7	12.5
West Midlands	5.9	15.4	24.1	20.5	14.6	8.2	7.6	8.9	12.3
North West	7.9	19.0	23.9	24.4	21.0	15.8	14.9	15.7	19.1
England	73.8	161.1	213.8	180.3	135.3	87.4	85.4	94.5	120.3
Wales	4.9	9.5	12.1	13.8	12.1	8.1	8.5	9.6	11.2
Scotland	11.6	16.3	20.0	21.7	21.6	18.3	18.9	18.5	19.9
Northern Ireland	0.7	2.0	2.8	3.8	4.5	4.1	4.3	5.2	6.5

1 Vacancies remaining unfilled, seasonally adjusted annual averages.

Source: Employment Department

5.26 Trade union membership[1]: by gender

Percentages[2]

	Males					Females				
	1990	1991	1992	1993	1994	1990	1991	1992	1993	1994
United Kingdom	43.3	42.2	39.6	38.3	36.5	32.4	32.6	31.9	31.7	30.8
North	59.4	58.0	51.2	47.1	46.9	43.8	43.3	40.4	42.0	39.8
Yorkshire & Humberside	46.2	48.0	44.1	40.5	39.2	37.7	36.5	36.0	35.1	33.1
East Midlands	44.0	43.0	38.2	39.8	35.4	34.1	34.1	31.0	31.3	29.1
East Anglia	32.6	32.6	33.2	32.1	31.2	21.9	22.6	25.2	24.5	22.2
South East	34.5	34.5	31.8	31.2	29.2	25.5	25.5	25.7	25.4	24.6
Greater London	37.2	36.9	34.1	34.1	30.4	30.1	30.3	30.7	28.5	29.4
Rest of South East	32.8	33.1	30.5	29.6	28.6	22.6	22.7	22.8	23.6	21.9
South West	40.4	38.3	35.5	34.9	30.7	25.1	25.5	26.0	24.9	25.3
West Midlands	47.1	44.2	42.6	39.2	39.1	33.0	34.8	32.3	31.0	32.0
North West	51.1	47.7	46.6	45.4	43.7	38.2	39.3	39.4	38.3	36.7
England	42.1	41.1	38.3	36.9	35.0	30.7	31.1	30.6	30.2	29.1
Wales	52.5	49.8	48.4	50.6	50.2	42.2	43.0	37.0	42.0	41.6
Scotland	48.9	46.6	43.6	42.1	40.4	39.7	38.7	38.7	38.8	37.4
Northern Ireland	50.5	50.6	48.4	49.0	48.7	44.9	43.7	42.8	42.0	42.4

1 For 1990 to 1992, three months to May of each year. For 1993 and 1994, three months to November for England, Wales and Scotland; three months to May for Northern Ireland. See
Appendix notes.
2 As a percentage of all employees in each region. Excludes those who did not state whether they were a member of a trade union/staff association.

Source: Labour Force Survey, Employment Department; Department of Economic Development,
Northern Ireland

6 Housing

Stock of dwellings
: The stock of dwellings in East Anglia rose by 18 per cent between 1981 and 1993, almost three times the rate of growth in the North West.

(Table 6.1)

Tenure
: The rate of owner-occupation in Scotland rose by 6 per cent between 1991 and 1993, a bigger rise than in any other region.

(Table 6.2)

Age of dwellings
: Wales has proportionately more older houses, with one in five dwellings built before 1891.

(Table 6.3)

Size of dwellings
: On average, the South West has the biggest houses and the North West the smallest.

(Table 6.4)

New homes
: In 1993, private developers built more than twice as many new homes per head of population in East Anglia as in the North

(Table 6.6)

: Northern Ireland is the only region where the public sector is building more new houses than housing associations are.

(Table 6.6)

Rents
: The average local authority rent was highest in the South East in April 1994 at £44 per week, and lowest in Scotland at £27 per week.

(Table 6.7)

Council house sales
: Local authorities in East Anglia have sold the largest proportion of their housing stocks since 1979, while those in the North West have sold the smallest proportion.

(Table 6.8)

House prices
: The North, Scotland and Northern Ireland are the only regions where house prices have risen each year since 1989.

(Table 6.9)

Homelessness
: Mortgage arrears accounted for 15 per cent of households accepted as homeless in East Anglia in 1993, compared with only 1 per cent in Northern Ireland.

(Table 6.12)

Council Tax bandings
: Almost ten times the proportion of residential properties in the North as in the South East was classified as Band A for Council Tax.

(Table 6.13)

Introduction

The tables in the first half of the chapter look at different aspects of the stock of dwellings. Between 1981 and 1993, East Anglia had the biggest percentage increase in stock, nearly three times the rate of growth in the North West (Table 6.1). However, the stock of dwellings is affected by a number of factors other than the building of new homes: some existing properties are converted, some are demolished under slum clearance legislation, to make way for new development or because they are defective, some are closed as unfit for habitation and others that were previously closed are made fit again. The North West accounted for about a third of the total losses to the housing stock in England between April 1981 and March 1993.

Looking more recently, slum clearance accounted for the removal of around 25,600 dwellings from Great Britain's housing stock between April 1989 and March 1993, of which over a third were in Scotland and nearly a quarter were in the North West. Only 1 per cent of slums cleared in this period were in East Anglia. Over the last ten years, slum clearance has generally declined each year in England and Wales, although large programmes of clearances in the South East in 1988/89 and, more importantly, 1990/91 and in the North West in 1989/90 disturbed this trend within those regions. In Scotland, the number of dwellings demolished or closed each year remained reasonably constant over the nine years to 1991/92, but doubled in 1992/93, to just under 3,700, almost two-thirds of the GB total.

The housing market generally reflects the state of the economy. Housing starts per head of population peaked in 1988 but, with the recession, fell each year up to 1992. The trend was reversed in 1993. As Table 6.6 shows, Housing Associations now build many more new homes than local authorities in any region of England or in Wales. Those built by local authorities are, in the main, specialised dwellings.

There was a boom in house prices in the late 1980s, but the early 1990s saw a fall in prices in real terms. Average dwelling prices as measured by *The Five per cent Sample Survey of Building Society Mortgages* are shown in Table 6.9. An alternative source of information on house prices which generally confirms the figures shown in

"The housing market the state

that table is the *Property Market Report* by the Valuation Agency of the Inland Revenue which comprises reports by the District Valuers based on average property values in the major towns of the regions. These reports indicate that in most regions of England and Wales house prices peaked in Spring 1989, although it was in Autumn of that year in Wales, Spring 1990 in Yorkshire and Humberside, and Spring 1991 in the Northern and North West regions. By Autumn 1994, the most notable falls were in East Anglia and the South West, where average values were down by 28 per cent on their peaks.

Across England and Wales as a whole, the volume of housing transactions in the year to October 1994 was nearly 14 per cent greater than for the corresponding period a year earlier, and was at a level not seen since 1991. However, local market intelligence suggests that this reflected primarily those whose moves were a necessity rather than those who chose to move.

The majority of homes are purchased with the aid of a mortgage, and average mortgage advances are shown in Table 6.10. The Department of Social Security's Family Resources Survey (FRS) found that, of those households in the South East that reported paying mortgages in 1993-94, 24 per cent had a loan of less than £25,000, compared with 62 per cent in the North and 60 per cent in Yorkshire and Humberside and Wales. At the other end of the scale, 14 per cent of households in the South East had mortgages of £60,000 or more, compared with 3 per cent in Yorkshire and Humberside and 4 per cent in the North, the East Midlands, Wales and Scotland. The FRS also found that one in 20 households with a mortgage were in a position of negative equity, and for one in every 100 the negative equity was in excess of £10,000.

Table 6.11 shows the trend in the number of mortgage possession actions entered and orders made in the courts in England, Wales and Northern Ireland. The figures do not indicate how many houses have been repossessed through the courts as not all orders result in the issue and execution of warrants of possession (see Appendix for further details). The regional breakdown relates to the location of the court rather than the address of the property.

generally reflects of the economy."

6.1 Stock of dwellings[1,2]

Thousands and percentages

| | Thousands | | | | | | Percentage increase |
	1976	1981	1986	1991	1992	1993	1981-1993
United Kingdom	20,598	21,580	22,601	23,702	23,874	24,056	11.5
North	1,169	1,214	1,249	1,287	1,294	1,301	7.2
Yorkshire & Humberside	1,829	1,901	1,960	2,031	2,044	2,058	8.3
East Midlands	1,393	1,484	1,558	1,646	1,661	1,676	12.9
East Anglia	692	754	807	870	880	890	18.0
South East	6,236	6,537	6,913	7,288	7,340	7,391	13.1
Greater London	2,640	2,682	2,801	2,928	2,945	2,959	10.3
Rest of South East	3,596	3,856	4,112	4,360	4,396	4,432	14.9
South West	1,613	1,728	1,853	1,983	2,000	2,015	16.6
West Midlands	1,840	1,941	2,016	2,089	2,102	2,117	9.1
North West	2,396	2,466	2,526	2,593	2,606	2,622	6.3
England	17,168	18,025	18,883	19,787	19,927	20,070	11.3
Wales	1,029	1,083	1,128	1,184	1,193	1,203	11.0
Scotland	1,921	1,970	2,050	2,158	2,174	2,193	11.2
Northern Ireland	480	502	540	573	580	590	17.5

1 At December.
2 See Appendix notes.

Source: Department of the Environment; Welsh Office; The Scottish Office Environment Department; Department of the Environment, Northern Ireland

6.2 Tenure of dwellings[1]

Percentages

| | Owner-occupied | | | Rented from local authority or New Town[2,3] | | | Rented from private owners or with job or business | | | Rented from housing association | | |
	1981	1991	1993	1981	1991	1993	1981	1991	1993	1981	1991	1993
United Kingdom	55	66	66	30	22	20	11	9	9	2	3	4
North	48	60	61	39	28	27	10	8	9	3	4	4
Yorkshire & Humberside	57	65	65	31	23	22	11	9	9	2	2	3
East Midlands	60	70	70	27	19	18	11	9	9	1	2	2
East Anglia	59	68	69	25	16	14	14	13	13	2	3	5
South East	59	67	67	26	18	17	12	11	12	3	4	5
Greater London	50	57	57	32	23	22	13	14	14	5	6	6
Rest of South East	65	73	73	23	14	13	11	10	10	2	3	4
South West	64	72	72	21	14	13	14	12	12	2	2	3
West Midlands	58	67	67	31	23	22	9	7	8	2	3	3
North West	60	67	68	29	21	21	9	8	8	2	4	4
England	59	67	67	28	20	19	11	10	10	2	3	4
Wales	62	71	72	28	18	18	9	8	8	1	3	3
Scotland	36	52	56	52	38	34	10	7	7	2	3	3
Northern Ireland	54	66	68	38	28	27	8	4	4	1	2	2

1 See Appendix notes.
2 Including Scottish Homes, formerly the Scottish Special Housing Association.
3 Northern Ireland Housing Executive in Northern Ireland.

Source: Department of the Environment; Welsh Office; The Scottish Office Environment Department; Department of the Environment Northern Ireland

6.3 Date of construction of dwellings, 1993[1]

Percentages

	Pre 1891	1891 -1918	1919 -1944	1945 -1970	Post 1970
Great Britain	14.1	12.6	19.1	31.4	22.8
North	11.0	14.5	19.0	34.8	20.7
Yorkshire & Humberside	12.8	14.7	20.7	31.7	20.1
East Midlands	12.6	11.5	18.1	31.6	26.1
East Anglia	18.7	7.4	12.7	29.7	31.6
South East	14.3	12.3	21.2	30.1	22.1
Greater London	18.2	17.5	27.2	22.0	15.1
Rest of S East	11.8	8.9	17.1	35.5	26.7
South West	19.2	9.4	14.9	30.0	26.5
West Midlands	10.9	10.8	21.5	35.2	21.7
North West	14.4	13.8	21.4	30.1	20.3
England	14.1	12.2	19.8	31.2	22.7
Wales	20.4	16.2	12.7	28.7	22.0
Scotland	10.0	14.4	16.0	34.8	24.4
Northern Ireland[2]	20.6		1.0	22.0	46.3

1 See Appendix notes.
2 1991 data for Northern Ireland.

Source: Department of the Environment; Welsh Office; The Scottish Office Environment Department; Northern Ireland Housing Executive

6.4 Average floor area of dwellings, 1991

Square metres

	Houses	Flats	All dwellings
North	81	56	77
Yorkshire & Humberside	81	58	77
East Midlands	85	55	82
East Anglia	87	55	84
South East	89	61	81
Greater London	87	61	74
Rest of South East	90	60	85
South West	91	65	85
West Midlands	80	57	76
North West	79	55	76
England	85	60	80
Wales[1]	134	96	131

1 1993 data for Wales. Based on external dimensions; see *1993 Welsh House Condition Survey* report for further details.

Source: Department of the Environment; Welsh Office

6.5 Renovations: by sector[1]

Thousands of dwellings[2]

	Grants paid to private owners and tenants[3,4]			Work completed for housing associations			Work completed for local authorities and new towns [3,5,6]		
	1981	1986	1993	1981	1986	1993	1981	1986	1993
United Kingdom	115.7	178.0	123.1	13.9	15.4	..	..	230.9	360.7
North	4.9	7.0	5.3	1.2	1.2	0.3	4.1	17.5	18.2
Yorkshire & Humberside	7.7	10.1	10.1	0.7	1.0	0.5	5.0	4.9	21.8
East Midlands	7.3	11.2	7.9	0.7	0.8	0.3	5.6	11.3	13.0
East Anglia	3.3	5.7	3.6	0.2	0.3	0.1	1.2	3.9	7.0
South East	20.6	39.0	24.5	3.6	4.2	3.2	20.1	52.5	92.9
Greater London	9.5	20.8	8.0	3.3	3.5	2.3	13.5	30.4	60.7
Rest of South East	11.2	18.2	16.5	0.3	0.6	0.9	6.7	22.1	32.2
South West	6.0	9.6	9.5	0.4	0.7	0.2	1.9	12.1	25.4
West Midlands	7.1	10.4	8.0	1.2	1.7	0.4	6.4	13.2	34.7
North West	12.1	20.2	11.8	3.2	2.8	0.8	8.5	15.2	35.6
England	68.9	113.3	80.8	11.2	12.7	5.8	52.9	133.7	248.7
Wales	7.1	18.6	16.0	0.7	0.9	0.3	..	2.8	23.2
Scotland	15.2	24.7	19.0	1.8	1.4	..	25.3	71.1	82.5
Northern Ireland[7]	24.5	21.4	7.3	0.2	0.4	0.1	..	23.3	6.3

1 See Appendix notes.
2 Welsh figures are for thousands of grants.
3 Figures for Scotland and Northern Ireland are for work approved.
4 In England grants paid under the *Housing Act 1985* and earlier legislation refer to the number of dwellings whereas grants paid under the *Local Government and Housing Act 1989* refer to the number of grants.
5 Including Scottish Homes, formerly the Scottish Special Housing Association.
6 Northern Ireland Housing Executive in Northern Ireland.
7 From 1986 the data exclude large numbers of small Belfast City Council grants. Part III of the *Housing (NI) Order 1992* became operative on 1 October 1992. Approvals continued to be issued under the *Housing (NI) Order 1983* until March 1993. Thereafter, approvals were only issued under the 1992 Order. Figures for 1993 could, therefore, include grants paid under both schemes and so may not be directly comparable with earlier years.

Source: Department of the Environment; Welsh Office; The Scottish Office Environment Department; Department of the Environment, Northern Ireland

6.6 New dwellings[1] completed: by sector

Thousands and rates per 1,000 population

	Thousands				Rate per 1,000 population			
	1981	1991	1992	1993	1981	1991	1992	1993
Private enterprise[2]								
United Kingdom	118.6	159.3	146.6	144.6	2.1	2.8	2.5	2.5
North	4.9	6.6	6.2	5.5	1.6	2.1	2.0	1.8
Yorkshire & Humberside	8.5	11.1	10.8	11.0	1.7	2.2	2.2	2.2
East Midlands	9.5	14.0	12.7	12.7	2.5	3.5	3.1	3.1
East Anglia	6.6	9.9	8.1	8.3	3.5	4.8	3.9	4.0
South East	35.0	44.8	41.8	37.7	2.1	2.5	2.4	2.1
Greater London	4.0	12.8	11.4	8.6	0.6	1.9	1.6	1.2
Rest of South East	30.9	31.9	30.4	29.1	3.0	3.0	2.8	2.7
South West	13.9	17.0	13.6	12.5	3.2	3.6	2.9	2.6
West Midlands	10.3	13.6	12.2	12.8	2.0	2.6	2.3	2.4
North West	10.3	14.2	14.2	14.2	1.6	2.2	2.2	2.2
England	98.9	131.2	119.5	114.9	2.1	2.7	2.5	2.4
Wales	5.1	7.2	7.0	6.3	1.8	2.5	2.4	2.2
Scotland	11.0	15.7	14.5	17.7	2.1	3.1	2.8	3.5
Northern Ireland	3.6	5.2	5.9	5.7	2.3	3.3	3.7	3.5
Housing associations								
United Kingdom	..	..	..	..	..	..	..	..
North	1.1	1.2	1.7	1.7	0.4	0.4	0.6	0.6
Yorkshire & Humberside	1.3	2.0	2.1	3.3	0.3	0.4	0.4	0.7
East Midlands	1.9	1.0	1.2	1.9	0.2	0.3	0.3	0.5
East Anglia	1.0	0.3	1.0	1.2	1.2	0.1	0.5	0.6
South East	4.7	5.4	7.7	11.5	0.2	0.3	0.4	0.6
Greater London	2.0	2.7	3.9	4.8	0.3	0.4	0.6	0.7
Rest of South East	2.7	2.7	3.7	6.7	0.2	0.2	0.3	0.6
South West	1.2	1.1	1.7	2.3	0.2	0.2	0.3	0.5
West Midlands	3.0	1.5	2.3	2.9	0.4	0.3	0.4	0.5
North West	2.7	2.8	3.0	4.4	0.4	0.4	0.5	0.7
England	16.8	15.3	20.8	29.2	0.3	0.3	0.4	0.6
Wales	0.5	2.5	2.5	2.9	0.2	0.9	0.8	1.0
Scotland	..	..	..	..	..	..	..	..
Northern Ireland	0.2	0.8	0.7	0.7	0.1	0.5	0.4	0.4
Local authorities, new towns and government departments[3]								
United Kingdom	68.6	11.2	5.7	3.3	1.2	0.2	0.1	0.1
North	3.3	0.2	0.1	-	0.1	0.1	-	- York-
shire & Humberside	5.3	0.2	0.3	-	0.2	0.0	0.1	-
East Midlands	3.6	0.7	0.3	0.1	0.2	0.2	0.1	-
East Anglia	2.2	0.6	0.4	0.1	0.7	0.3	0.2	0.1
South East	23.9	3.9	1.3	0.6	0.4	0.2	0.1	-
Greater London	13.4	0.7	0.2	0.1	0.3	0.1	-	-
Rest of South East	10.5	3.2	1.1	0.5	0.5	0.3	0.1	-
South West	2.8	1.1	0.5	-	0.4	0.2	0.1	-
West Midlands	5.2	1.0	0.4	0.2	0.2	0.2	0.1	-
North West	8.6	0.5	0.2	-	0.1	0.1	-	-
England	54.9	8.1	3.5	1.4	0.3	0.2	0.1	-
Wales	3.5	0.4	0.1	0.2	1.3	0.1	-	0.1
Scotland	7.1	1.7	1.0	0.9	1.4	0.3	0.2	0.2
Northern Ireland	2.9	1.0	1.1	0.8	1.9	0.6	0.7	0.5

1 Permanent dwellings only ie those with a life expectancy of 60 years or more. See Appendix notes.
2 Includes private landlords (persons or companies) and owner-occupiers.
3 Northern Ireland Housing Executive in Northern Ireland.

Source: Department of the Environment; Welsh Office; The Scottish Office Environment Department; Department of the Environment, Northern Ireland

6.7 Average weekly rents: by tenure, 1994[1]

£

	Private sector fair rents[2]	Local authorities[3]	Housing associa- tions[4]
North	28.8	30.2	33.2
Yorkshire & Humberside	31.9	27.6	34.8
East Midlands	35.6	30.0	38.8
East Anglia	38.3	34.3	36.4
South East	51.2	44.4	42.3
Greater London	50.9	47.1	42.7
Rest of South East	51.7	41.2	41.8
South West	46.8	37.1	40.7
West Midlands	34.0	32.7	36.2
North West	26.9	31.6	31.3
England	42.2	35.7	37.6
Wales	34.7	34.0	38.8
Scotland	..	26.6	28.5
Northern Ireland	..	29.6	..

1 See Appendix notes.
2 Figures relate to registered fair rents and include service charges which add about 3 per cent to the rent.
3 Unrebated rents at April 1994. Northern Ireland Housing Executive average unrebated rent for Northern Ireland.
4 Rents covering whole stock at 31 March 1994, from Housing Corporation returns.
Source: Department of the Environment; Welsh Office; The Scottish Office Environment Department; Department of the Environment, Northern Ireland

6.8 Sales of local authority dwellings[1]

Thousands and percentages

	Sales 1979 to 1993[2] (thousands)			Sales 1993 (thousands)			Stock at end- 1993[3] (thousands)	Total sales 1979 to 1993 as a percentage of stock at April 1979[3]
	Right-to-buy	Other	Total	Right-to-buy	Other	Total		
United Kingdom	1,469	450	1,920	60	34	95	4,748	28.8
North	113	6	119	4	-	4	344	25.6
Yorkshire & Humberside	123	21	144	3	4	8	459	23.9
East Midlands	109	15	124	3	-	3	305	28.8
East Anglia	40	36	76	2	11	13	124	38.0
South East	418	215	633	17	7	24	1,220	34.1
Greater London	181	75	255	7	2	9	650	28.2
Rest of South East	238	140	378	10	4	14	570	39.9
South West	103	26	129	4	6	9	259	33.3
West Midlands	138	24	162	4	-	4	463	25.9
North West	122	35	157	4	2	5	526	22.9
England	1,166	378	1,545	41	30	71	3,700	29.4
Wales	89	6	96	3	-	3	213	31.0
Scotland	214	9	223	16	-	17	677	24.8
Northern Ireland[4]	.	57	57	.	4	4	158	26.6

1 Includes shared ownership deals and dwellings transferred to housing associations and private developers. Excludes New Towns. Figures for Scotland exclude sales by Scottish Homes.
2 Figures relate to sales between April 1979 and December 1993. Right-to-buy sales are from October 1980.
3 See Appendix for details of the calculation of these figures.
4 The Northern Ireland Housing Executive is responsible for Public Sector housing in Northern Ireland. There is no "Right-to-buy" scheme in Northern Ireland; sales are conducted under the NIHE House Sales Scheme which started in 1980.
Source: Department of the Environment; Welsh Office; The Scottish Office Environment Department; Department of the Environment, Northern Ireland

6.9 Dwelling prices[1]

Indices and £ thousands

	Index of dwelling prices[2] (1990=100)								Building society borrowers average dwelling price, 1994 £ thousands)		
	1981	1986	1989	1990	1991	1992	1993	1994	All	Excluding LA sitting tenants	First-time buyers[3]
United Kingdom	37	57	101	100	99	95	93	94	63.1	65.9	48.1
North	41	56	88	100	101	105	107	110	49.4	52.8	37.3
Yorkshire & Humberside	37	52	92	100	104	102	103	100	53.4	54.9	40.5
East Midlands	36	53	100	100	98	96	93	94	54.6	56.1	42.7
East Anglia	37	59	112	100	97	92	88	88	58.5	60.0	46.4
South East	..	..	..	..	..	..	..	..	80.2	82.6	61.7
Greater London	33	61	102	100	96	86	85	89	85.2	88.2	68.9
Rest of South East	35	59	109	100	95	88	84	87	77.7	79.9	57.3
South West	37	58	110	100	97	91	88	89	62.9	64.3	49.6
West Midlands	37	49	98	100	100	97	96	96	59.1	61.1	46.0
North West	38	52	87	100	101	103	99	101	56.4	57.7	42.5
England	36	57	102	100	98	93	90	92	65.7	67.7	50.6
Wales	38	53	96	100	99	98	99	99	52.1	53.9	39.8
Scotland	46	66	90	100	108	113	117	118	50.6	59.7	35.2
Northern Ireland	62	82	95	100	107	109	114	118	38.7	41.6	30.5

1 See Appendix notes.
2 This index adjusts for the mix of dwellings (by size, type, and whether new or second hand) and excludes those bought at non-market prices.
3 Includes LA sitting tenants.

Source: Department of the Environment

6.10 Building societies: mortgage advances and income of borrowers, 1994[1]

	All borrowers				First-time buyers	
	Number of loans (thousands)	Average recorded income (£ thousand per annum)	Average percentage of price advanced	Percentage of advances over £30,000	Percentage of all loans	Average percentage of price advanced
United Kingdom	728	21.5	72.9	71.2	55.0	82.7
North	40	18.7	74.1	56.8	57.0	83.7
Yorkshire & Humberside	64	19.1	74.6	65.8	53.0	85.5
East Midlands	51	18.9	73.2	65.6	54.8	82.3
East Anglia	29	20.3	73.0	72.1	52.5	83.1
South East	238	25.8	71.9	83.0	54.4	81.3
Greater London	78	28.1	73.1	86.8	64.6	80.1
Rest of South East	161	24.7	71.2	81.2	49.9	82.3
South West	59	20.4	71.4	74.0	50.5	81.3
West Midlands	60	19.9	71.7	70.1	55.9	82.8
North West	70	19.7	75.1	70.1	56.4	86.5
England	612	22.0	72.6	73.9	54.3	82.6
Wales	30	18.7	74.9	65.3	57.2	84.4
Scotland	66	19.8	73.7	56.0	56.8	83.1
Northern Ireland	19	16.3	78.3	44.3	66.4	83.5

1 See Appendix notes.

Source: Department of the Environment

6.11 Residential properties: by Council Tax bandings[1], 1993-94

Percentages

	Percentage of residential properties classified to							
	Band A	Band B	Band C	Band D	Band E	Band F	Band G	Band H
North	57.6	14.6	14.0	7.0	3.7	1.8	1.1	0.2
Yorkshire & Humberside	47.3	19.4	16.3	7.8	4.9	2.5	1.7	0.1
East Midlands	39.5	22.7	18.3	9.5	5.3	2.7	1.9	0.2
East Anglia	22.8	28.0	23.0	12.7	7.1	3.7	2.4	0.2
South East	6.0	15.0	27.2	22.2	14.2	7.8	6.4	1.2
Greater London	2.9	13.0	26.7	25.2	15.9	7.9	6.6	1.8
Rest of South East	8.1	16.3	27.5	20.1	13.1	7.7	6.3	0.9
South West	16.4	24.5	23.7	15.4	10.3	5.6	3.8	0.4
West Midlands	33.5	25.0	19.2	10.1	6.1	3.4	2.3	0.2
North West	45.2	18.7	17.5	8.9	5.0	2.6	2.0	0.2
England	26.2	19.1	21.8	14.6	9.1	4.9	3.7	0.6
Wales	20.6	25.9	19.7	14.7	11.7	4.3	2.8	0.3
Scotland	27.3	25.9	15.6	10.9	10.8	5.3	3.7	0.5

1 See Appendix notes.

Source: Department of the Environment; Welsh Office; The Scottish Office Environment Department

6.12 County Court actions for mortgage possessions[1]

Thousands

	1991			1992			1993			1994		
	Actions entered	Orders made	Sus-pended orders	Actions entered	Orders made	Sus-pended orders	Actions entered	Orders made	Sus-pended orders	Actions entered	Orders made	Sus-pended orders
North	6.9	2.2	3.4	6.0	2.1	4.2	4.6	1.7	3.4	3.7	1.3	2.8
Yorkshire & Humberside	14.1	5.7	5.1	10.3	4.2	4.8	8.4	2.9	4.5	7.6	2.3	3.2
East Midlands	13.5	5.2	4.5	10.1	4.3	4.9	7.7	2.8	4.2	6.0	2.4	3.2
East Anglia	6.2	3.1	2.0	5.0	2.3	1.7	3.9	1.8	2.2	3.0	1.1	1.3
South East	79.9	33.0	30.3	59.5	25.6	29.3	48.9	19.3	25.8	35.5	14.8	19.2
Greater London	35.3	14.4	13.1	25.7	11.4	12.4	21.3	8.8	10.6	15.5	6.8	8.4
Rest of South East	44.6	18.6	17.2	33.3	14.2	16.8	27.7	10.5	15.2	20.0	8.0	10.8
South West	16.7	6.5	5.8	12.5	5.1	5.2	11.7	4.1	5.2	7.4	2.5	3.5
West Midlands	17.7	6.9	6.5	14.0	5.2	6.4	10.3	3.4	5.5	8.6	2.6	4.4
North West	21.4	7.3	8.1	17.2	6.3	8.1	14.1	4.9	7.8	11.7	3.6	5.8
England	176.4	69.9	65.6	134.6	55.3	64.6	109.7	40.7	58.7	83.5	30.7	43.3
Wales	10.2	4.0	3.5	7.6	3.4	3.7	6.4	2.3	3.6	4.4	1.5	2.3
Northern Ireland[2]	3.1	..	..	1.6	..	..	1.7	..	..	1.4	..	..

1 Local authority and private. See Appendix notes.
2 Mortgage possession actions are heard in Chancery Division of Northern Ireland High Court.

Source: Lord Chancellor's Department; Northern Ireland Court Service

6.13 Households accepted as homeless: by reason, 1993[1]

Percentages and numbers

	No longer willing or able to remain with		Break-down of relationship with partner	Mortgage arrears	Rent arrears or other reason for loss of rented or tied accommodation	Other reasons	Total number of cases (=100%)
	Parents	Relatives or friends					
United Kingdom	37		20	7	17	18	170,220
North	27	12	26	7	15	13	7,730
Yorkshire & Humberside	24	13	26	7	17	13	13,810
East Midlands	23	12	23	9	20	13	10,330
East Anglia	19	9	19	15	30	8	3,320
South East	24	17	14	8	20	17	51,060
Greater London	25	20	14	5	16	20	32,190
Rest of South East	22	11	15	13	28	11	18,870
South West	18	9	17	13	32	11	9,420
West Midlands	35	7	22	7	14	15	16,850
North West	25	14	21	6	13	21	19,860
England	25	13	19	8	19	16	132,380
Wales[2]	23	9	19	7	25	17	11,120
Scotland	37		32	2	4	25	19,200
Northern Ireland[3]	32		4	1	10	52	7,520

1 See Appendix notes.
2 Figures for Wales include 237 households made homeless in Aberconwy as a result of the flooding incident in Llandudno during June 1993.
3 A large proportion of the Northern Ireland total is classified as "Other reasons" due to differences in the definitions used.

Source: Department of the Environment; Welsh Office; The Scottish Office Environment Department;
Department of the Environment, Northern Ireland

# 7 Health

Infant deaths	Fewer babies die in East Anglia then anywhere else, with 4.8 deaths in the first year of life per thousand live births in 1993 compared with a high of 7.3 in Yorkshire and Humberside.
	(Table 7.2)
Tuberculosis	Over the past ten years, tuberculosis has been most prevalent in the North West and North East Thames Regional Health Authority (RHA) areas and least prevalent in the East Anglian, Wessex and South Western RHA areas.
	(Table 7.4)
Cancer	Allowing for the age structure of the population, the incidence of lung cancer is higher than the average for England and Wales in the northern parts of England and in Wales and lower than the average in the south western parts of England.
	(Chart 7.7)
Death rates	The highest death rates due to respiratory diseases are in the Mersey and North Western Regional Health Authority areas.
	(Table 7.10)
Smoking	Over a third of adults in Scotland smoked cigarettes in 1992 compared with about a quarter in the East Midlands and the South West.
	(Table 7.13)
Drinking	The North and the North West have the highest proportions of men, and East Anglia the highest proportion of women, drinking more than the recommended sensible levels.
	(Table 7.14)
Dental attendance	Adults in East Anglia and the South West are most likely to visit their dentist for a regular check-up, while those in the North, the West Midlands and Northern Ireland are least likely.
	(Table 7.15)
Screening	Nearly nine in every ten women in the target population in the Trent and South West Thames Regional Health Authority (RHA) areas were screened for cervical cancer in 1992-93, compared with just over seven in ten in the North West Thames RHA area.
	(Table 7.16)
Prescriptions	In 1993, the number of prescription items dispensed per person was highest in Wales and lowest in the Oxford Regional Health Authority area.
	(Table 7.18)
Hospital beds	The Mersey and Oxford Health Authorities have the highest rates of throughput per hospital bed of all the Regional Health Authorities in England.
	(Table 7.19)
Waiting lists	The South and West, and the North West Regional Health Authorities have the lowest proportions of patients waiting more than 12 months for admission to an NHS hospital.
	(Table 7.20)

Introduction

The regional breakdown within England of many of the tables in this chapter is the Regional Health Authority (RHA) areas, as administratively the NHS does not use the standard planning regions used throughout most of *Regional Trends*. On 1 April 1994 there was a reorganisation of the then 14 RHAs to form eight. Most of the statistics in this edition relate to periods before the reorganisation and so are shown on the basis of the old RHA structure. However, maps of both structures appear on page 232 of the Appendix. Due to differences in the collection of health statistics across the United Kingdom, it is not always possible to show national totals.

Tables 7.5 and 7.6 are drawn from the Health Survey for England 1993. This is the third in a series of surveys designed to monitor trends in the nation's health, in particular progress in achieving the targets in the *Health of the Nation* initiative in England. One of those targets is to reduce mean systolic blood pressure in the adult population by at least 5 mmHg by the year 2005. While the target focuses on systolic pressure, there is also interest in diastolic pressure. A summary measure to describe blood pressure which takes into account both systolic and diastolic pressure is used in Table 7.5. Where people were recorded as having high blood pressure, this means that they were in any of the three categories Normotensive treated, Hypertensive treated or Hypertensive untreated (detailed descriptions of the categories are in the Appendix). High blood pressure is strongly related to age. As the figures in Table 7.5 are not standardised for age, care should be taken in making regional comparisons.

Another of the targets in the *Health of the Nation* initiative is the reduction in the proportion of people who are obese. Specifically, the aim is to reduce the percentages of people aged between 16 and 64 who are obese from 8 per cent of men and 12 per cent of women in 1986/87 to no more than 6 and 8 per cent respectively by 2005. The measure most commonly used to classify obesity is the body mass index (BMI). The BMI is calculated as weight(kg)/ height(m)^2. In 1993, the average height for men was 1.74m and for women 1.61m while the average weight was 78.9kg for men and 66.6kg for women. These give mean BMIs of 25.9 and 25.7 respectively. Obesity is defined as BMI over 30. In 1993, 13 per cent of men and 16 per cent of women were classified as obese; the percentages were the same for the target group (people aged between 16 and 64).

"About one person in ....sometime

Regional Trends 30, © Crown copyright 1995

There was some evidence that women in RHAs in the north and midlands were more likely to be overweight, but not obese, than the average and those in the south of England less likely. However, among individual RHAs only the North Western RHA contained a significantly higher proportion of overweight women and the South East Thames RHA a significantly lower proportion. The West Midlands RHA was the only region where there was a higher proportion of men who were overweight or obese than would be expected by their age distribution alone.

About one person in three develops cancer - or strictly a malignant neoplasm - sometime in their life. For both males and females, just three sites (different ones for each gender) out of a total of 63 make up around half the cancer registrations each year. For men the three major cancer sites are lung, colorectal and prostate; for women they are breast, colorectal and lung. Chart 7.7 shows, for the RHAs of England and for Wales, the standardised registration ratios (SSR) for these cancer sites. The SRR is an index which allows ready comparison of incidence rates in populations with different age structures, as the incidence of cancer varies greatly with age. For each cancer, the 1989 registration rates for England and Wales are taken as the standards (with the genders considered separately). A more detailed explanation of the SRR is in the Appendix.

Tables 7.8 and 7.9 show cumulative reports of HIV-1 infected persons and AIDS cases reported in the United Kingdom. Reports of HIV infection reflect the uptake of testing and do not represent the total number of persons who are infected, since many of these will not have had a voluntary, confidential HIV antibody test. The regional reports do, however, indicate the distributions of all diagnosed infected persons in different parts of the United Kingdom.

Table 7.20 on hospital waiting lists presents figures on the basis of the new eight RHAs. The waiting lists take a snapshot of those waiting at a particular point in time. Most people required to wait for admission to hospital are admitted within a few months, but about half of patients (excluding live births) treated in hospitals are emergency cases and do not come from the waiting lists.

three develops cancer in their life."

7.1 Population and vital statistics: Health Authority Areas, 1993

Thousands and rates

	Population aged (mid-year estimates)(thousands)				Vital statistics (rates)				
	0-15	16-64	65 or over	All ages	Live births[1]	Still births[2,3]	Deaths[4]	Perinatal mortality[3,5]	Infant mortality[6]
United Kingdom	11,965.3	37,054.4	9,171.5	58,191.2	62.4	5.7	11.3	9.0	6.3
Northern	639.2	1,966.9	496.2	3,102.3	60.2	5.9	12.2	9.2	6.7
Yorkshire	772.3	2,348.9	587.2	3,708.3	62.7	6.3	11.4	9.6	7.0
Trent	961.2	3,040.2	764.2	4,765.6	61.7	5.3	11.4	8.6	7.0
East Anglian	415.6	1,320.1	359.0	2,094.7	60.3	4.5	11.1	7.1	4.8
North West Thames	705.8	2,334.6	480.4	3,520.7	62.5	5.9	9.3	8.8	5.7
North East Thames	794.4	2,460.4	557.5	3,812.2	67.0	6.1	10.3	9.8	6.5
South East Thames	744.7	2,350.3	622.7	3,717.6	63.9	5.8	11.7	9.3	6.2
South West Thames	570.5	1,932.3	496.5	2,999.3	59.7	5.1	11.2	8.0	5.5
Wessex	620.4	1,987.2	546.0	3,153.6	61.3	4.8	11.2	7.5	5.0
Oxford	555.4	1,696.0	342.0	2,593.3	61.4	6.0	9.0	9.1	5.7
South Western	645.2	2,070.2	616.3	3,331.7	60.0	5.2	12.0	8.1	6.1
West Midlands	1,113.8	3,360.9	815.1	5,289.8	64.2	6.0	11.0	9.9	7.1
Mersey	510.0	1,526.5	376.2	2,412.8	60.9	5.1	11.8	7.7	5.8
North Western	864.5	2,536.7	629.6	4,030.8	65.1	6.2	12.2	9.6	6.9
England	9,912.9	30,931.2	7,688.6	48,532.7	62.5	5.7	11.1	8.9	6.3
Wales	601.7	1,802.5	502.3	2,906.5	63.3	5.8	12.3	8.3	5.5
Scotland	1,032.2	3,315.4	772.6	5,120.2	57.4	6.4	12.5	9.6	6.5
Northern Ireland	418.5	1,005.2	208.1	1,631.8	71.0	5.2	9.6	8.8	7.1

1 Per 1,000 women aged 15-44.
2 Per 1,000 live and still births.
3 On 1 October 1992 the legal definition of a still birth was altered from a baby born dead after 28 completed weeks gestation or more to one born dead after 24 completed weeks gestation or more. The figures in this table are therefore not comparable with those in earlier editions.
4 Per 1,000 population.
5 Still births and deaths of infants under 1 week of age per 1,000 live and still births.
6 Deaths of infants under 1 year of age per 1,000 live births.

Source: Office of Population Censuses and Surveys; General Register Offices for Scotland and Northern Ireland

7.2 Still births, perinatal mortality and infant mortality

Rates

	Still births[1]				Perinatal mortality[2]				Infant mortality[3]		
	1971	1981	1993[4]	1993[4]	1971	1981	1993[4]	1993[4]	1971	1981	1993
United Kingdom	12.6	6.6	4.4	5.7	22.6	12.0	7.6	9.0	17.9	11.2	6.3
North	13.0	8.0	4.6	5.9	23.0	13.2	7.9	9.2	18.7	10.7	6.7
Yorkshire & Humberside	12.5	7.8	4.6	5.9	22.7	13.5	8.0	9.4	19.8	12.1	7.3
East Midlands	11.8	6.2	3.9	5.4	22.0	11.4	7.2	8.7	18.0	11.0	6.6
East Anglia	10.9	5.5	3.4	4.5	20.1	10.2	6.0	7.1	15.2	9.8	4.8
South East	11.3	5.9	4.4	5.7	20.5	10.7	7.6	8.9	15.9	10.4	5.9
Greater London	11.7	6.3	4.9	6.1	21.1	10.3	8.2	9.5	17.4	10.7	6.4
Rest of South East	11.0	5.7	4.1	5.4	19.8	11.1	7.1	8.5	14.8	10.1	5.4
South West	11.7	6.3	4.0	5.0	20.1	10.8	6.9	7.9	15.9	10.4	5.8
West Midlands	13.6	7.0	4.4	6.0	23.7	12.9	8.4	9.9	17.7	11.7	7.1
North West	14.5	6.7	4.5	5.8	25.6	12.4	7.7	9.0	19.8	11.2	6.5
England	12.4	6.5	4.3	5.7	22.1	11.7	7.6	8.9	17.5	10.9	6.3
Wales	14.2	7.3	4.5	5.8	24.4	14.1	7.0	8.3	18.4	12.6	5.5
Scotland	13.1	6.3	4.8	6.4	24.5	11.6	8.0	9.6	19.9	11.3	6.5
Northern Ireland	14.3	8.7	4.1	5.2	27.2	15.3	7.7	8.8	22.7	13.2	7.1

1 Rate per 1,000 live and still births, see Appendix notes.
2 Still births and deaths of infants under 1 week of age per 1,000 live and still births.
3 Deaths of infants under 1 year of age per 1,000 live births.
4 On 1 October 1992 the legal definition of a still birth was altered from a baby born dead after 28 completed weeks gestation or more to one born dead after 24weeks gestation or more. Figures are given on both the old and new definitions for continuity/comparison.

Source: Office of Population Censuses and Surveys; General Register Offices for Scotland and Northern Ireland

7.3 Consultations with an NHS general medical practitioner[1] and reports of limiting long-standing illness[2]: by age,1993

Percentages

| | Persons who consulted an NHS general medical practitioner[1] | | | | | | Persons who reported limiting long-standing illness[2] | | | | | |
	0-4	5-15	16-44	45-64	65 and over	All ages	0-4	5-15	16-44	45-64	65 and over	All ages
Great Britain	22	11	16	17	21	17	4	9	14	29	44	20
North	28	11	15	22	17	17	7	14	14	30	44	22
Yorkshire & Humberside	16	11	14	18	23	16	6	9	13	31	47	22
East Midlands	17	12	15	17	19	16	2	8	16	31	45	21
East Anglia	28	8	18	11	20	16	2	8	16	17	38	18
South East	22	10	15	15	20	16	5	8	13	25	44	19
Greater London	24	9	16	16	22	16	7	7	14	27	48	20
Rest of South East	21	10	15	15	18	15	4	8	13	25	41	18
South West	24	9	17	15	21	17	2	8	11	24	36	19
West Midlands	27	10	15	17	25	17	2	9	13	29	45	20
North West	21	13	17	19	23	18	4	7	14	34	48	22
England	22	11	16	17	21	16	4	8	14	28	44	20
Wales	29	11	18	19	22	19	3	12	14	32	45	22
Scotland	20	11	15	20	25	17	3	9	14	33	46	22
Northern Ireland	..	..	14	16	22	..	..	..	11	30	47	..

1 In the 14 days before interview.
2 See Appendix notes.

Source: General Household Survey; Continuous Household Survey, Northern Ireland

7.4 Notifications of tuberculosis

Rates per 100,000 population

	1983	1984	1985	1986	1987	1988	1989	1990	1991	1992	1993
United Kingdom	13.8	12.5	11.7	12.1	10.1	10.1	10.6	10.2	10.5	11.1	11.3
Northern	11.0	9.7	8.4	9.7	8.8	7.2	7.9	6.6	7.6	8.6	8.2
Yorkshire	15.0	13.0	11.5	12.1	9.8	11.1	11.5	11.9	13.3	10.6	12.6
Trent	11.9	11.3	11.6	12.3	11.1	11.4	10.5	9.6	9.5	8.9	10.9
East Anglia	5.5	4.9	5.1	4.6	4.5	3.9	3.6	4.7	4.0	3.7	3.4
North West Thames	28.3	25.4	21.9	24.4	19.0	20.6	21.4	18.1	21.6	25.0	24.2
North East Thames	20.5	17.9	18.8	16.7	16.2	15.5	18.4	17.8	20.0	22.4	21.1
South East Thames	12.6	12.5	12.2	9.4	8.0	8.8	10.1	10.4	9.9	10.3	11.4
South West Thames	11.0	8.8	8.5	10.1	8.2	7.7	6.6	8.5	7.6	8.0	9.1
Wessex	6.0	5.1	5.7	4.6	4.1	4.9	4.2	3.7	3.5	3.6	3.6
Oxford	7.6	9.0	7.0	6.0	8.0	7.5	7.5	6.4	7.2	7.5	8.2
South Western	5.9	5.7	4.4	4.6	4.2	4.5	4.2	3.5	3.6	4.1	4.7
West Midlands	17.4	16.4	15.7	16.5	12.7	12.8	16.1	13.9	15.6	16.5	14.9
Mersey	9.1	6.2	6.7	8.1	5.8	5.5	6.5	5.8	4.6	5.6	7.4
North Western	19.7	16.1	16.4	18.4	13.9	14.7	13.2	15.1	13.8	15.6	15.1
England	13.9	12.4	11.8	12.1	10.2	10.4	10.9	10.4	10.9	11.6	11.8
Wales	10.7	11.0	9.7	8.3	8.2	7.0	7.3	6.7	5.7	6.9	6.8
Scotland	16.1	14.3	13.8	14.3	11.0	10.4	10.5	11.0	10.7	10.9	10.8
Northern Ireland	10.6	10.4	5.3	6.9	6.3	5.4	5.9	8.2	6.0	5.2	5.5

Source: Office of Population Censuses and Surveys; The Scottish Office: Department of Health and Social Services, Northern Ireland

7.5 Blood pressure level[1]: by gender, 1993

Percentages

	Men[2]				Women[2]			
	Normotensive		Hypertensive		Normotensive		Hypertensive	
	Untreated	Treated	Treated	Untreated	Untreated	Treated	Treated	Untreated
Northern	88	2	3	6	83	5	3	9
Yorkshire	79	4	3	14	83	4	4	9
Trent	78	3	4	15	77	6	5	12
East Anglian	79	4	3	14	81	2	4	13
North West Thames	84	5	3	8	82	6	3	9
North East Thames	84	6	3	7	84	5	3	9
South East Thames	82	4	5	10	81	7	3	9
South West Thames	84	3	4	9	83	5	4	7
Wessex	79	4	3	14	80	4	6	10
Oxford	84	3	4	10	83	3	3	11
South Western	81	4	2	13	79	6	4	11
West Midlands	77	4	3	16	83	5	3	10
Mersey	79	5	4	12	79	5	2	14
North Western	77	5	4	15	78	6	6	11
England	81	4	4	12	81	5	4	10

1 Respondents were considered to be hypertensive if their systolic blood pressure was 160mHg or over or if their diastolic blood pressure was 95 mmHg or over. 'Treated' means taking medication for high blood pressure. See introductory text and Appendix notes.
2 Aged 16 or over.

Source: Health Survey for England, Office of Population Censuses and Surveys

7.6 Mean body mass index [1]: by gender and age, 1993

BMI[1]

	Men				Women			
	16-44	45-64	65 or over	All aged 16 or over	16-44	45-64	65 or over	All aged 16 or over
Northern	25.1	26.7	26.1	25.8	25.1	27.4	27.3	26.2
Yorkshire	25.7	26.7	26.7	26.2	24.5	26.7	26.5	25.5
Trent	25.5	27.0	26.2	26.1	24.8	27.4	26.8	26.0
East Anglian	25.2	27.0	26.3	26.0	25.2	26.8	26.2	25.9
North West Thames	24.8	26.7	27.1	25.7	24.3	26.3	26.2	25.2
North East Thames	24.6	26.8	27.2	25.6	25.0	27.0	26.8	25.8
South East Thames	25.4	26.9	26.7	26.1	24.3	26.7	26.2	25.4
South West Thames	24.8	26.3	26.0	25.5	24.2	26.2	26.3	25.2
Wessex	24.9	27.1	25.9	25.8	24.9	26.1	26.2	25.6
Oxford	25.3	26.5	25.9	25.8	24.8	26.5	25.8	25.4
South Western	25.2	26.8	26.3	25.9	24.4	26.4	26.8	25.5
West Midlands	25.6	27.6	26.8	26.5	25.0	27.2	26.5	26.0
Mersey	25.3	27.1	25.7	25.9	24.9	27.2	27.0	26.0
North Western	25.1	27.0	26.2	25.9	24.6	27.5	27.5	26.1
England	25.2	26.9	26.4	25.9	24.7	26.9	26.6	25.7

1 See introductory text and Appendix notes.

Source: Health Survey for England, Office of Population Censuses and Surveys

7.7 Cancer - standardised registration ratios for selected sites: by gender, 1989

Lung

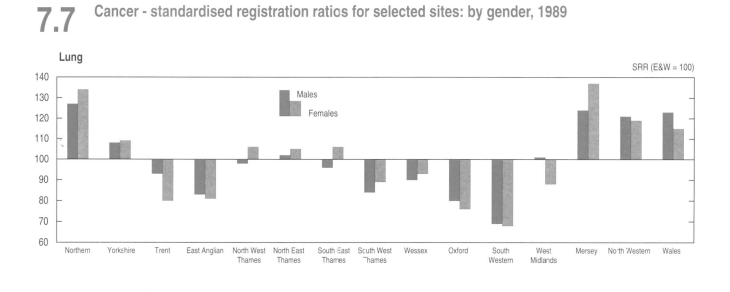

Colorectal

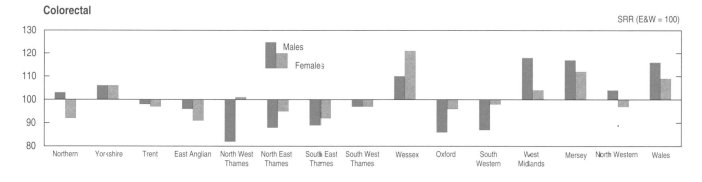

Breast

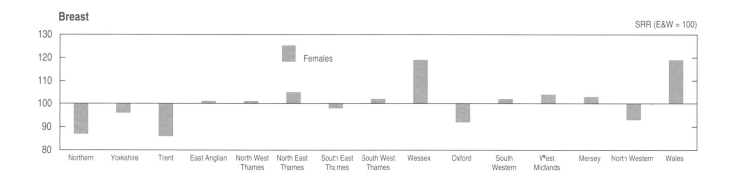

Prostrate

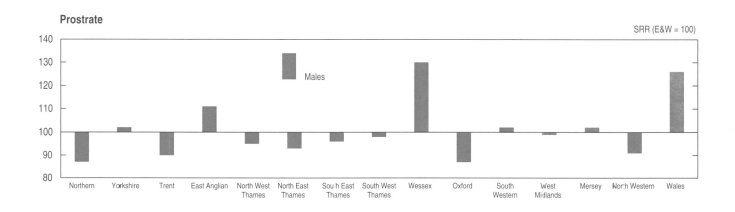

1 See Appendix notes.

Source: Office of Population Censuses and Surveys

7.8 Exposure category of HIV-1 infected persons: cumulative totals to 31 December 1994

Numbers

	Sexual intercourse			Injecting drug use			Other[3]/ undetermined[4]		Cases reported to 31 December 1994[5]
	Between men[1]	Between men and women				Blood[2]			
		Males	Females	Males	Females		Males	Females	
Region of first report									
United Kingdom	14,259	1,772	2,037	1,832	829	1,378	713	244	23,104
Northern	204	40	31	35	12	88	9	0	419
Yorkshire	318	56	60	41	27	73	13	5	593
Trent	335	77	47	44	15	77	5	7	607
East Anglian	153	37	31	48	17	33	9	2	330
North West Thames	5,036	302	412	295	133	59	186	53	6,484
North East Thames	3,016	441	524	191	124	184	244	65	4,818
South East Thames	1,743	218	295	178	80	134	74	38	2,761
South West Thames	446	108	155	50	12	36	38	15	861
Wessex	328	38	37	26	5	45	11	7	498
Oxford	263	55	67	42	16	111	9	1	564
South Western	311	55	41	47	11	36	13	5	519
West Midlands	412	64	63	37	11	161	19	4	771
Mersey	147	17	17	10	10	45	11	1	258
North Western	643	65	41	49	27	117	10	5	957
England	13,355	1,573	1,821	1,093	500	1,199	651	208	20,440
Wales	206	53	30	13	3	56	12	2	375
Scot and	629	135	172	723	323	103	47	34	2,166
Northern Ireland	69	11	14	3	3	20	3	0	123

1 Includes 313 male drug users who also had sexual intercourse with other men.
2 Blood/b ood factor and tissue recipients.
3 Includes mother to infant transmission.
4 See Appendix notes.
5 Components may not add to totals as in some cases gender was not recorded.

Source: Public Health Laboratory Service, Communicable Disease Surveillance Centre;
Scottish Centre for Infection and Environmental Health

7.9 Exposure category of AIDS cases: cumulative totals to 31 December 1994

Numbers

	Sexual intercourse			Injecting drug use			Other[3]/ undetermined[4]		Total reported to 31 December 1994	
	Between men[1]	Between men and women				Blood[2]				
		Males	Females	Males	Females		Males	Females	Cases	Deaths[5]
Region of first report										
United Kingdom	7,628	716	548	416	175	565	163	93	10,304	7,019
Northern	90	17	8	3	1	37	3	0	159	114
Yorkshire	146	24	13	9	7	43	4	4	250	185
Trent	165	27	9	11	3	19	4	4	242	171
East Anglian	91	15	9	14	4	13	1	1	148	97
North West Thames	3,148	156	114	75	35	43	38	17	3,626	2,454
North East Thames	1,522	160	149	48	25	68	36	28	2,036	1,229
South East Thames	854	89	87	40	16	67	20	9	1,182	825
South West Thames	266	48	49	9	5	14	16	9	416	286
Wessex	176	21	14	5	2	27	4	4	253	187
Oxford	142	21	13	14	2	52	6	1	251	172
South Western	161	18	7	3	2	19	5	2	217	162
West Midlands	158	23	16	2	5	39	5	1	249	184
Mersey	85	13	7	7	1	24	3	1	141	109
North Western	245	21	9	15	3	39	5	3	340	259
England	7,249	653	504	255	111	504	150	84	9,510	6,434
Wales	87	11	8	2	2	24	6	1	141	118
Scotland	258	47	32	158	62	33	6	8	604	429
Northern Ireland	34	5	4	1	0	4	1	0	49	38

1 Includes 165 male drug users who also had sexual intercourse with other men.
2 Blood/blood factor and tissue recipients.
3 Includes mother to infant transmissions.
4 See Appendix notes.
5 Deaths reported to the Communicable Disease Surveillance Centre and the Scottish Centre for Infection and Environmental Health to 31 December 1994.

Source: Public Health Laboratory Service, Communicable Disease Surveillance Centre;
Scottish Centre for Infection and Environmental Health

7.10 Age adjusted mortality rates[1]: by cause[2] and gender, 1993

Rate per 100,000 population

| | All circulatory diseases | | | All respiratory diseases | | | All injuries and poisonings | | | | |
	Total	Ischaemic heart disease	Cerebro-vascular disease	Total	Bronchitis and allied conditions	Cancer[3]	Total	Road traffic accidents	Suicides and open verdicts	All other causes	All causes
Males											
United Kingdom	496	319	92	165	69	293	42	9	16	114	1,109
Northern	539	360	101	177	79	337	41	9	15	113	1,207
Yorkshire	503	339	90	171	72	286	38	10	14	109	1,106
Trent	511	333	95	163	70	305	41	11	16	116	1,136
East Anglia	498	306	99	158	58	287	43	12	15	115	1,101
North West Thames	386	241	67	149	56	240	36	6	13	106	917
North East Thames	427	272	74	158	65	272	36	6	12	120	1,013
South East Thames	489	296	90	173	73	301	41	7	15	119	1,123
South West Thames	462	279	88	172	66	281	32	6	13	109	1,056
Wessex	494	318	88	150	60	287	35	8	14	119	1,085
Oxford	362	228	66	135	55	237	38	9	14	96	869
South Western	544	339	103	163	66	301	37	6	14	126	1,171
West Midlands	493	317	92	160	73	291	39	8	15	108	1,090
Mersey	511	337	93	185	75	316	39	8	14	107	1,157
North Western	541	358	99	190	87	299	44	7	16	111	1,185
England	485	311	89	165	69	289	39	8	14	113	1,090
Wales	560	371	97	179	77	325	43	8	15	115	1,223
Scotland	561	361	123	153	67	320	62	11	27	134	1,231
Northern Ireland	439	292	81	156	55	235	55	13	15	85	970
Females											
United Kingdom	518	259	151	186	44	257	24	3	5	157	1,142
Northern	560	302	156	200	57	286	25	3	5	159	1,230
Yorkshire	524	277	154	193	50	251	23	4	5	161	1,152
Trent	516	261	146	178	43	253	21	3	4	160	1,128
East Anglia	495	237	149	164	30	246	25	5	5	171	1,102
North West Thames	398	197	111	169	34	215	19	2	5	132	933
North East Thames	438	220	122	175	35	241	21	3	4	159	1,033
South East Thames	535	249	153	202	40	268	23	3	6	161	1,190
South West Thames	521	235	152	205	40	260	21	4	6	166	1,173
Wessex	507	244	150	186	35	257	22	3	4	175	1,147
Oxford	393	185	116	156	31	212	18	3	4	133	912
South Western	559	263	173	172	34	275	24	4	5	180	1,211
West Midlands	500	251	142	174	43	242	22	3	5	151	1,089
Mersey	542	280	147	215	56	274	21	4	4	143	1,195
North Western	582	303	168	215	66	265	24	3	5	162	1,248
England	507	252	146	186	43	253	22	3	5	158	1,126
Wales	584	297	161	200	47	278	24	3	4	150	1,236
Scotland	605	302	202	175	51	285	36	5	9	169	1,270
Northern Ireland	436	230	128	181	35	209	24	5	4	96	946

1 Adjusted for the age structure of the population. The 1993 data are not comparable with figures for 1992 and earlier years as published in previous editions of *Regional Trends* because of changes to the coding rules.
2 Deaths at ages under 28 days occurring in England and Wales can no longer be assigned an underlying cause of death.
3 Malignant neoplasms only.

Source: Office of Population Censuses and Surveys; General Register Offices for Scotland and Northern Ireland

7.11 Legal abortions performed to residents: by area of usual residence and gestation

Numbers and percentages

	Number of abortions					1993 Gestation (weeks)(percentages)				Total[1] (=100%) (numbers)
	1981	1986	1990	1991	1992	Under 9	9-12	13-16	17 and over	
Great Britain[2]	138,561	157,982	184,882	179,134	171,866	*39.8*	*49.2*	*7.7*	*3.3*	169,338
Northern	5,554	6,263	7,289	6,873	6,827	*33.0*	*55.6*	*7.9*	*3.5*	6,865
Yorkshire	7,472	8,517	10,221	10,136	9,675	*30.9*	*55.8*	*9.7*	*3.6*	9,491
Trent	9,837	10,791	12,509	12,641	12,222	*33.1*	*56.0*	*8.0*	*2.9*	12,348
East Anglian	3,913	4,662	5,112	4,776	4,785	*35.0*	*55.6*	*6.4*	*3.0*	4,589
North West Thames	14,797	15,770	18,465	17,929	16,668	*48.5*	*42.4*	*6.2*	*2.9*	16,402
North East Thames	14,296	17,103	22,015	20,797	19,840	*41.0*	*49.1*	*6.9*	*3.0*	19,211
South East Thames	11,299	13,802	16,748	15,675	15,399	*39.4*	*48.4*	*8.5*	*3.7*	14,880
South West Thames	8,728	10,183	11,778	11,594	10,601	*44.1*	*46.6*	*6.6*	*2.7*	10,068
Wessex	5,656	6,943	8,002	7,557	7,401	*35.3*	*53.6*	*7.6*	*3.5*	7,496
Oxford	5,645	6,838	8,074	7,693	7,495	*48.4*	*41.9*	*6.7*	*2.9*	7,233
South Western	6,109	6,812	7,903	7,575	7,368	*30.6*	*59.7*	*6.4*	*3.4*	7,388
West Midlands	14,208	15,785	18,380	17,692	16,692	*41.2*	*44.3*	*10.4*	*4.1*	16,307
Mersey	5,520	6,825	7,520	7,163	7,028	*43.1*	*48.8*	*5.8*	*2.4*	7,040
North Western	9,206	10,579	12,444	12,088	11,644	*39.3*	*48.6*	*8.4*	*3.6*	11,601
England	122,240	140,873	166,460	160,189	153,645	*39.6*	*49.4*	*7.7*	*3.3*	150,919
Wales	6,341	6,746	7,440	7,187	6,856	*31.4*	*55.8*	*8.8*	*3.9*	6,924
Scotland	9,980	10,363	10,982	11,758	11,365	*48.1*	*42.6*	*6.5*	*2.8*	11,495

1 Totals include cases where gestation was not stated.
2 Excludes a small number of abortions performed in Scotland on women normally resident in England and Wales.

Source: Office of Population Censuses and Surveys; The Scottish Office

7.12 Drug addicts notified[1]

Numbers

	All addicts notified, 1981	New addicts notified						All addicts notified, 1993
		1981	1986	1990	1991	1992	1993	
United Kingdom	3,311	2,248	5,325	6,923	8,007	9,663	11,561	27,976
North	33	19	89	102	97	125	276	526
Yorkshire & Humberside	139	100	207	299	464	911	1,202	2,205
East Midlands	105	64	69	182	150	228	280	699
East Anglia	65	37	128	168	203	242	274	789
South East	2,178	1,462	2,322	2,836	3,085	3,462	3,927	10,349
Greater London	1,688	1,152	1,747	2,120	2,352	2,468	2,861	7,678
Rest of South East	490	310	575	716	733	994	1,066	2,671
South West	122	90	286	394	477	694	939	1,904
West Midlands	116	88	187	308	359	432	597	1,222
North West	234	155	1,299	1,958	2,212	2,445	2,685	7,353
England	2,992	2,015	4,587	6,247	7,047	8,539	10,180	25,047
Wales	61	34	112	137	224	237	310	659
Scotland	249	192	616	525	727	868	1,045	2,220
Northern Ireland	9	7	10	14	9	19	26	50

1 Number of addicts notified throughout the year. Under the *Misuse of Drugs (Notification of and Supply to Addicts) Regulations 1973*, doctors are required to notify the Chief Medical Officer at the Home Office with particulars of people whom they consider, or suspect, to be addicted to any of the 14 controlled drugs.

Source: Home Office

7.13 Cigarette smoking amongst people aged 16 or over: by gender

Percentages

	All smokers						Heavy smokers[1]					
	Males			Females			Males			Females		
	1980	1986	1992	1980	1986	1992	1980	1986	1992	1980	1986	1992
Great Britain	42	35	29	37	31	28	21	15	12	13	10	9
North	44	38	28	39	33	32	26	16	13	17	11	13
Yorkshire & Humberside	44	35	28	38	32	28	20	14	12	14	11	10
East Midlands	44	33	27	35	29	23	22	15	11	13	8	7
East Anglia	40	36	30	32	28	25	20	13	11	9	9	6
South East	41	34	30	35	30	26	19	14	11	12	8	7
Greater London	44	36	32	36	31	26	21	14	13	13	10	7
Rest of South East	40	32	28	34	29	26	18	13	11	11	8	7
South West	36	31	28	32	27	23	15	13	12	11	7	7
West Midlands	40	38	28	35	31	25	19	17	12	12	10	7
North West	45	34	29	41	35	30	25	15	12	16	9	9
England	42	34	29	36	31	27	20	14	12	13	9	8
Wales	45	33	32	39	30	33	25	14	12	16	10	8
Scotland	46	37	34	42	35	34	27	19	16	16	15	13
Northern Ireland	..	35	31	..	31	29	..	17	16	..	10	11

1 People smoking 20 cigarettes or more a day.

Source: General Household Survey; Northern Ireland, Continuous Household Survey

7.14 Alcohol consumption[1] amongst people aged 16 or over: by gender, 1992

Percentages

	Consumption levels of males (units per week)				Consumption levels of females (units per week)			
	Non-drinker	Low (<1 - 10)	Moderate (11 - 21)	High (22+)	Non-drinker	Low (<1 - 7)	Moderate (8 - 14)	High (15+)
Great Britain	7	46	21	26	12	62	15	11
North	5	37	25	32	12	58	16	13
Yorkshire & Humberside	8	41	22	29	13	58	16	13
East Midlands	6	49	19	27	14	59	15	12
East Anglia	3	55	22	20	9	63	14	14
South East	8	48	21	23	13	63	13	11
Greater London	11	46	20	23	18	60	12	10
Rest of South East	5	50	21	24	10	64	14	12
South West	6	48	22	24	9	64	16	11
West Midlands	6	49	20	25	14	63	15	8
North West	6	41	21	32	11	60	16	13
England	6	46	21	26	12	61	15	12
Wales	5	43	24	28	14	62	13	11
Scotland	7	45	22	26	14	63	16	8
Northern Ireland	24	36	22	18	34	46	14	6

1 See Appendix notes.

Source: General Household Survey; Nothern Ireland, Continuous Household Survey

7.15 Dental attendance

Percentages

	Percentage of adults[1] who said that they went to the dentist for a regular check-up						Percentage of children who had been to the dentist[2]		
	1987		1989		1993		1987	1989	1993
	Males	Females	Males	Females	Males	Females			
Great Britain	40	56	41	56	44	59	65	67	67
North	28	49	35	52	40	53	61	59	60
Yorkshire & Humberside	39	57	39	56	43	61	62	62	61
East Midlands	42	60	43	63	45	63	70	71	66
East Anglia	49	59	51	60	53	68	74	73	79
South East	40	55	41	54	43	56	66	67	67
Greater London	35	48	33	44	36	47	58	64	60
Rest of South East	43	59	46	60	46	61	70	69	71
South West	49	65	50	61	55	66	69	76	74
West Midlands	42	56	40	57	40	54	60	69	68
North West	40	57	39	55	41	61	63	59	67
England	41	57	42	56	44	59	65	67	67
Wales	39	51	40	54	41	57	69	63	66
Scotland	35	55	36	54	42	57	62	69	67
Northern Ireland	35	52	33	51	38	55	58	57	..

1 Adults with some natural teeth.
2 For a check-up or to get used to the dentist.

Source: General Household Survey; Northern Ireland, Continuous Household Survey

7.16 Cervical and breast cancer: screening and age adjusted death rates[1]

Percentages and rates

	Breast screening program percentage of target population[2] screened			Cervical screening Deaths from cervical cancer[3]			programmes percentage of women invited for screening who attended[4]			Deaths from breast cancer[3]		
	1990-91	1991-92	1992-93	1991	1992	1993	1990-91	1991-92	1992-93	1991	1992	1993
United Kingdom	..	..	..	8.4	8.3	7.5	68	72	72	68.9	67.8	64.9
Northern	79	84	86	9.4	8.4	9.5	75	75	75	66.3	65.7	62.2
Yorkshire	81	85	87	9.3	9.2	8.1	68	74	72	62.0	61.8	63.2
Trent	83	88	89	9.6	8.1	7.8	76	77	78	69.6	70.5	66.1
East Anglia	83	86	87	7.6	6.8	5.4	74	81	79	69.6	70.9	72.9
North West Thames	58	65	72	6.4	8.0	5.6	60	58	61	70.2	64.6	56.5
North East Thames	50	64	79	7.3	8.6	6.4	60	61	61	73.8	67.6	63.7
South East Thames	61	70	80	7.2	8.9	8.1	70	71	70	71.6	69.8	70.1
South West Thames	66	78	89	6.2	5.4	6.6	70	67	68	70.3	71.0	67.8
Wessex	86	88	86	7.8	5.8	6.0	76	79	76	69.9	69.4	67.6
Oxford	82	85	88	8.5	6.3	4.5	81	77	76	72.2	74.1	57.3
South West	84	87	86	5.5	9.5	7.0	69	75	77	70.9	68.4	71.4
West Midlands	81	84	84	7.6	9.0	7.0	69	72	70	73.0	70.8	64.2
Mersey	79	82	84	11.6	9.7	10.0	73	69	72	62.6	68.5	62.9
North West	79	84	86	11.0	9.1	9.3	74	73	76	67.0	63.0	62.4
England	74	80	83	8.2	8.2	7.3	68	72	72	69.4	68.1	64.8
Wales	73	79	85	11.4	9.1	9.1	79	77	75	64.9	69.1	70.8
Scotland	74	78	82	8.7	9.1	8.4	70	72	71	63.8	62.2	63.6
Northern Ireland	51	68	81	7.1	6.1	5.6	56	63	65	65.6	59.1	56.6

1 The death rates shown are adjusted for the age structure of the population. See Appendix notes.
2 Women aged 20-64 years. The calculation of the data for England and Wales involves subtracting the number of women with 'recall ceased' (women who as a result of surgery etc do not require screening) from the target population. In Northern Ireland, women who are known to have had a smear in the last five years are excluded. In Scotland, this information is not yet collected centrally and is an estimate based on local health board data.
3 Deaths per 100,000 women aged 20 or over.
4 Women aged 50-64 years.

Source: Office of Population Censuses and Surveys; General Register Offices for Scotland and Northern Ireland; Department of Health; Welsh Office; The Scottish Office; Department of Health and Social Services, Northern Ireland

7.17 Contributions of selected foods to nutritional intakes (household food), 1992-1993[1]

	Percentage of fat and energy derived from										Total intake[2] per persons per day		Per-centage of food energy derived from fat
	Liquid & processed milk & cream		Meat & meat products		Cooking & spreading fats		Fruit, vegetables & vegetable products		Bread				
	Fat	Energy	Fat	Energy	Fat	Energy	Fat	Energy	Fat	Energy	Fat (grams)	Energy (Kcal)	
Great Britain	10.9	10.5	25.1	15.3	31.0	13.0	6.9	14.4	2.8	15.4	85	1,840	41.4
North	10.0	9.9	27.5	17.1	29.8	12.6	7.0	14.3	3.1	14.3	85	1,840	41.6
Yorkshire & Humberside	10.3	9.8	24.4	14.9	32.7	13.7	6.6	13.7	2.7	12.9	90	1,940	41.5
East Midlands	11.1	10.6	23.8	14.2	33.7	13.9	6.6	14.1	2.7	13.5	86	1,900	40.9
East Anglia/South East[3]	10.8	10.5	24.7	15.0	30.2	12.7	7.4	14.9	2.7	13.5	85	1,830	41.5
Greater London	10.9	10.3	24.9	15.1	30.5	12.8	7.0	14.8	2.6	13.0	83	1,790	41.5
South West	11.6	11.1	23.3	14.2	32.2	13.5	6.6	14.7	2.7	12.9	86	1,860	41.4
West Midlands	10.5	10.1	26.5	16.1	30.9	13.0	6.9	14.2	2.8	14.5	85	1,850	41.6
North West	11.0	10.5	26.4	16.0	31.1	13.0	6.4	13.9	2.9	14.0	84	1,840	41.2
England	10.8	10.4	25.1	15.3	31.1	13.0	6.9	14.4	2.7	13.2	85	1,850	41.4
Wales	11.5	10.9	24.7	14.8	31.2	12.9	6.5	14.4	3.0	14.4	82	1,800	40.7
Scotland	11.1	10.7	25.5	16.0	29.9	12.7	6.8	14.0	3.0	14.5	82	1,780	41.8

1 See Appendix notes.
2 Total intake from all household food, excluding household consumption of soft and alcoholic drinks and confectionery.
3 Data shown are averages for East Anglia and the South East combined.

Source: National Food Survey, Ministry of Agriculture, Fisheries and Food

7.18 Pharmaceutical services[1], 1991 and 1993[2]

	Prescription items dispensed (millions)		Percentage of prescription items exempt from charge[3,4]		Number of prescriptions items per person		Average net ingredient cost[5] (£ per person)		Average net ingredient cost[5] (£ per prescription item)	
	1991	1993	1991	1993	1991	1993	1991	1993	1991	1993
United Kingdom	499.9	547.8	..	..	8.6	9.4	53.63	66.82	6.20	7.11
Northern	28.7	31.1	81.5	83.3	9.3	10.0	57.43	70.09	6.19	7.00
Yorkshire	33.6	36.4	81.0	82.7	9.1	9.8	53.39	65.51	5.84	6.68
Trent	41.6	45.8	80.3	82.1	8.8	9.6	52.27	65.21	5.97	6.82
East Anglian	16.6	18.4	77.8	79.8	8.0	8.8	50.70	64.90	6.36	7.37
North West Thames	25.6	28.2	76.9	80.1	7.3	8.0	48.11	60.40	6.55	7.54
North East Thames	30.1	33.3	80.5	83.5	7.9	8.7	50.32	66.64	6.33	7.62
South East Thames	29.8	32.9	79.9	82.6	8.0	8.9	49.96	62.84	6.21	7.10
South West Thames	21.6	23.5	76.7	79.2	7.2	7.8	48.87	61.22	6.75	7.80
Wessex	23.4	25.6	78.2	80.4	8.0	8.6	51.61	62.89	6.43	7.29
Oxford	17.7	19.6	74.3	76.8	6.9	7.6	47.08	58.00	6.80	7.68
South Western	28.4	31.3	79.8	81.8	8.2	8.9	52.15	64.79	6.39	7.29
West Midlands	45.8	50.3	81.1	83.2	8.7	9.5	52.06	63.95	5.93	6.73
Mersey	23.7	25.7	83.2	84.9	9.8	10.7	59.02	73.92	6.01	6.94
North Western	39.9	43.3	81.8	83.6	10.0	10.8	58.35	70.96	5.83	6.56
England	406.5	445.4	80.0	82.1	8.4	9.2	52.27	65.08	6.20	7.09
Wales	31.2	34.3	..	83.9	10.8	11.5	63.03	77.70	5.82	6.75
Scotland	46.0	50.0	85.6	87.3	9.0	9.8	67.97	73.00	6.43	7.47
Northern Ireland	16.2	18.0	91.2	91.9	9.9	10.9	63.75	79.30	6.43	7.23

1 Figures relate to NHS prescriptions items dispensed by community pharmacists, and appliance contractors, dispensing doctors and prescriptions submitted by prescribing doctors for items personally administered.
2 Figures for Wales relate to the financial year 1993-94.
3 Figures for the English regions, England and Wales exclude prescriptions for which prepayment certificates have been purchased. For Scotland and Northern Ireland they are included.
4 For England figures relate to items dispensed by community pharmacists and appliance contractors only. Items dispensed by dispensing doctors and personal administration are not analysed into exempt, non exempt or other categories and are therefore excluded. Personally administered items are free of charge.
5 Net ingredient cost is the cost of medicines before any discounts and does not include any dispensing costs or fees.

Source: Department of Health; Welsh Office; The Scottish Office; Department of Health and Social Services, Northern Ireland

7.19 Hospital activity[1], year ending 31 March 1994

	In-patients (all specialities)						Total out-patient attend-ances[2] (thousands)	Total accident & Emerg-ency attend-ances (thousands)
	Average daily available beds per 1,000 population	Cases[1] treated per available bed	Cases[1] treated per 1,000 population	Finished consultant episodes[1] (thousands)	Percent-age of FCEs[1] in NHS Trusts	Day cases (thousands)		
United Kingdom	5.0	..	..	..	..	2,674.4	48,252.7	16,294.7
Northern	5.5	32.5	179.3	556.1	45	151.5	2,655.6	899.5
Yorkshire	4.7	37.2	176.2	653.4	92	163.9	2,988.3	1,024.8
Trent	4.3	37.0	160.4	764.2	79	185.3	3,609.3	1,159.8
East Angliian	4.6	34.7	159.9	335.0	78	81.7	1,526.0	388.6
North West Thames	4.2	30.4	128.3	451.7	79	145.1	2,545.0	920.6
North East Thames	4.7	34.6	161.4	615.1	75	158.2	3,351.7	1,079.6
South East Thames	3.7	40.7	152.1	565.3	75	147.6	3,024.7	1,070.4
South West Thames	5.0	29.3	146.3	438.7	79	119.7	2,196.7	768.1
Wessex	4.1	38.0	156.0	492.0	75	128.1	2,053.5	723.7
Oxford	3.4	42.0	144.3	374.2	50	87.4	1,662.6	527.7
South Western	4.5	37.7	169.5	564.9	88	139.1	2,234.0	911.0
West Midlands	4.1	39.7	164.5	870.0	46	207.2	3,955.9	1,583.6
Mersey	4.4	42.6	186.7	450.4	99	122.3	2,086.3	837.8
North Western	5.3	35.6	188.0	757.9	36	225.1	3,583.9	1,285.5
England[3]	4.5	36.4	164.5	7,983.5	69	2,106.4	38,232.6	13,288.7
Wales	6.0	30.0	174.8	508.0	54	204.4	2,525.2	964.5
Scotland	8.6	21.6	186.0	952.3	46	285.0	6,144.8	1,424.9
Northern Ireland	6.7	26.6	177.6	289.9	64	78.6	1,350.1	616.6

1 Finished consultant episodes in England. Data for Wales, Scotland and Northern Ireland relate to discharges and deaths. See Appendix notes.
2 Consultant out-patient attendances in Scotland.
3 Special Health Authorities are not shown separately but are included in England totals.

Source: Department of Health; Welsh Office; The Scottish Office; Department of Health and Social Services, Northern Ireland

7.20 NHS hospital waiting lists[1,2], at 30 September 1994

Thousands and percentages

	Ordinary admissions					Day case admissions				
		Months waited (percentages)			Patients admitted from the waiting list per month[3] (thousands)		Months waited (percentages)			Patients admitted from the waiting list per month[3] (thousands)
	Total waiting (thousands)	Less than 6	6 but less than 12	12 or over		Total waiting (thousands)	Less than 6	6 but less than 12	12 or over	
United Kingdom	745.9	92.5		7.5	170.5	499.1	..	..	..	183.4
Northern and Yorkshire	88.6	63.9	26.6	9.4	21.7	60.8	76.9	18.3	4.8	21.8
Trent	58.3	69.1	24.5	6.4	11.7	36.8	80.3	16.1	3.6	12.3
Anglia and Oxford	65.0	70.2	24.6	5.2	13.3	37.3	80.9	16.2	2.8	12.0
North Thames	100.9	61.3	27.0	11.7	18.1	71.4	71.5	21.4	7.1	22.8
South Thames	86.1	62.8	27.3	10.0	15.2	66.0	73.4	20.8	5.8	19.0
South and West	72.0	75.1	22.1	2.7	19.2	49.7	83.6	15.3	1.1	17.9
West Midlands	63.5	66.6	26.6	6.8	12.1	49.2	77.1	19.0	3.8	13.2
North West	93.4	71.3	25.8	2.9	21.0	70.5	82.1	16.6	1.3	25.2
England[4]	628.8	67.2	25.7	7.1	132.7	442.3	77.8	18.3	4.0	144.7
Wales	42.8	87.5		2.5	13.2	16.6	..	..	..	20.0
Scotland[5]	51.7	78.9	16.3	4.8	17.0	28.1	83.0	11.1	5.9	12.1
Northern Ireland	22.7	64.4	22.2	13.4	7.5	12.1	75.1	15.8	9.0	6.6

1 The regional breakdown for England is on the basis of the Regional Health Authorities which came into existence on 1 April 1994. See introductory text and the opening paragraph to the chapter Appendix notes.
2 Data are provider based ie people waiting to be admitted to hospitals in the region/country.
3 Monthly average for the three months ending 30 September 1994 for England and for the 12 months ending 30 September 1994 for Northern Ireland. For Wales, figures are based on admissions from waiting list plus booked admissions in the six months ending 30 September 1994. For Scotland figures are based on total planned removals from the waiting list in the year ending 30 September 1994.
4 Includes figures for Special Health Authorities.
5 Figures refer to true waiting lists only: they exclude repeat and deferred waiting lists.

Source: Department of Health; Welsh Office; The Scottish Office; Department of Health and Social Services, Northern Ireland

7.21 Children looked after by local authorities, year ending 31 March 1993[1]

	Total children looked after per thousand resident population[2,3]			Manner of accommodation (percentages)			Number of children looked after[4] (=100%)
	Children admitted	Ceased to be looked after	Looked after[4]	Foster homes	Community homes	Other	
North	3.1	3.3	4.7	58.8	17.1	24.1	3,300
Yorkshire & Humberside	2.8	3.2	4.9	62.5	14.9	22.5	5,600
East Midlands	2.4	3.0	4.5	59.2	12.0	28.7	4,200
East Anglia	2.2	2.4	3.8	70.4	7.2	22.4	1,800
South East	2.6	2.8	4.5	57.3	12.4	30.3	17,600
Greater London	3.3	3.5	5.9	54.8	12.6	32.6	8,900
Rest of South East	2.1	2.3	3.5	59.8	12.2	28.0	8,600
South West	2.9	3.1	4.0	70.8	8.3	21.0	4,100
West Midlands	2.5	2.8	4.9	62.9	12.3	24.8	6,000
North West	2.8	3.2	5.3	57.5	16.7	25.8	8,000
England	2.7	2.9	4.6	60.7	12.8	26.5	51,000
Wales[5]	3.8	3.7	4.0	58.4	11.6	29.9	3,165
Northern Ireland	2.3	2.4	4.4	61.0	13.0	26.0	2,063

1 English regional figures are estimates which take account of missing or incomplete data. These estimated figures are rounded to the nearest hundred; the England total is rounded to the nearest thousand.
2 Rates are based on mid-1992 estimates of population aged under 18 for the English regions, England and Northern Ireland, and aged 20 or under for Wales
3 Children may be included more than once if they started to be looked after more than once during the year.
4 At 31 March. For Northern Ireland, data relate to children in care excluding children home on trial.
5 Figures include 99 children aged 18 or over.

Source: Department of Health; Welsh Office; Department of Health and Social Services, Northern Ireland

7.22 Children and young people on child protection registers: by age and by category of abuse, at 31 March 1993

	Percentage aged					Number of children registers[1] (= 100%)	Rate per 10,000 children aged under 18	Percentage of children in each category of abuse[2]				
	Under 1	1-4	5-9	10-15	16 or over			Neglect	Physical injury	Sexual abuse	Emotional abuse	Grave concern
North	7	30	29	30	4	3,108	43.8	29	40	25	13	2
Yorkshire & Humberside	8	31	32	26	3	4,309	37.7	21	37	27	7	15
East Midlands	7	31	30	29	3	2,833	30.6	19	40	33	10	3
East Anglia	7	31	27	32	3	825	17.8	20	37	38	11	-
South East	7	29	31	29	4	10,828	27.5	31	34	23	13	6
Greater London	6	28	32	30	4	5,701	37.8	36	39	21	14	1
Rest of South East	7	30	31	29	3	5,127	21.0	26	28	26	13	11
South West	6	31	32	27	3	2,700	26.8	28	35	30	15	1
West Midlands	7	31	31	28	4	3,873	31.4	22	36	20	7	25
North West	8	33	30	26	3	3,948	26.1	25	41	26	6	9
England	7	30	31	28	3	32,500	29.6	26	37	26	11	8
Wales	8	31	33	25	3	1,789	26.8	23	37	20	9	15
Northern Ireland	5	30	31	28	5	1,345	28.9	31	12	14	9	36

1 Includes a small number of unborn children. Figure for the South West also includes estimates for missing data and therefore it, together with the England total, has been rounded to the nearest hundred.
2 The totals of the percentages exceed 100 as children in mixed categories are counted more than once. Northern Ireland data exclude 30 children registered in the 'Other' category.

Source: Department of Health; Welsh Office; Department of Health and Social Services, Northern Ireland

7.23 People in residential care homes for the elderly and adults with physical disabilities[1]: by sector and by age, as at 31 March 1994[2]

	Percentage of residents in			Percentage of residents aged				Number of Number of residents
	Local authority homes	Voluntary homes	Private homes	Under 65	65 to 84	85 or over	residents (all ages) (= 100%)	(all ages) per 1,000 population
North	32	10	57	4	49	47	15,559	5.1
Yorkshire & Humberside	32	9	59	4	46	50	25,548	5.1
East Midlands	31	9	60	4	45	51	18,445	4.6
East Anglia	30	12	58	3	40	57	10,573	5.1
South East							81,765	
Greater London	39	29	32	3	43	54	21,406	3.1
Rest of South East	19	21	60	5	41	53	60,359	5.7
South West	14	16	70	4	42	54	34,033	7.3
West Midlands	31	12	56	5	47	49	23,030	4.4
North West	20	22	58	5	48	47	35,160	5.5
England	25	17	58	4	44	52	244,113	5.1
Wales[3]	40	9	51	4	47	49	13,234	4.6
Scotland[4]	52	27	21	4	47	49	15,629	3.1

1 Includes people with sensory disabilities.
2 As at 31 March 1993 for Wales and Scotland.
3 Excludes 81 residents in voluntary homes for people with visual disabilities.
4 Total includes holiday/respite residents. Age breakdown is based on long-stay residents only.

Source: Department of Health; Welsh Office; The Scottish Office

7.24 Health Authorities' gross current expenditure and capital additions[1,2], 1992-93

Percentages and thousands

	Current expenditure				Capital additions (£ thousand)	Total expenditure (£ thousand)
	Percentage spent on			Total current expenditure (£ thousand) (= 100%)		
	Purchase of health care	Other services	Headquarters administ- ration			
Great Britain	92.7	3.7	3.4	25,414,380	1,572,468	26,986,848
Northern	90.6	5.6	3.8	1,287,275	73,531	1,360,806
Yorkshire	88.3	6.8	4.8	1,459,379	66,052	1,525,431
Trent	92.4	4.4	3.2	1,839,712	135,952	1,975,664
East Anglian	89.7	6.7	3.6	770,402	54,727	825,129
North West Thames	92.0	4.5	3.6	1,594,497	105,782	1,700,279
North East Thames	95.2	1.4	3.3	1,801,760	137,600	1,939,360
South East Thames	95.6	1.6	2.8	1,649,110	119,172	1,768,282
South West Thames	95.1	1.5	3.4	1,331,177	61,222	1,392,399
Wessex	90.0	5.0	5.0	1,135,439	66,282	1,201,721
Oxford	90.5	3.9	5.6	882,532	66,567	949,099
South Western	91.4	6.0	2.6	1,297,878	56,623	1,354,501
West Midlands	90.0	6.8	3.2	2,032,748	146,044	2,178,792
Mersey	93.0	2.0	4.9	1,022,066	25,720	1,047,786
North Western	93.0	4.3	2.6	1,706,329	108,137	1,814,466
England[3]	92.1	4.2	3.7	20,112,873	1,303,908	21,416,781
Wales	95.2	0.6	4.1	1,370,651	117,219	1,487,870
Scotland	94.8	3.2	2.0	3,930,856	151,341	4,082,197

1 See Appendix notes.
2 Regiona figures for England relate to directly managed units and therefore exclude NHS Trusts.
3 Includes Special Health Authorities.

Source: Department of Health; Welsh Office; The Scottish Office

7.25 Health Service staff[1]

Thousands and rates

	Total whole-time equivalents (thousands)				Rate per 10,000 population			
	1981	1986	1991	1993	1981	1986	1991	1993
United Kingdom	1,064.2	1,050.0	1,052.5	1,023.5	188.8	184.7	182.1	175.9
Northern	56.4	56.2	56.7	51.7	181.1	182.5	183.9	166.6
Yorkshire	65.2	62.9	62.2	61.7	181.5	174.6	170.0	166.4
Trent	77.5	78.3	80.4	78.5	168.8	169.1	171.1	164.8
East Anglian	31.2	32.2	33.9	33.3	164.5	161.6	162.3	158.9
North West Thames[2]	65.7	58.6	55.3	50.1	189.7	167.9	155.4	142.4
North East Thames[2]	72.6	72.4	71.4	65.1	196.4	192.5	190.2	170.7
South East Thames[2]	71.4	65.5	64.7	58.5	198.5	181.0	175.7	157.2
South West Thames[2]	55.1	49.1	46.6	46.8	182.2	165.6	154.1	156.0
Wessex	45.7	46.4	48.3	48.9	166.2	161.3	161.8	155.0
Oxford	36.2	35.6	35.4	37.7	155.6	143.7	138.2	145.3
South West	56.4	55.9	56.8	56.0	184.3	175.9	172.1	168.2
West Midlands	88.6	88.8	89.1	87.0	170.9	171.4	169.6	164.4
Mersey	47.3	45.1	42.6	40.0	192.6	187.0	176.9	165.6
North West	78.1	77.9	76.0	72.8	193.3	195.1	190.0	180.7
England[3]	861.0	841.8	847.2	817.6	183.9	178.1	176.2	168.5
Wales	49.5	52.1	53.6	55.1	176.0	184.6	185.5	189.5
Scotland	114.0	117.6	113.0	114.4	221.4	229.6	221.3	223.4
Northern Ireland	39.7	38.5	38.7	36.4	258.2	245.7	241.7	223.1

1 Includes staff in Family Health Service Authorities for the four countries, but not for the English Regional Health Authorities. Locum medical and dental staff
and agency nurses are excluded throughout. Figures for Wales and Scotland exclude nurses in training. See Appendix notes.
2 London ambulance service staff have been apportioned between the four Thames regions on the basis of population.
3 England figures do not equal the sum of the regions because of the inclusion of Special Health Authorities, Family Health Service Authorities and Other Statutory Authorities.

Source: Department of Health; Welsh Office; The Scottish Office;
Department of Health and Social Services, Northern Ireland

7.26 Primary health care nursing services: by category of staff[1]

Rates

	Community psychiatric nurses			Midwives			Health visitors[2]			District nurses[3]		
	1981	1986	1993	1981	1986	1993	1981	1986	1993	1981	1986	1993
Northern	0.19	0.51	1.14	0.71	0.82	0.79	1.98	2.24	2.24	3.33	2.64	2.83
Yorkshire	0.19	0.55	1.03	0.72	0.90	0.97	1.91	2.06	2.26	3.07	1.95	1.70
Trent	0.22	0.56	0.68	0.96	1.03	1.01	1.87	2.06	1.99	3.01	2.10	1.78
East Anglian	0.26	0.53	0.77	1.02	1.10	0.87	1.73	1.88	1.62	2.90	1.86	1.53
North West Thames	0.20	0.48	0.74	0.50	0.66	0.55	2.08	2.32	2.12	2.55	1.81	1.77
North East Thames	0.26	0.36	0.92	0.65	0.74	0.62	1.76	1.97	2.02	2.68	1.71	1.79
South East Thames	0.10	0.58	0.74	0.64	0.87	0.69	1.91	2.31	1.72	3.44	1.95	1.68
South West Thames	0.45	0.71	0.81	0.57	0.70	0.66	2.24	2.16	1.98	3.30	2.18	2.03
Wessex	0.30	0.61	0.89	0.60	0.77	0.73	2.00	2.11	2.02	2.88	2.16	2.10
Oxford	0.30	0.49	0.74	0.72	0.77	0.63	1.97	2.27	2.53	3.15	1.99	2.33
South West	0.31	0.46	1.16	0.44	0.68	1.07	1.98	2.14	1.98	3.03	1.88	1.78
West Midlands	0.10	0.49	0.79	0.81	0.94	0.87	1.94	2.16	1.99	3.09	2.01	1.92
Mersey	0.37	0.65	0.99	0.88	1.01	0.85	1.98	2.08	2.05	3.08	2.16	1.99
North West	0.19	0.57	1.10	0.92	1.17	1.05	2.25	2.94	2.78	3.79	2.49	2.21
England[4]	0.23	0.54	0.89	0.73	0.87	0.83	1.97	2.21	2.10	3.10	2.07	1.95
Wales	0.28	..	..	0.67	..	..	1.94	..	..	4.31	.	..
Scotland	..	..	0.69	0.28	0.37	0.55	2.87	3.12	3.25	4.47	4.73	3.99
Northern Ireland	..	0.61	0.75	0.37	0.75	0.98	2.86	2.99	3.27	4.14	3.84	4.42

1 Whole-time equivalents, rate per 10,000 population. Agency nurses and midwives are excluded. Figures for Northern Ireland include all qualified nurses
working in the area concerned.
2 Within Great Britain, includes health visitors in both the community and school health services (except that in Scotland, health visitors in schools are excluded in 1993), HV fieldwork teachers,
TB visitors with HV certificates, dual/triple posts (HV/DN/Midwife) and bank health visitors. Excludes HV students. In Scotland Bank Nurses and nurses in training are excluded.
3 Within Great Britain, includes District Nurse Practical Work Teachers, SRN, SSEN, and SEN Assisting District Nurses, dual posts (DN/Midwife) and Bank District Nurses. Excludes DN
students. In 1993 figures for England include Senior Nurses 6-8 and clinical grades G-I in the District Nursing Service, District Nurses, District Nurse Practical Work Teachers, holders of
dual post (DN/Midwife), and Bank District Nurses. In Scotland Bank nurses are excluded.
4 England totals include staff in Special Health Authorities and Family Health Service Authorities.

Source: Department of Health; Welsh Office; The Scottish Office;
Department of Health and Social Services, Northern Ireland

7.27 General practitioners: numbers and list sizes, 1993[1]

Numbers and percentages

| | General Medical Practitioners | | | | | | General Dental Practitioners | | |
| | | | GP fundholders[2] | | | | | Persons registered with a dentist as a | |
	Number of unrestricted principals[3]	Average list size	Number of funds	Number of practices	Number of GPs	Number of opticians[4]	Number of dentists[5]	percentage of the population[6]	Average list size
United Kingdom	32,426	1,850	1,324	1,478	7,234	..	19,012	59	1,800
Northern	1,671	1,878	69	73	391	414	909	60	2,047
Yorkshire	2,023	1,861	108	121	632	587	1,113	63	2,085
Trent	2,516	1,915	138	160	740	762	1,302	61	2,231
East Anglian	1,162	1,750	48	50	274	366	611	63	2,146
North West Thames	1,982	2,024	88	96	457	942	1,457	56	1,364
North East Thames	2,057	2,004	48	52	248	886	1,228	55	1,711
South West Thames	2,013	1,951	77	90	388	811	1,258	57	1,368
South East Thames	1,598	1,948	66	70	361	780	1,370	55	1,494
Wessex	1,669	1,779	54	59	352	584	953	62	1,937
Oxford	1,409	1,887	74	78	448	518	837	55	1,697
South Western	2,067	1,706	69	76	403	535	1,238	64	1,820
West Midlands	2,755	1,958	131	138	687	819	1,454	59	2,143
Mersey	1,274	1,940	84	101	424	444	773	64	2,004
North Western	2,093	1,937	66	85	335	649	1,270	62	1,958
England	26,289	1,902	1,120	1,249	6,140	6,619	15,773	60	1,834
Wales	1,702	1,736	71	74	385	530	843	58	2,015
Scotland	3,475	1,542	113	132	610	981	1,851	51	1,408
Northern Ireland	960	1,763	20	23	99	254	545	60	1,806

1 As at 1 October 1993 for England, Wales and Scotland and at 30 September 1993 for Northern Ireland.
2 Figures for the English Regional Health Authorities and for England relate to 1 April 1993. For Scotland comprises preparatory fundholders, small practice pilots and full fundholders.
3 See Appendix notes.
4 Figures relate to the number of optometrists and Opthalmic Medical Practitioners who have a contract with a Family Health Services Authority (FHSA) at 31 December 1993 or Scottish Health Board at 31 March 1994 to carry out an NHS sight test. For Northern Ireland, the figure relates to the the number of OMPs and Opticians registered with the Central Services Agency to carry out NHS sight tests. As some practitioners have contracts in more than one region, the sum of the regions does not equal the England total. Similarly, as some practitioners have contracts in more than one country, it is not possible to add the figures for the four countries to obtain a UK total.
5 At 30 September 1993. For England, Wales and Scotland includes principals, assistants and trainees; for Northern Ireland includes principals and trainees. Some dentists may have contracts with more than one FHSA. These dentists have been counted only once, in the region which includes the FHSA in which they hold their main contract.
6 The number of patients registered with a dentist in the region expressed as a percentage of the population of the region. This is not a precise measure of the proportion registered as some residents of one region may be registered with a dentist in another region.

Source: Department of Health; Welsh Office; The Scottish Office;
Department of Health and Social Services, Northern Ireland.

8 Living Standards

Household income

Average weekly household income in 1993 was highest in the South East, at £424, and lowest in the North, at £291.

(Table 8.1)

Savings

Only one household in seven in the North owned stocks and shares in 1993-94, around half the rate of the South West.

(Table 8.3)

Income tax

The average rate of tax payable was highest in the South East in 1992-93 at 19 per cent, over 3 percentage points higher than in Northern Ireland and Wales, which had the lowest rates.

(Table 8.5)

Benefits

In 1993-94, 23 per cent of households in the North and in the West Midlands received Family Credit or Income Support, compared with only 15 per cent in East Anglia.

(Table 8.6)

Three quarters of pensioners in the North West take advantage of a concessionary fare scheme, compared with only one quarter in East Anglia.

(Chart 8.7)

Household expenditure

Average weekly household expenditure in 1993 ranged from £238 in the West Midlands to £321 in the South East.

(Table 8.11)

Households in the South East spent most, proportionately, on housing in 1993 and least on fuel, light and power and on food, while those in Northern Ireland spent least on housing and most on fuel, light and power and on food.

(Table 8.11)

Household food consumption

In 1992-93, people in the North ate the most meat and meat products, those in Yorkshire and Humberside ate the most fish, those in the South West ate the most vegetables, while those in East Anglia and the South East ate the most fruit.

(Table 8.13)

Consumer goods

Households in the South East are most likely to have a deep freezer, compact disc player, video or home computer, and those in Northern Ireland are least likely.

(Table 8.14)

More than one in five households in the South West own a dishwasher, compared with less than one in ten in the North.

(Table 8.14)

Leisure

People in the Central Scotland ITV region watched an average of more than 27 hours of television each week in 1994 nearly five hours more than those in London, who watched the least.

(Table 8.15)

Introduction

This chapter focuses on the way we live. Income is one of the major factors affecting our standard of living and the first two tables look at the source and distribution of household income. The chapter goes on to look at income tax payable, benefits, household expenditure, ownership of consumer durables, and some aspects of how we spend our leisure time.

Tables 8.3 and 8.6 are sourced by the Department of Social Security's Family Resources Survey (FRS). This new survey was launched in October 1992 to assist in the forecasting of benefit expenditure and other analytical work required to support policy initiatives and evaluation. Although the DSS is primarily interested in information about the groups for which it provides financial support - the unemployed, sick or disabled people, the elderly, lone parents and less well-off families, the FRS questionnaire covers all types of households. In the first full year of the survey's operation - April 1993 to March 1994 - responses were achieved from over 26,000 households across Great Britain. The survey is mainly about household incomes, but there are detailed questions covering a variety of subjects which have a bearing on household income, including the number and age of children in the household, and any disability which may affect benefit entitlement.

Table 8.6 shows the proportions of households in receipt of certain benefits, but the FRS also recorded the levels of benefits received and found regional variations. Those households receiving some benefits, for example those related to sickness or unemployment, may experience changes in their circumstances at some point in the future, but for some elderly people their standard of living is determined by the amount of retirement pension they receive. The FRS found that about two thirds of single pensioners claiming (state) retirement pension in Wales received less than £60 per week in 1993/94, compared with just under half in the West Midlands. Of pensioner couples, about half of those claiming retirement pension in the South East, South West and East Midlands received less than £100 per week, compared with around two-thirds in the North and Scotland.

The rates of domestic disconnections of electricity, gas and water, where the reason for disconnection is non-payment of the account or standing charge, are shown at Tables 8.8, 8.9 and 8.10. Care should be taken when making comparisons on each

"Income is one of affecting our

of these tables, as the decision to disconnect the supply for debt is subject to the policy of each individual utility company. Companies will not now disconnect supplies if a satisfactory offer of payment is received (eg payment by instalments). These tables therefore provide an indication of the level of financial hardship encountered by households.

Table 8.17, drawn from the 1992 General Household Survey (GHS), looks at the proportion of people undertaking voluntary work. Because of sampling error in the GHS, it is not appropriate to rank individual regions according to their participation rates, but it can be seen that the highest proportions of people undertaking voluntary work were in the regions in the south of England, except for Greater London, and the lowest in the north of England and in Wales.

Voluntary work is defined as unpaid work (except for expenses) done through a group or on behalf of an organisation of some kind, but not for a trade union or political party; examples of the types of work which may be done are collecting money door-to-door, sponsored walks, visiting people in institutions such as hospitals or prisons, giving legal or financial advice or running a youth club. The average time spent on voluntary activities by those who had done them in the four weeks before interview was 15.6 hours - just under four hours per week. This suggests that in an average week about 20 million hours of voluntary work are performed by adults in Great Britain. Those doing voluntary work are not drawn predominantly from those who it might be thought would have more time available, such as those without children, the unemployed, and perhaps the recently retired; on the contrary, these are the groups least likely to do voluntary work.

The Central Statistical Office sometimes receives requests for the Retail Prices Index (RPI) on a regional basis. This information is not available. The RPI is designed to measure price **changes** over time rather than the differences in price **levels** between different groups within the reference population, which is what is generally required. It would be possible (with perhaps some enlargement of the sample of price collections) to compile indices which showed regional changes in prices, but in practice these indices would move in much the same way as the UK index.

the major factors
standard of living...."

8.1 Household income: by source, 1980-1981 and 1993[1]

Percentages and £

	Percentage of average gross weekly household income						Average gross weekly household income[3] (£) (= 100%)
	Wages and salaries	Self employ- ment	Invest- ments	Annuities and pensions[2]	Social security benefits[3]	Other income	
1980-1981							
United Kingdom	72.9	6.1	3.6	3.0	13.2	1.2	150.5
North	73.2	4.1	2.3	3.0	16.7	0.7	136.0
Yorkshire & Humberside	72.7	4.4	2.6	2.6	16.5	1.3	130.3
East Midlands	75.3	6.1	3.0	2.5	12.4	0.8	141.8
East Anglia	71.5	7.6	3.9	3.0	13.1	0.9	143.8
South East	75.0	6.3	4.3	3.1	10.0	1.4	173.3
Greater London	75.2	5.7	4.7	2.6	10.1	1.7	172.8
Rest of South East	74.8	6.7	4.0	3.3	10.0	1.2	173.7
South West	64.4	7.7	6.1	4.6	15.1	2.2	140.9
West Midlands	75.4	5.1	3.4	2.6	12.7	0.6	146.7
North West	72.8	6.0	3.1	2.7	14.4	1.0	148.0
England	73.4	6.0	3.8	3.0	12.7	1.2	152.7
Wales	68.2	6.9	3.0	3.9	17.2	0.8	138.6
Scotland	71.8	7.4	2.8	2.7	14.1	1.3	144.2
Northern Ireland	66.7	6.1	2.1	1.9	22.7	0.5	119.2
1993							
United Kingdom	64.7	8.3	5.1	6.2	13.9	1.9	353.0
North	60.6	8.7	3.8	5.8	19.2	1.9	291.1
Yorkshire & Humberside	66.6	6.1	3.7	6.0	15.2	2.5	317.7
East Midlands	65.5	9.4	4.9	5.8	13.3	1.2	341.7
East Anglia	59.8	10.2	5.7	6.5	15.1	2.7	346.9
South East	66.3	8.8	6.0	6.4	10.4	2.1	423.6
Greater London	65.6	9.8	6.3	5.5	10.0	2.8	431.7
Rest of South East	66.7	8.2	5.8	7.0	10.6	1.7	419.2
South West	61.7	8.4	6.4	7.1	14.5	1.8	330.5
West Midlands	59.9	10.7	5.0	5.0	17.8	1.4	301.0
North West	64.6	7.6	4.3	6.4	15.8	1.4	335.2
England	64.5	8.6	5.3	6.2	13.5	1.9	358.5
Wales	57.2	8.4	4.7	8.4	19.6	1.8	306.1
Scotland	69.4	5.5	4.0	5.3	13.8	2.0	334.1
Northern Ireland[4]	63.7	7.2	3.3	4.2	20.5	1.1	302.7

1 See Appendix notes. These figures are comparable with those published in *Regional Trends 29*, but not with those published in earlier editions, as they exclude an element for imputed income from owner/rent-free occupation of accommodation, which was previously classified under 'other income'.

2 Excluding social security benefits.

3 The figures cannot be compared directly between years. From 1984 all rent/rates/community charge rebates and allowances and housing benefit are excluded from gross income.

4 Northern Ireland data for 1993 are calculated from an enhanced sample, but the United Kingdom figures are calculated from the main Family Expenditure Survey sample. See Appendix notes.

Source: Family Expenditure Survey, Central Statistical Office; Department of Finance and Personnel, Northern Ireland

8.2 Distribution of household income, 1993[1]

Percentages and £

	Percentage of households in each weekly income group								Average gross weekly income (£)	
	Under £80	£80 but under £125	£125 but under £175	£175 but under £275	£275 but under £375	£375 but under £475	£475 but under £650	£650 or over	Per house-hold	Per person
United Kingdom	11.7	11.8	9.8	16.5	13.8	12.1	11.7	12.7	353.0	142.5
North	16.4	11.4	11.4	16.9	14.3	13.0	10.6	6.0	291.1	119.2
Yorkshire & Humberside	12.8	9.8	9.8	19.2	13.4	15.5	11.5	7.9	317.7	126.4
East Midlands	9.7	10.7	9.9	17.5	16.3	12.6	12.8	10.5	341.7	134.1
East Anglia	9.5	16.2	7.5	17.8	16.6	13.8	5.1	13.4	346.9	140.4
South East	9.8	11.3	7.8	14.8	12.1	11.9	12.4	20.0	423.3	174.0
Greater London	12.2	11.9	7.5	13.5	11.6	10.7	11.6	20.9	431.7	187.0
Rest of South East	8.5	11.0	7.9	15.4	12.4	12.5	12.9	19.5	419.2	167.5
South West	9.8	11.2	11.2	18.6	14.4	12.0	13.0	9.8	330.5	133.2
West Midlands	12.6	15.4	12.2	16.2	15.9	12.1	7.8	7.9	301.0	120.3
North West	13.5	11.7	11.2	14.8	13.9	10.8	12.8	11.5	335.2	136.7
England	11.4	11.8	9.7	16.3	13.8	12.4	11.5	13.2	358.5	145.2
Wales	13.8	11.2	13.5	16.4	14.7	10.6	11.2	8.6	306.1	122.3
Scotland	13.4	11.5	8.3	17.6	14.5	10.8	13.7	10.3	334.1	135.9
Northern Ireland[2]	14.8	13.9	12.6	16.5	12.3	8.7	10.6	10.5	302.7	106.2

1 See Appendix notes.
2 Northern Ireland data are calculated from an enhanced sample, but the United Kingdom figures are calculated from the main Family Expenditure Survey sample.

Source: Family Expenditure Survey, Central Statistical Office; Department of Finance and Personnel, Northern Ireland

8.3 Households[1]: by type of saving, 1993-94

Percentages[2]

	Accounts						Other savings				
	Current[3]	Post Office	TESSA	Other building society[4]	Other bank	Other account[5]	Gilts or unit trusts	Stocks & shares	National Savings	Save As You Earn	Premium Bonds
Great Britain	78	14	10	58	20	4	8	22	7	2	32
North	69	13	7	53	17	3	7	15	5	1	25
Yorkshire & Humberside	74	12	11	55	20	3	7	19	6	2	29
East Midlands	78	15	10	61	23	3	7	20	7	2	34
East Anglia	86	20	10	61	24	3	9	22	8	2	42
South East	83	16	11	64	16	4	9	26	9	2	37
Greater London	78	14	9	59	14	4	8	24	8	2	33
Rest of South East	86	17	12	67	17	4	10	28	9	2	39
South West	87	19	12	67	19	4	10	28	9	2	40
West Midlands	74	12	8	59	18	4	7	18	5	2	29
North West	76	14	10	54	19	2	7	19	7	2	30
England	79	15	10	60	18	4	8	22	7	2	34
Wales	75	13	7	50	16	2	4	16	5	1	25
Scotland	66	9	8	43	33	3	7	17	5	1	21

1 Households in which at least one member has an account. See Appendix notes.
2 As a percentage of all households.
3 A current account may be either a bank or building society account.
4 All building society accounts excluding current accounts and TESSAs.
5 All accounts yielding interest but excluding high street bank and building society accounts.

Source: Family Resources Survey, Department of Social Security

8.4 Distribution of income liable to assessment for tax, 1992-93[1]

Percentages and thousands

	Percentage of individuals in each income range								Individuals with incomes of £3,445 or more (= 100%) (thousands)
	£3,445-£4,999	£5,000-£7,499	£7,500-£9,999	£10,000-£14,999	£15,000-£19,999	£20,000-£29,999	£30,000-£49,999	£50,000 and over	
United Kingdom[2]	12.7	17.7	15.1	22.8	14.0	11.5	4.5	1.6	27,200
North	14.7	19.6	15.5	22.8	13.3	10.3	3.0	0.7	1,370
Yorkshire & Humberside	14.1	20.3	16.6	22.1	12.8	9.8	3.3	1.1	2,250
East Midlands	13.6	19.5	15.5	21.2	14.3	10.8	3.7	1.2	1,850
East Anglia	12.5	16.0	16.5	23.9	14.0	11.7	4.0	1.3	1,000
South East	10.5	15.2	13.3	22.9	15.0	14.0	6.4	2.7	8,830
Greater London	9.2	14.3	12.3	23.4	15.9	14.9	6.7	3.2	3,300
Rest of South East	11.2	15.8	13.8	22.6	14.5	13.4	6.3	2.4	5,530
South West	14.2	18.6	14.6	23.8	12.6	10.7	4.3	1.2	2,310
West Midlands	11.6	19.1	15.8	25.1	13.5	10.1	3.6	1.2	2,390
North West	14.8	18.7	16.5	22.6	13.4	9.7	3.4	0.9	2,850
England	12.5	17.6	14.9	23.0	14.0	11.7	4.7	1.7	22,800
Wales	14.2	18.9	17.7	20.8	14.2	10.3	3.0	0.7	1,210
Scotland	13.5	18.5	15.7	22.7	13.5	11.0	3.9	1.1	2,410
Northern Ireland	15.9	19.3	16.5	21.3	14.5	8.9	2.8	0.9	608

1 See Appendix notes.
2 Figures for United Kingdom include members of HM Forces and others who are liable to some UK tax but reside overseas on a long-term basis. In addition the United Kingdom total includes a very small number of individuals who could not be allocated to a region.

Source: Survey of Personal Incomes, Board of Inland Revenue

8.5 Income tax payable, 1992-93[1]

	Lower rate (20%)		Basic rate (25%)		Tax in excess of basic rate (40%)		Total tax payable (£ million)	Total annual income (£ million)	Average rate of tax payable (%)	Average amount of tax payable(£)
	Number of individuals (thousands)	Amount (£ million)	Number of individuals (thousands)	Amount (£ million)	Number of individuals (thousands)	Amount (£ million)				
United Kingdom[2]	25,700	9,340	21,200	51,100	1,710	4,920	65,400	383,000	17.1	3,080
North	1,270	460	1,020	2,070	56	110	2,640	17,100	15.5	2,580
Yorkshire & Humberside	2,080	750	1,690	3,490	100	280	4,510	28,500	15.9	2,680
East Midlands	1,740	630	1,410	3,090	92	240	3,960	24,400	16.2	2,820
East Anglia	946	350	791	1,780	56	140	2,270	13,700	16.6	2,870
South East	8,430	3,110	7,200	21,300	835	2,770	27,200	144,000	18.9	3,770
Greater London	3,190	1,180	2,750	8,870	338	1,340	11,400	57,400	19.8	4,140
Rest of South East	5,240	1,930	4,460	12,400	497	1,440	15,800	86,400	18.3	3,540
South West	2,150	780	1,760	3,950	129	340	5,060	30,900	16.4	2,880
West Midlands	2,260	830	1,890	4,020	119	300	5,150	31,600	16.3	2,720
North West	2,650	960	2,140	4,370	120	280	5,600	35,800	15.7	2,620
England	21,500	7,860	17,900	44,000	1,510	4,460	56,400	326,000	17.3	3,150
Wales	1,120	400	902	1,830	48	100	2,330	15,100	15.4	2,580
Scotland	2,280	820	1,830	4,030	126	270	5,130	31,700	16.2	2,800
Northern Ireland	578	200	442	910	22	60	1,170	7,510	15.6	2,650

1 See Appendix notes. As figures are rounded, components may not add to totals.
2 Figures for United Kingdom include members of HM Forces and others who are liable to some UK tax but reside overseas on a long-term basis. In addition the United Kingdom total includes a very small number of individuals who could not be allocated to a region.

Source: Survey of Personal Incomes, Board of Inland Revenue

8.6 Households in receipt of benefit[1]: by type of benefit, 1993-94

Percentages[2]

	Family Credit or Income Support	Housing Benefit	Council Tax Benefit	Unemploy- ment Benefit	Retirement pension	Sickness, Invalidity or Disablement Benefits[3]	Child Benefit or One Parent Benefit	Any Benefit
Great Britain	20	20	21	3	29	12	32	76
North	23	26	27	3	29	18	33	81
Yorkshire & Humberside	22	22	25	3	30	14	31	78
East Midlands	19	17	19	3	31	12	31	75
East Anglia	15	16	20	4	31	10	31	74
South East	18	18	17	3	27	8	32	72
Greater London	22	23	19	3	24	8	33	72
Rest of South East	15	14	16	2	29	8	32	72
South West	17	15	18	3	30	8	32	76
West Midlands	23	20	21	3	29	13	33	77
North West	22	21	25	2	30	17	34	80
England	19	19	20	3	29	11	32	75
Wales	21	19	22	3	29	18	31	80
Scotland	21	27	22	3	27	15	33	78

1 Households in which at least one member is currently in receipt of benefit. See Appendix notes.
2 As a percentage of all households.
3 Sickness Benefit, Invalidity Benefit, Disability Living Allowance (Care and Mobility components), Severe Disablement Allowance, Industrial Injuries Disability Benefit, War Disablement Benefit and Attendance Allowance.

Source: Family Resources Survey, Department of Social Security

8.7 Pensioners' concessionary fare scheme: availability and take-up, 1991-1993[1]

Pensioners with scheme avaliable[2]   **Take-up rate[3]**

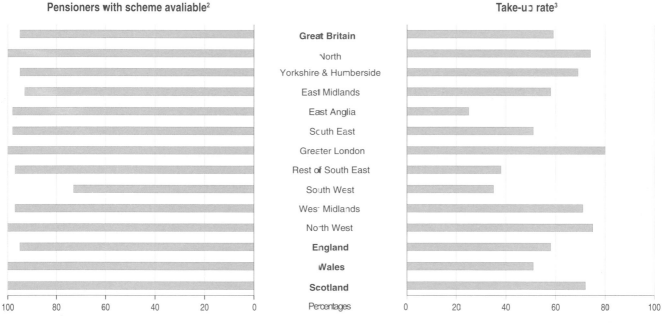

1 Average of the three years.
2 As a percentage of the total population aged 60/65 (females/males) or over.
3 Those who applied for concessionary fares as a percentage of those to whom schemes were available.

Source: National Travel Survey, Department of Transport

8.8 Domestic disconnections of electricity supply, 1992/93 and 1993/94

| | Rates[1] | |
	1992/93	1993/94
United Kingdom[2]	67	16
Northern	184	14
NORWEB	27	20
Yorkshire	111	24
East Midlands	21	17
Eastern	36	20
London	37	10
SEEBOARD	69	6
Southern	64	9
South Western	80	6
Midlands	55	12
Manweb	35	2
SWALEC	28	7
Scottish Power	72	5
Hydro-Electric	100	48
Northern Ireland	305	120

1 Rate per 100,000 domestic credit customers.
2 UK data are not official, but have been calculated by Central Statistical Office from the Great Britain and Northern Ireland base data.

Source: Office of Electricity Regulation; Northern Ireland Electricity

8.9 Domestic disconnections of gas supply

| | Percentages[1] | | | |
	1991	1992	1993	1994
Great Britain	0.11	0.09	0.09	0.09
Northern	0.17	0.11	0.09	0.12
North Eastern	0.11	0.07	0.11	0.11
East Midlands	0.11	0.10	0.12	0.10
Eastern	0.12	0.06	0.09	0.14
South Eastern	0.09	0.09	0.10	0.09
North Thames	0.20	0.24	0.21	0.14
Southern	0.09	0.05	0.04	0.05
South Western	0.04	0.03	0.03	0.03
West Midlands	0.11	0.09	0.07	0.09
North Western	0.09	0.06	0.07	0.08
Wales	0.13	0.06	0.05	0.06
Scotland	0.06	0.07	0.08	0.08

1 As a percentage of all domestic credit customers.

Source: British Gas

8.10 Domestic disconnections of water supply

| | Rates[1] | | |
	1991/92	1992/93	1993/94
Northumbria	9.9	7.4	3.7
Yorkshire	14.5	10.4	7.0
Central	15.0	9.7	4.0
Eastern	8.5	4.2	7.3
Southern	19.4	30.0	21.5
Thames	4.7	8.2	6.8
South West	6.8	5.3	2.6
Wessex	5.1	3.2	2.5
North West	8.1	1.9	1.4
Wales	26.3	21.5	5.3
England & Wales	11.0	9.5	6.3

1 Rate per 10,000 domestic customers.

Source: Office of Water Services (OFWAT)

8.11 Household expenditure: by commodity and service, 1993[1]

£ per week and percentages

	Housing	Fuel, light & power	Food	Alcohol and tobacco	Clothing and footwear	House-hold goods and services	Motoring and fares	Leisure goods and services	Miscellan-eous and personal goods and services	Average house-hold expend-iture	Average expend-iture per person
£ per week											
United Kingdom	44.9	13.2	50.0	17.5	17.4	38.5	43.2	38.8	13.1	276.7	111.7
North	36.9	13.0	47.0	19.8	16.0	36.2	34.9	30.9	11.2	245.9	100.7
Yorkshire & Humberside	38.8	13.1	48.0	21.0	17.6	33.1	43.5	35.2	12.8	263.1	104.6
East Midlands	42.3	13.6	49.2	17.1	15.3	36.5	39.7	36.1	12.5	262.2	102.9
East Anglia	44.1	12.6	48.1	12.1	15.8	35.8	46.1	34.1	11.9	260.5	105.5
South East	58.6	13.2	54.1	16.7	19.0	47.3	48.8	48.0	15.5	321.1	131.9
Greater London	61.6	12.3	53.2	16.2	19.4	45.5	46.5	50.8	16.5	322.0	139.4
Rest of South East	57.0	13.7	54.5	16.9	18.7	48.3	50.1	46.5	15.0	320.6	128.1
South West	43.0	12.8	49.2	15.6	14.8	36.8	46.7	35.6	13.6	268.1	108.1
West Midlands	36.5	12.7	44.8	14.9	14.1	32.2	39.1	32.9	11.2	238.2	95.2
North West	41.1	13.2	47.2	19.4	18.4	35.4	38.5	37.6	11.2	261.8	106.8
England	46.7	13.1	49.9	17.3	17.2	39.3	43.8	39.6	13.3	280.1	113.4
Wales	39.2	13.9	48.7	18.0	17.6	33.9	37.7	30.6	9.9	249.5	99.7
Scotland	35.4	13.5	49.8	19.8	19.1	33.9	41.3	38.1	14.0	264.8	107.8
Northern Ireland[2]	25.1	16.3	54.0	17.5	18.4	33.5	46.6	30.3	11.9	253.5	89.0
As a percentage of average weekly household expenditure											
United Kingdom	*16.2*	*4.8*	*18.1*	*6.3*	*6.3*	*13.9*	*15.6*	*14.0*	*4.8*	*100.0*	
North	*15.0*	*5.3*	*19.1*	*8.1*	*6.5*	*14.7*	*14.2*	*12.6*	*4.6*	*100.0*	
Yorkshire & Humberside	*14.7*	*5.0*	*18.2*	*8.0*	*6.7*	*12.6*	*16.6*	*13.4*	*4.9*	*100.0*	
East Midlands	*16.1*	*5.2*	*18.8*	*6.5*	*5.8*	*13.9*	*15.1*	*13.8*	*4.8*	*100.0*	
East Anglia	*16.9*	*4.9*	*18.5*	*4.7*	*6.1*	*13.7*	*17.7*	*13.1*	*4.6*	*100.0*	
South East	*18.3*	*4.1*	*16.8*	*5.2*	*5.9*	*14.7*	*15.2*	*14.9*	*4.8*	*100.0*	
Greater London	*19.1*	*3.8*	*16.5*	*5.0*	*6.0*	*14.1*	*14.4*	*15.8*	*5.1*	*100.0*	
Rest of South East	*17.8*	*4.3*	*17.0*	*5.3*	*5.8*	*15.1*	*15.6*	*14.5*	*4.7*	*100.0*	
South West	*16.1*	*4.8*	*18.3*	*5.8*	*5.5*	*13.7*	*17.4*	*13.3*	*5.1*	*100.0*	
West Midlands	*15.3*	*5.3*	*18.8*	*6.2*	*5.9*	*13.5*	*16.4*	*13.8*	*4.7*	*100.0*	
North West	*15.7*	*5.0*	*18.0*	*7.4*	*7.0*	*13.5*	*14.7*	*14.4*	*4.3*	*100.0*	
England	*16.7*	*4.7*	*17.8*	*6.2*	*6.1*	*14.0*	*15.6*	*14.1*	*4.7*	*100.0*	
Wales	*15.7*	*5.6*	*19.5*	*7.2*	*7.1*	*13.6*	*15.1*	*12.3*	*4.0*	*100.0*	
Scotland	*13.4*	*5.1*	*18.8*	*7.5*	*7.2*	*12.8*	*15.6*	*14.4*	*5.3*	*100.0*	
Northern Ireland[2]	*9.9*	*6.4*	*21.3*	*6.9*	*7.3*	*13.2*	*18.4*	*11.9*	*4.7*	*100.0*	

1 See Appendix notes.
2 Northern Ireland data are calculated from an enhanced sample, but the United Kingdom figures are calculated from the main Family Expenditure Survey sample.

Source: Family Expenditure Survey, Central Statistical Office; Department of Finance and Personnel, Northern Ireland

8.12 Expenditure on foods bought for household consumption: selected foods and total, 1992-1993[1]

£ per person per week

	Liquid and processed milk and cream	Cheese	Eggs	Uncooked carcass meat and poultry	Meat products	Fish	Vegetables and vegetable products[2]	Fresh and other fruit	Bread	Total household food[3]
Great Britain	1.44	0.47	0.18	1.67	1.83	0.70	1.85	1.03	0.69	13.07
North	1.31	0.35	0.18	1.53	1.96	0.64	1.71	0.75	0.73	12.22
Yorkshire & Humberside	1.37	0.43	0.18	1.59	1.84	0.74	1.76	0.94	0.69	12.83
East Midlands	1.43	0.43	0.16	1.49	1.61	0.65	1.64	0.89	0.67	12.00
East Anglia/South East[4]	1.54	0.54	0.19	1.77	1.84	0.80	2.06	1.29	0.68	14.17
South West	1.53	0.50	0.18	1.59	1.55	0.58	1.71	0.99	0.67	12.44
West Midlands	1.35	0.47	0.18	1.76	1.68	0.61	1.74	0.87	0.67	12.15
North West	1.38	0.39	0.16	1.62	1.93	0.68	1.74	0.83	0.71	12.56
England	1.45	0.48	0.18	1.67	1.79	0.71	1.86	1.04	0.69	13.10
Wales	1.42	0.41	0.19	1.56	1.63	0.63	1.79	0.90	0.71	12.25
Scotland	1.36	0.44	0.20	1.72	2.28	0.66	1.74	1.02	0.74	13.34

1 See Appendix notes.
2 Including tomatoes, fresh potatoes and potato products.
3 Excluding soft and alcoholic drinks and confectionery.
4 Data shown are averages for East Anglia and the South East combined.

Source: National Food Survey, Ministry of Agriculture, Fisheries and Food

8.13 Household consumption of selected foods, 1980-1981 and 1992-1993[1]

Grams per person per week[2]

	Liquid and processed milk and cream		Meat and meat products		Fish		Vegetables & vegetable products[3]		Fresh and other fruit		Bread	
	1980-1981	1992-1993	1980-1981	1992-1993	1980-1981	1992-1993	1980-1981	1992-1993	1980-1981	1992-1993	1980-1981	1992-1993
Great Britain	2,556	2,195	1,128	953	139	143	2,438	2,174	794	934	885	756
North	2,386	2,104	1,199	1,056	159	147	2,600	2,249	618	741	1,006	801
Yorkshire & Humberside	2,386	2,130	1,066	955	153	160	2,435	2,199	624	881	890	764
East Midlands	2,670	2,317	1,066	896	142	142	2,461	2,269	717	866	921	788
East Anglia/South East[4]	2,556	2,192	1,140	936	133	151	2,393	2,166	953	1,103	777	697
South West	2,613	2,346	1,083	908	116	129	2,495	2,314	868	953	868	726
West Midlands	2,613	2,127	1,134	994	142	126	2,390	2,165	743	840	893	830
North West	2,556	2,215	1,174	995	130	147	2,489	2,171	680	785	972	796
England	2,556	2,201	1,128	955	139	144	2,441	2,197	802	948	868	750
Wales	2,726	2,283	1,091	920	145	140	2,775	2,214	760	825	975	796
Scotland	2,613	2,164	1,145	947	136	128	2,217	1,916	720	875	998	783

1 See Appendix notes.
2 Except equivalent millilitres of milk and cream. Data have been converted from imperial measures using factors of 28.35 grams per ounce and 568 millilitres per pint.
3 Including tomatoes, fresh potatoes and potato products.
4 Data shown are averages for East Anglia and the South East combined.

Source: National Food Survey, Ministry of Agriculture, Fisheries and Food

8.14 Households with selected durable goods, 1980-1981 and 1992-1993[1]

Percentages

	Microwave oven	Wash-ing machine	Tumble drier	Dish-washer	Refrig-erator[2]	Deep freezer[2]	Tele-phone	Tele-vision	Compact disc player	Video	Home comp-uter	Central heating
				Percentage of households in sample having								
1980-1981												
Great Britain	..	77	22	4	93	47	73	97	..	..	..	58
North	..	88	19	1	89	42	64	98	..	..	..	64
Yorkshire &												
Humberside	..	84	24	2	89	40	68	97	.	..	..	52
East Midlands	..	84	22	3	93	45	73	98	.	..	..	65
East Anglia	..	80	27	5	92	59	73	98	.	..	..	68
South East	..	69	23	6	96	55	80	96	.	..	..	62
Greater London	..	61	20	4	95	50	79	95	.	..	..	54
Rest of South East	..	75	25	7	96	59	80	97	.	..	..	67
South West	..	72	22	5	93	54	72	96	.	..	..	57
West Midlands	..	77	21	2	91	42	71	97	.	..	..	54
North West	..	77	21	2	92	40	71	98	.	..	..	54
England	..	76	22	4	93	48	74	97	.	..	..	59
Wales	..	81	23	2	91	50	67	98	.	..	..	52
Scotland	..	83	24	3	91	39	74	97	..	..	..	51
Northern Ireland	..	70	..	..	85	..	57	91	..	..	..	37
1992-1993												
Great Britain	60	88	49	16	..	86	89	98	36	72	23	83
North	62	91	46	9	..	84	83	98	34	72	24	91
Yorkshire &												
Humberside	62	89	47	12	..	82	88	98	32	69	22	75
East Midlands	60	91	52	14	..	87	90	99	35	73	22	88
East Anglia	57	86	49	16	..	84	91	98	37	70	23	86
South East	59	85	49	20	..	88	93	98	40	74	25	86
Greater London	53	82	43	16	..	84	92	98	38	72	23	83
Rest of South East	62	88	53	23	..	90	93	99	42	74	27	88
South West	62	87	51	21	..	88	93	98	34	70	23	82
West Midlands	61	87	49	12	..	86	87	98	33	73	23	77
North West	62	87	47	12	..	85	86	99	34	73	24	77
England	60	87	49	16	..	86	90	98	36	72	24	83
Wales	66	88	48	14	..	87	86	98	31	71	24	85
Scotland	58	90	50	14	..	80	86	98	33	72	20	83
Northern Ireland	54	88	34	15	98	71	82	97	21	64	17	87

1 See Appendix notes.
2 Fridge freezers are attributed to both Refrigerator and Deep freezer.

Source: General Household Survey; Family Expenditure Survey and Continuous Household Survey, Department of Finance and Personnel, Northern Ireland

8.15 Average weekly television viewing[1]: by age, 1992 and 1994

Hours[2]

| | 1992 | | | | | 1994 | | | | |
| | Persons aged | | | | All persons aged 4 or over | Persons aged | | | | All persons aged 4 or over |
	4-15	16-34	35-64	65 or over		4-15	16-34	35-64	65 or over	
United Kingdom[3]	19.6	23.4	27.5	37.7	26.7	18.4	22.1	25.9	35.9	25.2
Yorkshire	19.7	23.1	28.7	34.8	26.6	17.8	22.2	26.7	34.1	25.3
North East	20.0	24.8	30.5	34.0	27.4	17.0	21.4	27.5	33.2	24.9
East	17.5	20.1	23.2	32.0	22.8	17.5	19.0	23.1	32.9	22.6
London	19.0	21.5	24.8	36.4	24.6	16.0	18.7	23.1	35.4	22.5
South, South East and Channel Islands	17.5	21.4	24.3	32.8	24.0	17.8	20.3	23.2	34.1	23.4
South West	17.7	22.2	24.2	31.4	24.1	18.0	21.5	24.4	30.5	23.7
Midlands	18.6	22.8	25.3	38.7	25.5	17.8	21.7	24.1	33.5	23.8
North West	19.4	23.3	28.3	39.7	27.1	17.8	22.0	25.6	37.0	25.0
Wales and West	18.8	23.0	26.6	30.5	25.0	18.4	21.5	25.1	33.3	24.2
Border	20.0	26.8	27.4	37.0	27.5	16.6	21.0	27.0	30.1	24.1
Central Scotland	19.9	25.2	32.6	41.8	29.8	18.8	24.2	28.9	39.1	27.3
Northern Scotland	19.3	20.2	26.5	41.5	26.1	20.0	21.7	24.3	30.7	24.0
Ulster	22.9	25.7	29.7	36.3	27.8	19.3	23.9	27.6	37.1	26.0

1 Including timeshift, ie viewing of broadcast material recorded at home and played back within seven days of recording.
2 Per person in UK private households containing a television set in working order.
3 Figures for the regions exclude viewing of other regions' broadcasts, whereas figures for the United Kingdom include all viewing, and are therefore higher.

Source: Broadcasters' Audience Research Board Ltd

8.16 Adults taking a holiday[1]: by region of domicile, 1994

1 A holiday is defined as four or more nights away from home.

Source: British Tourist Authority

8.17 Participation in voluntary work[1]: by gender, 1992

Percentages

	Males	Females	Total
Great Britain	21	27	24
North	14	20	17
Yorkshire & Humberside	17	22	20
East Midlands	21	29	25
East Anglia	24	35	30
South East	24	28	26
Greater London	19	24	22
Rest of South East	27	31	29
South West	28	34	31
West Midlands	20	22	21
North West	21	26	23
England	22	27	25
Wales	15	22	19
Scotland	19	25	23

1 People who had done voluntary work in the year before interview.

Source: General Household Survey, Office of Population Censuses and Surveys

9 Crime and Justice

Crime rates

Recorded crime fell in all regions in 1993 except Yorkshire and Humberside, the East Midlands, the South West and the West Midlands.

(Table 9.1)

Yorkshire and Humberside had the highest recorded crime rate in England and Wales in 1993, more than one and a half times the rate in East Anglia, which had the lowest.

(Table 9.1)

Victims

Householders in the North, Yorkshire and Humberside, the West Midlands and the North West faced higher than average risks of crime against their property in 1993.

(Table 9.2)

Clear-up rates

Within England and Wales, police forces in the North West and in Wales were the most successful at clearing up crime in 1993, with over a third of recorded offences cleared up.

(Table 9.4)

Offenders

The North has proportionately the most known young offenders aged under 18, and the North West has the most aged 18 or over.

(Table 9.6)

Police in the North are less likely than those in other regions to caution the under 18s for an indictable offence, while police in the South West are the most likely.

(Table 9.7)

Sentences

People found guilty in a Crown Court in Yorkshire and Humberside or in the South West are more likely than those in other regions of England or in Wales to receive a community penalty.

(Table 9.9)

Judges in Crown Courts in the West and East Midlands are the most likely to impose an immediate custodial sentence.

(Table 9.9)

Police manpower

There is one police officer or full-time Reserve for every 140 people in Northern Ireland, compared with one officer for every 533 people in East Anglia.

(Table 9.14)

Fear of crime

Nearly two fifths of people in the North are worried about their car being stolen, compared with just over one fifth in the South West.

(Table 9.15)

People in Yorkshire and Humberside and the West Midlands are the most likely to worry about the possibility of burglary, and people in East Anglia are the least likely.

(Table 9.15)

Introduction

There are important differences between both the legal systems and the crime recording systems in England and Wales, Scotland and Northern Ireland. Figures are therefore not directly comparable in some of the tables and so it has not always been possible to include figures for the United Kingdom. A map of the police force areas in England and Wales is included in the Appendix on page 232. Figures for Greater London include the Metropolitan Police and the City of London Force throughout.

There are two main measures of crime. One is the statistics of offences recorded by the police (see Table 9.1), but these measure only a proportion of the total number of crimes committed because not all crimes are reported to the police. The other measure is crime surveys - the British Crime Survey (BCS) in England and Wales and the Scottish Crime Survey in Scotland -which ask people directly about their experience as victims, whether or not they told the police about it (see Table 9.2). However, surveys cover only a selection of crime types and are subject to sampling error. Hence neither measure accurately records the scale of crime.

In 1993, 5.5 million notifiable offences were recorded by the police in England and Wales, 1 per cent fewer than in 1992. Nevertheless, the number of offences recorded has risen from around 1 per 100 population in the 1950s to 5 per 100 population in the 1970s to 10.8 per 100 population in 1993. Not all crimes measured by the BCS fall into categories which can be compared with offences recorded by the police, but for those which do, the survey estimated 11.6 million offences in 1993 against 3.1 million recorded offences of the same type. In all, the BCS estimated a total of 18 million crimes against householders and their property in 1993. The survey figures indicate a shallower increase in crime than the recorded offence figures where categories can be compared; recorded offences rose by 111 per cent between 1981 and 1993, whereas the survey suggests an increase of 77 per cent. It further suggests that overall there has been an increase in the reporting of offences to the police in recent years, from 31 per cent in 1981 to 43 per cent in 1991, but dropping back to 41 per cent in 1993.

About 95 per cent of crimes recorded by the police are crimes against property. Although serious crimes of violence attract media attention, they are comparatively rare and a higher proportion of them are cleared up by the police. Home Office research demonstrates that in times of low or negative economic growth property crime rises at a faster rate and violent crime rises relatively slowly (or falls).

"....serious crimes of violence..

Crime rates can be expressed in terms of incidence (the number of crimes per head of population) or prevalence (the number of victims per head). Prevalence figures are lower than those for incidence as some people are victims more than once over a year. The BCS estimates that, of those victimised in 1993, about half were victims more than once.

Table 9.2 looks at the incidence and prevalence of household crime as measured by the BCS and its Scottish equivalent. Risks of crime are not spread evenly across the population. The likelihood of experiencing burglary and theft involving vehicles is much higher for households in inner city areas, council and rented accommodation, and flats. In general, risks are highest in the northern regions of England and lowest in the South outside London, the East Midlands and East Anglia. Elderly householders are much less at risk than other household types. Risks of contact crime - that is woundings, common assaults, robberies and "snatch" thefts from the person - are highest for men and younger people. Someone's risk of contact crime is also related to the features of their area and household type which emerge as important for household crime.

In England and Wales, an offence is said to be cleared up by primary means if a person has been charged, summonsed or cautioned, or by secondary means if the offence is admitted and could be taken into consideration by the court, or in some cases, if there is sufficient evidence to charge a person but the case is not proceeded with, for example because the victim is unable to give evidence or the offender is under the age of criminal responsibility (ten in England and Wales and Northern Ireland compared with eight in Scotland). Some offences have high clear-up rates because there is a high likelihood of the victim being able to identify the offender, for example most sexual offences, or because the knowledge of the offence directly identifies the offender, for example handling stolen goods, going equipped for stealing and trafficking in controlled drugs.

Chart 9.3 and Table 9.4 show the clear-up rates by primary and secondary means combined. In 1993, the four police forces with the highest clear-up rates through primary means alone were Gwent (35 per cent), Dyfed-Powys (31), Dorset (25) and Wiltshire (24).

..are comparatively rare...."

9.1 Notifiable offences recorded by the police[1]: by offence group, 1981 and 1993, and percentage change, 1992-1993

Rates per 100,000 population and percentages

	Violence against the person	Sexual offences	Burglary	Robbery	Theft and handling stolen goods	Fraud and forgery	Criminal damage[2]	Other[3]	Total[2,3]
1981									
North	229	36	1,861	16	3,612	155	894	10	6,813
Yorkshire & Humberside	245	46	1,608	20	3,192	140	854	18	6,122
East Midlands	265	49	1,327	19	3,160	192	746	20	5,780
East Anglia	155	38	879	11	2,750	143	510	23	4,510
South East	177	36	1,370	75	3,444	263	815	20	6,200
Greater London	218	36	1,988	154	4,683	429	1,128	29	8,666
Rest of South East	146	36	907	15	2,515	139	580	13	4,352
South West	149	36	868	14	2,507	198	508	13	4,293
West Midlands	231	43	1,566	34	3,012	137	773	15	5,810
North West	217	41	1,937	37	3,615	298	890	23	7,057
England	203	40	1,457	43	3,265	217	783	18	6,026
Wales	187	31	1,284	13	2,643	179	711	10	5,057
Scotland[4]	154	40	1,847	81	3,882	414	1,191	271	7,880
Northern Ireland	154	21	1,338	178	1,660	170	343	82	3,946
1993									
North	417	54	3,426	59	6,016	274	2,688	77	13,009
Yorkshire & Humberside	419	63	4,218	95	6,132	261	1,877	89	13,154
East Midlands	503	67	2,950	75	5,603	309	1,811	74	11,393
East Anglia	334	55	2,028	31	4,507	249	1,022	70	8,296
South East	393	68	2,120	162	5,310	361	1,783	81	10,278
Greater London	536	87	2,366	331	6,072	464	2,373	92	12,321
Rest of South East	290	55	1,944	40	4,765	287	1,361	73	8,815
South West	337	61	2,302	60	5,176	345	1,156	78	9,516
West Midlands	407	53	3,044	129	4,990	276	1,598	56	10,552
North West	367	48	2,861	133	5,521	333	1,917	100	11,281
England	397	61	2,703	118	5,410	321	1,756	80	10,846
Wales	458	63	2,136	26	4,643	253	1,969	79	9,626
Scotland[4]	270	72	1,911	109	4,891	463	1,644	1,246	10,605
Northern Ireland	282	73	964	106	2,032	340	175	87	4,058
Percentage change 1992-1993									
North	-4	3	-5	13	-5	-2	-5	23	-5
Yorkshire & Humberside	-2	7	13	18	-	5	4	-3	5
East Midlands	-1	1	12	13	-6	9	1	11	-
East Anglia	4	-5	4	-2	-5	-3	-8	-3	-3
South East	4	5	-4	2	-4	-10	3	4	-3
Greater London	5	9	-9	4	-4	-14	2	1	-4
Rest of South East	2	2	-	-9	-5	-5	4	8	-2
South West	7	23	1	30	-1	-3	8	18	1
West Midlands	-2	-	-	17	-1	12	6	-4	1
North West	1	2	-2	18	-7	-8	-4	-8	-5
England	1	5	1	9	-4	-4	1	3	-1
Wales	1	13	-4	11	-6	2	2	24	-3
Scotland[4]	-16	11	-14	-18	-8	-15	-9	8	-8
Northern Ireland	12	22	-8	-7	-3	1	14	14	-2

1 See Appendix notes.
2 The Northern Ireland figures excludes criminal damage valued at £100 or less in 1981 and £200 or less from 1992.
3 In England and Wales, offences of trafficking in controlled drugs were included only from January 1983.
4 Figures for Scotland are not comparable with those for England, Wales and Northern Ireland because of the differences in the legal system, recording practices and classification.

Source: Home Office; The Scottish Office Home and Health Department;
Royal Ulster Constabulary

9.2 Offences committed against households, 1993[1,2]

Rates and percentages

	Offences per 10,000 households[3]				Percentage of households[3] victimised at least once			
	Vandalism	Burglary[4]	Vehicle thefts[5]	All household offences[6]	Vandalism	Burglary[4]	Vehicle thefts[5]	All household offences[6]
North	1,710	962	4,168	7,168	9.8	7.6	28.8	38.7
Yorkshire & Humberside	1,707	1,167	3,130	6,895	10.3	8.8	22.0	35.5
East Midlands	1,126	612	2,425	4,573	7.3	5.1	17.6	28.5
East Anglia	1,680	654	1,650	5,236	10.7	5.4	13.1	39.6
South East	1,774	759	2,503	5,679	10.7	5.5	17.9	31.1
Greater London	1,691	1,271	3,072	6,180	10.1	8.4	21.1	31.6
Rest of South East	1,823	461	2,228	5,388	11.0	3.9	16.4	30.8
South West	1,332	656	2,521	5,206	9.4	5.2	18.5	30.7
West Midlands	1,449	869	2,978	6,196	9.5	6.6	20.0	34.6
North West	1,861	1,176	3,539	7,163	10.1	8.8	22.9	35.1
England	1,634	855	2,793	5,995	10.0	6.5	19.6	32.6
Wales	1,650	743	3,077	5,938	9.5	5.9	20.9	31.7
Scotland	1,048	607	1,188	3,716	6.5	4.9	11.4	21.9

1 See Appendix notes.
2 Data for Scotland relate to 1992.
3 The vehicle theft risks are based on owners, not households.
4 The term used in Scotland is housebreaking. The figures include attempts at burglary/housebreaking.
5 Comprises theft of vehicles, thefts from vehicles and associated attempts.
6 Comprises the three individual categories plus thefts of bicycles and other household property.

Source: British Crime Survey, Home Office; Scottish Crime Survey, The Scottish Office Home and Health Department

9.3 Notifiable offences recorded by the police and proportion cleared up[1,2] :by police force area, 1993

Offences recorded (rates per 100 population)
- 12 or over
- 10 – 11
- 8 – 9
- 7 or fewer

Offences cleared up (percentages)
- 35 or over
- 28 – 34
- 22 – 27
- 21 or under

1 See Appendix notes.
2 Excluding criminal damage valued at £20 or less in England and Wales and £200 or less in Northern Ireland.

Source: Home Office; Royal Ulster Constabulary

9.4 Notifiable offences cleared up by the police[1,2]: by offence group, 1993

Percentages

	Violence against the person	Sexual offences	Burglary	Robbery	Theft and handling stolen goods	Fraud and forgery	Criminal damage[3]	Trafficking in controlled drugs	Other[4]	Total[3,4]
North	79	84	17	29	24	58	19	99	99	25
Yorkshire & Humberside	77	73	11	27	19	47	14	90	99	19
East Midlands	80	76	23	33	26	45	18	98	99	28
East Anglia	82	79	21	38	28	53	20	83	97	29
South East	71	66	16	16	18	44	12	88	92	21
Greater London[5]	65	59	14	14	13	42	9	85	89	17
Rest of South East	78	75	17	31	23	48	16	90	96	24
South West	83	79	15	25	19	61	20	85	93	23
West Midlands	77	74	25	24	25	39	16	94	96	27
North West	73	79	30	25	33	72	21	99	95	34
England	76	73	19	21	23	51	16	91	95	25
Wales	88	93	27	50	33	54	21	100	99	34
Scotland[6]	77	77	16	27	24	75	19	100	98	34
Northern Ireland	62	74	20	15	34	62	35	93	81	36

1 See Appendix notes.
2 Some offences cleared up in 1993 may have been initially recorded in an earlier year.
3 The Northern Ireland figure excludes criminal damage valued at £200 or less.
4 The Northern Ireland figure incudes Offences against the State.
5 The Metropolitan police use a different method for assessing the clear-up rate, hence the lower figures.
6 Figures for Scotland are not comparable with those for England, Wales and Northern Ireland because of the differences in the legal system, recording practices and classification.

Source: Home Office; The Scottish Office Home and Health Department; Royal Ulster Constabulary

9.5 Firearms

Numbers

	Operations in which firearms were issued to the police[1]					Offences recorded by the police in which firearms were reported to have been used				
	1986	1990	1991	1992	1993	1986	1990	1991	1992	1993
Great Britain	2,627	2,925	3,783	4,627	5,723	10,888	11,857	14,017	15,255	15,718
North	62	229	395	386	473	561	704	755	808	740
Yorkshire & Humberside	107	239	269	487	616	1,161	1,369	1,494	1,948	2,146
East Midlands	36	54	108	109	230	973	796	904	1,078	1,044
East Anglia	46	85	186	232	171	221	361	378	413	328
South East	1,956	1,798	2,162	2,566	3,297	3,641	4,320	5,386	5,496	5,454
Greater London	1,728	1,436	1,591	1,931	2,608	2,404	2,764	3,706	3,584	3,513
Rest of South East	228	362	571	635	689	1,237	1,556	1,680	1,912	1,941
South West	63	131	157	139	157	281	300	285	263	416
West Midlands	49	117	156	266	339	1,020	949	1,063	1,328	1,372
North West	116	179	186	223	266	1,179	1,187	1,411	1,605	2,065
England	2,435	2,832	3,619	4,408	5,549	9,037	9,986	11,676	12,939	13,565
Wales	18	42	103	71	76	326	387	453	366	386
Scotland	174	51	61	148	98	1,525	1,484	1,888	1,950	1,767

1 In England and Wales, operations where police shots were fired were 1 in 1986, 3 in 1990, 5 in 1991, 12 in 1992 and 6 in 1993.

Source: Home Office; The Scottish Office Home and Health Department

9.6 Offenders found guilty or cautioned: by type of offence and age, 1981 and 1993

Rates per 100,000 population

	1981						1993					
	Violence against the person	Sexual off-ences	Burglary, robbery and theft[1]	Drugs off-ences	Other indict-able off-ences[2]	All indict-able off-ences	Violence against the person	Sexual off-ences	Burglary, robbery and theft[1]	Drugs off-ences	Other indict-able off-ences[2]	All indict-able off-ences
Age 10-13												
North	87	12	2,368	0	125	2,592	160	18	1,728	11	89	2,005
Yorkshire & Humberside	77	28	2,226	0	100	2,431	131	17	1,187	7	81	1,423
East Midlands	98	21	1,865	0	123	2,107	157	22	1,014	6	80	1,280
East Anglia	50	17	2,248	0	98	2,414	69	7	785	9	49	919
South East	40	7	1,381	-	74	1,502	70	7	760	8	59	905
Greater London	35	3	1,189	1	55	1,284	64	4	629	13	33	743
Rest of South East	43	9	1,509	0	86	1,647	75	9	847	5	76	1,012
South West	41	13	1,323	0	86	1,463	47	7	653	8	58	773
West Midlands	72	22	1,877	0	96	2,067	149	15	1,154	4	70	1,393
North West	67	12	2,233	-	86	2,397	136	19	1,031	14	80	1,279
England	61	14	1,801	-	91	1,967	106	12	963	8	68	1,159
Wales	62	14	1,754	0	111	1,941	99	12	1,098	8	103	1,319
Age 14-17												
North	437	60	4,717	11	442	5,667	780	64	4,021	278	420	5,563
Yorkshire & Humberside	453	96	4,236	10	382	5,177	641	56	3,530	230	405	4,862
East Midlands	495	110	3,783	7	418	4,812	716	81	3,043	156	288	4,284
East Anglia	371	66	3,144	35	370	3,986	489	45	2,695	329	278	3,836
South East	370	49	3,232	41	341	4,033	447	36	2,499	403	321	3,706
Greater London	455	29	3,829	76	331	4,721	448	27	2,447	604	326	3,853
Rest of South East	313	62	2,831	17	347	3,571	445	42	2,532	276	318	3,613
South West	353	62	2,877	26	361	3,679	393	44	2,327	216	235	3,215
West Midlands	409	89	3,656	12	369	4,536	628	66	3,217	177	417	4,505
North West	454	49	4,505	28	449	5,486	657	46	3,149	412	455	4,719
England	409	66	3,679	26	381	4,560	557	50	2,913	310	352	4,183
Wales	361	52	3,952	21	465	4,852	627	54	3,339	248	455	4,723
Age 18-20												
North	517	40	3,138	83	648	4,426	604	36	3,151	612	859	5,261
Yorkshire & Humberside	523	63	2,850	68	644	4,147	533	27	2,739	511	820	4,629
East Midlands	592	86	2,336	70	584	3,668	624	60	2,598	417	695	4,394
East Anglia	402	58	1,997	143	603	3,202	494	35	2,377	827	586	4,318
South East	471	38	2,506	188	630	3,833	352	29	2,231	974	662	4,248
Greater London	564	36	3,259	292	766	4,917	338	29	2,167	1,382	801	4,717
Rest of South East	402	39	1,948	111	530	3,029	361	28	2,275	700	568	3,932
South West	416	58	2,139	134	550	3,298	364	33	2,432	607	553	3,988
West Midlands	533	70	2,402	59	628	3,692	570	47	2,728	474	953	4,771
North West	527	41	3,210	112	733	4,623	552	38	3,064	896	1,084	5,635
England	496	51	2,603	127	635	3,913	471	36	2,573	744	771	4,594
Wales	461	51	2,695	121	706	4,035	668	42	3,048	699	1,051	5,507
Age 21 or over												
North	86	15	499	18	137	756	112	14	452	66	164	808
Yorkshire & Humberside	92	19	510	17	144	782	119	12	401	68	162	762
East Midlands	115	16	432	16	147	726	137	14	371	51	156	729
East Anglia	69	15	384	34	130	633	99	13	370	82	152	716
South East	75	17	440	56	168	756	74	14	378	122	165	753
Greater London	92	21	553	97	213	976	77	16	449	188	225	955
Rest of South East	63	14	355	25	133	590	71	12	326	74	122	606
South West	63	16	387	27	139	633	72	12	339	82	126	631
West Midlands	95	16	441	16	150	718	129	18	393	58	184	782
North West	92	18	561	24	173	868	112	16	539	107	223	997
England	84	17	461	34	156	752	98	14	403	92	170	776
Wales	80	14	466	27	162	749	127	16	420	100	197	861

1 Includes handling stolen goods.
2 Includes fraud and forgery.

Source: Home Office

9.7 Offences resulting in a police caution[1,2]: by offence group and age, 1993

Percentages

	Violence against the person	Sexual offences	Burglary	Robbery	Theft and handling stolen goods	Fraud and forgery	Criminal damage	Drug offences	Other indict-able offences	Total indict-able offences	Summary offences[3]
Persons aged 10-17											
North	64	69	46	15	74	73	45	86	28	66	63
Yorkshire & Humberside	67	72	50	19	78	78	39	84	30	68	73
East Midlands	69	78	53	33	80	72	63	86	36	72	72
East Anglia	69	84	54	21	85	80	59	91	28	77	77
South East	72	78	56	33	84	81	73	92	43	77	76
Greater London	70	59	46	29	79	81	32	91	39	71	77
Rest of South East	74	85	63	43	87	81	82	92	48	82	75
South West	68	79	60	38	87	77	71	95	33	79	69
West Midlands	66	75	59	40	82	85	48	88	29	72	72
North West	69	71	54	23	77	76	68	87	31	70	70
England	69	75	54	30	81	79	61	90	34	73	72
Wales	56	79	56	37	76	66	61	91	24	68	66
Persons aged 18 or over											
North	19	30	6	1	30	22	4	48	3	23	11
Yorkshire & Humberside	26	26	5	1	29	20	5	40	4	22	7
East Midlands	31	35	7	1	34	27	8	48	6	27	8
East Anglia	24	30	8	5	35	17	4	63	5	30	10
South East	36	38	8	2	39	31	22	62	7	36	19
Greater London	34	37	5	1	38	33	4	64	6	35	24
Rest of South East	37	39	10	4	41	29	34	58	8	36	10
South West	30	37	9	2	41	31	25	65	10	36	11
West Midlands	27	41	12	2	40	36	11	58	9	31	14
North West	29	40	6	-	31	28	28	53	3	27	18
England	30	37	8	2	36	29	16	57	6	31	15
Wales	11	17	4	1	26	13	10	55	7	21	9

1 Persons who on admission of guilt were given formal oral cautions by the police.
2 Those cautioned as a percentage of persons found guilty or cautioned.
3 Excluding motoring offences for which written warnings were issued.

Source: Home Office

9.8 Persons[1] against whom charge proved at courts in Scotland: by sentence[2], 1993

Percentages and numbers

	Absolute discharge	Admon-isment/ caution	Fine	Probation	Immediate custodial sentence	Otherwise dealt with	Total (= 100%) (numbers)
High court							
Crimes	1	4	2	6	82	5	1,090
Offences	6	8	12	9	56	8	97
Sheriff courts							
Crimes	-	11	43	10	24	13	34,130
Offences	-	9	77	3	7	4	48,140
District courts							
Crimes	-	17	66	3	11	3	17,074
Offences	-	10	88	-	1	-	61,049

1 Including companies.
2 See Appendix notes.

Souce: The Scottish Office Home and Health Department

9.9 Persons[1] found guilty of indictable[2] and summary offences[3]: by court and type of sentence[4], 1993

	Result as a percentage of number of persons sentenced						Persons convicted	
	Absolute or conditional discharge	Fine	All community penalties	Fully suspended sentence	Immediate custodial sentence[5]	Otherwise dealt with	Rate[6]	Numbers (= 100%)
Crown Court: indictable offences								
North	8	5	35	3	45	3	1.5	4,180
Yorkshire & Humberside	7	5	40	2	42	4	1.7	7,216
East Midlands	6	5	32	4	52	2	1.4	4,798
East Anglia	6	5	31	3	51	3	1.1	2,048
South East	6	7	33	3	49	2	1.3	20,390
Greater London	6	7	34	3	48	2	1.9	12,136
Rest of South East	5	6	32	4	51	2	0.9	8,254
South West	6	6	39	2	43	3	1.0	4,032
West Midlands	6	4	33	2	53	2	1.4	6,340
North West	6	4	33	3	51	2	2.0	11,092
England	6	5	34	3	49	2	1.4	60,096
Wales	7	4	34	2	51	2	1.6	3,974
Northern Ireland	2	3	11	22	62	1	0.8	1,117
Magistrates' Courts: indictable offences								
North	29	37	26	-	6	2	6.9	18,549
Yorkshire & Humberside	26	37	27	-	5	3	6.1	26,305
	26	36	27	-	6	4	5.4	19,265
East Anglia	24	44	23	-	5	4	5.1	9,319
South East	25	44	23	-	6	3	4.5	69,335
Greater London	22	49	20	-	6	2	5.3	34,087
Rest of South East	27	39	25	-	5	3	3.9	35,248
South West	26	38	27	-	6	2	4.0	16,789
West Midlands	25	41	26	-	6	2	5.6	25,416
North West	28	41	23	-	6	2	7.0	38,914
England	26	41	25	-	6	3	5.3	223,892
Wales	28	45	20	-	5	2	7.1	17,967
Northern Ireland	18	31	16	17	17	1	5.7	7,798
Magistrates' Courts: summary offences								
North	12	83	2	-	1	2	13.4	36,188
Yorkshire & Humberside	11	84	3	-	1	2	9.6	41,706
East Midlands	11	82	3	-	1	3	9.5	33,690
East Anglia	10	85	2	-	0	3	7.8	14,311
South East	9	87	2	-	1	1	10.1	156,604
Greater London	8	88	2	-	1	1	14.1	90,999
Rest of South East	10	85	3	-	1	2	7.3	65,605
South West	12	80	4	-	1	2	6.6	27,833
West Midlands	9	86	3	-	1	1	9.8	44,665
North West	12	82	3	-	1	2	10.6	58,506
England	10	84	3	-	1	2	9.8	413,503
Wales	10	86	2	-	0	1	13.6	34,371
Northern Ireland	13	55	4	7	3	18	3.1	4,302

1 Companies etc. are included for Northern Ireland.
2 Includes indictable motoring offences.
3 Excludes summary motoring offences.
4 See Appendix notes.
5 Includes Young Offender Institutions and unsuspended imprisonment.
6 Rate per 1,000 population aged 10 or over.

Source: Home Office; Northern Ireland Office

9.10 Seizures of controlled drugs[1]: by type of drug, 1993[2]

Number of seizures

	Class A drugs					Class B drugs		
	Heroin	Cocaine	LSD	MDMA (Ecstasy)	All class A drugs[3]	Cannabis	Ampheta-mines	All class B drugs[3]
United Kingdom	3,679	2,983	2,513	2,341	12,102	69,349	11,639	77,068
North	76	28	151	111	394	2,568	822	3,139
Yorkshire & Humberside	241	90	203	163	719	3,741	1,087	4,461
East Midlands	78	77	196	113	460	3,205	870	3,790
East Anglia	36	10	43	35	134	1,205	241	1,359
South East	1,488	1,932	690	978	5,251	24,145	3,340	26,384
Greater London	1,346	1,813	411	660	4,361	15,582	1,903	17,007
Rest of South East	142	119	279	318	890	8,563	1,437	9,377
South West	185	65	232	247	799	5,053	1,087	5,673
West Midlands	103	101	152	120	483	4,218	615	4,621
North West	732	140	226	232	1,336	6,553	1,325	7,495
England	3,225	2,917	1,962	2,027	10,523	57,195	9,589	63,589
Wales	86	21	156	55	353	3,806	663	4,165
Scotland	366	43	338	205	1,126	7,875	1,314	8,790
Northern Ireland	2	2	57	54	100	473	73	524

1 See Appendix notes.
2 Seizures of drugs made by Custom and Excise are included against each country but not counted against each region.
3 Since a seizure may involve more than one type of drug, and drugs other than those listed are included, figures for individual drugs cannot be added together to produce totals.

Source: Home Office

9.11 Persons found guilty, cautioned or dealt with by compounding[1] for drug offences: by type of drug, 1993

Rates per 100,000 population

	Class A drugs					Class B drugs		
	Heroin	Cocaine	LSD	MDMA (Ecstasy)	All class A drugs	Cannabis	Ampheta-mines	All class B drugs
United Kingdom	4	3	3	3	13	99	13	109
North	1	1	5	4	11	74	17	86
Yorkshire & Humberside	5	1	5	4	16	80	19	93
East Midlands	-	1	3	2	8	60	11	70
East Anglia	2	2	3	3	12	103	15	112
South East	5	5	3	4	17	133	12	142
Greater London	10	10	4	6	31	211	13	222
Rest of South East	1	1	2	2	8	83	11	91
South West	2	2	3	3	11	88	16	101
West Midlands	1	1	3	2	8	67	10	73
North West	10	2	4	3	20	119	17	135
England	4	4	3	3	15	106	14	116
Wales	2	5	3	1	13	113	15	123
Scotland	2	-	2	2	7	58	10	66
Northern Ireland	-	-	2	1	7	13	2	14

1 HM Customs and Excise cases dealt with by the payment of a penalty in lieu of prosecution. Persons so dealt with are included against each country but are not counted against each region.

Source: Home Office

9.12 Offences[1] of driving etc after consuming alcohol or drugs[2]: custodial sentences and average fines, 1987 and 1993

	1987					1993				
	Total pro- ceedings (numbers)	Total findings of guilt (numbers)	Percentage attracting custodial sentence	Average length of sentence (months)	Average fine(£)[3]	Total pro- ceedings (numbers)	Total findings of guilt (numbers)	Percentage attracting custodial sentence	Average length of sentence (months)	Average fine(£)[3]
United Kingdom	147,576	131,205	2.9	3.0	229	119,863	104,122	4.1	3.1	244
North	7,649	6,784	3.3	3.2	179	6,360	5,651	4.3	3.3	199
Yorkshire & Humberside	14,606	12,900	3.7	2.8	226	9,513	8,439	5.7	3.0	267
East Midlands	9,292	8,415	3.6	2.9	225	6,837	5,791	7.0	2.3	279
East Anglia	3,856	3,570	2.3	2.5	228	3,134	2,829	3.6	3.1	267
South East	48,486	41,595	2.5	2.9	251	37,932	32,076	4.6	2.9	268
Greater London	22,988	18,851	2.2	3.0	251	18,610	15,094	5.5	2.9	257
Rest of South East	25,498	22,744	2.7	2.9	251	19,322	16,982	3.7	3.0	277
South West	10,080	9,203	2.9	2.7	221	8,007	7,128	4.0	3.2	247
West Midlands	12,578	11,003	3.2	3.0	222	12,034	10,421	5.7	3.3	240
North West	15,844	14,292	3.7	2.9	217	15,047	13,330	5.8	3.0	242
England	122,391	107,762	3.0	2.9	231	98,864	85,665	5.1	3.0	255
Wales	8,142	7,331	2.3	3.4	202	6,294	5,533	4.0	3.5	218
Scotland[4]	13,000	12,409	3.1	3.2	229	9,943	9,117	3.8	3.3	232
Northern Ireland	4,043	3,703	1.2	7.2	86	4,762	3,807	1.5	5.7	97

1 The table relates to the total number of offences of which people were found guilty, not the number of people.
2 See Appendix notes.
3 Where a fine was the principle penalty. Figures for 1987 relate to the average fine revalued to 1993 prices as estimated by the general index of retail prices.
4 Data for 1987 include 20 cases where the length of sentence is not known and 368 cases where the amount of the fine is not known. Corresponding figures for 1993 are 17 and 60 cases respectively.

Source: Home Office; The Scottish Office Home and Health Department;
Royal Ulster Constabulary

9.13 Persons aged 21 or over sentenced to immediate imprisonment: by length of sentence imposed for principal offence, 1987 and 1993

Percentages and numbers

	1987				1993			
	Length of sentence			Number of persons sentenced to immediate imprisonment (= 100%)	Length of sentence			Number of persons sentenced to immediate imprisonment (= 100%)
	One year or less	Over 1 year but less than 4 years	4 years and over		One year or less	Over 1 year but less than 4 years	4 years and over	
United Kingdom	73	21	6	59,163	75	18	8	55,518
North	73	22	5	2,907	71	21	7	2,445
Yorkshire & Humberside	72	22	6	4,735	72	21	7	3,917
East Midlands	68	26	7	3,519	73	20	7	3,382
East Anglia	69	26	5	1,526	69	24	8	1,367
South East	67	24	9	17,508	69	21	10	14,825
Greater London	66	24	10	10,375	70	20	10	8,759
Rest of South East	68	24	8	7,133	68	22	11	6,066
South West	74	22	4	2,998	77	17	6	2,799
West Midlands	66	27	7	5,100	72	22	7	4,360
North West	74	21	6	7,554	74	19	7	7,575
England	69	23	7	45,847	71	20	8	40,670
Wales	72	24	4	2,174	73	20	7	2,510
Scotland	90	6	3	9,293	89	7	4	10,763
Northern Ireland	75	17	8	1,849	72	15	13	1,575

Source: Home Office; The Scottish Office Home and Health Department;
Northern Ireland Office

9.14 Police manpower: by type, 1993[1]

| | Regular police[2] | | | | | Special constables and civilian staff (rates per 1,000 regular police) | | |
| | | Percentage of which | | Population per officer[3] | Hectares per officer | Special con- stables[4] | Civilian staff[5] | Traffic wardens (numbers) |
	Number	Ethnic minorities	Women officers					
United Kingdom[6]	151,332	1.3	12.6	383	160	158	374	5,694
North	7,577	0.6	11.7	409	203	166	354	194
Yorkshire & Humberside	11,364	1.3	12.3	440	136	187	367	334
East Midlands	8,349	2.2	12.2	487	187	249	364	259
East Anglia	3,916	0.9	11.7	533	321	262	368	124
South East	49,273	1.8	13.9	359	55	112	457	2,602
Metropolitan Police	27,605	2.4	14.0	268	7	59	528	1,750
City of London	884	1.2	13.2	4	-	101	361	61
Other forces in S.E.	20,784	1.0	13.8	496	121	183	366	791
South West	9,647	0.6	11.9	492	247	284	388	420
West Midlands	12,251	2.4	15.3	431	106	218	363	372
North West	16,723	1.4	13.6	383	44	117	353	504
England	119,100	1.6	13.3	406	110	163	402	4,809
Wales	6,438	0.5	10.6	450	323	188	351	190
Scotland[7]	14,139	0.2	11.0	362	545	134	286	545
Northern Ireland[8]	11,655	..	8.1	140	122	119	208	150

1 At 31 December.
2 Includes full-time Reserves in Northern Ireland.
3 Based on mid-1992 population estimates.
4 These are part-time Reserves in Northern Ireland.
5 Part-time staff counted as half full-time except for the Metropolitan Police which is actual full-time equivalent.
6 Great Britain for ethnic minorities.
7 For traffic wardens, part-time staff are counted as half full-time.
8 The figure for civilian staff relates to those who work to the Chief Constable and not to those who work to the Police Authority for Northern Ireland.

Source: Home Office; The Scottish Office Home and Health Department; Royal Ulster Constabulary

9.15 Fear of crime and feelings of insecurity: by gender, 1994[1,2]

Percentages

| | Worry about falling victim of specific crimes: percentage feeling 'very' worried | | | | | | | Feelings of insecurity, walking alone at night: percentage feeling 'very' or 'fairly' unsafe | | | |
| | Theft of a car[3] | | Burglary | | Mugging | | Rape | Men | | Women | |
	Men	Women	Men	Women	Men	Women	Women	16-59	60 or over	16-59	60 or over
North	38	40	27	42	16	34	27	11	33	52	66
Yorkshire & Humberside	33	34	30	34	16	32	28	12	31	49	67
East Midlands	25	33	18	31	9	27	20	11	15	47	53
East Anglia	25	21	15	17	10	20	23	9	21	50	54
South East	24	25	19	27	12	28	26	12	29	51	69
Greater London	25	27	24	31	16	33	32	17	35	54	67
Rest of South East	23	24	17	25	11	24	23	10	26	49	70
South West	23	21	16	23	9	20	22	9	23	41	60
West Midlands	33	35	28	35	18	31	26	15	31	55	65
North West	26	31	22	32	14	34	27	14	36	52	60
England	27	29	22	30	13	29	25	12	28	50	64
Wales	35	38	20	31	13	28	24	13	31	51	62
Scotland	..	..	16	24	11	25	30	19	37	48	60

1 See Appendix notes.
2 Data for Scotland relate to 1993.
3 Base excludes 'not applicable' and 'don't know' responses.

Source: British Crime Survey, Home Office; Scottish Crime Survey, The Scottish Office Home and Health Department

10 Transport

Cars

New car registrations in the West Midlands in 1994 were 13 per cent higher than in 1993, while in Scotland and East Anglia they were down by 2 and 3 per cent respectively.

(Table 10.1)

Three quarters of all households in East Anglia have access to a car, compared with only three fifths of households in the North.

(Table 10.2)

Road accidents

Within Great Britain, the fall in fatal and serious road casualties between the average for 1981-1985 and 1993 ranged from 24 per cent in the North West to 51 per cent in the South West.

(Table 10.3)

On average, people in the North and Wales are least likely to be involved in a fatal or serious road accident, while those in East Anglia are the most likely.

(Table 10.4)

Buses

Apart from London, households in the North and the North West have the most frequent bus services on average, while those in East Anglia have the least frequent.

(Table 10.5)

Journeys

On average, people living in Wales travel the shortest distance to work, while those in the South East commute the furthest.

(Chart 10.6)

Someone living in East Anglia travels an average of 2,200 miles per year more - that is 40 per cent further - than someone living in the North.

(Tables 10.7 and 10.8)

A third of all travel in the South East is for commuting or business purposes compared with less than a quarter in the South West.

(Table 10.7)

People in the East Midlands and Wales travelled, on average, more than 30 per cent further each year between 1991 and 1993 than they had done in 1985/86, double the increase travelled in the North and Yorkshire and Humberside.

(Table 10.8)

Expenditure on roads

Kilometre for kilometre, more money is spent on roads in the South East than in any other region of England and Wales.

(Table 10.9)

Freight traffic

Over half the freight carried by rail in 1993-94 started its journey in Yorkshire and Humberside or in the East Midlands.

(Table 10.10)

Introduction

The transport chapter has a dual nature: it is concerned with both social and economic policy. Whether or not people have access to transport is a social indicator, while transport is an important factor in the economy of a region.

Table 10.1 looks at the trend in the number of cars licensed. In 1992 the source for this information within Great Britain changed from the Annual Vehicle Census conducted by the Driver and Vehicle Licensing Agency to the Vehicle Information Database held by the Department of Transport . Minor technical changes in the methods used to determine if vehicles were properly licensed on "census" day were introduced with the change of source. Under the new system, more careful examination is made of vehicles that had complicated licensing histories, for example late payment, cheques that failed to clear, changes in taxation class, refunds or incorrect levels of duty paid.

In addition, there was a change involving vehicles where the keeper was unknown or not properly registered. Previously such vehicles were allocated to counties and regions on the basis of the previous keeper. The new system created a separate category for 'address of current keeper unknown'. These vehicles are therefore included in the United Kingdom total, but not in the regions. The result of these two changes is a small decrease in the estimated licensed stock. Figures for 1992 are shown on both the old and new basis for comparison. Neither the new registration data nor the stock data for Northern Ireland are affected by these changes.

The Government has adopted a target of reducing the total number of road casualties in Great Britain by a third from the 1981-1985 baseline average by the year 2000. Tables 10.3 and 10.4, which look at serious and fatal road casualties, and fatal and serious road accidents respectively, therefore compare data for 1993, the latest year available, with the 1981-1985 average.

Motorways are the safest roads on which to travel, with only a small proportion of accidents occurring on them: in 1993, 3 per cent of accidents in Great Britain as a whole were on motorways, 9 per cent were on trunk roads, 38 per cent on principal roads and the remaining 50 per cent on other roads. There were, of course, regional variations in these proportions. For example, motorways accounted for nearly 5 per

"Motorways are the safest

cent of all accidents in the South East region excluding London, compared with only 1 per cent in London and less than 2 per cent in the Northern region, Scotland and Wales. However, this does not automatically mean that motorways located in the South East outside of London are more dangerous than motorways elsewhere. There are two factors to bear in mind when making regional comparisons of this kind: firstly the length of different types of road within a region and secondly the amount of traffic using those different road types. The North, Wales and Scotland each has only a small share of the motorway network in Great Britain relative to their size. Together they account for 562 kilometres of motorway - 18 per cent of the total network - while there are 567 kilometres just in the South East outside London. And looking at the distribution of traffic on our major roads, only around 14 per cent of traffic in the North, Wales and Scotland is on motorways, less than half the proportion in the South East outside London. The Appendix notes contain further points to consider in making regional comparisons of road accidents.

Several of the tables in this chapter are drawn from the National Travel Survey, a household survey designed to provide information on personal travel in Great Britain. Table 10.8 shows that the average distance travelled in Great Britain over the period 1991-1993 was just under 6,500 miles per person, 22 per cent higher than the average in 1985/86. Again there were regional variations around this average. Time spent travelling averaged 361 hours (or 15 days) per person per year, across the country as a whole. This was only 7 per cent higher than the average time spent travelling in 1985/ 86 (337 hours or 14 days). The increase in mileage travelled since 1985/86 is therefore mainly due to the increased use of faster forms of transport such as the car, as well as increases in the average speeds of the various modes of travel.

Ownership of a car may be an indication of wealth, but it may equally reflect need - for example in rural areas. The proportion of adults licensed to drive a car continues to rise. Over the period 1991-1993, 81 per cent of men and 53 per cent of women in Great Britain held a full driving licence. Not surprisingly, the South West which has the highest proportion of households with access to a car, had the highest proportion of adults with a full licence - 89 per cent of men and 60 per cent of women. Similarly, the regions with the lowest proportions of households with a car - namely the North, Yorkshire and Humberside and Scotland - had the lowest proportions of adults with a full driving licence.

roads on which to travel...."

10.1 Motor cars currently licensed and new registrations

Thousands

	Currently licensed[1]					New registrations				
	1981	1991	1992[2]	1992[2,3]	1993[3]	1981	1991[3]	1992[3]	1993[3]	1994[3]
United Kingdom	15,701	20,727	21,174	20,937	21,256	1,524	1,666	1,664	1,846	1,983
North	699	920	945	917	931	68	68	70	77	79
Yorkshire & Humberside	1,185	1,605	1,653	1,607	1,632	124	114	114	126	131
East Midlands	1,030	1,408	1,440	1,398	1,423	96	113	113	130	138
East Anglia	604	864	876	853	856	55	67	64	65	63
South East	5,336	6,827	6,930	6,730	6,829a	535	582	568	626	689
Greater London	1,966	2,357	2,362	2,287	2,302	216	247	235	245	274
Rest of South East	3,370	4,470	4,568	4,443	4,527	319	335	334	381	415
South West	1,427	1,922	1,967	1,916	1,948	110	109	113	113	120
West Midlands	1,496	2,038	2,083	2,023	2,067	145	192	195	215	244
North West	1,615	2,145	2,184	2,120	2,176	152	163	165	190	210
England	13,392	17,729	18,078	17,565	17,862	1,284	1,408	1,401	1,542	1,674
Wales	753	992	1,016	981	974	59	56	57	66	67
Scotland	1,119	1,532	1,587	1,537	1,574	126	127	130	146	143
Northern Ireland	437	474	493	493	500	55	66	65	69	77

1 At 31 December.
2 The definition of vehicles licensed changed in Great Britain in 1992. See introductory text.
3 Figure for United Kingdom includes motor vehicles where the county of the registered keeper is unknown.

Source: Annual Vehicle Census/ Vehicle Information Database, Department of Transport;
Department of the Environment, Northern Ireland

10.2 Household ownership of cars[1] and vehicle age

Percentages and numbers

	1981			1986			1993		
	Percentage of households with regular use of			Percentage of households with regular use of			Percentage of households with regular use of		
	One car only	Two or more cars	Average vehicle age (years)[2]	One car only	Two or more cars	Average vehicle age (years)[2]	One car only	Two or more cars	Average vehicle age (years)[2]
Great Britain	45	15	6.1	45	18	5.4	45	23	6.7
North	41	10	5.4	41	11	5.5	43	17	6.3
Yorkshire & Humberside	43	12	5.5	43	13	5.5	46	19	6.3
East Midlands	47	15	6.0	47	18	6.0	47	22	6.8
East Anglia	51	18	6.3	50	19	6.2	53	22	7.0
South East	46	19	6.3	45	21	6.1	44	27	6.9
Greater London	42	14	6.1	42	15	5.9	42	20	6.9
Rest of South East	48	22	6.4	48	26	6.2	45	31	6.9
South West	51	18	7.1	50	22	7.0	46	28	7.3
West Midlands	46	16	6.0	42	17	6.1	43	23	6.3
North West	42	13	5.7	43	16	5.7	43	21	6.4
England	45	16	6.1	45	18	5.4	45	24	6.8
Wales	47	15	6.3	48	15	6.3	46	24	6.9
Scotland	40	11	5.0	41	13	5.0	44	16	5.9
Northern Ireland	46	14	..	48	14	..	46	20	4.3

1 Includes cars and light vans normally available to the household.
2 Average vehicle age is computed using year of first registration.

Source: Department of Transport; Department of Finance and Personnel, Northern Ireland; Department of the
Environment , Northern Ireland

10.3 Fatal and serious road casualties[1]: by type of road user, 1993 and percentage change over 1981-1985 average[2]

Numbers and percentages

	Pedestrians		Pedal cyclists		Motor cyclists & their passengers		Other drivers & their passengers		All road users	
	1993	% change over 1981-85 average	1993	% change over 1981-85 average	1993	% change over 1981-85 average	1993	% change over 1981-85 average	1993	% change over 1981-85 average
Great Britain	12,658	-33	3,796	-37	6,879	-67	25,491	-26	48,824	-39
North	779	-21	164	-23	203	-75	1,032	-29	2,178	-37
Yorkshire & Humberside	1,206	-30	387	-21	583	-68	2,427	-22	4,603	-33
East Midlands	760	-36	301	-41	614	-66	2,265	-21	3,940	-38
East Anglia	344	-25	263	-35	391	-65	1,462	-19	2,460	-35
South East	4,012	-33	1,295	-37	2,488	-63	7,679	-23	15,474	-38
Greater London	2,303	-28	511	-14	946	-50	2,659	+4	6,419	-22
Rest of South East	1,709	-39	784	-46	1,542	-68	5,020	-33	9,055	-45
South West	744	-42	320	-48	742	-72	2,110	-39	3,916	-51
West Midlands	1,191	-37	324	-44	612	-68	2,387	-32	4,514	-43
North West	1,709	-17	392	-21	589	-61	2,015	-7	4,705	-24
England	10,745	-31	3,446	-36	6,222	-66	21,377	-24	41,790	-38
Wales	465	-42	118	-42	257	-71	1,350	-31	2,190	-43
Scotland	1,448	-45	232	-50	400	-71	2,764	-37	4,844	-46
Northern Ireland	415	..	59	..	112	..	1,282	..	1,868	-21

1 See Appendix notes.
2 Used as a basis for the government target of reducing total road casualties in Great Britain by a third by the year 2000.

Source: Department of Transport; Welsh Office; The Scottish Office Environment Department; Royal Ulster Constabulary

10.4 Fatal and serious road accidents[1], 1981-1985 average[2] and 1993

Numbers and rates

	1981-1985 average			1993			
	Total	Per 100,000 population	Per 100,000 vehicles[1]	Total	Per 100,000 population	Per 100,000 vehicles[1]	Per billion vehicle kms[3]
Great Britain	67,839	124	336	41,502	73	174	81
North	2,930	94	322	1,876	60	169	68
Yorkshire & Humberside	5,714	116	353	3,810	76	188	88
East Midlands	5,334	138		3,289	81	189	83
East Anglia	3,075	160	354	1,984	95	185	85
South East	21,566	126	310	13,565	76	169	89
Greater London	7,588	112	304	5,842	84	218	201
Rest of South East	13,978	136	314	7,723	71	145	58
South West	6,697	151	339	3,290	69	138	62
West Midlands	6,525	126	337	3,769	71	153	75
North West	5,503	86	265	4,168	65	163	74
England	57,344	122	323	35,751	74	167	81
Wales	3,083	110	314	1,748	60	179	71
Scotland	7,412	144	510	4,003	78	254	90
Northern Ireland	..	..	..	1,378	85	234	95

1 See Appendix notes.
2 Used as a basis for the government target of reducing road casualties in Great Britain by a third by the year 2000.
3 Major roads only, ie motorways, A(M)roads and A roads.

Source: Department of Transport; Welsh Office, The Scottish Office Environment Department; Royal Ulster Constabulary

10.5 Frequency of bus service, 1985-86 and 1991-1993[1]

Percentages[2]

	At least every 15 minutes		At least every 30 minutes		At least every hour		At least daily		Less than daily		Don't know	
	1985-86	1991-1993	1985-86	1991-1993	1985-86	1991-1993	1985-86	1991-1993	1985-86	1991-1993	1985-86	1991-1993
Great Britain	28	33	36	33	16	13	10	7	1	2	8	13
North	35	47	40	31	14	7	5	4	2	0	5	12
Yorkshire & Humberside	34	29	35	41	16	12	8	4	1	0	6	14
East Midlands	18	22	37	30	21	22	11	12	1	4	11	11
East Anglia	15	18	20	20	22	17	25	18	8	7	10	20
South East	27	35	38	31	16	14	8	6	1	1	10	14
Greater London	51	64	39	27	3	2	0	0	0	0	7	8
Rest of South East	13	18	37	33	24	21	13	9	1	1	12	18
South West	19	28	25	25	21	17	21	14	4	4	10	12
West Midlands	31	36	36	34	14	9	8	5	2	3	9	13
North West	39	38	41	42	10	9	3	2	0	0	6	9
England	28	33	36	32	16	13	9	7	1	2	9	13
Wales	10	24	41	32	25	17	14	11	1	3	9	14
Scotland	31	37	38	34	15	11	10	8	0	1	6	8

1 Data for three year period combined. See Appendix notes.
2 Percentage of households with bus service.

Source: National Travel Survey, Department of Transport

10.6 Travel to work[1]: average distance travelled and time taken, 1991-1993

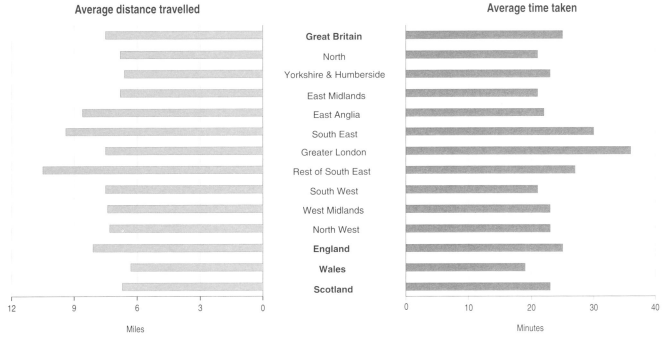

Average distance travelled   **Average time taken**

1 By region of residence. See Appendix notes.

Source: National Travel Survey, Department of Transport

10.7 Distance travelled per person per year[1]: by journey purpose, 1991-1993[2]

Percentages and miles

	Commuting	Business	Education	Shopping	Other personal business	Leisure	Total distance travelled (=100%) (miles)
Great Britain	19	10	3	12	14	42	6,473
North	18	9	3	15	15	40	5,342
Yorkshire & Humberside	17	9	2	14	13	45	5,516
East Midlands	15	12	3	12	15	43	6,822
East Anglia	21	11	4	13	13	38	7,561
South East	21	12	3	11	13	41	7,133
Greater London	21	9	3	9	13	45	5,423
Rest of South East	21	13	3	11	13	39	8,168
South West	15	9	3	11	15	46	7,240
West Midlands	19	10	3	11	12	45	6,169
North West	20	9	2	13	14	42	5,723
England	19	11	3	12	14	42	6,567
Wales	14	11	3	15	14	42	6,093
Scotland	17	9	3	13	14	43	5,788

1 Figures relate to region of residence of the traveller and therefore some journeys may have been undertaken outside of this region.
2 See Appendix notes.

Source: National Travel Survey, Department of Transport

10.8 Distance travelled per person per year[1]: by mode of transport[2], 1991-1993[3]

Miles and percentages

	Walk		Cars & other road vehicles[4]		Bus & coach		Rail & other public[5]		All modes of transport	
	1991/93	Percentage change 1985/86-1991/93	1991/93	Percentage change 1985/86-1991/93	1991/93	Percentage change 1985/86-1991/93	1991/93	Percentage change 1985/86-1991/93	1991/93	Percentage change 1985/86-1991/93
Great Britain	212	-13	5,489	27	368	-10	405	13	6,473	22
North	228	-3	4,265	19	..	..	..	..	5,342	15
Yorkshire & Humberside	198	-28	4,579	23	511	-18	..	..	5,516	15
East Midlands	233	-2	6,144	37	..	..	..	..	6,822	32
East Anglia	191	-7	6,621	19	..	..	..	..	7,561	23
South East	210	-13	5,894	23	299	-	730	2	7,133	18
Greater London	246	-13	3,953	11	408	-2	816	1	5,423	7
Rest of South East	189	-14	7,068	29	233	1	678	2	8,168	24
South West	206	-4	6,483	25	..	..	..	..	7,240	22
West Midlands	188	-14	5,458	25	371	9	..	..	6,169	21
North West	227	-10	4,845	32	415	-16	..	..	5,723	22
England	211	-12	5,581	26	354	-9	421	12	6,567	21
Wales	169	-24	5,462	40	..	..	..	..	6,093	31
Scotland	247	-14	4,615	33	553	-5	..	..	5,788	24

1 Figures relate to region of residence of the traveller and therefore some journeys may have been undertaken outside of this region.
2 Sample sizes in some regions are too small to provide reliable bus/rail estimates.
3 See Appendix notes.
4 Includes other private transport.
5 Includes London Underground and other forms of public transport.

Source: National Travel Survey, Department of Transport

10.9 Public expenditure on roads, 1992-93

£ million

	Motorways and trunk roads				Local roads			
	New construction and improvement	Public lighting and maintenance	Total	Expenditure per 1,000 kilometres	New construction and improvement	Public lighting and maintenance	Total	Expenditure per 1,000 kilometres
North	49.2	37.2	86.4	88.9	50.0	98.8	148.8	6.7
Yorkshire & Humberside	56.1	99.2	155.3	146.0	107.2	141.6	248.8	8.8
East Midlands	86.6	49.8	136.4	96.6	69.4	108.9	178.3	6.5
East Anglia	120.2	27.2	147.4	169.0	37.8	69.5	107.3	5.4
South East	627.3	251.0	878.3	327.2	390.8	521.0	911.8	13.4
Greater London	125.9	82.5	208.4	510.8	86.7	239.1	325.8	25.2
Rest of South East	501.4	168.5	669.9	294.3	304.1	281.9	586.0	10.6
South West	117.8	54.1	171.9	122.7	88.4	147.4	235.8	5.0
West Midlands	166.1	70.0	236.1	188.4	97.9	134.3	232.2	8.0
North West	100.8	73.9	174.7	180.7	128.8	175.6	304.4	12.1
England	1,324.2	662.4	1,986.6	186.9	970.3	1,397.1	2,367.4	8.9
Wales	176.2	23.2	199.4	116.6	103.3	136.4	239.7	7.5
Northern Ireland[1]	..	..	..	..	24.0	66.8	140.3	5.8

1 Figures for motorways and trunk roads are included in local roads total.

Source: Department of Transport; Welsh Office; Department of the Environment, Northern Ireland

10.10 Road haulage[1] and rail freight traffic[2]

Million tonnes

	Road haulage						Rail freight				
	1989	1990	1991	1992	1993	1994	1989-90	1990-91	1991-92	1992-93	1993-94
Loading region											
United Kingdom	1,742	1,686	1,547	1,505	1,575	1,641	142.6	137.7	135.4	122.0	102.4
North	103	104	97	86	90	102	14.2	14.2	12.9	11.9	8.8
Yorkshire & Humberside	172	179	179	176	182	186	36.0	36.1	42.9	41.0	34.5
East Midlands	178	167	149	145	155	165	29.3	28.2	25.9	24.2	20.4
East Anglia	92	89	83	80	86	83	2.2	2.0	1.6	1.3	1.5
South East	383	376	313	309	313	343	9.6	8.6	5.8	4.8	5.2
Greater London	93	104	74	67	76	80	3.3	3.6	2.7	2.2	1.6
Rest of South East	290	272	239	242	237	263	6.3	5.0	3.1	2.6	3.6
South West	149	131	136	120	122	129	12.2	9.9	9.9	9.3	9.0
West Midlands	178	164	143	142	157	152	7.3	6.4	6.1	4.5	3.5
North West	181	180	165	162	171	185	7.9	8.2	7.4	5.5	3.3
England	1,436	1,390	1,265	1,220	1,278	1,347	118.6	113.6	112.5	102.6	86.2
Wales	113	95	92	87	89	96	14.5	14.2	13.7	12.2	11.2
Scotland	154	160	148	157	158	155	9.4	9.8	9.0	7.0	5.0
Northern Ireland	39	41	42	41	50	43	0.0	0.0	0.0	0.0	0.0

1 Traffic carried by UK registered vehicles only. International road haulage is considered to be loaded at the port of entry. Includes weight of containers.
2 Excludes international traffic. Includes weight of containers.

Source: Department of Transport

11 Environment

Weather

Average rainfall in the north and west of the United Kingdom is about double that for the rest of the country.

(Chart 11.1)

Water pollution

Within England and Wales, the South Western region and Wales have the cleanest rivers and canals overall.

(Table 11.2)

In 1993, prosecutions for water pollution incidents were more likely in Northern Ireland than elsewhere in the United Kingdom.

(Table 11.3)

The North West coastal region has the poorest record of bathing waters complying with EC standards, while Northern Ireland, South Western and Anglian regions have the best records.

(Table 11.4)

Air pollution

Black smoke and sulphur dioxide concentrations have reduced greatly in most parts of the United Kingdom since the early 1970s, but there are still significant local variations.

(Table 11.5)

Acidity

The areas where critical loads for freshwater and soil acidity are exceeded occur mainly in the upland areas of the north and west of the United Kingdom.

(Chart 11.7)

Radiation

The South West is the region most affected by high levels of radon.

(Chart 11.8)

Land

Ten per cent of the agricultural land in East Anglia and the South East was set-aside in 1994, compared with less than 1 per cent in Wales and Northern Ireland.

(Table 11.9)

Nearly a quarter of the land in the North and about a fifth in Yorkshire and Humberside and Wales is designated as National Parks.

(Chart 11.10)

Wales and the South West together account for about three quarters of the Heritage Coasts in England and Wales.

(Chart 11.10)

Introduction

Over recent years, there has been a growing awareness of environmental issues. In the Department of the Environment's latest survey of public attitudes to the environment, undertaken in 1993, the environment was mentioned as the most important issue for the government to deal with by 22 per cent of respondents, almost three times as many as in the corresponding survey of 1986. Only unemployment and health were mentioned as the most important issue by more respondents.

Variations in rainfall and river flow can have a considerable effect on freshwater quality. Lower than average rainfall and low river flows are likely to have an adverse effect on river quality. High rainfall can also adversely affect quality by causing greater leaching of pollutants from the soil into freshwaters. However, increased river flows can lead to a dilution of the effect of point sources of pollution. Table 11.2 looks at the chemical quality of rivers and canals in England and Wales. The classification system differs from that used in previous editions of *Regional Trends* and so this table is not directly comparable with earlier versions. Details of the new classification system are in the Appendix.

Table 11.5 shows mean daily concentrations of sulphur dioxide and black smoke at 12 sites selected on a regional basis from the 155-site EC Directive network which monitors these pollutants. In many towns and cities, concentrations have fallen substantially over the last 20 years or so. The widespread introduction of smoke control programmes has reduced black smoke concentrations at most sites. In areas like Barnsley, Mansfield and Belfast, where coal is commonly used for domestic heating, the decline has been less than for other areas.

Acid deposition is often cited as a cause of damage to historic buildings, soils, lakes and forests. Two main gases contribute to acid deposition - sulphur dioxide (SO_2) and oxides of nitrogen, which are produced by the burning of a wide range of fuels. However, the amount of damage caused depends not only on the acidity of precipitation reaching the ground, but on the sensitivity of the environment to acidity. Enhanced deposition of acidic compounds from the atmosphere, caused by man-made emissions of SO_2, nitrogen oxide and ammonia, can add to the acidification of soils and freshwaters, thereby adversely affecting these ecosystems in some sensitive areas.

"Over recent years, there

awareness of

153

The risk of harmful effects on soil and freshwater ecosystems from acid deposition is assessed using a concept known as 'critical loads', which assumes that there are damage thresholds for the response of different ecosystems to acidic deposition. The critical load for a particular ecosystem-pollutant combination is defined as the highest deposition load of the pollutant that the ecosystem can stand without long-term damage occurring. Chart 11.7 shows where critical loads for soils and freshwaters, based on SO_2 and in the case of freshwaters nitrogen deposition, were exceeded. The most vulnerable soils and freshwaters are generally in the upland areas of north and west Britain.

Radon accounts for half of the average overall dose of radioactivity received by the UK population. The health hazard associated with radon is from its radioactive decay products. These may be inhaled and deposited in the lungs where radiation from them can damage lung tissue, and may increase the risk of lung cancer. Current estimates suggest that one in 20 of UK deaths from lung cancer each year are attributable to radon.

A national survey conducted by the National Radiological Protection Board (NRPB), based on a stratified sample of 2,300 dwellings, found the average indoor concentration of radon gas to be 20 Bq/m^3 (equivalent to an average annual dose of 1.3 mSv for members of the UK public). Parts of the United Kingdom have been designated as Radon Affected Areas, that is areas where more than 1 in 100 homes are estimated to have radon concentrations above the NRPB recommended action level of 200Bq/m^3. Above this level, NRPB recommend that actions be taken to limit exposure of householders to high levels of radon. Chart 11.8 shows the radon Affected Areas across the whole of the United Kingdom.

National Parks, Areas of Outstanding Natural Beauty in England and Wales and Northern Ireland and National Scenic Areas in Scotland are the major areas designated by legislation to protect their landscape importance. Other areas, such as National Nature Reserves, Special Protection Areas, Marine Nature Reserves and Ramsar Sites, are protected for their value as wildlife habitat, in particular for endangered species. Chart 11.10 shows the distribution across the United Kingdom of these and other protected areas.

has been a growing environmental issues."

11.1 Mean annual temperature and rainfall, 1961 to 1990

**Mean annual temperature
(degrees celsius)**

Mean annual rainfall (mm)

Source: Meteorological Office

11.2 Rivers and canals: by quality[1], 1988-1990 and 1991-1993[2]

Percentages and kilometres

	1988-1990					1991-1993				
	Quality (percentages)				Total length (= 100%) (kms)	Quality (percentages)				Total length (= 100%) (kms)
	Good	Fair	Poor	Bad		Good	Fair	Poor	Bad	
North West	42	31	21	7	3,190	55	29	13	3	5,520
Northumbria & Yorkshire[3]	58	24	14	4	4,350	58	25	15	2	5,260
Severn Trent	33	47	18	2	5,870	38	46	12	3	6,240
Anglian	18	63	17	2	4,570	24	60	15	1	4,590
Thames	37	46	16	1	3,530	45	47	7	1	3,700
Southern	44	44	11	1	2,190	50	41	8	1	2,210
South Western[3]	64	29	5	1	6,650	72	23	4	1	6,740
England	43	40	14	3	30,360	50	37	11	2	34,260
Wales[4]	79	16	3	1	3,960	86	11	2	-	5,010

1 The basis of the surveys from which these data are derived differs from earlier surveys, results of which were published in previous editions of *Regional Trends*. See Appendix notes.
2 Averages of three years' data combined.
3 In 1993, the Northumbria and Yorkshire regions amalgamated, as did the Wessex and South West regions.
4 NRA Welsh region. Data do not include all Wales as regional boundaries are based on catchment areas not national or county boundaries.

Source: Department of the Environment; National Rivers Authority

11.3 Water pollution incidents: by type, 1993[1]

Numbers

	Industrial		Sewage and water related		Agricultural		Other		Total		Number of prose-cutions[4]
	All	Major[2]	All[3]	Major[2]	All	Major[2]	All	Major[2]	All	Major[2]	
United Kingdom	7,113	..	..	..	4,050	..	12,213	..	30,257	.	676
North West	1,335	26	1,066	25	403	11	852	15	3,656	77	92
Northumbria & Yorkshire[5]	1,092	24	726	19	148	7	1,676	11	3,642	61	60
Severn Trent	727	29	1,327	16	391	15	2,431	33	4,876	93	66
Anglian	601	6	586	1	356	0	1,082	3	2,625	10	64
Thames	397	1	421	0	132	2	1,121	2	2,071	5	36
Southern	203	3	227	0	68	0	857	4	1,355	7	11
South Western[5]	767	12	1,124	5	943	24	1,295	7	4,129	48	44
England	5,122	101	5,477	66	2,441	59	9,314	75	22,354	301	373
Wales[6]	880	10	898	9	442	4	725	7	2,945	30	46
Scotland	801	..	..	..	663	..	1,617	..	3,081	..	91
Northern Ireland	310	60	501	0	504	106	562	0	1,877	166	166

1 Data relate to substantiated reports of pollution only. Figures for Scotland relate to the financial year 1993-94. The NRA regional boundaries are based on river catchment areas and not county borders.
2 Major incidents are those corresponding to Category 1 in the NRA's pollution incidents classification scheme. For Northern Ireland major incidents also correspond to Category 2. See Appendix notes.
3 Not summarised separately for Scotland - included in other sectors.
4 For England and Wales total prosecutions includes cases concluded and prosecutions outstanding. Prosecutions concluded relate to cases which had been brought to court by the 31 March 1994. In Scotland, this figure relates to the number of incidents referred to the Procurator Fiscal.
5 In 1993, the Northumbrian and Yorkshire regions amalgamated, as did the Wessex and South West regions.
6 NRA Welsh Region.

Source: National Rivers Authority; The Scottish Office Environment Department; Environment Service, Department of the Environment, Northern Ireland

11.4 Five year record of compliance with EC Bathing Water Directive[1] for coliform standards[2]: by coastal region, 1990 to 1994[3]

Percentages and numbers

	Percentage of bathing waters complying						Number of bathing waters (= 100%)
	In all 5 years	In 4 years	In 3 years	In 2 years	In 1 year only	In no years	
United Kingdom	56	18	7	7	7	5	457
North West	12	12	15	12	27	21	33
Northumbria & Yorkshire[4]	52	18	9	11	7	4	56
Anglian	82	3	3	0	6	6	33
Thames	33	33	33	0	0	0	3
Southern	51	21	6	9	9	4	67
South Western[4]	63	21	5	5	5	2	175
England	56	18	7	7	8	5	367
Wales[5]	53	18	10	10	8	2	51
Scotland	43	13	13	9	4	17	23
Northern Ireland	75	25	0	0	0	0	16

1 76/160/EEC.
2 At least 95 per cent of samples must have counts not exceeding the mandatory limit values for total and faecal coliforms.
3 Based on bathing waters in 1994. For each new bathing water identified after 1990, it has been assumed that its compliance record in earlier years accords with that for the first year that the bathing water was identified.
4 In 1993, the Northumbrian and Yorkshire regions amalgamated, as did the Wessex and South West regions.
5 NRA Welsh Region.

Source: Department of the Environment; National Rivers Authority; The Scottish Office Environment Department; Environment Service, Department of the Environment, Northern Ireland

11.5 Atmospheric pollution[1,2]

	Black smoke				Sulphur dioxide			
	Micrograms per cubic metre			Percentage change 1972-73 to 1993-94	Micrograms per cubic metre			Percentage change 1972-73 to 1993-94
	1972-73	1982-83	1993-94		1972-73	1982-83	1993-94	
Newcastle	254	89	56	-78	418	184	56	-87
Barnsley	476	204	78	-84	320	198	189	-41
Mansfield Woodhouse	441	251	79	-82	282	192	120	-57
Norwich	266	67	35	-87	169	49	32	-81
Stepney	162	69	22	-86	582	228	71	-88
Slough	114	39	16	-86	175	69	48	-73
Plymouth	109	54	20	-82	139	63	30	-78
Stoke-on-Trent	552	142	54	-90	382	147	108	-72
Manchester	362	45	75	-79	449	134	62	-86
Cardiff	214	54	38	-82	201	65	43	-79
Glasgow	265	115	42	-84	232	110	43	-81
Belfast	409	128	72	-82	240	103	160	-33

1 One site chosen for each UK region and Greater London.
2 Figures shown are for 98th percentile daily mean concentrations ie the level which is exceeded by the highest 2 per cent of daily mean concentrations during the year.

Source: National Environmental Technology Centre

11.6 Air pollution: emissions of sulphur dioxide[1] and nitrogen oxides[2], 1994[3]

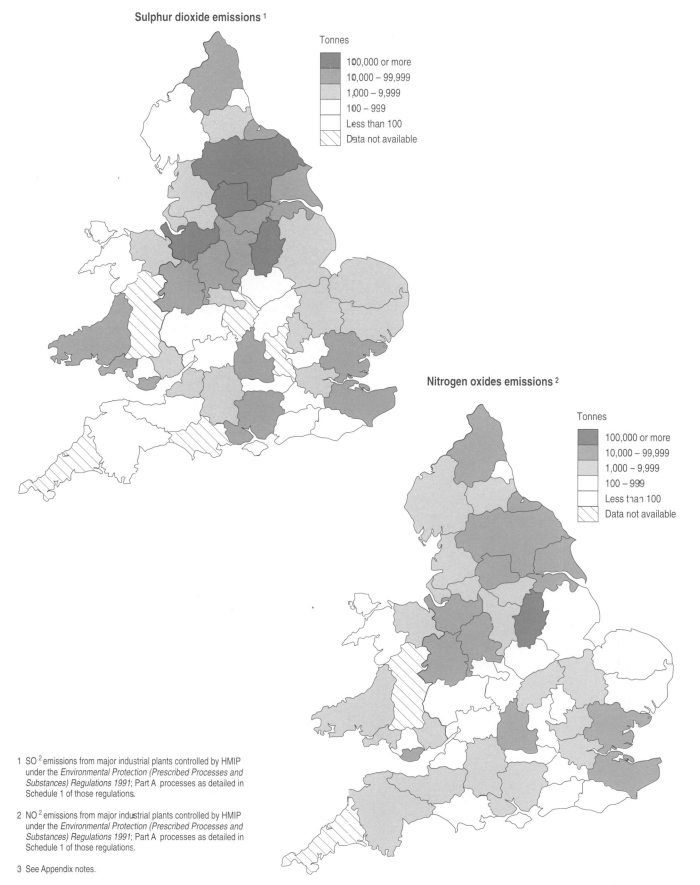

Sulphur dioxide emissions [1]

Tonnes

- 100,000 or more
- 10,000 – 99,999
- 1,000 – 9,999
- 100 – 999
- Less than 100
- Data not available

Nitrogen oxides emissions [2]

Tonnes

- 100,000 or more
- 10,000 – 99,999
- 1,000 – 9,999
- 100 – 999
- Less than 100
- Data not available

1 SO $_2$ emissions from major industrial plants controlled by HMIP under the *Environmental Protection (Prescribed Processes and Substances) Regulations 1991*; Part A processes as detailed in Schedule 1 of those regulations.

2 NO $_2$ emissions from major industrial plants controlled by HMIP under the *Environmental Protection (Prescribed Processes and Substances) Regulations 1991*; Part A processes as detailed in Schedule 1 of those regulations.

3 See Appendix notes.

Source: HM Inspectorate of Pollution

11.7 Critical loads for acidity of soils and freshwaters

**Areas[1] where critical loads for acidity of soils
are exceeded by annual mean total non-marine
sulphur deposition, 1989-1992**

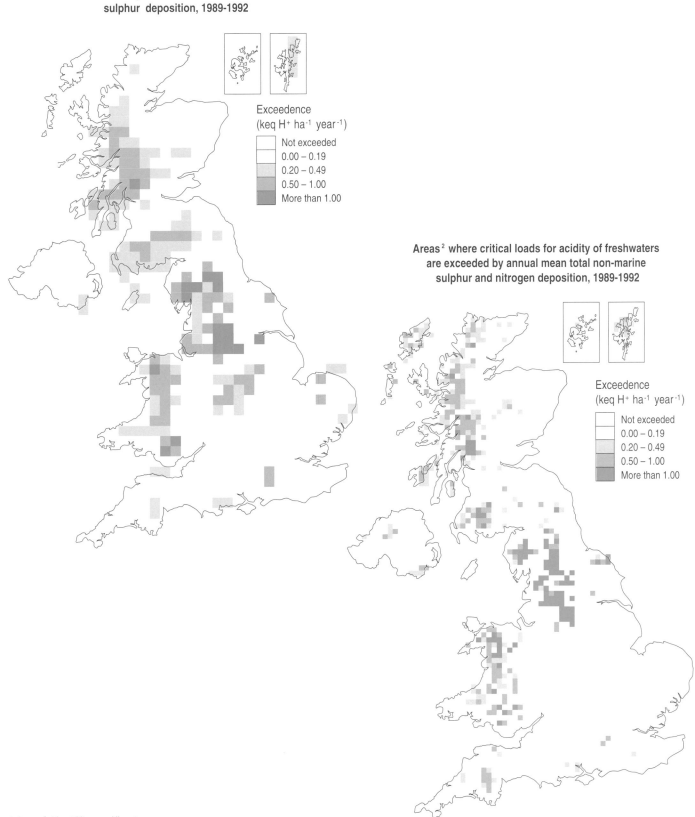

Exceedence
(keq H+ ha-1 year-1)

- Not exceeded
- 0.00 – 0.19
- 0.20 – 0.49
- 0.50 – 1.00
- More than 1.00

**Areas[2] where critical loads for acidity of freshwaters
are exceeded by annual mean total non-marine
sulphur and nitrogen deposition, 1989-1992**

Exceedence
(keq H+ ha-1 year-1)

- Not exceeded
- 0.00 – 0.19
- 0.20 – 0.49
- 0.50 – 1.00
- More than 1.00

1 Areas of at least 20 square kilometres.
2 Areas of at least 10 square kilometres.

Source: National Environmental Technology Centre; Institute of Terrestrial Ecology

11.8 Radon Affected Areas, 1993

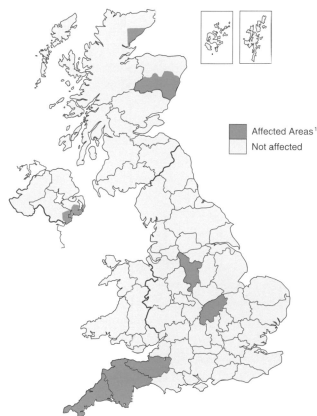

Affected Areas[1]

Not affected

1 Areas where at least 1 per cent of homes have radon concentrations above 200 Bq/m[3].

Source: National Radiological Protection Board

11.9 Agricultural land use[1], June 1992 and 1994

Percentages and thousand hectares

	Percentage of agricultural land in 1992 covered by				Total area on agri- cultural holdings (thousand hectares) (= 100%) 1992	Percentage of agricultural land in 1994 covered by				Total area on agri- cultural holdings (thousand hectares) (= 100%) 1994
	Total arable land[2]	All grass five years old and over (incl- uding sole right rough grazing)	Set aside land[3]	All other land on agri- cultural holdings including woodland[4]		Total arable land[2]	All grass five years old and over (incl- uding sole right rough grazing)	Set aside land	All other land on agri- cultural holdings including woodland[4]	
United Kingdom	38.2	57.3	0.9	3.7	17,281	34.5	57.2	4.2	4.1	17,258
North	26.9	70.1	0.5	2.6	1,042	24.0	70.5	2.6	3.0	1,050
Yorkshire & Humberside	57.8	38.9	0.6	2.7	1,108	50.9	39.1	6.9	3.1	1,104
East Midlands	71.0	25.2	1.2	2.7	1,240	62.3	25.4	9.1	3.1	1,247
East Anglia	82.8	10.3	1.5	5.3	1,013	73.3	10.8	10.1	5.8	1,018
South East	63.8	26.0	3.1	7.0	1,690	56.0	26.4	10.0	7.5	1,684
South West	40.9	53.5	1.4	4.3	1,823	37.1	53.8	4.2	4.8	1,837
West Midlands	52.2	43.1	0.9	3.8	968	47.8	42.9	5.2	4.1	966
North West	31.3	65.6	0.4	2.5	450	29.2	65.8	2.0	2.9	448
England	54.4	40.1	1.4	4.2	9,423	48.4	40.4	6.6	4.6	9,443
Wales	15.0	81.4	0.2	3.4	1,509	14.1	81.8	0.4	3.8	1,509
Scotland	18.8	77.9	0.5	2.7	5,297	17.4	77.3	1.8	3.5	5,259
Northern Ireland	23.4	72.6	..	4.0	1,052	23.9	73.0	0.2	3.0	1,048

1 Data include estimates for minor holdings except for Scotland and the regions of England.
2 Crops, bare fallow and all grass under five years old.
3 The figure shown against the United Kingdom is for Great Britain.
4 In Great Britain this includes farm roads, yards, buildings (except glasshouses), ponds and derelict land. In Northern Ireland it includes land under bog, water, roads, buildings etc and wasteland not used for agriculture.

Source: Ministry of Agriculture, Fisheries and Food; Welsh Office; The Scottish Office Agriculture and Fisheries Department; Department of Agriculture for Northern Ireland

11.10 Protected areas, as at 31 December 1994

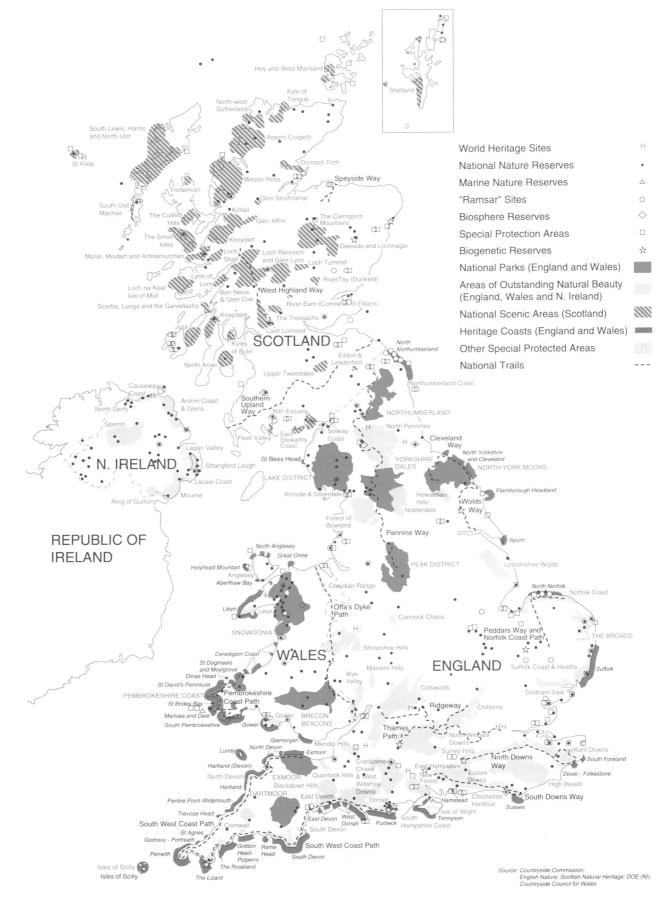

World Heritage Sites .... H

National Nature Reserves .... •

Marine Nature Reserves .... △

"Ramsar" Sites .... ○

Biosphere Reserves .... ◇

Special Protection Areas .... □

Biogenetic Reserves .... ☆

National Parks (England and Wales) .... ▓

Areas of Outstanding Natural Beauty
(England, Wales and N. Ireland) ▒

National Scenic Areas (Scotland) ▨

Heritage Coasts (England and Wales) ▰

Other Special Protected Areas ░

National Trails ----

*Source: Countryside Commission;
English Nature; Scottish Natural Heritage; DOE (NI);
Countryside Council for Wales*

12 Regional Accounts

Gross domestic product

The South East accounts for more than a third of UK GDP.

(Table 12.1)

GDP per head relative to the UK average increased significantly between 1989 and 1993 in Scotland and Northern Ireland while the South East's share declined.

(Table 12.1)

Only in the South East was GDP per head over £10,000 in 1993; it was lowest in Wales and in Northern Ireland at around £7,800 and £7,600 respectively.

(Table 12.1)

Income from employment accounted for about two thirds of total GDP in all regions in 1993; the proportion was highest in Scotland and lowest in East Anglia, the South West and Wales.

(Table 12.2)

Just over 29 per cent of GDP in the East Midlands, but only 16 per cent in the South East, came from manufacturing in 1993, the highest and lowest proportions.

(Table 12.3)

A third of the South East's GDP in 1993 was generated by financial and business services, compared with about a sixth in the North, Wales and Northern Ireland.

(Table 12.3)

Household income/ disposable income

Households in Northern Ireland, Wales and the North benefited most from the redistributive effects of the tax and benefit system in 1993, whilst those in the South East contributed the most.

(Chart 12.5)

Personal income/ disposable income

Personal income per head in 1993 was more than 10 per cent below the UK average in Northern Ireland, Wales and the North, while in the South East it was 13 per cent above the UK average.

(Table 12.8)

Personal disposable income per head in 1993 was highest in the South East at £8,700 and lowest in Wales and the North, at about £7,200.

(Table 12.9)

Consumers' expenditure

The South East has the highest consumers' expenditure per head, at more than £8,000 per person in 1993, while Northern Ireland has the lowest, at just under £6,000.

(Table 12.10)

Introduction

The regional accounts provide a breakdown of the main components of the national accounts into the standard regions and counties (local authority regions in Scotland). The national accounts are published each year in the CSO's Blue Book - United Kingdom National Accounts. This chapter covers estimates for the standard regions; county estimates of GDP and household income can be found in Chapter 14.

Scotland, Wales, Northern Ireland and the regions of England are all different in size, character, industrial structure and economic performance. Scotland has the largest area, but a small population relative to its size; the North West has the smallest area, but the second largest population. The South East is very densely populated and, as it is also large in area, its population of over 17 million is nearly three times as large as any other region. Northern Ireland at the other extreme has a population of only 1.6 million. These large variations in regions' populations are, of course, reflected in the sizes of regional GDP and incomes.

Because of the wide variation in the sizes of regions, comparisons of regional accounts aggregates such as GDP and total personal income are usually made in terms of amounts per head. It is important to note, however, that in regions where the population has increased or decreased significantly, the growth in total regional income or expenditure may be quite different to the growth per head. Furthermore the level of income per head is determined both by the earnings of the working population and the proportion of dependants. Northern Ireland households, for example, have a high proportion of children; over a quarter of the population was aged 15 or under in 1992 compared with about a fifth in most regions. This depresses income and expenditure per head in the Province relative to other regions.

UK GDP is defined as the total sum of all incomes earned from productive activity in the United Kingdom. Regional GDP should thus be defined as the sum of incomes earned from productive activity in the region, so that the income of commuters should be included in the region where they work. However the estimates of regional GDP are not compiled on this basis; they include regional estimates of income from employment on a residence basis, because this is the basis of the more reliable data source (the 1 per cent sample of Department of Social Security (DSS) records). This has a significant effect on the estimates for Greater London and the Rest of the South East, but is assumed not to introduce any significant distortion for the other regions.

Estimates of GDP by region are at factor cost. They measure the income of factors of production and exclude the value of taxes on expenditure such as VAT, but

"....a breakdown of the..

include subsidies. Thus the effect of the 1984 miners' strike on regional GDP is restricted to the effect on miners' income from employment; the value of government subsidy to the coal industry is included in profits and therefore in GDP.

All the items are measured in current prices which means that increases over time reflect inflation as well as real growth. Trends in total GDP per head cannot be analyzed easily without deflating the data. However, there are no regional or county price indices, which could be used to remove the effect of inflation from the figures. Comparisons of trends can therefore be based only either on the difference between regional increases at current prices or on movements in the amount relative to the UK average. Both approaches would be misleading if the rate of inflation in any region were different from the national average.

In the regional accounts it is usual to look at changes per head relative to the UK average over time. However this obscures the effect of changes in population size and area. In counties where the population is increasing most rapidly, growth in total GDP would be expected to grow relatively strongly; conversely, counties with a low or negative population growth would be expected to grow more slowly. Cambridgeshire, for example, has experienced a relatively high rate of population growth and total GDP is certainly growing faster than the UK average; the same is not necessarily true of GDP per head.

Personal income is the income both actual and imputed of the personal sector, which comprises not only households, but also individuals living in hostels and other institutions. unincorporated businesses such as farms, the funds of pension and life assurance schemes, private trusts and all private non-profit making bodies such as universities, trade unions and charities. Personal disposable income is thus not a measure of the spending power of households.

The regional accounts, although calculated as reliably as possible, cannot be regarded as accurate to the last digit shown. They are based partly on sample surveys and the quality of the results therefore varies according to sample size. This means that the results for areas with smaller populations such as the Isle of Wight and the Borders region of Scotland are subject to a greater degree of uncertainty than those for more populated areas. an assessment of the quality of the regional and county estimates was published in *Economic Trends*, November 1990.

..national accounts into regions...."

12.1 Gross domestic product[1], factor cost: current prices

	1984	1985	1986	1987	1988	1989	1990	1991	1992	1993
£ million										
United Kingdom	280,653	307,902	328,272	360,675	401,428	441,759	478,886	495,900	516,027	546,120
North	13,143	14,611	15,597	17,211	18,914	20,937	22,278	23,468	24,508	25,640
Yorkshire & Humberside	21,051	23,517	25,959	28,098	31,042	34,308	36,968	38,630	39,937	42,287
East Midlands	17,613	19,611	21,457	23,613	26,409	29,454	31,689	33,114	34,430	36,190
East Anglia	9,178	10,124	11,347	12,368	14,044	15,695	17,144	17,777	18,702	19,699
South East	91,380	101,824	113,506	125,371	141,983	156,825	170,157	175,026	181,539	190,622
Greater London	38,379	43,051	48,000	53,134	59,054	65,119	70,695	73,023	76,125	79,926
Rest of South East	53,001	58,773	65,505	72,237	82,929	91,706	99,463	102,003	105,415	110,696
South West	19,518	21,732	24,241	26,850	30,240	33,350	36,312	37,916	39,724	42,598
West Midlands	21,822	24,469	26,734	29,384	33,322	36,503	39,872	41,290	43,227	45,533
North West	27,750	30,586	33,430	36,239	40,528	44,291	47,613	48,886	50,628	53,832
England	221,455	246,473	272,270	299,136	336,482	371,363	402,032	416,107	432,696	456,401
Wales	10,950	11,862	13,328	14,834	17,077	18,604	20,032	20,856	21,247	22,761
Scotland	22,900	25,315	27,364	29,806	32,842	36,134	39,852	41,905	44,304	46,614
Northern Ireland	5,675	6,263	6,932	7,423	8,311	9,225	10,130	11,037	11,515	12,360
United Kingdom less Continental Shelf and statistical discrepancy	260,979	289,912	319,893	351,198	394,712	435,325	472,046	489,905	509,762	538,135
Continental Shelf	18,504	17,990	8,379	9,477	6,716	6,434	6,840	5,995	6,265	7,668
Statistical discrepancy (income adjustment)	1,170	-	-	-	-	-	-	-	-	317
As a percentage of United Kingdom *less* Continental Shelf and statistical discrepancy										
United Kingdom	100.0	100.0	100.0	100.0	100.0	100.0	100.0	100.0	100.0	100.0
North	5.0	5.0	4.9	4.9	4.8	4.8	4.7	4.8	4.8	4.8
Yorkshire & Humberside	8.1	8.1	8.1	8.0	7.9	7.9	7.8	7.9	7.8	7.9
East Midlands	6.7	6.8	6.7	6.7	6.7	6.8	6.7	6.8	6.8	6.7
East Anglia	3.5	3.5	3.5	3.5	3.6	3.6	3.6	3.6	3.7	3.7
South East	35.0	35.1	35.5	35.7	36.0	36.0	36.0	35.7	35.6	35.4
Greater London	14.7	14.8	15.0	15.1	15.0	15.0	15.0	14.9	14.9	14.9
Rest of South East	20.3	20.3	20.5	20.6	21.0	21.1	21.1	20.8	20.7	20.6
South West	7.5	7.5	7.6	7.6	7.7	7.7	7.7	7.7	7.8	7.9
West Midlands	8.4	8.4	8.4	8.4	8.4	8.4	8.4	8.4	8.5	8.5
North West	10.6	10.6	10.5	10.3	10.3	10.2	10.1	10.0	9.9	10.0
England	84.9	85.0	85.1	85.2	85.2	85.3	85.2	84.9	84.9	84.8
Wales	4.2	4.1	4.2	4.2	4.3	4.3	4.2	4.3	4.2	4.2
Scotland	8.8	8.7	8.6	8.5	8.3	8.3	8.4	8.6	8.7	8.7
Northern Ireland	2.2	2.2	2.2	2.1	2.1	2.1	2.1	2.3	2.3	2.3
£ per head										
United Kingdom *less* Continental Shelf and statistical discrepancy	4,622	5,121	5,636	6,169	6,917	7,606	8,222	8,497	8,789	9,248
North	4,249	4,734	5,064	5,594	6,159	6,813	7,244	7,609	7,909	8,265
Yorkshire & Humberside	4,292	4,797	5,298	5,734	6,318	6,944	7,465	7,797	7,984	8,434
East Midlands	4,546	5,032	5,474	5,990	6,652	7,365	7,885	8,226	8,476	8,864
East Anglia	4,732	5,153	5,697	6,142	6,903	7,676	8,326	8,501	8,954	9,408
South East	5,340	5,923	6,574	7,240	8,186	9,021	9,747	9,969	10,255	10,728
Greater London	5,681	6,362	7,085	7,848	8,768	9,638	10,405	10,734	11,025	11,528
Rest of South East	5,117	5,638	6,245	6,849	7,817	8,629	9,327	9,485	9,762	10,215
South West	4,375	4,829	5,336	5,852	6,526	7,168	7,781	8,027	8,370	8,934
West Midlands	4,216	4,721	5,160	5,653	6,400	6,998	7,639	7,858	8,191	8,608
North West	4,339	4,789	5,244	5,689	6,369	6,943	7,453	7,665	7,911	8,395
England	4,716	5,232	5,762	6,310	7,078	7,787	8,404	8,657	8,944	9,404
Wales	3,901	4,219	4,724	5,230	5,977	6,475	6,952	7,226	7,330	7,831
Scotland	4,450	4,928	5,343	5,830	6,447	7,098	7,810	8,205	8,668	9,104
Northern Ireland	3,660	4,020	4,424	4,712	5,266	5,827	6,375	6,922	7,151	7,574
£ per head, United Kingdom *less* Continental Shelf and statistical discrepancy = 100										
United Kingdom	100.0	100.0	100.0	100.0	100.0	100.0	100.0	100.0	100.0	100.0
North	91.9	92.5	89.9	90.7	89.0	89.6	88.1	89.6	90.0	89.4
Yorkshire & Humberside	92.9	93.7	94.0	92.9	91.3	91.3	90.8	91.8	90.8	91.2
East Midlands	98.4	98.3	97.1	97.1	96.2	96.8	95.9	96.8	96.4	95.8
East Anglia	102.4	100.6	101.1	99.6	99.8	100.9	101.3	100.1	101.9	101.7
South East	115.5	115.7	116.7	117.4	118.4	118.6	118.5	117.3	116.7	116.0
Greater London	122.9	124.2	125.7	127.2	126.8	126.7	126.5	126.3	125.4	124.7
Rest of South East	110.7	110.1	110.8	111.0	113.0	113.5	113.4	111.6	111.1	110.5
South West	94.7	94.3	94.7	94.9	94.3	94.2	94.6	94.5	95.2	96.6
West Midlands	91.2	92.2	91.6	91.6	92.5	92.0	92.9	92.5	93.2	93.1
North West	93.9	93.5	93.1	92.2	92.1	91.3	90.6	90.2	90.0	90.8
England	102.0	102.2	102.2	102.3	102.3	102.4	102.2	101.9	101.8	101.7
Wales	84.4	82.4	83.8	84.8	86.4	85.1	84.6	85.0	83.4	84.7
Scotland	96.3	96.2	94.8	94.5	93.2	93.3	95.0	96.6	98.6	98.4
Northern Ireland	79.2	78.5	78.5	76.4	76.1	76.6	77.5	81.5	81.4	81.9

1 See Appendix notes.

Source: Central Statistical Office

12.2 Factor incomes in the gross domestic product[1], factor cost: current prices

£ million

	Income from employment	Income from self-employment	Gross trading profits and surpluses	*Less* stock appreciation	Rent[2]	Gross domestic product
1990						
United Kingdom	312,358	61,138	68,561	6,131	42,960	478,886
North	14,815	2,271	3,771	354	1,776	22,278
Yorkshire & Humberside	24,254	4,765	5,739	548	2,759	36,968
East Midlands	20,645	4,357	4,404	436	2,719	31,689
East Anglia	10,727	2,922	2,190	217	1,521	17,144
South East	114,664	21,490	18,420	1,783	17,367	170,157
Greater London	48,194	7,987	6,974	614	8,154	70,695
Rest of South East	66,470	13,502	11,446	1,169	9,213	99,463
South West	23,292	6,237	3,769	488	3,502	36,312
West Midlands	26,556	4,870	5,525	615	3,536	39,872
North West	31,459	5,049	7,824	758	4,039	47,613
England	266,412	51,960	51,641	5,199	37,218	402,032
Wales	12,397	2,883	3,433	284	1,604	20,032
Scotland	26,989	4,724	5,398	503	3,244	39,852
Northern Ireland	6,560	1,571	1,253	149	895	10,130
Continental Shelf	.	.	6,835	-5	.	6,840
Statistical discrepancy (income adjustment)	..	..	..	..	..	-
1991						
United Kingdom	329,609	58,639	60,592	2,010	49,070	495,900
North	15,715	2,339	3,548	110	1,976	23,468
Yorkshire & Humberside	25,867	4,677	5,067	176	3,195	38,630
East Midlands	21,782	4,200	4,227	183	3,089	33,114
East Anglia	11,341	2,809	1,950	73	1,751	17,777
South East	119,520	20,328	15,930	502	19,749	175,026
Greater London	50,039	7,694	6,194	183	9,280	73,023
Rest of South East	69,482	12,635	9,736	318	10,469	102,003
South West	24,690	5,804	3,496	182	4,108	37,916
West Midlands	27,995	4,709	4,745	258	4,098	41,290
North West	33,112	4,838	6,646	249	4,539	48,886
England	280,023	49,703	45,609	1,733	42,504	416,107
Wales	13,306	2,709	3,098	79	1,821	20,856
Scotland	29,027	4,654	4,681	188	3,731	41,905
Northern Ireland	7,253	1,573	1,253	54	1,013	11,037
Continental Shelf	.	.	5,951	-44	.	5,995
Statistical discrepancy (income adjustment)	..	..	..	..	..	-
1992						
United Kingdom	342,215	59,482	62,762	1,832	53,400	516,027
North	16,399	2,306	3,699	61	2,166	24,508
Yorkshire & Humberside	26,882	4,732	4,973	148	3,499	39,937
East Midlands	22,479	4,230	4,555	200	3,366	34,430
East Anglia	11,934	2,810	2,107	71	1,922	18,702
South East	123,419	20,380	16,891	397	21,246	181,539
Greater London	51,652	7,938	6,893	129	9,772	76,125
Rest of South East	71,767	12,442	9,999	268	11,474	105,415
South West	25,653	6,044	3,666	160	4,522	39,724
West Midlands	29,163	4,872	4,949	264	4,507	43,227
North West	34,292	4,998	6,525	195	5,008	50,628
England	290,220	50,371	47,365	1,496	46,236	432,696
Wales	13,838	2,693	2,823	78	1,971	21,247
Scotland	30,509	4,821	5,112	194	4,057	44,304
Northern Ireland	7,647	1,598	1,197	64	1,136	11,515
Continental Shelf	.	.	6,265	-	.	6,265
Statistical discrepancy (income adjustment)	..	..	..	..	..	-
1993						
United Kingdom	352,896	61,346	77,106	2,359	56,814	546,120
North	16,761	2,414	4,261	95	2,298	25,640
Yorkshire & Humberside	27,805	4,867	6,072	163	3,706	42,287
East Midlands	23,266	4,334	5,186	174	3,579	36,190
East Anglia	12,317	2,798	2,573	43	2,054	19,699
South East	126,014	21,219	21,474	660	22,575	190,622
Greater London	52,685	8,002	9,153	290	10,376	79,926
Rest of South East	73,328	13,218	12,322	370	12,198	110,696
South West	27,056	6,304	4,640	209	4,808	42,598
West Midlands	30,129	4,924	5,970	301	4,812	45,533
North West	35,595	5,156	8,092	304	5,292	53,832
England	298,943	52,017	58,268	1,949	49,123	456,401
Wales	14,471	2,743	3,576	103	2,073	22,761
Scotland	31,418	4,925	6,116	232	4,387	46,614
Northern Ireland	8,065	1,660	1,505	101	1,231	12,360
Continental Shelf	.	.	7,642	-26	.	7,668
Statistical discrepancy (income adjustment)	..	..	..	..	..	317

1 See Appendix notes.
2 Including imputed charges for consumption of non-trading capital.

Source: Central Statistical Office

12.3 Gross domestic product by industry groups[1], factor cost: current prices

£ million

North / Yorkshire & Humberside

	1990	1991	1992	1993	1990	1991	1992	1993
	North				Yorkshire & Humberside			
Agriculture, hunting, forestry and fishing	446	435	491	572	757	754	785	882
Mining, quarrying inc oil and gas extraction	366	427	404	371	596	735	696	625
Manufacturing[2]	6,965	6,836	7,144	7,425	10,668	10,204	10,337	11,046
Electricity, gas, water	564	707	669	711	935	1,210	1,202	1,252
Construction	1,724	1,688	1,593	1,522	2,786	2,567	2,410	2,346
Distribution, hotels and catering; repairs	2,762	3,067	3,150	3,327	5,640	6,145	6,270	6,714
Transport, storage and communication	1,665	1,710	1,693	1,811	2,789	2,948	2,959	3,236
Financial & business services,etc[3]	3,511	3,704	4,083	4,409	6,291	6,655	7,334	7,953
Public administration and defence[4]	1,328	1,443	1,728	1,764	2,145	2,348	2,553	2,550
Education, social work and health services	2,405	2,755	2,882	2,999	3,826	4,237	4,751	4,893
Other services	1,233	1,278	1,320	1,394	2,053	2,151	2,214	2,412
Adjustment for financial services	-690	-581	-651	-666	-1,520	-1,325	-1,574	-1,622
Total	22,278	23,468	24,508	25,639	36,967	38,630	39,937	42,287

East Midlands / East Anglia

	1990	1991	1992	1993	1990	1991	1992	1993
	East Midlands				East Anglia			
Agriculture, hunting, forestry and fishing	857	895	892	1,069	901	890	898	993
Mining, quarrying inc oil and gas extraction	636	817	764	640	71	87	106	128
Manufacturing[2]	9,665	9,437	10,031	10,582	4,067	3,846	4,028	4,306
Electricity, gas, water	790	1,012	965	943	362	505	517	557
Construction	2,315	2,147	1,981	1,957	1,399	1,246	1,144	1,082
Distribution, hotels and catering; repairs	4,539	4,822	5,037	5,257	2,545	2,616	2,675	2,831
Transport, storage and communication	2,153	2,315	2,290	2,469	1,559	1,675	1,888	1,959
Financial & business services,etc[3]	5,687	6,040	6,404	6,888	3,567	3,698	4,014	4,350
Public administration and defence[4]	2,010	2,125	1,917	1,949	1,068	1,221	1,452	1,482
Education, social work and health services	2,712	2,982	3,538	3,694	1,558	1,772	1,889	1,913
Other services	1,371	1,434	1,549	1,686	896	948	934	1,000
Adjustment for financial services	-1,047	-912	-937	-944	-849	-727	-845	-903
Total	31,689	33,114	34,430	36,190	17,144	17,777	18,702	19,699

South East / Greater London

	1990	1991	1992	1993	1990	1991	1992	1993
	South East				Greater London			
Agriculture, hunting, forestry and fishing	1,252	1,235	1,235	1,418	46	44	44	52
Mining, quarrying inc oil and gas extraction	352	403	500	617	148	161	171	205
Manufacturing[2]	28,976	27,786	28,774	30,358	9,669	9,487	9,979	10,590
Electricity, gas, water	3,062	3,928	3,988	4,243	1,127	1,397	1,383	1,482
Construction	12,116	10,833	10,076	9,902	4,196	3,743	3,516	3,479
Distribution, hotels and catering; repairs	25,013	25,618	26,351	27,672	10,325	10,294	11,006	11,378
Transport, storage and communication	17,462	18,244	19,263	20,120	8,354	8,703	9,102	9,502
Financial & business services,etc[3]	57,122	56,892	59,935	63,682	28,290	27,946	29,252	31,163
Public administration and defence[4]	11,335	12,097	13,307	13,555	4,360	4,622	5,035	5,051
Education, social work and health services	13,958	15,821	17,122	17,579	5,878	6,587	7,011	7,137
Other services	11,275	11,779	11,746	12,227	5,532	5,838	5,914	6,117
Adjustment for financial services	-11,766	-9,610	-10,758	-10,751	-7,230	-5,800	-6,287	-6,232
Total	170,157	175,025	181,539	190,622	70,694	73,023	76,125	79,926

Rest of South East / South West

	1990	1991	1992	1993	1990	1991	1992	1993
	Rest of South East				South West			
Agriculture, hunting, forestry and fishing	1,206	1,191	1,191	1,365	1,340	1,376	1,462	1,644
Mining, quarrying inc oil and gas extraction	205	242	328	412	222	344	395	480
Manufacturing[2]	19,307	18,298	18,795	19,768	7,634	7,362	7,578	8,143
Electricity, gas, water	1,935	2,531	2,605	2,761	1,076	1,412	1,360	1,354
Construction	7,920	7,090	6,560	6,422	3,056	2,604	2,440	2,395
Distribution, hotels and catering; repairs	14,688	15,324	15,346	16,294	5,562	5,891	6,177	6,589
Transport, storage and communication	9,109	9,541	10,161	10,617	2,498	2,538	2,694	2,864
Financial & business services,etc[3]	28,832	28,946	30,683	32,519	8,328	8,595	9,206	10,257
Public administration and defence[4]	6,975	7,475	8,271	8,504	3,358	3,697	4,072	4,334
Education, social work and health services	8,080	9,234	10,111	10,442	3,399	3,883	4,252	4,374
Other services	5,742	5,940	5,833	6,110	1,996	2,042	2,145	2,334
Adjustment for financial services	-4,536	-3,810	-4,470	-4,519	-2,157	-1,828	-2,056	-2,170
Total	99,462	102,002	105,414	110,696	36,312	37,916	39,724	42,598

12.3 *(continued)*

£ million

	1990	1991	1992	1993	1990	1991	1992	1993
	West Midlands				North West			
Agriculture, hunting, forestry and fishing	833	870	908	1,028	471	480	505	550
Mining, quarrying inc oil and gas extraction	246	298	252	242	100	114	99	101
Manufacturing[2]	13,132	12,410	12,737	13,225	14,937	14,132	14,223	15,260
Electricity, gas, water	823	1,054	1,055	1,179	1,146	1,368	1,302	1,374
Construction	2,713	2,498	2,453	2,462	3,126	2,908	2,712	2,697
Distribution, hotels and catering; repairs	5,607	5,961	6,301	6,607	6,966	7,172	7,652	8,011
Transport, storage and communication	2,647	2,844	3,046	3,171	3,955	4,174	4,323	4,513
Financial & business services,etc[3]	7,707	8,120	8,944	9,697	9,463	9,771	10,500	11,408
Public administration and defence[4]	1,980	2,203	2,322	2,322	2,580	2,821	2,968	3,044
Education, social work and health services	3,755	4,317	4,585	4,829	4,514	5,167	5,667	5,996
Other services	1,949	2,032	2,107	2,316	2,567	2,701	2,829	3,051
Adjustment for financial services	-1,521	-1,318	-1,482	-1,545	-2,212	-1,923	-2,151	-2,173
Total	39,872	41,290	43,227	45,533	47,613	48,886	50,627	53,832
	England				Wales			
Agriculture, hunting, forestry and fishing	6,859	6,935	7,175	8,156	461	468	459	493
Mining, quarrying inc oil and gas extraction	2,590	3,225	3,215	3,203	173	203	159	161
Manufacturing[2]	96,045	92,011	94,851	100,345	5,904	5,811	5,447	6,081
Electricity, gas, water	8,759	11,196	11,058	11,614	625	751	814	868
Construction	29,236	26,491	24,809	24,362	1,448	1,318	1,303	1,310
Distribution, hotels and catering; repairs	58,634	61,292	63,613	67,008	2,800	2,967	3,088	3,225
Transport, storage and communication	34,728	36,448	38,156	40,142	1,409	1,404	1,399	1,519
Financial & business services,etc[3]	101,675	103,477	110,420	118,645	3,072	3,307	3,630	4,019
Public administration and defence[4]	25,804	27,955	30,320	30,999	1,601	1,681	1,729	1,730
Education, social work and health services	36,127	40,935	44,686	46,277	2,105	2,468	2,727	2,861
Other services	23,339	24,364	24,844	26,420	1,058	1,060	1,118	1,179
Adjustment for financial services	-21,763	-18,224	-20,453	-20,771	-623	-581	-622	-684
Total	402,031	416,106	432,694	456,400	20,033	20,858	21,249	22,761
	Scotland				Northern Ireland			
Agriculture, hunting, forestry and fishing	1,199	1,121	1,186	1,214	404	439	462	510
Mining, quarrying inc oil and gas extraction	756	986	973	1,067	32	42	42	48
Manufacturing[2]	9,302	8,775	9,153	9,497	2,140	2,237	2,192	2,371
Electricity, gas, water	937	1,164	1,226	1,291	262	277	241	221
Construction	3,158	3,002	3,001	2,886	687	659	647	664
Distribution, hotels and catering; repairs	5,356	5,878	6,294	6,450	1,287	1,420	1,541	1,665
Transport, storage and communication	3,374	3,587	3,713	3,911	560	612	638	691
Financial & business services,etc[3]	7,261	7,719	8,437	9,113	1,630	1,775	1,969	2,179
Public administration and defence[4]	2,914	3,088	3,516	3,687	1,357	1,532	1,695	1,783
Education, social work and health services	5,085	5,741	5,952	6,499	1,387	1,613	1,697	1,820
Other services	2,355	2,527	2,736	2,894	704	725	758	799
Adjustment for financial services	-1,846	-1,683	-1,884	-1,895	-320	-294	-367	-390
Total	39,852	41,905	44,304	46,614	10,130	11,037	11,515	12,360
	United Kingdom							
Agriculture, hunting, forestry and fishing	8,923	8,964	9,282	10,373				
Mining, quarrying inc oil and gas extraction	3,550	4,455	4,389	4,479				
of which Continental Shelf	6,840	5,995	6,265	7,668				
Manufacturing[2]	113,392	108,834	111,644	118,294				
Electricity, gas, water	10,583	13,388	13,339	13,994				
Construction	34,529	31,470	29,760	29,221				
Distribution, hotels and catering; repairs	68,076	71,558	74,536	78,348				
Transport, storage and communication	40,071	42,051	43,905	46,263				
Financial & business services,etc[3]	113,638	116,277	124,456	133,956				
Public administration and defence[4]	31,676	34,257	37,260	38,199				
Education, social work and health services	44,704	50,757	55,062	57,457				
Other services	27,456	28,676	29,455	31,292				
Adjustment for financial services	-24,552	-20,782	-23,326	-23,741				
Statistical discrepancy (income adjustment)	-	-	-	317				
Total	478,886	495,900	516,027	546,120				

1 Gross domestic product is shown for each industry after deducting stock appreciation. See Appendix notes.
2 Definition of manufacturing as revised in SIC 92.
3 Financial intermediation, real estate, renting, business activities, including rent on dwellings.
4 Public administration, national defence and compulsory social security.

Source: Central Statistical Office

12.4 Shares of gross domestic product

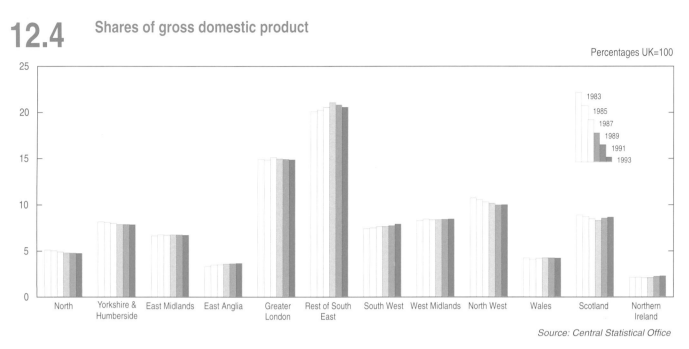

Percentages UK=100

Source: Central Statistical Office

12.5 Household total and disposable income per head, 1993

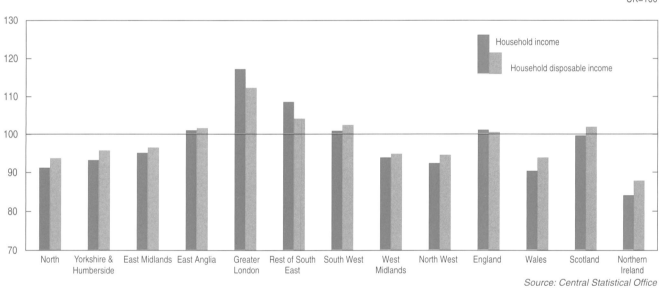

UK=100

Source: Central Statistical Office

12.6 Consumers' expenditure per head

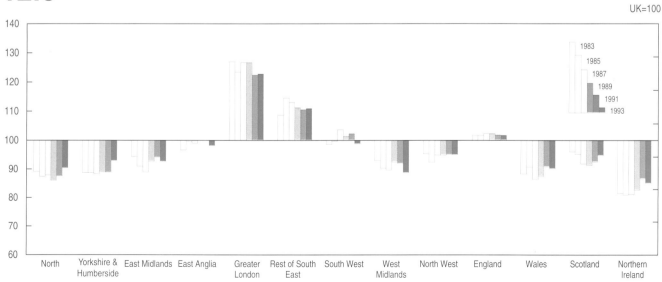

UK=100

Source: Central Statistical Office

Regional Trends 30, © Crown copyright 1995

12.7   Gross domestic fixed capital formation: by selected industry groups

£ million

	Agriculture forestry and fishing	Energy, mining and water[1]	Manufacturing[2]	Transport and communication[3]	Dwellings	Total of industries shown
1989						
United Kingdom	1,485	7,993	14,248	9,066	22,988	55,785
North	78	279	1,413	319	1,063	3,152
Yorkshire & Humberside	124	673	1,259	599	1,844	4,502
East Midlands	117	481	893	500	1,749	3,741
East Anglia	109	230	477	234	1,042	2,092
South East	148	1,473	3,463	4,186	7,382	16,654
South West	206	523	758	769	2,386	4,647
West Midlands	123	441	1,476	709	1,954	4,705
North West	52	443	2,029	670	2,109	5,303
England	956	4,557	11,768	7,986	19,529	44,796
Wales	133	294	1,068	279	1,164	2,938
Scotland	261	473	1,150	601	1,708	4,198
Northern Ireland	134	151	262	200	587	1,334
Continental shelf	.	2,519	.	.	.	2,519
1990						
United Kingdom	1,368	9,442	14,226	8,711	21,439	55,186
North	72	359	1,414	328	1,049	3,221
Yorkshire & Humberside	113	655	1,291	550	1,717	4,327
East Midlands	106	525	985	479	1,538	3,632
East Anglia	101	263	452	255	769	1,839
South East	137	1,663	3,251	4,073	6,642	15,771
South West	187	525	758	684	1,918	4,072
West Midlands	109	473	1,388	617	1,832	4,424
North West	48	463	2,291	649	2,221	5,673
England	874	4,933	11,829	7,635	17,686	42,959
Wales	107	437	1,068	303	1,184	3,100
Scotland	254	624	1,012	590	2,013	4,493
Northern Ireland	133	125	317	183	556	1,314
Continental shelf	.	3,321	.	.	.	3,321
1991						
United Kingdom	1,063	11,563	13,183	8,405	18,501	52,718
North	48	393	1,437	339	925	3,146
Yorkshire & Humberside	76	733	1,182	568	1,432	3,995
East Midlands	80	593	1,109	451	1,365	3,603
East Anglia	76	242	340	241	718	1,616
South East	101	1,845	3,255	3,791	5,239	14,233
South West	161	531	651	615	1,651	3,610
West Midlands	96	555	1,184	601	1,661	4,096
North West	31	431	1,733	688	1,990	4,873
England	669	5,333	10,892	7,294	14,980	39,172
Wales	79	347	809	302	937	2,474
Scotland	214	833	1,172	625	2,045	4,890
Northern Ireland	102	130	309	183	540	1,264
Continental shelf	.	4,919	.	.	.	4,919
1992						
United Kingdom	1,070	12,311	12,163	8,249	18,692	52,485
North	56	382	1,137	366	943	2,883
Yorkshire & Humberside	97	747	1,285	603	1,426	4,159
East Midlands	96	635	1,246	498	1,397	3,873
East Anglia	91	353	402	254	733	1,832
South East	120	2,244	2,631	3,606	5,475	14,077
South West	121	427	713	581	1,692	3,535
West Midlands	73	427	848	563	1,697	3,608
North West	47	833	1,748	659	1,949	5,236
England	701	6,043	10,010	7,131	15,312	39,202
Wales	89	297	768	283	991	2,428
Scotland	165	931	1,089	643	1,852	4,681
Northern Ireland	116	107	295	192	536	1,246
Continental shelf	.	4,923	.	.	.	4,928

1 Includes extraction of mineral oil and natural gas, mining and quarrying, electricity, gas and water.
2 Definition of manufacturing as revised in SIC 92.
3 Excluding sea and air transport.

Source: Central Statistical Office

12.8 Total personal income

	£ million					£ per head					£ per head index UK=100
	1989	1990	1991	1992	1993	1989	1990	1991	1992	1993	1993
United Kingdom	442,421	486,690	518,383	551,511	575,511	7,730	8,477	8,992	9,509	9,890	100.0
North	20,774	22,894	24,825	26,442	27,455	6,760	7,444	8,049	8,533	8,850	89.5
Yorkshire and Humberside	35,276	38,580	41,315	43,737	45,667	7,140	7,791	8,339	8,743	9,108	92.1
East Midlands	29,887	32,373	34,194	36,101	37,774	7,473	8,056	8,494	8,888	9,252	93.5
East Anglia	16,008	17,536	18,861	20,150	20,891	7,829	8,517	9,019	9,647	9,977	100.9
South East	155,902	171,957	181,248	191,884	198,836	8,968	9,850	10,323	10,839	11,190	113.1
Greater London	63,734	71,330	75,964	80,056	83,074	9,433	10,498	11,166	11,595	11,982	121.2
Rest of South East	92,168	100,627	105,285	111,828	115,762	8,672	9,437	9,790	10,356	10,683	108.0
South West	35,526	38,681	41,460	44,483	46,790	7,636	8,289	8,778	9,372	9,813	99.2
West Midlands	37,580	41,542	44,566	47,644	49,664	7,205	7,959	8,481	9,028	9,389	94.9
North West	45,058	49,451	52,509	55,743	58,618	7,063	7,741	8,234	8,710	9,141	92.4
England	376,010	413,014	438,977	466,184	485,695	7,885	8,634	9,132	9,636	10,008	101.2
Wales	18,976	20,770	22,426	23,771	25,156	6,605	7,208	7,769	8,201	8,655	87.5
Scotland	37,249	41,861	44,812	48,452	50,609	7,317	8,204	8,787	9,480	9,885	99.9
Northern Ireland	10,186	11,046	12,168	13,103	14,051	6,434	6,951	7,639	8,137	8,611	87.1

Source: Central Statistical Office

12.9 Personal disposable income[1]

	£ million					£ per head					£ per head index UK=100
	1989	1990[2]	1991[2]	1992[2]	1993[2]	1989	1990[2]	1991[2]	1992[2]	1993[2]	1993
United Kingdom	352,905	379,330	407,794	438,514	462,178	6,166	6,607	7,074	7,561	7,942	100.00
North	17,009	18,278	19,952	21,426	22,479	5,535	5,943	6,469	6,914	7,246	91.2
Yorkshire and Humberside	28,658	30,705	33,096	35,352	37,288	5,801	6,201	6,680	7,067	7,437	93.6
East Midlands	24,048	25,443	27,019	28,831	30,526	6,013	6,331	6,712	7,098	7,477	94.1
East Anglia	12,851	13,696	14,883	16,129	16,867	6,285	6,652	7,117	7,722	8,055	101.4
South East	121,538	129,936	138,164	147,797	154,628	6,991	7,443	7,869	8,349	8,702	109.6
Greater London	50,104	53,990	58,033	61,828	64,813	7,416	7,946	8,531	8,955	9,348	117.7
Rest of South East	71,434	75,946	80,130	85,969	89,815	6,721	7,122	7,451	7,961	8,288	104.4
South West	28,742	30,374	32,866	35,719	37,988	6,178	6,509	6,958	7,526	7,967	100.3
West Midlands	30,271	32,755	35,420	38,265	40,318	5,803	6,276	6,741	7,251	7,622	96.0
North West	36,515	39,067	41,777	44,970	47,801	5,724	6,115	6,551	7,027	7,454	93.9
England	299,631	320,254	343,177	368,489	387,895	6,283	6,695	7,139	7,617	7,992	100.6
Wales	15,390	16,603	18,350	19,575	20,893	5,357	5,762	6,357	6,753	7,189	90.5
Scotland	29,405	33,230	35,958	39,319	41,293	5,776	6,513	7,051	7,693	8,065	101.5
Northern Ireland	8,479	9,243	10,309	11,132	12,097	5,356	5,817	6,472	6,913	7,413	93.3

1 Total personal income less United Kingdom taxes on income, national insurance etc contributions, community charge, net current transfers abroad and miscellaneous current transfers.
2 Community Charge was introduced in Scotland from 1989 and in England and Wales from 1990. Council Tax replaced Community Charge in April 1993. Community Charge and Council Tax are now additional deductions in the calculation of personal disposable income and hence there is a discontinuity in both the regional and national series.

Source: Central Statistical Office

12.10 Consumers' expenditure

	1984	1985	1986	1987	1988	1989[1]	1990[1]	1991[1]	1992[1]	1993[1]
£ million										
United Kingdom	198,820	217,485	241,553	265,290	299,449	327,363	347,527	364,972	382,240	405,640
North	9,438	10,360	11,693	12,595	13,888	15,113	15,966	17,090	18,237	19,553
Yorkshire and Humberside	15,442	16,696	18,272	20,172	22,908	25,136	26,246	27,877	30,222	32,497
East Midlands	12,753	13,624	14,803	16,344	18,686	21,215	23,121	24,005	24,817	26,385
East Anglia	6,623	7,520	8,536	9,293	10,587	11,686	12,440	13,250	13,816	14,322
South East	70,616	77,940	87,233	95,527	107,324	116,562	122,634	127,939	134,663	143,088
Greater London	29,799	32,071	36,241	39,984	45,192	48,948	51,238	52,700	55,227	59,314
Rest of South East	40,818	45,869	50,992	55,543	62,132	67,613	71,396	75,240	79,436	83,774
South West	15,451	17,247	19,698	22,161	24,892	26,967	28,949	30,570	31,372	32,838
West Midlands	16,761	17,985	19,643	21,732	24,863	27,612	29,237	30,608	31,275	32,721
North West	21,096	22,684	25,343	28,196	31,734	34,631	36,579	38,387	39,844	42,466
England	168,182	184,055	205,220	226,019	254,882	278,923	295,171	309,726	324,247	343,870
Wales	8,780	9,803	10,640	11,421	12,966	14,364	15,590	16,612	17,336	18,269
Scotland	17,499	18,780	20,194	21,896	24,819	26,598	28,613	29,896	31,413	33,830
Northern Ireland	4,359	4,848	5,500	5,954	6,782	7,478	8,152	8,738	9,244	9,671
As a percentage of United Kingdom										
United Kingdom	100.0	100.0	100.0	100.0	100.0	100.0	100.0	100.0	100.0	100.0
North	4.7	4.8	4.8	4.7	4.6	4.6	4.6	4.7	4.8	4.8
Yorkshire and Humberside	7.8	7.7	7.6	7.6	7.7	7.7	7.6	7.6	7.9	8.0
East Midlands	6.4	6.3	6.1	6.2	6.2	6.5	6.7	6.6	6.5	6.5
East Anglia	3.3	3.5	3.5	3.5	3.5	3.6	3.6	3.6	3.5	3.5
South East	35.5	35.8	36.1	36.0	35.8	35.6	35.3	35.1	35.2	35.3
Greater London	15.0	14.7	15.0	15.1	15.1	15.0	14.7	14.4	14.4	14.6
Rest of South East	20.5	21.1	21.1	20.9	20.7	20.7	20.5	20.6	20.8	20.7
South West	7.8	7.9	8.2	8.4	8.3	8.2	8.3	8.4	8.2	8.1
West Midlands	8.4	8.3	8.1	8.2	8.3	8.4	8.4	8.4	8.2	8.1
North West	10.6	10.4	10.5	10.6	10.6	10.6	10.5	10.5	10.4	10.5
England	84.6	84.6	85.0	85.2	85.1	85.2	84.9	84.9	84.8	84.8
Wales	4.4	4.5	4.4	4.3	4.3	4.4	4.5	4.6	4.5	4.5
Scotland	8.8	8.6	8.4	8.3	8.3	8.1	8.2	8.2	8.2	8.3
Northern Ireland	2.2	2.2	2.3	2.2	2.3	2.3	2.3	2.4	2.4	2.4
£ per head										
United Kingdom	3,521	3,841	4,255	4,660	5,247	5,720	6,053	6,331	6,591	6,971
North	3,051	3,357	3,796	4,094	4,522	4,918	5,192	5,541	5,885	6,303
Yorkshire and Humberside	3,149	3,406	3,729	4,116	4,663	5,088	5,300	5,627	6,042	6,481
East Midlands	3,292	3,496	3,776	4,146	4,707	5,305	5,753	5,963	6,110	6,462
East Anglia	3,415	3,827	4,286	4,615	5,204	5,715	6,042	6,336	6,615	6,840
South East	4,127	4,534	5,053	5,516	6,188	6,705	7,025	7,287	7,607	8,053
Greater London	4,411	4,739	5,349	5,906	6,710	7,245	7,541	7,747	7,999	8,555
Rest of South East	3,941	4,400	4,861	5,266	5,857	6,362	6,695	6,996	7,356	7,731
South West	3,464	3,832	4,336	4,830	5,372	5,796	6,204	6,472	6,610	6,887
West Midlands	3,238	3,470	3,791	4,181	4,775	5,294	5,602	5,825	5,926	6,186
North West	3,299	3,552	3,976	4,426	4,987	5,428	5,726	6,019	6,226	6,622
England	3,582	3,907	4,343	4,768	5,362	5,849	6,170	6,443	6,702	7,085
Wales	3,128	3,486	3,772	4,027	4,538	4,999	5,411	5,755	5,981	6,286
Scotland	3,401	3,656	3,943	4,283	4,872	5,225	5,608	5,862	6,146	6,607
Northern Ireland	2,811	3,112	3,510	3,780	4,298	4,724	5,130	5,485	5,712	5,926
£ per head, United Kingdom = 100										
United Kingdom	100.0	100.0	100.0	100.0	100.0	100.0	100.0	100.0	100.0	100.0
North	86.6	87.4	89.2	87.8	86.2	86.0	85.8	87.5	89.3	90.4
Yorkshire and Humberside	89.4	88.7	87.6	88.3	88.9	89.0	87.6	88.9	91.7	93.0
East Midlands	93.5	91.0	88.7	89.0	89.7	92.8	95.0	94.2	92.7	92.7
East Anglia	97.0	99.6	100.7	99.0	99.2	99.9	99.8	100.1	100.4	98.1
South East	117.2	118.0	118.7	118.4	117.9	117.2	116.0	115.1	115.4	115.5
Greater London	125.3	123.4	125.7	126.7	127.9	126.7	124.6	122.4	121.4	122.7
Rest of South East	111.9	114.6	114.2	113.0	111.6	111.2	110.6	110.5	111.6	110.9
South West	98.4	99.8	101.9	103.6	102.4	101.3	102.5	102.2	100.3	98.8
West Midlands	92.0	90.3	89.1	89.7	91.0	92.6	92.5	92.0	89.9	88.7
North West	93.7	92.5	93.4	95.0	95.0	94.9	94.6	95.1	94.5	95.0
England	101.7	101.7	102.1	102.3	102.2	102.3	101.9	101.8	101.7	101.6
Wales	88.8	90.8	88.6	86.4	86.5	87.4	89.4	90.9	90.7	90.2
Scotland	96.6	95.2	92.7	91.9	92.8	91.4	92.6	92.6	93.3	94.8
Northern Ireland	79.8	81.0	82.5	81.1	81.9	82.6	84.8	86.6	86.7	85.0

1 Figures are not comparable with earlier years due to the introduction of the community charge in 1989 in Scotland and in 1990 in England and Wales.

Source: Central Statistical Office

12.11 Consumers' expenditure: by broad function, 1993

	£ million						£ per head index UK = 100
	Food, drink and tobacco	Housing and fuel	Other	Consumers' expenditure in the UK[1]	Total consumers' expenditure[2]	£ per head	
United Kingdom	81,551	76,934	238,164	396,649	405,640	6,971	100.0
North	4,455	3,379	10,952	18,786	19,553	6,303	90.4
Yorkshire & Humberside	7,099	5,749	18,489	31,337	32,497	6,481	93.0
East Midlands	5,467	5,125	14,902	25,494	26,385	6,462	92.7
East Anglia	2,686	2,768	8,691	14,144	14,322	6,840	98.1
South East	25,939	27,924	88,432	142,296	143,088	8,053	115.5
Greater London	10,532	11,608	38,580	60,720	59,314	8,555	122.7
Rest of South East	15,407	16,316	49,852	81,576	83,774	7,731	110.9
South West	6,598	6,593	18,837	32,027	32,838	6,887	98.8
West Midlands	6,666	6,794	17,981	31,440	32,721	6,186	88.7
North West	8,983	7,904	24,269	41,156	42,466	6,622	95.0
England	67,892	66,235	202,552	336,680	343,870	7,085	101.6
Wales	3,976	3,610	10,063	17,649	18,269	6,286	90.2
Scotland	7,567	5,370	20,159	33,095	33,830	6,607	94.8
Northern Ireland[3]	2,116	1,719	5,390	9,225	9,671	5,926	85.0

1 Expenditure by UK households and foreign residents in the UK.
2 Expenditure by UK consumers, including private non-profit-making bodies serving persons and UK households abroad but excluding expenditure in the UK by foreign residents in the UK.
3 In 1993, the community charge operated in Great Britain, but domestic rates continued in Northern Ireland. Thus Northern Ireland figures are not comparable with those for Great Britain.

Source: Central Statistical Office

13 Industry and Agriculture

Gross domestic product

The East Midlands, the West Midlands and the North derived the highest proportion of their GDP from manufacturing and the lowest proportion from services of all the regions in 1993.

(Chart 13.1)

East Anglia, followed by Northern Ireland, derived a greater percentage of its GDP from agriculture in 1993 than any other region.

(Chart 13.15)

Businesses

Over a third of Northern Ireland's businesses are involved in agriculture, hunting, forestry or fishing, more than ten times the proportion in the South East.

(Table 13.2)

The West Midlands Metropolitan County and Leicestershire have the highest proportions of their businesses in manufacturing industry of all the counties.

(Chart 13.3)

In 1993, Northern Ireland was the only region where the number of businesses registering for VAT exceeded the number deregistering.

(Table 13.11)

Manufacturing

The level of gross value added in manufacturing in 1992 ranged from £21.300 per person employed in Northern Ireland to £28,100 in the South East.

(Table 13.4)

Assisted areas

Government expenditure on preferential assistance to industry in Assisted Areas rose in all regions in 1993-94 except in Wales.

(Table 13.7)

Construction

New work accounted for 60 per cent of the value of construction contractors' output in Wales in 1994, compared with a little over 50 per cent in the South East.

(Table 13.12)

Economic size of farms

Half of the total business activity of Northern Ireland's farms is found on small holdings, compared with only a tenth in East Anglia.

(Table 13.17)

Crops

The East Midlands had the highest yield of wheat, and Yorkshire and Humberside the highest yield of barley, in 1993.

(Table 13.18)

Animals

The South West and Scotland each account for 18 per cent of the cattle in the United Kingdom, Yorkshire and Humberside accounts for 23 per cent of the pigs and Wales for 26 per cent of the sheep.

(Table 13.19)

Introduction

Many of the tables in this chapter deal with the productivity of, and investment in manufacturing, a major sector of the UK economy in terms of its contribution to the gross domestic product (GDP). Although manufacturing's share of GDP has been slowly declining for many years, it still accounted for over a fifth in 1992-93. Agriculture, although small in terms of its contribution to overall GDP, is nevertheless important to some regions, notably East Anglia, the South West and Northern Ireland.

Information from the Inter-Departmental Business Register (IDBR) is included in *Regional Trends* for the first time at Table 13.2 and Charts 13.3 and 13.16. The IDBR is a structured list of business units for the selection, mailing and grossing of statistical inquiries, combining the Central Statistical Offices's VAT-based business register and the Employment Department's employment statistics system. This information is provided at legal unit level, that is businesses registered for VAT purposes. Businesses generally register for VAT giving their Head Office address, but may have individual local units, for example shops or factories, in other regions. It is estimated that there are around 3.2 million business enterprises operating in the United Kingdom, some of which are single-person or part-time enterprises, but only those registered for VAT (around 1.6 million enterprises) are included in these items.

Data on projects which have successfully attracted inward investment appear at Table 13.6. It should be noted that these figures are based on information provided to the Invest in Britain Bureau of the Department of Trade and Industry by companies at the time of the announcement of the decision to invest. There is no requirement to notify the department, and so the figures include only those projects where the Invest in Britain Bureau or its regional partners were involved, or which have come to their notice. They also take no account of subsequent developments.

Some areas of Great Britain are classified as Development or Intermediate Assisted Areas and are thus eligible for assistance from the UK government. Eligibility depends on various factors, the principal being the level of unemployment. The Assisted Area map was last revised in August 1993 and has resulted in small parts of East Anglia and the South East becoming eligible for assistance for the first time. Chart 13.8 shows the

"....manufacturing's has been

Assisted Area map as it is currently. Information on the regional allocation of European Community Structural Funds is given at Table 13.10; these Funds are allocated according to specific objectives, details of which can be found in the Appendix.

Expenditure on Research and Development (R&D) in the United Kingdom is shown in *Regional Trends* for the first time at Table 13.14. This table shows R&D performed in the United Kingdom by the business, government and higher education sectors. Between 1989 and 1993, R&D expenditure on defence decreased by 34 per cent in real terms, whilst that for civil purposes increased by 9 per cent in real terms. In terms of funding, in 1993, government spent almost £4.5 billion on R&D in all sectors, accounting for around a third of the total, whereas in 1981 almost half of UK R&D was government funded. In real terms, government funding fell by a fifth over this period, while funding by business enterprise increased by more than 50 per cent. Funding from overseas, whilst accounting for only around 12 per cent of total 1993 expenditure, was almost double the 1981 level in real terms.

A new table on agricultural holdings by economic size appears as Table 13.17. Whereas the size of agricultural holdings table in previous editions of *Regional Trends* allowed for comparison of the land under cultivation and size of holdings, it made no allowance for the quality of the land or the purpose to which it was put or for the intensity of land use. Thus no inference could be made of the contribution to the local economy: for example, it was impossible to compare a hill farm, where a large amount of land is necessary to support a relatively small number of sheep, with a poultry farm where a large number of livestock can be kept within a small area.

The concept of Economic Size Units (ESUs) was introduced to allow realistic comparison, both domestically and throughout the European Communities. Under this system, a standard value is calculated for each crop or type of livestock, currently by reference to average 1987-1989 values; the economic worth of each holding is then assessed by applying these values to the areas of each crop and numbers of livestock held. In basic terms, a farm of more than 8 ESUs is taken to be a full-time holding.

share of GDP
slowly declining...."

13.1 Percentage of gross domestic product[1] derived from manufacturing and services, 1993

Manufacturing

Manufacturing as a percentage of total GDP
- 29.0 or over
- 25.0 to 28.9
- 21.0 to 24.9
- 17.0 to 20.9
- 16.9 or less

Services

Services as a percentage of total GDP
- 85.0 or over
- 80.0–84.9
- 75.0–79.9
- 70.0 to 74.9
- 69.9 or under

1 Factor cost at current prices. See Appendix notes.

Source: Central Statistical Office

13.2 Classification of businesses, 1994[1]

Percentages and thousands

	Agriculture, hunting, forestry & fishing	Mining & quarrying, energy, water supply & manu-facturing	Constr-uction	Distribution, hotels & catering, repairs	Transport & communi-cations	Financial intermediation, real estate, renting & business activities	Other services	Total number of local units[2] (=100%) (thousands)
United Kingdom	10.0	10.1	12.2	34.4	4.3	19.9	9.2	1,569
North	14.6	8.5	11.7	39.1	4.9	13.5	7.6	60
Yorkshire & Humberside	10.0	11.1	12.6	39.4	5.3	14.1	7.6	118
East Midlands	11.0	13.1	12.9	35.8	5.1	14.5	7.6	107
East Anglia	15.0	9.6	13.5	31.2	4.6	16.5	9.6	63
South East	3.0	9.5	11.8	31.0	4.0	29.1	11.7	557
South West	16.4	8.7	13.1	33.7	3.7	16.2	8.2	145
West Midlands	9.2	14.4	12.9	35.7	4.3	15.9	7.7	134
North West	5.0	11.4	11.9	41.4	4.8	17.2	8.2	141
England	7.7	10.5	12.3	34.4	4.4	21.2	9.5	1,325
Wales	23.3	7.5	12.6	35.6	4.4	10.2	6.5	76
Scotland	17.5	7.7	12.2	34.5	3.8	15.8	8.5	116
Northern Ireland	34.6	7.6	11.0	31.3	3.2	7.3	5.1	51

1 Legal unit basis, ie by location of VAT registration. Classification based on VAT trade codes.
2 Includes the small number of businesses for which no industrial classification is held on register.

Source: Inter-Departmental Business Register, Central Statistical Office

13.3 Manufacturing and service industry legal units as a percentage of total legal units: by county, 1994

Manufacturing

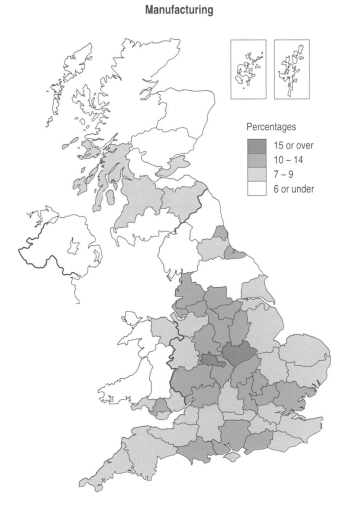

Services

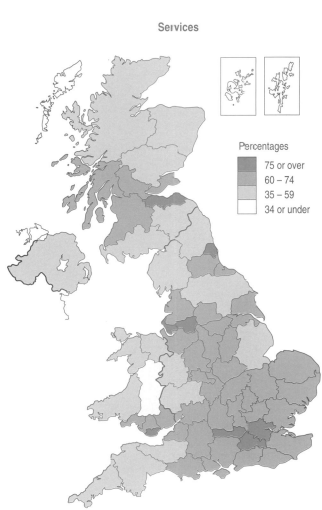

Source: Inter-Departmental Business Register, Central Statistical Office

13.4 Net capital expenditure and gross value added in manufacturing[1], 1981 and 1992

| | Net capital expenditure | | | | Gross value added | | | | | |
| | £ million | | As a percentage of UK | | £ million | | As a percentage of UK | | £ per person employed | |
	1981	1992	1981	1992	1981	1992	1981	1992	1981	1992
United Kingdom	5,493	12,094	100.0	100.0	57,935	108,144	100.0	100.0	10,027	24,752
North	358	837	6.5	6.9	3,576	6,329	6.2	5.8	10,631	25,839
Yorkshire & Humberside	453	1,244	8.3	10.3	5,118	9,636	8.8	8.9	9,191	22,495
East Midlands	398	1,284	7.2	10.6	4,339	9,684	7.5	9.0	8,775	22,698
East Anglia	167	421	3.0	3.5	1,864	3,920	3.2	3.6	10,629	24,914
South East	1,355	2,550	24.7	21.1	16,406	28,381	28.3	26.2	10,976	28,112
South West	342	745	6.2	6.2	3,864	7,378	6.7	6.8	10,326	23,005
West Midlands	532	1,232	9.7	10.2	6,567	12,727	11.3	11.8	8,874	22,048
North West	766	1,662	14.0	13.7	7,836	13,585	13.5	12.6	10,069	25,302
England	4,371	9,976	79.6	82.5	49,570	91,642	85.6	84.7	10,014	24,756
Wales	371	730	6.8	6.0	2,216	5,359	3.8	5.0	9,415	25,546
Scotland	617	1,074	11.2	8.9	5,100	8,799	8.8	8.1	10,701	25,333
Northern Ireland	134	314	2.4	2.6	1,049	2,344	1.8	2.2	9,070	21,269

1 SIC Divisions 2-4. See Appendix notes.

Source: Annual Census of Production, Central Statistical Office

13.5 Gross value added in manufacturing[1]: by size of local unit, 1992

Percentages and £ million

| | Percentage of gross value added by number employed[2] | | | | | | | Total (= 100%) (£ million) |
	1-24	25-49	50-99	100-199	200-499	500-999	1,000 or over	
United Kingdom	13.2	7.9	10.2	13.6	21.9	14.0	19.3	108,144
North	7.4	5.5	7.7	11.9	23.5	17.4	26.5	6,329
Yorkshire & Humberside	12.0	8.4	11.8	16.0	23.1	15.0	13.7	9,636
East Midlands	12.4	8.1	11.2	15.3	24.5	12.9	15.7	9,684
East Anglia	13.4	8.3	12.1	16.1	26.3	16.1	7.7	3,920
South East	16.6	8.6	9.6	11.7	19.7	13.6	20.2	28,381
South West	14.5	8.5	11.1	14.5	25.4	11.1	14.9	7,378
West Midlands	13.9	8.8	11.0	13.0	19.2	10.2	23.9	12,727
North West	10.8	6.6	9.5	14.4	21.9	12.9	24.0	13,585
England	13.5	8.0	10.3	13.5	21.8	13.3	19.6	91,642
Wales	9.9	6.2	9.7	13.5	25.9	15.4	19.4	5,359
Scotland	11.0	7.7	10.1	13.8	20.3	21.0	16.2	8,799
Northern Ireland	16.8	7.4	9.2	14.0	20.3	12.1	20.2	2,344

1 SIC Divisions 2-4. See Appendix notes.
2 Average numbers employed during the year, including full and part-time employees and working proprietors.

Source: Annual Census of Production, Central Statistical Office

13.6 Direct inward investment[1]: project successes[2]

Numbers

	Manufacturing					Non-manufacturing				
	1984	1986	1991	1992	1993	1984	1986	1991	1992	1993
United Kingdom	258	236	275	261	280	82	125	85	61	103
North East	24	26	20	30	30	6	7	11	7	5
Yorkshire & Humberside	7	13	19	28	37	0	1	3	6	13
East Midlands	9	9	6	1	11	0	6	2	2	9
East[3]	..	..	5	2	3	..	..	7	6	8
South East[3]	30	22	19	10	8	36	43	13	8	8
South West	13	8	3	6	11	2	4	3	1	0
West Midlands	11	37	33	36	49	4	40	17	6	19
North West	29	27	59	33	17	13	10	16	5	7
England	123	142	164	146	166	61	111	72	41	69
Wales	47	45	68	61	43	4	6	5	15	24
Scotland	59	33	27	42	57	15	6	2	0	0
Northern Ireland	29	16	16	12	14	2	2	6	5	10

1 See introduction to chapter.
2 A project success is defined as a case where an overseas company specifies an interest and successfully completes investment in a UK company. The regions used in this table are DTI
   regions; please see map on page 233.
3 Prior to 1990, figures for the East are included with those for the South East.

Source: Invest in Britain Bureau, Department of Trade and Industry

13.7 Government expenditure on regional preferential assistance to industry[1]

£ million

	1986-87	1987-88	1988-89	1989-90	1990-91	1991-92	1992-93	1993-94
Great Britain[2]	746.2	556.2	615.7	539.3	497.3	427.8	364.0	394.4
North East	137.3	109.3	134.1	117.0	85.0	63.8	48.3	52.7
Yorkshire & Humberside	41.9	38.8	50.2	32.4	29.4	18.2	13.7	35.6
East Midlands	10.7	9.4	8.8	9.5	5.5	2.6	1.2	1.9
East	0.0	0.0	0.0	0.0	0.0	0.0	0.0	-
South East	0.0	0.0	0.0	0.0	0.0	0.0	0.0	-
South West	23.0	14.8	14.7	10.7	9.0	8.3	8.2	9.5
West Midlands	10.6	19.3	26.2	19.9	18.0	8.7	10.8	14.4
North West	129.6	79.0	82.3	74.3	57.5	49.5	36.8	40.3
England	353.1	270.6	316.3	263.8	204.4	151.1	119.0	154.4
Wales	150.7	132.4	148.2	131.7	133.7	153.9	140.6	118.8
Scotland	242.4	153.2	151.2	143.8	159.2	122.8	104.4	121.2
Northern Ireland[2]	146.7	127.2	137.4	126.0	134.9	138.3	119.1	133.3

1 The regions used in this table are DTI regions; please see map on page 233.
2 The system of assistance available in Northern Ireland is not comparable with that operating in Great Britain, and thus UK figures are not produced. See Appendix notes.

Source: Department of Trade and Industry

13.8 Areas qualifying for preferential assistance to industry [1]

Development Areas
Intermediate Areas

1 At 1 August 1993.

Source: Department of Trade and Industry

13.9 Areas qualifying for EC Structural Funds[1]

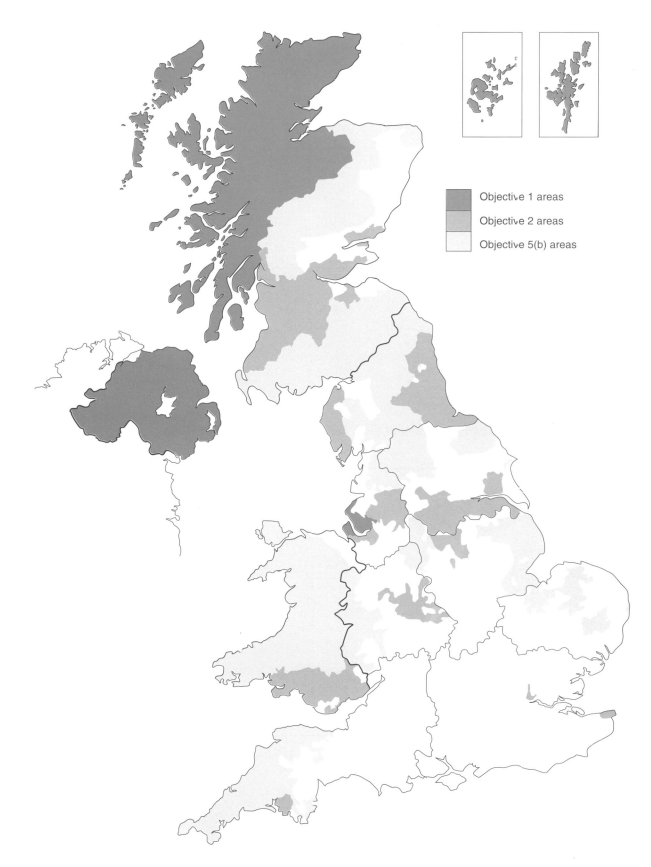

Objective 1 areas
Objective 2 areas
Objective 5(b) areas

1 From 1 January 1994.

Source: Department of Trade and Industry

13.10 Allocation of EC Structural Funds[1]

Million ECUs[2]

	Objective 1[3]			Objective 2[3]			Objective 5b[3]		
	1994	1995	1996	1994	1995	1996	1994	1995	1996
United Kingdom	324	350	375	687	714	736	97	127	147
North	.	.	.	107	111	115	5	7	8
Yorkshire & Humberside	.	.	.	101	105	108	7	9	10
East Midlands	.	.	.	25	26	27	7	9	11
East Anglia	.	.	.	.	.	.	7	9	11
South East	.	.	.	28	29	30	.	.	.
Greater London	.	.	.	24	25	26	.	.	.
Rest of South East	.	.	.	5	5	5	.	.	.
South West	.	.	.	9	10	10	26	34	39
West Midlands	.	.	.	119	124	128	5	7	8
North West	112	121	130	106	110	113	1	1	2
England	112	121	130	496	515	531	59	77	89
Wales	.	.	.	60	63	65	22	29	33
Scotland	43	46	49	131	136	140	17	22	25
Northern Ireland	169	183	196	.	.	.	.	.	.

1 Only allocations resulting from the Commission Single Programming Documents are shown. Allocations resulting from Community Initiatives had not been announced at the time of going to press.
2 The average sterling value of the ECU in 1994 was 1.2924.
3 See Appendix notes.

Source: Department of Trade and Industry

13.11 Business registrations and deregistrations[1]

Thousands

	Net change (registrations *less* deregistrations)								Regist-rations 1993[2]	Deregist-rations 1993[2]	Stock end-93[2]
	1986	1987	1988	1989	1990[2]	1991[2]	1992	1993[2]			
United Kingdom	27.0	41.0	68.0	80.0	55.0	3.0	-42.0	-28.0	190.0	218.0	1,572.3
North	0.5	1.1	1.7	2.3	1.6	0.1	-1.4	-0.8	6.3	7.2	59.8
Yorkshire & Humberside	0.7	1.9	4.4	5.3	3.3	0.6	-2.8	-1.5	13.6	15.2	118.5
East Midlands	1.4	3.0	4.6	5.1	3.1	0.2	-2.1	-1.4	12.3	13.7	108.5
East Anglia	1.3	2.1	3.0	3.0	1.4	-	-1.9	-1.1	6.7	7.8	63.8
South East	15.3	20.6	31.1	35.8	24.0	0.8	-18.8	-9.7	77.9	87.6	548.7
Greater London	5.1	6.9	10.9	14.8	9.2	2.0	-8.0	-2.1	35.5	37.6	227.3
Rest of South East	10.2	13.7	20.1	21.0	14.8	-1.2	-10.8	-7.6	42.4	50.1	321.4
South West	3.1	4.9	7.5	7.5	3.7	-1.4	-5.8	-3.6	15.8	19.4	147.6
West Midlands	1.6	2.8	5.3	6.5	4.2	-	-3.3	-3.1	15.5	18.6	133.5
North West	0.3	1.1	4.3	6.4	6.1	1.5	-3.6	-4.4	17.7	22.1	141.0
England	24.2	37.4	61.9	71.9	47.4	1.9	-39.8	-25.8	165.9	191.6	1,321.4
Wales	0.5	1.5	3.1	3.2	2.1	-0.4	-2.3	-1.8	7.2	9.0	79.7
Scotland	1.9	1.8	2.4	3.9	4.2	0.9	-0.5	-1.1	12.9	14.0	116.9
Northern Ireland	0.5	0.3	0.6	1.0	1.3	0.6	0.5	0.7	4.0	3.3	54.3

1 Businesses registered for VAT. See Appendix notes.
2 Figures for 1990, 1991 and 1993 include adjustments to allow for the effects of changes introduced in the 1990, 1991 and 1993 budgets.

Source: Department of Trade and Industry

13.12 Construction: value at current prices of contractors' output[1]

£ million and percentages

	Total work (£ million)					Of which new work (percentages)				
	1981	1986	1992	1993	1994	1981	1986	1992	1993	1994
Great Britain	18,859	28,935	43,735	42,797	45,802	63.9	56.7	55.9	54.3	54.1
North	915	1,376	1,946	1,863	2,132	70.6	62.3	57.4	56.4	58.7
Yorkshire & Humberside	1,566	2,131	3,566	3,468	3,703	61.1	49.1	54.6	52.9	53.3
East Midlands	1,197	1,824	2,934	3,019	3,294	62.9	52.6	54.9	56.4	56.6
East Anglia	822	1,215	1,801	1,786	1,973	66.3	58.2	55.0	50.7	52.7
South East	6,963	11,162	15,617	14,970	15,561	63.9	60.2	54.9	52.7	51.6
Greater London	3,010	4,354	6,296	5,646	6,106	63.6	60.9	59.8	55.0	55.9
Rest of South East	3,954	6,808	9,321	9,325	9,455	64.2	59.8	51.6	51.2	48.8
South West	1,406	2,509	3,914	3,781	4,045	61.6	53.8	54.7	54.6	54.5
West Midlands	1,428	2,394	3,730	3,7`6	4,037	58.2	53.8	55.5	52.4	52.7
North West	1,845	2,683	3,984	4,1`7	4,575	62.4	53.6	54.4	55.2	55.1
England	16,143	25,293	37,492	36,720	39,320	63.2	56.8	55.0	53.5	53.4
Wales	894	1,074	2,082	1,826	2,174	71.0	51.1	61.0	56.0	59.8
Scotland	1,822	2,568	4,161	4,251	4,309	67.0	58.1	61.4	60.5	57.1

1 Output of contractors, including estimates of unrecorded output by small firms and self-employed workers, classified to construction in the Standard Industrial Classification (revised 1980).
For new work, figures are for the region in which the site is located; for repair and maintenance, figures are for the region in which the reporting unit is based.

Source: Department of the Environment

13.13 Deep mined coal

	Output of saleable coal[1] (million tonnes)			Average number of wage-earners[1] on colliery books (thousands)			Output per manshift[1] (tonnes)		
	1985-86	1991-92	1992-93	1985-86	1991-92	1992-93	1985-86	1991-92	1992-93
Great Britain	87.6	70.6	61.4	154.6	52.3	38.4	2.72	5.31	6.34
North East	9.5	7.6	6.0	19.7	7.8	5.6	2.23	3.74	4.17
North Yorkshire[2]	13.9	.	.	22.8	.	.	3.04	.	.
Selby[2]	.	14.3	15.7	.	7.5	5.4	.	7.48	10.96
South Yorkshire[2]	12.5	13.4	11.0	22.0	10.7	7.9	2.90	5.12	5.73
Nottinghamshire	18.7	17.2	15.3	27.2	13.0	10.3	3.21	5.26	5.91
Midlands and Wales[3]	28.9	15.9	11.4	54.1	12.0	7.9	2.54	5.15	5.88
England and Wales	83.4	68.4	59.4	145.9	50.9	37.1	2.75	5.30	6.37
Scotland	4.2	2.2	2.0	8.8	1.4	1.3	2.21	5.85	5.51
Percentage of GB total									
Great Britain	100.0	100.0	100.0	100.0	100.0	100.0			
North East	10.8	10.7	9.8	12.8	14.8	14.6			
North Yorkshire[2]	15.9	.	.	14.8	.	.			
Selby[2]	.	20.2	25.6	.	14.3	14.0			
South Yorkshire[2]	14.2	19.0	17.9	14.2	20.5	20.6			
Nottinghamshire	21.3	24.4	24.9	17.6	24.8	26.8			
Midlands and Wales[3]	33.0	22.6	18.6	35.0	23.0	20.6			
England and Wales	95.2	96.8	96.8	94.3	97.4	96.6			
Scotland	4.8	3.2	3.2	5.7	2.6	3.4			

1 See Appendix notes.
2 North Yorkshire ceased to operate as a separate area in October 1991. Its operations were transferred to Selby (a new area) and South Yorkshire areas. Data from 1991-92 onwards for North Yorkshire are included in the revised areas; hence data for South Yorkshire from 1991-92 onwards are not comparable with earlier years.
3 The three areas of Central, Western and South Wales have been replaced by a single amalgamated Midlands and Wales area. 1985-86 figures also include Kent.

Source: Department of Trade and Industry

13.14 Expenditure on Research & Development, 1993

£ million

	R&D performed within		
	Businesses	Government[1]	Higher education institutions
United Kingdom	9,069	1,893	2,266
North	132	18	72
Yorkshire & Humberside	230	36	149
East Midlands	790	51	121
East Anglia	257	113	147
South East	5,098	1,027	1,012
South West	553	224	96
West Midlands	721	138	111
North West	892	60	171
England	8,672	1,666	1,879
Wales	112	29	71
Scotland	245	182	277
Northern Ireland	39	15	38

1 Figures include estimates of NHS and local authorities' R&D.

Source: Central Statistical Office

13.15 Percentage of gross domestic product[1] derived from agriculture, 1993

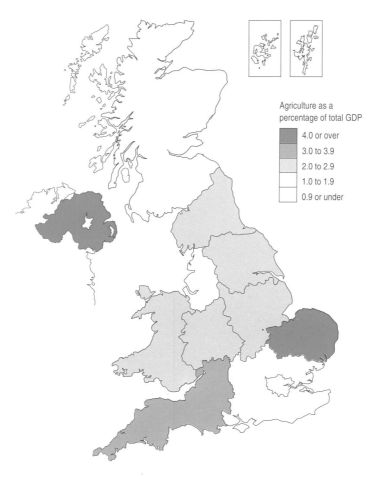

Agriculture as a percentage of total GDP

- 4.0 or over
- 3.0 to 3.9
- 2.0 to 2.9
- 1.0 to 1.9
- 0.9 or under

1 Factor cost at current prices. See Appendix notes.

Source: Central Statistical Office

13.16 Agricultural legal units as a percentage of total legal units: by county, 1994

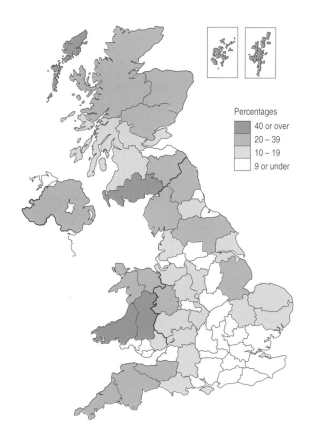

Percentages

- 40 or over
- 20 – 39
- 10 – 19
- 9 or under

Source: Inter-Departmental Business Register, Central Statistical Office

13.17 Agricultural holdings[1]: by economic size[2], 1993

Percentages and thousands

	Percentage of total holdings					Total holdings (=100%) (thou-sands)	Percentage of total ESUs					Total ESUs (=100%) (thou-sands)
	Less than 8 ESU	8-39 ESU	40-99 ESU	100-199 ESU	200 or more ESU		Less than 8 ESU	8-39 ESU	40-99 ESU	100-199 ESU	200 or more ESU	
United Kingdom	43.7	29.6	18.0	6.4	2.3	244.2	2.8	17.1	31.8	24.1	24.2	8,758.4
North	33.1	31.4	27.1	7.6	1.7	11.8	2.0	17.6	44.1	25.9	10.5	464.2
Yorkshire & Humberside	37.4	28.1	22.2	8.6	3.5	17.1	1.8	13.6	30.7	25.0	29.0	790.8
East Midlands	36.0	29.1	20.9	9.3	4.7	17.2	1.6	11.6	25.2	24.5	37.0	909.0
East Anglia	31.2	30.4	20.0	10.4	8.0	12.5	1.1	9.8	19.2	21.1	48.9	853.8
South East	47.1	26.6	14.8	7.6	4.2	26.3	2.4	12.5	23.3	25.2	36.6	1,098.9
South West	47.5	25.7	18.0	6.8	1.9	36.6	2.9	15.8	34.8	27.4	19.2	1,224.6
West Midlands	43.1	28.4	18.8	7.6	2.5	19.7	2.5	15.8	32.3	28.3	21.1	731.5
North West	45.1	26.2	19.7	6.6	1.6	12.2	2.8	16.7	38.2	27.6	14.7	404.3
England	41.8	27.7	19.4	7.9	3.3	153.4	2.1	13.8	29.5	25.5	29.1	6,477.1
Wales	47.5	33.8	16.1	2.7	0.3	29.9	4.6	31.9	43.3	15.2	4.9	663.2
Scotland	44.2	27.4	19.6	6.9	1.9	32.1	2.6	16.9	36.7	27.2	16.5	1,117.3
Northern Ireland	50.0	37.7	10.7	1.5	0.1	28.8	9.4	41.2	36.3	10.9	2.2	500.8

1 Excluding minor holdings. Land in Great Britain let out under short-term lets is attributed to the lessor, but land so let out in Northern Ireland is attributed to the lessee.
2 Economic size is measured by European Size Units (ESUs), which are an estimate of the financial potential of the holding in terms of the margins which might be expected from crops and stock. The margins used are gross margins standardised at average 1987-1989 values. The threshhold of 8 ESU is judged to be the minimum for full-time holdings. See introductory text.

Source: Ministry of Agriculture, Fisheries and Food; Welsh Office; The Scottish Office Agriculture and Fisheries Department; Department of Agriculture for Northern Ireland

13.18 Areas and estimated yields of selected crops[1], 1988-1992[2] and 1993

Thousand hectares and tonnes per hectare

	Areas (thousand hectares)						Estimated yields (tonnes per hectare)					
	Wheat		Barley		Rape (for oilseed)		Wheat		Barley		Rape (for oilseed)	
	1988-1992	1993	1988-1992	1993	1988-1992[3]	1993	1988-1992	1993	1988-1992	1993	1988-1992[3]	1993
United Kingdom	2,006	1,759	1,548	1,164	384	377	6.8	7.3	5.2	5.2	2.9	2.7
North	65	71	81	58	20	21	7.2	7.2	5.3	5.4	..	..
Yorkshire & Humberside	246	235	166	117	51	39	7.2	7.6	5.6	6.0	..	..
East Midlands	393	339	152	105	84	72	6.9	7.7	5.2	5.7	..	..
East Anglia	339	297	183	148	42	32	7.1	7.6	5.4	5.6	..	..
South East	467	375	216	150	93	96	6.4	7.1	5.3	5.4	..	..
South West	193	159	175	129	19	27	6.2	6.7	5.0	5.0	..	..
West Midlands	151	133	112	82	23	24	6.4	7.1	5.0	5.4	..	..
North West	22	22	35	25	4	4	6.2	6.6	4.8	4.9	..	..
England	1,879	1,631	1,121	816	336	315	6.7	7.4	5.2	5.5	2.9	2.8
Wales	11	12	41	33	1	1	6.0	6.5	4.4	5.0	2.7	2.8
Scotland	110	109	346	276	46	60	7.8	7.2	5.2	4.6	3.3	2.1
Northern Ireland	6	7	39	39	1	1	6.8	5.6	4.5	3.6	2.8	1.6

1 Figures for England, Wales and Northern Ireland include estimates for minor holdings; figures for English regions exclude minor holdings and hence their sum may be less than the England total. Figures for Scotland exclude minor holdings. See Appendix notes.
2 Five-year average.
3 The figures for Scotland and Northern Ireland are the four year average of 1989-1992. The figure for yield for Wales is for 1992 only.

Source: Ministry of Agriculture, Fisheries and Food; Welsh Office; The Scottish Office Agriculture and Fisheries Department; Department of Agriculture for Northern Ireland

13.19 Livestock on agricultural holdings, June 1993[1]

Thousands

	Cattle and calves			Sheep and lambs	Pigs	Poultry	
	Total herd[2]	Dairy cows	Beef cows			Total fowls[3]	Total laying flock[4]
United Kingdom	11,729	2,667	1,751	43,901	7,754	130,045	32,695
North	880	171	157	5,121	199	3,321	770
Yorkshire & Humberside	646	151	86	2,670	1,818	13,469	2,158
East Midlands	622	144	71	1,726	637	13,371	4,509
East Anglia	200	35	33	294	1,453	13,428	2,361
South East	736	185	87	2,102	786	17,221	5,869
South West	2,096	661	185	4,223	871	15,513	4,771
West Midlands	921	268	92	3,005	423	13,511	3,516
North West	598	247	36	1,118	313	6,767	2,243
England	6,750	1,863	757	20,448	6,518	96,851	26,397
Wales	1,340	304	214	11,256	108	5,429	927
Scotland	2,062	231	502	9,586	534	14,775	2,250
Northern Ireland	1,578	269	278	2,611	594	12,991	3,121

1 Figures for England, Wales and Northern Ireland include minor holdings; figures for English regions exclude minor holdings and hence their sum may be less than the England total. Figures for Scotland exclude minor holdings. See Appendix notes.
2 Includes bulls, in-calf heifers and fattening cattle and calves.
3 Excludes ducks, geese and turkeys.
4 Excludes growing pullets (from day-old to point of lay).

Source: Ministry of Agriculture, Fisheries and Food; Welsh Office; The Scottish Office Agriculture and Fisheries Department; Department of Agriculture for Northern Ireland

13.20 Agricultural gross domestic fixed capital formation[1]

£ million

	Plant and machinery			Vehicles			Buildings and works			Total		
	1981	1986	1993	1981	1986	1993	1981	1986	1993	1981	1986	1993
United Kingdom	361	495	540	96	112	179	523	432	418	980	1,039	1,137
North	15	29	25	7	8	9	22	26	25	43	63	60
Yorkshire & Humberside	28	46	43	13	13	16	42	42	43	83	101	102
East Midlands	39	57	57	9	10	14	40	25	33	88	92	104
East Anglia	38	53	53	9	9	13	39	23	31	85	85	97
South East	53	74	68	13	13	17	55	32	40	121	119	125
South West	44	60	64	8	11	16	60	31	50	113	102	129
West Midlands	28	36	39	5	7	9	38	18	30	71	62	78
North West	13	21	21	6	6	8	20	18	22	40	45	51
England	258	377	369	71	78	103	316	214	274	645	669	747
Wales	18	30	24	8	10	25	58	42	48	83	82	98
Scotland	59	56	93	10	14	24	79	76	38	149	145	154
Northern Ireland	27	33	54	7	10	27	69	100	57	103	143	138

1 See Appendix notes.

Source: Ministry of Agriculture, Fisheries and Food; Welsh Office; The Scottish Office Agriculture and Fisheries Department; Department of Agriculture for Northern Ireland

13.21 Output and income from agriculture

£ million

	Gross output[1]			Net product[2]			Total income from farming[3]		
	1986	1991	1993	1986	1991	1993	1986	1991	1993
United Kingdom	12,129	13,933	15,612	4,198	4,995	6,280	1,980	2,300	3,939
North	647	782	897	190	231	344	83	135	254
Yorkshire & Humberside	1,157	1,360	1,523	398	435	521	205	214	318
East Midlands	1,328	1,628	1,816	486	625	749	260	351	505
East Anglia	1,376	1,558	1,707	568	642	711	361	365	463
South East	1,869	1,993	2,172	724	823	954	311	233	478
South West	1,674	1,898	2,193	444	518	800	133	144	482
West Midlands	1,124	1,278	1,447	354	427	575	154	205	372
North West	644	762	837	238	302	349	114	152	224
England	9,370	10,746	12,017	3,402	4,002	5,003	1,620	1,800	3,095
Wales	809	912	1,015	238	268	339	131	138	232
Scotland	1,328	1,525	1,719	414	481	637	138	186	363
Northern Ireland	733	878	1,005	144	243	301	90	177	248

1 Gross output figures for each region include the sale of store stock out of the region; thus the sum of components will exceed the totals shown. See Appendix notes.
2 Defined as gross product *less* depreciation of buildings and works and plant, machinery and vehicles.
3 Total income from agriculture for the group with an entrepreneurial interest in the industry (farmers and spouses, non-principal partners and directors and their spouses and family workers).

Source: Ministry of Agriculture, Fisheries and Food; The Scottish Office Agriculture and Fisheries Department; Department of Agriculture for Northern Ireland

14 Sub-regional statistics

Standard regions and counties of England and Wales

Counties

Former Metropolitan counties and Greater London

1 Tyne & Wear
2 Merseyside
3 Greater Manchester
4 West Yorkshire
5 South Yorkshire
6 West Midlands
7 Greater London

Local Authority regions of Scotland and Boards of Northern Ireland

Western
Isles

Orkney Islands

Shetland Islands

Highland

Grampian

SCOTLAND

Tayside

Fife

Central

Central
Clydesdale
Conurbation

Lothian

Borders

Strathclyde

North
Eastern

Belfast

Western

South
Eastern

Southern

Dumfries & Galloway

NORTHERN
IRELAND

1 Education and Library Boards. For Health and Social Services Boards and travel-to-work areas see Appendix.

14.1 Vital and social statistics

	Live births per 1,000 population 1993	Deaths per 1,000 population 1993	Perinatal mortality rate[1] 1991-1993	Infant mortality rate[2] 1991-1993	Percentage of live births outside marriage		Children looked after by LAs[3] per 1,000 population[4] aged under 18 1993
					1981	1993	
United Kingdom	13.1	11.3	7.8	6.8	12.5	31.7	..
North	12.4	12.2	8.3	7.5	13.2	37.2	4.7
Cleveland	13.9	10.8	7.7	7.7	16.3	43.0	..
Cumbria	11.9	12.5	8.7	7.0	10.1	28.8	3.9
Durham	12.2	12.6	7.3	7.1	11.3	36.1	..
Northumberland	11.5	12.7	9.6	7.9	8.2	28.4	3.4
Tyne & Wear	12.3	12.5	8.7	7.7	14.9	40.4	6.0
Yorkshire & Humberside	13.0	11.4	7.9	7.5	13.5	34.0	4.9
Humberside	12.7	11.3	7.8	6.7	15.1	39.8	..
North Yorkshire	11.4	12.3	7.2	6.0	8.5	24.3	..
South Yorkshire	13.1	11.7	8.4	7.9	12.7	36.5	4.5
West Yorkshire	13.7	11.0	7.9	8.1	14.6	33.0	6.9
East Midlands	12.7	11.1	8.0	7.1	12.6	32.1	4.5
Derbyshire	12.6	11.7	6.5	6.1	11.1	31.8	..
Leicestershire	13.0	10.1	9.0	7.8	12.3	28.9	3.0
Lincolnshire	11.6	12.4	9.3	7.5	10.6	30.8	..
Northamptonshire	12.9	10.1	7.8	7.4	12.0	30.5	4.7
Nottinghamshire	12.9	11.2	7.8	6.9	15.6	36.9	5.8
East Anglia	12.2	11.1	6.3	5.2	9.5	27.4	3.8
Cambridgeshire	13.0	9.4	6.4	5.0	8.8	25.2	4.7
Norfolk	11.5	12.2	6.3	5.1	9.9	29.8	4.0
Suffolk	12.2	11.5	6.1	5.4	9.8	27.2	2.7
South East	13.7	10.4	7.4	6.2	12.6	29.3	4.5
Bedfordshire	15.2	8.8	7.7	5.9	10.2	26.4	4.3
Berkshire	13.9	8.5	7.2	6.0	8.9	23.3	4.3
Buckinghamshire	13.6	8.5	6.6	7.2	8.2	23.6	..
East Sussex	11.4	15.0	7.0	6.1	12.7	33.6	5.1
Essex	13.0	10.7	6.9	5.6	9.0	28.0	3.5
Greater London	15.1	9.9	8.1	6.9	17.2	32.9	5.9
Hampshire	13.0	10.2	7.1	5.6	10.0	27.2	3.1
Hertfordshire	13.4	9.5	6.5	4.8	8.4	24.3	..
Isle of Wight	10.6	15.8	7.3	6.0	13.2	34.1	3.9
Kent	13.1	11.5	7.6	6.4	10.4	31.2	..
Oxfordshire	13.1	8.9	6.8	4.9	8.4	22.7	3.8
Surrey	12.0	10.5	5.8	4.5	7.2	20.8	2.1
West Sussex	11.3	13.8	6.9	5.4	7.9	25.9	4.2
South West	11.9	11.9	6.7	5.9	10.3	28.9	4.0
Avon	12.6	10.8	6.9	5.9	11.6	30.0	..
Cornwall[5]	11.1	13.1	7.5	6.1	9.6	30.2	3.9
Devon	11.2	12.8	6.6	6.4	10.7	30.5	4.5
Dorset	10.9	13.5	6.1	5.4	9.7	27.8	4.1
Gloucestershire	12.3	11.1	6.8	6.0	10.7	28.2	3.0
Somerset	11.7	12.0	6.8	5.1	9.1	28.8	4.0
Wiltshire	13.2	10.2	6.5	6.2	9.5	25.6	3.8
West Midlands	13.2	11.0	9.1	8.0	12.8	33.1	4.9
Hereford & Worcs.	11.9	11.0	7.9	7.2	9.2	29.1	4.4
Shropshire	12.5	10.6	8.3	7.4	9.6	30.9	3.9
Staffordshire	12.2	10.9	8.0	7.5	8.9	31.1	4.6
Warwickshire	11.7	11.0	9.1	6.6	9.7	27.6	4.2
West Midlands (Met. county)	14.3	11.0	9.9	8.6	16.0	35.9	5.3
North West	13.2	12.1	7.9	7.0	15.5	38.2	5.3
Cheshire	12.4	10.8	6.4	6.4	9.6	30.2	..
Greater Manchester	13.8	11.9	8.7	7.4	17.3	39.7	..
Lancashire	13.0	12.8	8.2	7.8	12.9	34.6	5.2
Merseyside	12.8	12.5	6.9	5.9	18.2	44.0	6.0
England	13.1	11.1	7.7	6.7	12.9	32.0	4.6

Regional Trends 30, © Crown copyright 1995

14.1 *(continued)*

	Live births per 1,000 population . 1993	Deaths per 1,000 population 1993	Perinatal mortality rate[1] 1991-1993	Infant mortality rate[2] 1991-1993	Percentage of live births outside marriage		Children looked after by LAs[3] per 1,000 population[4] aged under 18 1993
					1981	1993	
Wales (Counties)	12.6	12.3	7.3	6.0	11.2	35.2	4.6
Clwyd	12.2	12.9	6.5	6.0	9.3	33.6	3.2
Dyfed	11.0	13.0	6.8	5.9	9.1	29.0	4.4
Gwent	13.4	11.5	7.7	6.8	11.6	37.5	5.7
Gwynedd	11.9	13.8	6.5	4.7	11.2	33.8	3.3
Mid-Glamorgan	13.3	12.2	7.9	5.8	11.5	39.1	5.0
Powys	11.7	12.5	6.7	6.7	8.0	27.3	3.0
South Glamorgan	13.7	10.8	7.7	6.0	16.3	36.3	6.1
West Glamorgan	12.0	12.9	7.3	6.2	9.4	35.3	4.3
Scotland (LA Regions)	12.4	12.5	9.1	6.8	12.2	31.3	..
Borders	10.8	13.2	6.9	5.0	9.7	22.9	..
Central	12.2	12.0	9.0	6.9	11.2	29.9	..
Dumfries & Galloway	11.6	13.2	9.5	8.4	10.4	27.3	..
Fife	12.2	11.7	8.7	6.2	11.0	30.7	..
Grampian	12.5	11.1	8.3	5.1	10.6	24.9	..
Highland	12.3	11.6	9.2	6.6	11.3	30.9	..
Lothian	12.4	11.8	9.6	6.8	11.8	29.9	..
Strathclyde	12.6	13.0	9.4	7.4	12.9	34.0	..
Tayside	12.0	13.6	7.9	6.0	14.9	34.3	..
Islands	11.6	14.0	8.7	6.9	8.1	21.6	..
Northern Ireland (Boards)[6]	15.3	9.6	8.5	6.8	7.0	21.9	4.4
Belfast	14.8	11.9	8.0	6.3	11.6	35.9	..
South Eastern	13.9	9.3	7.8	6.2	4.9	19.0	5.4
Southern	16.3	9.0	8.5	6.7	4.6	15.5	3.1
North Eastern	14.5	9.1	9.1	6.1	8.0	20.8	4.1
Western	17.3	8.9	8.9	9.0	5.9	20.6	4.3

1 Still births and deaths of infants under 1 week of age per 1,000 live and still births, 3 year average. On 1 October 1992 the legal definition of a still birth was altered from a baby born dead after 28 weeks completed gestation or more, to one born dead after 24 weeks gestation or more. To enable comparisons to be made, the figures given are all by the *old* definition.
2 Deaths of infants under 1 year of age per 1,000 live births, 3 year average.
3 As at 31 March. Legislation in Scotland relating to children in care is different from that in England, and no comparable Scottish statistics are available. Figures for the English regions and metropolitan counties are estimates which take account of missing or incomplete data. Figures for Northern Ireland relate to children in care excluding children home on trial.
4 For England & Wales population figures used are based on 1992 mid-year estimates.
5 Figures for the Isles of Scilly are included with Cornwall.
6 Education and Library Boards, except for Children looked after figures which relate to Health and Social Services Board Areas. See Appendix notes.

Source: Office of Population and Censuses Surveys; Welsh Office; General Register Offices for Scotland and Northern Ireland; Department of Health; Department of Health and Social Services, Northern Ireland

14.2 Education

	Day nursery places[1] per 1,000 pop. aged under 5 years[2] March 1993	Children under 5 in education (percentages) Jan. 1993[3]	Pupil/teacher ratio January 1993[3]		Pupils aged 16 partici- pating in education (percentages)		Percentage of 16 year olds[5] in schools 1992/9		Percentage of 17-19 year olds[6] 1992/93
			Primary schools	Secondary schools	Jan. 1986[4]	Jan. 1993	with no graded results	with 5 or more A-Cs at GCSE	with 2 or more A levels[7]
United Kingdom	..	51	22.1	15.7	67	78	7	39	22
North	26.1	77	22.7	16.1	61	71	8	35	18
Cleveland	38.3	92	23.5	15.7	66	73	10	31	19
Cumbria	24.8	58	22.3	15.3	73	75	6	41	21
Durham	13.7	77	22.7	16.3	60	70	7	34	16
Northumberland	13.6	74	23.8	17.8	63	68	6	41	23
Tyne & Wear	29.8	77	22.1	16.0	54	69	10	32	17
Yorkshire & Humberside	31.8	64	22.3	16.1	63	74	8	34	18
Humberside	28.9	61	23.1	16.3	63	73	8	31	17
North Yorkshire	43.6	50	22.6	15.7	70	82	4	47	23
South Yorkshire	15.8	66	22.6	16.0	65	68	9	32	16
West Yorkshire	38.9	68	21.8	16.2	61	74	10	32	17
East Midlands	34.0	51	22.7	15.8	68	75	6	37	27
Derbyshire	37.4	61	22.9	15.4	72	75	5	38	19
Leicestershire	29.9	39	22.5	15.8	65	76	6	38	21
Lincolnshire	25.5	43	23.1	15.8	70	74	6	39	22
Northamptonshire	47.0	49	22.6	16.6	68	79	5	38	21
Nottinghamshire	31.3	57	22.6	15.7	67	73	7	33	18
East Anglia	27.3	37	22.1	16.1	60	76	5	41	20
Cambridgeshire	42.4	44	23.0	16.5	58	80	6	41	22
Norfolk	23.1	35	21.8	15.6	58	74	6	39	19
Suffolk	15.8	32	21.4	16.1	65	74	3	43	20
South East	45.4	40	21.9	16.2	62	83	7	39	22
Bedfordshire	40.9	48	21.7	17.1	72	82	5	38	23
Berkshire	40.1	31	22.8	16.0	66	88	5	44	26
Buckinghamshire	19.8	31	22.8	16.7	65	80	5	47	27
East Sussex	49.2	38	22.3	15.9	61	83	7	42	23
Essex	15.7	23	23.1	16.9	57	74	6	39	24
Greater London	64.4	55	21.1	15.8	59	80	9	34	18
Hampshire	21.6	21	21.9	16.1	59	78	5	42	23
Hertfordshire	14.8	50	22.1	15.7	76	95	6	45	26
Isle of Wight	7.1	41	22.1	17.2	76	84	4	35	19
Kent	63.3	36	23.9	17.0	66	81	6	39	23
Oxfordshire	39.1	22	21.6	16.7	60	85	5	45	20
Surrey	32.4	26	21.7	15.8	64	86	5	47	25
West Sussex	29.3	22	22.1	16.4	67	84	4	47	26
South West	34.2	37	22.7	16.5	65	82	4	42	21
Avon	46.8	52	22.7	16.2	60	86	6	37	20
Cornwall	18.3	45	23.3	16.7	75	81	4	42	22
Devon	32.0	28	22.8	16.2	62	77	5	41	21
Dorset	23.8	37	23.2	17.0	58	83	4	44	22
Gloucestershire	47.2	32	21.9	17.1	71	86	4	45	26
Somerset	34.9	35	22.5	16.3	73	82	3	44	20
Wiltshire	27.0	25	22.6	16.3	65	80	4	43	20
West Midlands	43.1	58	22.8	16.2	68	76	7	35	19
Hereford & Worcs.	62.1	21	21.8	16.9	74	79	5	40	21
Shropshire	37.0	35	22.0	15.3	77	82	4	43	20
Staffordshire	51.4	57	24.7	16.9	71	74	6	36	20
Warwickshire	35.7	49	22.3	16.3	77	81	5	40	24
West Midlands (met county)	37.7	72	22.6	15.8	63	74	9	30	17
North West	50.8	64	23.0	15.8	72	75	9	37	19
Cheshire	53.0	53	23.9	16.6	78	81	5	44	26
Greater Manchester	53.1	69	22.9	15.5	70	71	10	35	18
Lancashire	61.5	52	22.8	15.9	69	75	7	39	19
Merseyside	34.6	72	23.0	15.9	75	76	12	32	18
England	40.6	51	22.4	16.1	65	78	7	38	20

Regional Trends 30, © Crown copyright 1995

14.2   *(continued)*

	Day nursery places[1] per 1,000 pop. aged under 5 years[2] March 1993	Children under 5 in education (percent-ages) Jan. 1993[3]	Pupil/teacher ratio January 1993[3]		Pupils aged 16 partici-pating in education (percentages)		Percentage of 16 year olds[5] in schools 1992/9		Percentage of 17-19 year olds[6] 1992/93
			Primary schools	Secondary schools	Jan. 1986[4]	Jan. 1993	with no graded results	with 5 or more A-Cs at GCSE	with 2 or more A levels[7]
Wales (counties)	28.6	71	22.1	15.7	65	63	6	37	30
Clwyd	64.2	81	23.5	15.6	66	72	4	37	28
Dyfed	23.8	67	19.5	16.0	65	83	4	44	31
Gwent	16.6	70	23.4	15.6	61	76	5	32	24
Gwynedd	23.4	45	21.1	14.4	68	74	5	39	26
Mid-Glamorgan	12.0	74	23.5	15.9	73	76	7	29	25
Powys	32.9	54	20.6	14.7	78	77	5	40	24
South Glamorgan	39.8	62	22.0	16.3	57	79	10	35	31
West Glamorgan	23.7	89	21.3	15.7	65	79	6	35	32
Scotland (LA regions)	42.5	43	19.3	12.6	84	83	7	48	26
Borders	41.0	27	18.0	12.0	85	80	3	60	26
Central	42.7	51	20.0	13.3	84	82	5	49	27
Dumfries & Galloway	27.5	42	18.6	12.0	92	77	4	56	30
Fife	20.9	58	19.3	13.3	93	100	6	48	25
Grampian	39.0	42	18.9	12.5	81	80	7	50	27
Highland	8.0	23	17.0	11.8	80	84	5	52	27
Lothian	56.7	54	19.8	12.7	80	78	9	47	29
Strathclyde	46.1	40	19.8	12.8	83	79	8	45	24
Tayside	48.8	43	19.7	12.2	83	76	9	48	29
Islands	24.6	30	13.4	9.8	87	97	3	63	31
Northern Ireland (Boards)[8]	15.8	45	21.6	15.1	60	95	6	48	35
Belfast[9]	..	..	21.7	14.7	..	..	7	52	..
South Eastern[9]	20.5	..	21.7	15.1	..	..	3	46	..
Southern	12.0	..	21.1	15.4	..	..	6	51	..
North Eastern	15.7	..	21.8	14.8	..	..	5	47	..
Western	9.8	..	21.6	15.4	..	..	7	46	..

1 Local authority provided and registered day nurseries only. A small number of places provided by facilities exempt from registration are excluded. Figures for day nursery places for England and some local authorities are estimates.
2 Population data used are mid-1992.
3 September 1992 for Scotland and October 1992 for Northern Ireland.
4 Data for Scotland relate to 1984/85.
5 Aged 16 at the end of the school year, as a percentage of all 15 year olds in schools. Year 4 pupils in Scotland, and Year 12 in Northern Ireland.
6 Aged 17-19 at the end of the school year in England and Wales as a percentage of the 18 year old population. The figures for Scotland are not strictly comparable with those for England and Wales; pupils in Scotland mostly sit Highers one year earlier and the figures relate to the results of pupils in Year S5 as a percentage of the 17 year old population.
7 3 or more SCE Higher Grades in Scotland. Two AS levels are equivalent to one 'A' level.
8 Education and library boards, except for day nursery information which refers to health and social services board areas.
9 South Eastern figure for day nursery places includes Belfast.

Source: Department of Health; Department for Education; Welsh Office; The Scottish Office Education Department;
Department of Health and Social Services, Northern Ireland;
Department of Education, Northern Ireland

14.3 Economic statistics

	Claimant unemploy-ment rate[1] (January 1995) (percentages)	Manufacturing 1992				Gross domestic product[2]			
		£ per employee index (UK=100)		Employ-ment (thou-sands)	Average wages/ salaries[4]	1981		1991	
		Net capital expen-diture[3]	Gross value added			£ million[5]	£ per head index UK=100[6]	£ million[5]	£ per head Index UK=100[6]
United Kingdom	8.9	100.0	100.0	4,369.1	14,146	206,422	100.0	488,971	100.0
North	11.3	123.5	104.4	245.0	14,196	10,720	93.9	23,671	90.5
Cleveland	14.0	92.1	110.0	43.2	14,932	2,069	99.0	4,221	89.3
Cumbria	8.1	83.5	97.5	44.7	14,303	1,830	103.8	4,679	112.7
Durham	10.0	127.4	115.3	49.5	13,786	1,940	86.6	4,054	79.1
Northumberland	11.1	119.7	94.0	17.7	12,929	955	87.1	1,982	76.1
Tyne & Wear	12.1	156.9	101.2	89.9	14,265	3,927	92.8	8,734	91.5
Yorkshire & Humberside	9.4	104.9	90.9	428.4	13,308	16,627	92.3	38,527	91.7
Humberside	10.5	175.9	108.5	82.2	14,443	2,733	87.0	7,135	96.2
North Yorkshire	6.3	127.3	95.6	42.7	13,328	2,393	96.5	6,051	99.0
South Yorkshire	12.0	83.5	84.1	99.7	13,088	4,465	92.5	8,787	80.2
West Yorkshire	8.5	82.0	86.1	203.7	12,952	7,036	92.9	16,553	94.5
East Midlands	8.4	108.7	91.7	426.6	12,882	13,696	97.0	33,168	97.1
Derbyshire	9.0	197.0	95.7	105.2	13,315	3,038	90.7	7,181	90.1
Leicestershire	6.8	74.1	88.9	120.8	12,753	3,262	103.7	7,903	104.6
Lincolnshire	8.6	71.6	81.8	42.6	12,544	1,860	91.8	4,586	91.2
Northamptonshire	6.6	91.5	95.5	64.8	13,355	1,775	91.0	5,061	101.6
Nottinghamshire	10.3	82.8	92.7	93.2	12,387	3,762	103.3	8,438	98.0
East Anglia	7.0	96.6	100.7	157.4	14,200	6,706	96.6	17,796	100.4
Cambridgeshire	6.0	92.5	107.9	57.3	15,135	2,261	104.4	6,173	108.7
Norfolk	8.0	99.6	100.0	50.4	13,546	2,404	93.5	6,107	94.8
Suffolk	6.7	98.6	93.0	49.7	13,785	2,040	92.6	5,517	98.3
South East	8.5	91.3	113.6	1,009.6	15,722	72,655	116.6	174,673	117.3
Bedfordshire	7.7	74.6	109.6	51.0	15,457	1,768	94.6	4,562	100.7
Berkshire	5.4	87.2	126.4	50.0	16,792	2,928	115.2	8,234	129.0
Buckinghamshire	5.7	76.5	103.6	54.1	15,475	1,919	91.6	6,155	113.4
East Sussex	10.5	77.6	92.4	24.8	13,605	1,971	80.9	4,750	78.2
Essex	9.2	74.9	91.7	94.7	15,477	4,793	88.2	10,843	82.6
Greater London	10.1	92.2	120.6	330.2	16,043	37,080	148.7	84,510	146.5
Hampshire	6.8	107.7	106.1	111.8	15,565	5,812	106.6	13,798	103.1
Hertfordshire	6.2	71.5	122.9	77.5	16,659	3,752	106.2	8,625	102.8
Isle of Wight	12.2	92.7	87.1	6.2	13,389	328	75.9	759	70.7
Kent	9.1	119.3	117.1	85.0	15,077	4,776	87.8	12,009	92.0
Oxfordshire	5.1	115.8	118.8	37.8	15,297	1,859	93.6	5,157	104.9
Surrey[7]	..	94.4	115.9	44.6	15,531	3,484	93.5	9,420	107.3
West Sussex	5.9	83.0	115.0	42.0	15,288	2,185	89.5	5,850	96.7
South West	8.1	83.9	92.9	320.7	13,973	14,985	93.4	37,784	94.3
Avon	8.0	95.2	96.3	66.4	15,284	3,494	102.7	8,505	104.2
Cornwall	11.3	56.6	87.9	22.6	12,137	1,208	77.3	2,937	72.9
Devon	9.0	89.1	91.7	57.0	13,282	3,130	88.5	7,679	87.1
Dorset	8.1	60.3	82.8	39.0	13,538	1,913	87.3	5,037	89.6
Gloucestershire	7.0	71.6	94.6	49.6	14,110	1,895	102.3	4,609	100.9
Somerset	7.2	68.0	93.7	39.4	13,590	1,445	91.6	3,651	91.7
Wiltshire	5.8	120.8	98.2	46.8	14,380	1,901	98.9	5,365	110.0
West Midlands	8.8	77.1	89.1	577.2	13,430	17,265	90.9	41,183	92.4
Hereford & Worcs.	7.1	77.6	86.3	58.8	12,789	1,893	81.2	4,943	85.0
Shropshire	6.7	116.0	87.5	38.1	12,923	1,127	80.8	3,176	90.8
Staffordshire	7.5	77.2	87.0	120.5	12,806	3,188	85.4	7,542	84.9
Warwickshire	6.4	91.1	104.5	46.4	14,133	1,541	88.2	4,038	97.2
West Midlands (Met county)	10.4	70.2	88.3	313.4	13,747	9,515	97.2	21,484	96.7
North West	9.2	111.9	102.2	536.9	14,497	22,349	94.5	48,880	90.4
Cheshire	7.0	210.9	128.1	93.9	17,208	3,648	106.8	8,493	103.6
Greater Manchester	8.9	94.8	97.1	223.6	13,608	9,169	95.6	20,155	92.8
Lancashire	7.1	64.2	91.5	137.1	13,794	4,561	89.9	11,139	93.3
Merseyside	13.4	124.8	104.7	82.3	14,988	4,971	89.1	9,092	74.4
England	8.8	97.4	100.0	3,701.8	14,263	175,003	102.0	415,681	102.0

14.3 *(continued)*

	Claimant unemploy-ment rate[1] (January 1995) (percentages)	Manufacturing 1992				Gross domestic product[2]			
		£ per employee index (UK=100)		Employ-ment (thou-sands)	Average wages/ salaries[4]	1981		1991	
		Net capital expen-diture[3]	Gross value added			£ million[5]	£ per head index UK=100[6]	£ million[5]	£ per head Index UK=100[6]
Wales (counties)	9.2	125.7	103.2	209.8	13,806	8,639	83.8	20,833	85.1
Clwyd	7.8	137.9	112.9	40.4	14,439	1,038	72.0	3,247	92.5
Dyfed[8]	9.1	145.6	80.7	12.9	12,350	1,368	84.1	3,006	75.5
Gwent	9.3	108.2	106.7	47.8	14,005	1,313	81.1	3,257	85.9
Gwynedd	11.1	72.4	69.9	8.0	12,002	662	78.1	1,555	76.4
Mid-Glamorgan	10.8	99.5	92.1	47.4	13,035	1,501	75.7	3,186	69.4
Powys	5.4	54.4	78.5	8.3	11,125	..	..	..	..
South Glamorgan	8.8	132.6	107.4	20.4	14,538	1,480	103.7	3,819	110.9
West Glamorgan	9.0	215.4	129.4	24.6	15,517	1,277	93.7	2,762	88.3
Scotland (LA Regions)	9.0	111.7	102.4	347.3	13,896	18,349	96.7	41,485	95.8
Borders	5.6	66.0	78.3	9.8	11,492	340	91.6	719	81.5
Central	9.5	365.2	112.8	20.4	14,509	1,032	103.0	2,029	87.7
Dumfries & Galloway	9.2	66.0	110.7	9.7	12,840	515	96.6	1,085	86.6
Fife	11.2	76.8	93.4	29.3	13,940	1,246	99.6	2,509	84.7
Grampian	5.2	92.1	97.9	33.9	13,590	2,116	119.1	5,893	134.8
Highland[9]	10.2	88.9	105.8	9.7	16,230	983	98.7	2,040	87.3
Lothian	7.4	106.3	106.2	48.9	14,113	2,855	104.0	7,038	110.5
Strathclyde	10.3	92.9	104.6	156.6	14,000	7,935	89.7	17,209	88.3
Tayside	8.8	145.3	96.0	27.2	13,339	1,327	91.3	2,962	89.0
Islands	7.3	86.3	85.1	2.1	12,006	..	..	.	..
Northern Ireland (Boards)	12.3	103.0	85.9	110.2	11,642	4,431	78.7	10,972	81.1
Belfast	..	..	..	..	..	..	..	..	..
South Eastern	..	..	..	..	..	..	..	..	..
Southern	..	..	..	..	..	..	..	..	..
North Eastern	..	..	..	..	..	..	..	..	..
Western	..	..	..	..	..	..	..	..	..

1 Claimant unemployed. Not adjusted to take account of seasonal influences.
2 County level GDP data are consistent with the National figures published inn the CSO Blue Book 1993 (HMSO). Estimates for the Scottish regions have been revised reflecting improved methodology.
3 New building work *plus* acquisitions *less* disposals of land and existing buildings, vehicles and plant and machinery. Includes expenditure on establishments where production had not started before the end of the year.
4 Includes employers' National Insurance contributions, overtime, bonuses and redundancy payments.
5 United Kingdom data exclude Continental Shelf and the statistical discrepancy which in 1991 were £5,863 million and -£10 million respectively.
6 County GDP indices are based on United Kingdom excluding Continental Shelf region.
7 Unemployment rates cannot be calculated for Surrey since it does not meet the self-containment criteria for a local labour market.
8 GDP figures include Powys.
9 GDP figures include Islands.

Source: Employment Department; Central Statistical Office

14.4 Income

	Average gross weekly full-time earnings[1] (£) April 1994						Household income 1992		Household disposable income 1992	
	Males			Females						
		10 per cent earned			10 per cent earned			£ per head		£ per head
	Total	Less than	More than	Total	Less than	More than	£ million	(UK =100)	£ million	(UK =100)
United Kingdom	361.0	..	..	260.8	..	..	531,148	100.0	436,504	100.0
North	327.8	170.8	517.6	237.0	129.6	389.5	25,856	91.1	21,862	93.8
Cleveland	334.7	174.7	515.2	226.8	117.4	376.0	4,531	88.4	3,859	91.6
Cumbria	343.0	173.9	544.9	227.0	132.4	371.7	4,567	101.8	3,814	103.4
Durham	320.6	169.2	490.0	238.6	126.7	399.0	4,731	85.1	4,031	88.2
Northumberland	318.2	166.2	523.2	234.6	129.6	380.0	2,799	99.5	2,327	100.7
Tyne & Wear	323.5	169.7	513.6	243.4	133.4	398.6	9,228	88.8	7,831	91.7
Yorkshire & Humberside	329.5	173.5	513.1	238.4	132.3	392.1	42,378	92.5	35,591	94.5
Humberside	332.3	180.5	518.5	225.8	127.3	377.4	7,399	91.7	6,202	93.5
North Yorkshire	315.7	159.9	499.6	232.2	128.7	388.7	7,168	108.3	5,907	108.6
South Yorkshire	324.2	172.1	504.7	233.9	132.0	382.4	10,350	86.7	8,838	90.0
West Yorkshire	335.3	176.4	521.2	246.4	136.3	399.0	17,461	91.1	14,645	93.0
East Midlands	325.0	175.5	496.9	230.5	128.2	377.6	35,221	94.7	29,321	95.9
Derbyshire	325.9	175.0	479.6	227.2	126.9	380.3	7,695	88.7	6,352	89.1
Leicestershire	327.8	178.2	514.2	232.5	127.5	396.3	8,041	97.3	6,714	98.9
Lincolnshire	307.5	170.5	487.2	221.9	126.9	399.5	5,452	99.8	4,579	102.0
Northamptonshire	339.2	189.8	500.7	235.6	134.7	365.2	5,329	98.6	4,369	98.4
Nottinghamshire	322.0	167.8	507.1	231.5	128.1	376.9	8,703	92.7	7,306	94.7
East Anglia	334.8	179.9	527.4	241.6	136.5	397.9	19,495	101.9	16,178	102.9
Cambridgeshire	351.6	185.5	547.0	257.9	142.9	406.2	6,591	106.2	5,418	106.2
Norfolk	318.3	175.8	507.1	235.4	134.0	382.3	7,138	102.2	5,997	104.5
Suffolk	333.3	175.0	518.7	225.1	125.0	390.5	5,765	97.2	4,763	97.7
South East	419.4	196.5	691.3	301.1	159.0	466.2	183,495	113.2	145,219	109.0
Bedfordshire	379.0	196.5	587.7	261.2	151.9	384.0	5,181	105.4	4,189	103.7
Berkshire	439.9	200.0	748.2	288.3	172.2	447.4	7,884	113.6	6,025	105.6
Buckinghamshire	393.9	191.0	642.4	276.5	153.5	421.2	6,749	114.1	5,204	107.1
East Sussex	327.8	162.2	538.9	254.2	139.4	398.8	6,655	100.9	5,513	101.7
Essex	369.7	187.8	596.9	266.4	143.6	412.5	15,291	107.3	12,119	103.5
Greater London	467.3	211.9	784.9	336.5	179.4	515.6	75,131	118.8	59,074	113.7
Hampshire	368.7	187.2	591.5	252.4	146.5	383.9	15,421	106.1	12,518	104.8
Hertfordshire	391.7	192.5	654.4	276.0	149.5	425.7	10,993	120.7	8,610	115.1
Isle of Wight	291.4	154.7	428.4	..	..	..	1,044	90.8	894	94.5
Kent	347.3	177.2	554.1	253.9	135.7	406.7	14,306	101.6	11,614	100.3
Oxfordshire	365.9	184.9	586.5	261.7	147.5	398.2	5,742	106.8	4,639	105.0
Surrey	423.3	202.3	698.6	291.0	158.9	467.5	11,974	126.1	9,047	116.0
West Sussex	376.2	177.7	618.5	274.0	159.7	440.7	7,123	109.2	5,774	107.7
South West	343.9	174.8	539.9	245.4	136.8	398.3	43,791	100.8	36,443	102.0
Avon	358.9	182.7	568.9	256.0	147.1	404.2	8,865	100.0	7,224	99.1
Cornwall	292.2	152.3	473.9	221.4	122.0	376.0	3,952	90.8	3,326	93.0
Devon	316.9	162.7	504.6	235.5	133.1	387.1	9,484	99.1	8,043	102.3
Dorset	339.0	176.4	527.6	243.7	142.3	394.7	6,435	105.8	5,380	107.6
Gloucestershire	366.8	182.4	571.0	257.1	135.6	420.7	5,118	103.2	4,223	103.7
Somerset	328.1	171.5	518.5	235.5	131.4	422.9	4,264	98.6	3,595	101.1
Wiltshire	372.5	192.8	616.2	251.3	148.6	395.1	5,672	106.9	4,654	106.7
West Midlands	336.2	174.5	522.4	236.5	132.5	384.9	44,923	93.0	37,239	93.8
Hereford & Worcs.	318.3	166.1	494.2	242.5	138.6	400.0	6,492	102.7	5,302	102.1
Shropshire	308.4	165.6	500.3	221.5	123.7	376.5	3,505	92.7	2,932	94.4
Staffordshire	316.2	168.7	491.8	229.0	131.5	384.3	9,152	95.0	7,637	96.5
Warwickshire	351.7	184.9	519.6	234.8	129.7	404.9	4,715	104.7	3,776	102.0
West Midlands (Met county)	348.1	179.3	541.2	240.2	134.0	381.7	21,059	87.4	17,592	88.9
North West	343.9	175.2	544.1	243.6	135.7	394.0	53,744	91.7	45,243	93.9
Cheshire	374.7	188.0	593.9	248.7	141.2	384.5	8,902	100.5	7,268	99.9
Greater Manchester	342.1	173.0	551.4	246.2	137.0	398.1	21,428	90.9	18,138	93.7
Lancashire	326.8	169.3	500.1	230.1	128.7	377.5	11,876	91.8	10,074	94.7
Merseyside	338.4	180.6	536.1	248.0	139.6	399.6	11,539	87.2	9,763	89.7
England	367.0	181.0	589.3	264.6	140.4	422.7	448,903	101.3	367,096	100.8

14.4 *(continued)*

	Average gross weekly full-time earnings[1] (£) April 1994						Household income 1992		Household disposable income 1992	
	Males			Females						
		10 per cent earned			10 per cent earned			£ per head		£ per head
	Total	Less than	More than	Total	Less than	More than	£ million	(UK =100)	£ million	(UK =100)
Wales (counties)	320.9	167.6	499.9	239.0	131.6	398.9	23,558	88.8	20,060	92.0
Clwyd	331.0	169.5	513.3	230.7	123.3	381.8	3,409	89.8	2,875	92.2
Dyfed[2]	304.0	163.1	482.1	..	..	..	3,769	87.5	3,210	90.7
Gwent	307.8	169.5	461.7	222.7	122.2	365.8	3,626	88.1	3,098	91.6
Gwynedd	315.3	160.8	492.5	..	..	..	2,090	95.2	1,800	99.8
Mid-Glamorgan	308.3	161.6	491.2	244.1	131.5	423.1	3,964	79.7	3,362	82.3
Powys	288.1	157.4	456.7	..	..	..	..	..	..	..
South Glamorgan	339.6	179.4	542.2	255.8	145.3	412.7	3,619	96.3	3,098	100.3
West Glamorgan[3]	330.2	162.5	509.2	239.4	136.4	398.5	3,083	90.7	2,618	93.7
Scotland (LA regions)	335.6	175.0	541.4	244.1	132.5	394.9	46,347	99.0	38,770	100.8
Borders	..	..	..	..	..	..	971	101.2	799	101.3
Central	344.0	179.1	561.7	236.6	129.7	369.8	2,313	92.6	1,963	95.7
Dumfries & Galloway	296.3	169.7	474.7	..	..	..	1,254	92.6	1,069	96.0
Fife	321.1	181.4	489.6	223.3	124.2	369.9	3,117	97.3	2,617	99.4
Grampian	382.1	181.7	655.2	250.3	134.8	402.3	5,120	107.0	4,185	106.4
Highland[4]	320.9	172.3	535.9	226.0	121.8	393.7	2,399	94.4	2,002	95.8
Lothian	335.7	173.8	542.0	261.5	144.5	412.1	7,661	111.5	6,369	112.8
Strathclyde	332.3	175.7	527.2	245.3	133.6	393.7	19,741	94.1	16,604	96.3
Tayside	317.8	166.4	513.3	226.4	124.9	369.9	3,772	104.4	3,163	106.5
Northern Ireland (Boards)	319.2	152.8	546.4	236.7	120.4	399.0	12,340	83.3	10,579	86.9
Belfast	..	..	..	..	..	..	..	..	..	..
South Eastern	..	..	..	..	..	..	..	..	..	..
Southern	..	..	..	..	..	..	..	..	..	..
North Eastern	..	..	..	..	..	..	..	..	..	..
Western	..	..	..	..	..	..	..	..	..	..

1 For these columns, in England, Wales and Scotland, ".." indicates cells for which no reliable estimates are available. See Appendix notes to Labour market chapter.
2 Earnings figures exclude Llanelli. Income figures include Powys.
3 Earnings figures include Llanelli.
4 Includes Islands.

Source: New Earnings Survey, Employment Department; Central Statistical Office

15.1 Area and population, 1993

	Persons Area (sq km)	per sq km	Population (thousands)			Total population percentage change 1981-1993	Total Period Fertility Rate (TPFR)[1]	Stand-ardised Mortality Ratio (SMR)[2]	Percentage of population aged			
			Males	Females	Total				Under 5	5-15	16 up to pension age[3]	Pension age[3] or over
UNITED KINGDOM	241,752	241	28,473.6	29,717.6	58,191.2	3.6	1.76	100	6.7	13.9	61.2	18.2
North	15,415	201	1,513.6	1,588.7	3,102.3	-0.5	1.74	112	6.5	14.1	60.7	18.7
Cleveland	597	938	273.6	285.9	559.5	-1.9	1.91	114	7.1	15.6	60.6	16.7
Hartlepool *	94	980	44.7	47.2	92.0	-3.1	1.91	117	7.0	15.2	60.2	17.6
Langbaurgh *	245	587	70.2	73.7	143.9	-4.7	1.93	113	6.8	15.2	60.3	17.7
Middlesbrough *	54	2,707	71.6	74.2	145.8	-3.2	1.91	115	7.4	16.2	60.4	16.1
Stockton-on-Tees *	204	872	87.1	90.7	177.8	2.2	1.88	112	7.1	15.8	61.2	15.9
Cumbria	6,824	72	240.1	250.0	490.2	1.9	1.77	102	6.2	13.3	60.2	20.4
Allerdale	1,258	77	47.2	49.0	96.2	0.5	1.91	110	6.1	13.5	60.0	20.4
Barrow-in-Furness	78	940	36.2	37.1	73.3	-0.2	2.00	105	7.1	13.5	61.0	18.4
Carlisle	1,040	99	50.0	52.9	102.9	1.9	1.76	104	6.3	13.4	60.2	20.1
Copeland	738	97	35.6	35.8	71.4	-2.1	1.67	112	6.5	14.6	61.3	17.5
Eden	2,156	22	23.1	23.7	46.8	8.2	1.56	100	5.9	12.8	60.5	20.8
South Lakeland	1,554	64	48.0	51.6	99.6	4.9	1.63	90	5.3	12.2	58.5	24.0
Durham	2,429	250	297.2	310.4	607.5	-0.6	1.73	116	6.4	14.0	61.0	18.6
Chester-le-Street	68	798	26.5	27.4	53.9	2.5	1.52	104	6.3	13.6	63.3	16.8
Darlington	197	507	48.6	51.6	100.2	1.6	1.92	119	6.8	13.9	59.8	19.5
Derwentside	271	321	42.3	44.6	86.9	-1.7	1.76	128	6.3	13.7	60.4	19.7
Durham	187	473	43.7	44.6	88.3	0.5	1.39	103	5.5	13.7	64.4	16.5
Easington	145	682	48.2	50.5	98.7	-2.8	1.92	123	7.2	14.8	59.8	18.3
Sedgefield	217	421	44.9	46.5	91.4	-2.2	1.83	116	6.7	14.5	60.9	18.0
Teesdale	840	29	12.0	12.3	24.3	-2.1	1.71	103	5.3	12.4	59.9	22.4
Wear Valley	505	126	30.9	32.9	63.8	-0.4	1.71	114	6.2	13.9	59.6	20.3
Northumberland	5,026	61	149.8	157.5	307.2	2.6	1.77	110	5.9	14.0	60.4	19.7
Alnwick	1,079	28	14.7	15.6	30.3	4.9	1.81	97	5.5	13.7	58.7	22.1
Berwick-upon-Tweed	972	28	12.9	13.8	26.7	2.2	1.56	95	5.3	12.9	57.6	24.2
Blyth Valley	70	1,149	39.5	41.2	80.7	3.7	1.84	119	6.4	15.1	62.8	15.7
Cast e Morpeth	619	81	24.4	25.7	50.1	0.4	1.71	108	5.0	13.9	60.7	20.4
Tynedale	2,219	26	28.0	29.5	57.5	6.4	1.77	110	5.8	14.1	59.2	20.8
Wansbeck	67	927	30.2	31.7	61.9	-1.1	1.74	118	6.4	13.4	60.1	20.1
Tyne and Wear	540	2,106	553.0	584.9	1,137.9	-1.5	1.65	115	6.5	13.8	60.8	18.8
Gateshead *	143	1,416	98.8	104.0	202.9	-4.9	1.69	122	6.3	13.2	61.1	19.4
Newcastle-upon-Tyne *	112	2,552	139.5	145.8	285.3	0.4	1.52	111	6.4	12.9	62.4	18.3
North Tyneside *	84	2,327	93.3	101.4	194.8	-1.9	1.70	111	6.2	13.7	59.5	20.7
South Tyneside *	64	2,457	76.3	80.9	157.2	-2.9	1.78	114	6.5	14.4	58.9	20.2
Sunderland *	138	2,163	145.0	152.8	297.8	0.2	1.70	119	6.9	15.0	61.0	17.1
YORKSHIRE & HUMBERSIDE	15,411	325	2,460.6	2,553.4	5,014.1	1.9	1.79	103	6.7	13.9	60.9	18.4
Humberside	3,508	252	433.9	450.6	884.4	3.1	1.80	102	6.7	14.2	60.3	18.7
Beverley	404	287	56.2	59.7	115.8	8.3	1.60	89	5.6	13.2	61.1	20.1
Boothferry	646	101	32.2	33.1	65.3	7.6	1.77	106	6.3	13.9	61.2	18.6
Cleethorpes	164	431	34.7	35.8	70.5	2.8	1.71	98	6.6	14.4	60.4	18.6
East Yorkshire	1,043	84	42.7	45.1	87.8	16.7	1.76	101	5.8	13.0	58.4	22.8
Glanford	580	125	36.0	36.7	72.7	8.6	1.62	105	6.0	14.0	61.9	18.1
Great Grimsby	28	3,258	44.6	46.8	91.5	-1.3	1.93	106	7.7	15.6	58.9	17.9
Holderness	538	97	25.7	26.5	52.2	12.2	1.72	103	5.5	14.8	61.4	18.3
Kingston upon Hull *	71	3,750	132.0	135.9	267.9	-2.1	1.87	105	7.5	14.3	60.7	17.5
Scunthorpe	34	1,802	29.8	31.0	60.8	-8.4	2.11	104	7.4	15.6	58.3	18.7
North Yorkshire	8,309	87	351.1	370.7	721.8	6.6	1.67	97	6.0	13.1	60.4	20.5
Craven	1,179	43	24.5	26.5	50.9	6.5	1.75	97	5.7	13.4	57.4	23.5
Hambleton	1,311	62	40.5	41.1	81.6	8.6	1.79	93	6.1	13.3	61.8	18.8
Harrogate	1,333	110	70.0	76.5	146.5	4.2	1.72	101	5.7	12.9	60.5	20.8
Richmondshire	1,319	35	23.3	22.5	45.8	5.3	1.81	97	7.0	13.5	62.5	17.1
Ryedale	1,597	58	45.5	47.0	92.6	8.2	1.67	89	5.3	13.2	59.8	21.6
Scarborough	817	133	51.5	57.1	108.7	6.2	1.75	93	5.9	12.7	56.8	24.6
Selby	725	127	45.5	46.3	91.8	15.0	1.67	97	6.2	14.0	62.8	17.1
York	29	3,528	50.3	53.7	104.0	1.8	1.45	103	6.5	12.4	61.6	19.5

15.1 *(continued)*

	Persons Area (sq km)	per sq km	Population (thousands)			Total population percentage change 1981-1993	Total Period Fertility Rate (TPFR)[1]	Standardised Mortality Ratio (SMR)[2]	Percentage of population aged			
			Males	Females	Total				Under 5	5-15	16 up to pens on age[3]	Pension age[3] or over
South Yorkshire	**1,559**	**838**	**644.4**	**661.9**	**1,306.2**	*-0.8*	**1.77**	**106**	*6.7*	*13.4*	*61.3*	*18.6*
Barnsley *	328	688	111.1	114.8	225.9	*-*	1.79	112	*6.7*	*13.7*	*61.1*	*18.4*
Doncaster *	581	504	144.2	148.5	292.7	*0.6*	1.90	106	*7.0*	*14.7*	*60.4*	*18.0*
Rotherham *	283	905	126.1	129.7	255.7	*1.2*	1.89	108	*7.0*	*14.3*	*61.4*	*17.3*
Sheffield *	367	1,448	263.0	268.9	531.9	*-2.9*	1.66	102	*6.3*	*12.2*	*61.9*	*19.5*
West Yorkshire	**2,034**	**1,033**	**1,031.3**	**1,070.3**	**2,101.6**	*1.7*	**1.82**	**104**	*7.0*	*14.4*	*61.2*	*17.5*
Bradford *	366	1,310	235.9	244.1	480.0	*3.3*	2.09	107	*7.7*	*15.9*	*59.6*	*16.8*
Calderdale	363	533	93.9	99.3	193.7	*0.4*	1.90	111	*6.9*	*14.3*	*60.2*	*18.5*
Kirklees *	410	942	188.8	197.0	385.8	*2.3*	1.83	106	*7.0*	*14.6*	*61.2*	*17.3*
Leeds *	562	1,290	356.4	368.1	724.5	*0.9*	1.64	97	*6.7*	*13.3*	*62.1*	*17.9*
Wakefield	333	954	156.3	161.2	317.5	*1.1*	1.82	110	*6.9*	*14.1*	*61.9*	*17.1*
EAST MIDLANDS	**15,627**	**261**	**2,014.9**	**2,068.0**	**4,082.9**	*6.0*	**1.75**	**101**	*6.6*	*13.9*	*61.3*	*18.3*
Derbyshire	**2,629**	**362**	**469.9**	**481.1**	**950.9**	*4.0*	**1.78**	**104**	*6.5*	*13.5*	*61.2*	*18.8*
Amber Valley	265	429	56.3	57.4	113.7	*3.9*	1.59	101	*5.8*	*12.9*	*61.7*	*19.6*
Bolsover	160	445	35.2	36.0	71.2	*0.3*	1.70	105	*6.4*	*13.1*	*60.5*	*20.0*
Chesterfield	66	1,532	49.5	51.7	101.2	*3.3*	1.87	112	*6.2*	*12.9*	*60.9*	*20.0*
Derby *	78	2,930	113.1	115.6	228.6	*5.2*	1.86	103	*7.3*	*13.9*	*60.6*	*18.2*
Derbyshire Dales	795	86	33.7	34.8	68.6	*1.0*	1.69	95	*5.5*	*12.9*	*60.2*	*21.4*
Erewash	109	981	53.1	54.1	107.2	*3.5*	1.90	102	*6.8*	*13.4*	*61.6*	*18.1*
High Peak	540	161	42.8	44.2	87.0	*5.5*	1.78	110	*7.0*	*14.1*	*61.8*	*17.1*
North East Derbyshire	277	358	49.2	49.9	99.1	*3.1*	1.74	103	*5.9*	*13.4*	*61.7*	*19.0*
South Derbyshire	338	220	37.0	37.3	74.3	*8.6*	1.67	111	*6.1*	*14.2*	*62.6*	*17.1*
Leicestershire	**2,551**	**357**	**451.2**	**459.1**	**910.3**	*6.0*	**1.73**	**97**	*6.8*	*14.3*	*61.9*	*17.1*
Blaby	130	651	42.4	42.6	85.0	*10.1*	1.79	87	*6.6*	*13.7*	*63.6*	*16.0*
Charnwood	279	546	76.2	76.3	152.5	*8.8*	1.59	92	*6.3*	*13.7*	*63.3*	*16.7*
Harborough	593	118	34.7	35.2	70.0	*13.8*	1.70	100	*6.2*	*14.4*	*62.0*	*17.3*
Hinckley and Bosworth	297	328	48.4	49.3	97.6	*10.9*	1.73	95	*6.2*	*13.9*	*62.3*	*17.5*
Leicester *	73	3,946	142.3	146.9	289.3	*2.2*	1.82	105	*7.9*	*15.2*	*60.3*	*16.7*
Melton	481	96	22.9	23.3	46.2	*6.2*	1.82	93	*6.5*	*13.7*	*62.1*	*17.7*
North West Leicestershire	279	296	41.2	41.6	82.8	*4.6*	1.73	101	*6.4*	*14.0*	*61.5*	*18.2*
Oadby and Wigston	24	2,274	26.2	27.3	53.5	*0.8*	1.49	81	*6.2*	*13.6*	*62.5*	*17.7*
Rutland	394	85	16.8	16.6	33.4	*1.3*	1.57	87	*5.6*	*14.8*	*62.3*	*17.2*
Lincolnshire	**5,921**	**102**	**294.4**	**307.0**	**601.4**	*8.7*	**1.78**	**99**	*6.0*	*13.3*	*59.5*	*21.3*
Boston	362	150	26.5	27.7	54.2	*3.3*	1.73	94	*5.9*	*12.9*	*59.4*	*21.8*
East Lindsey	1,760	69	58.9	61.9	120.8	*14.6*	1.81	99	*5.5*	*12.3*	*56.9*	*25.3*
Lincoln	36	2,396	41.8	43.7	85.5	*11.8*	1.83	105	*7.2*	*13.4*	*60.9*	*18.5*
North Kesteven	922	88	39.8	41.4	81.2	*1.2*	1.75	101	*5.7*	*13.1*	*59.9*	*21.3*
South Holland	742	93	34.0	35.3	69.3	*11.3*	1.77	101	*5.3*	*12.1*	*59.2*	*23.3*
South Kesteven	943	120	55.1	57.6	112.7	*14.5*	1.73	93	*6.2*	*14.6*	*60.6*	*18.6*
West Lindsey	1,156	67	38.2	39.4	77.6	*-0.1*	1.86	98	*5.8*	*14.3*	*60.0*	*19.8*
Northamptonshire	**2,367**	**250**	**291.9**	**299.9**	**591.9**	*11.2*	**1.76**	**98**	*7.1*	*14.8*	*61.5*	*16.6*
Corby	80	658	26.0	26.8	52.8	*0.5*	1.86	112	*7.7*	*15.9*	*60.8*	*15.6*
Daventry	666	96	31.7	32.0	63.7	*9.7*	1.78	94	*6.7*	*14.6*	*62.5*	*16.2*
East Northamptonshire	510	136	34.4	34.9	69.3	*11.1*	1.77	94	*6.5*	*14.6*	*61.0*	*17.9*
Kettering	233	336	38.5	40.1	78.5	*9.9*	1.74	95	*6.8*	*14.0*	*61.1*	*18.1*
Northampton	81	2,318	91.8	95.4	187.2	*17.9*	1.77	100	*7.6*	*14.7*	*61.6*	*16.1*
South Northamptonshire	634	113	36.0	35.9	71.9	*11.7*	1.63	97	*6.5*	*15.5*	*62.1*	*15.9*
Wellingborough	163	419	33.6	34.7	68.3	*5.6*	1.74	99	*7.0*	*14.8*	*61.0*	*17.2*
Nottinghamshire	**2,160**	**476**	**507.5**	**520.9**	**1,028.4**	*3.4*	**1.73**	**104**	*6.6*	*13.6*	*61.7*	*18.1*
Ashfield	110	1,000	54.2	55.6	109.8	*2.9*	1.65	106	*6.6*	*13.6*	*61.8*	*17.9*
Bassetlaw	637	166	52.4	53.1	105.5	*2.5*	1.77	105	*6.4*	*13.5*	*62.1*	*18.1*
Broxtowe	81	1,365	54.7	55.8	110.6	*5.9*	1.57	94	*6.1*	*13.0*	*63.1*	*17.8*
Gedling	120	933	54.9	57.1	112.0	*3.5*	1.65	97	*6.0*	*13.4*	*62.3*	*18.2*
Mansfield	77	1,328	50.4	51.7	102.1	*2.2*	1.94	104	*6.8*	*14.6*	*60.4*	*18.1*
Newark and Sherwood	651	160	51.4	53.0	104.4	*3.6*	1.75	102	*6.2*	*14.0*	*60.9*	*18.8*
Nottingham *	75	3,788	139.6	143.0	282.6	*1.6*	1.78	110	*7.5*	*13.5*	*61.3*	*17.6*
Rushcliffe	409	248	49.8	51.6	101.5	*9.1*	1.68	103	*5.8*	*13.4*	*62.2*	*18.6*

15.1 *(continued)*

	Persons Area (sq km)	per sq km	Population (thousands)			Total population percentage change 1981-1993	Total Period Fertility Rate (TPFR)[1]	Stand-ardised Mortality Ratio (SMR)[2]	Percentage of population aged			
			Males	Females	Total				Under 5	5-15	16 up to pension age[3]	Pension age[3] or over
EAST ANGLIA	12,570	167	1,032.1	1,061.8	2,093.9	*10.6*	1.74	91	*6.4*	*13.5*	*60.5*	*19.7*
Cambridgeshire	3,400	201	339.3	343.4	682.6	*15.8*	1.69	92	*6.7*	*13.8*	*63.0*	*16.4*
Cambridge	41	2,797	57.4	56.5	113.8	*12.7*	1.21	84	*5.4*	*10.3*	*68.2*	*16.1*
East Cambridgeshire	655	95	30.8	31.3	62.1	*15.0*	1.67	87	*6.4*	*13.6*	*60.7*	*19.3*
Fenland	546	143	38.5	39.5	78.0	*17.3*	1.87	97	*6.3*	*13.0*	*59.3*	*21.3*
Huntingdonshire	923	161	73.8	74.9	148.8	*19.1*	1.81	98	*7.5*	*14.8*	*64.0*	*13.8*
Peterborough	333	470	77.2	79.2	156.4	*16.6*	2.02	98	*7.4*	*15.5*	*61.4*	*15.7*
South Cambridgeshire	902	137	61.6	62.0	123.6	*13.5*	1.72	87	*6.4*	*14.4*	*62.8*	*16.4*
Norfolk	5,372	142	375.4	389.6	765.1	*8.8*	1.75	91	*5.9*	*12.8*	*59.2*	*22.1*
Breckland	1,305	85	54.5	56.3	110.8	*14.5*	1.80	93	*6.2*	*13.3*	*58.8*	*21.7*
Broadland	552	196	53.4	55.1	108.5	*10.6*	1.69	94	*5.5*	*12.9*	*60.6*	*21.0*
Great Yarmouth	174	511	43.2	45.6	88.8	*9.1*	1.88	100	*6.3*	*13.5*	*58.2*	*22.0*
Kings Lynn and West Norfolk	1,429	92	65.0	66.6	131.6	*7.8*	1.91	93	*6.0*	*12.6*	*58.4*	*23.1*
North Norfolk	965	97	45.6	48.1	93.7	*12.4*	1.73	84	*5.1*	*12.1*	*55.4*	*27.3*
Norwich	39	3,281	62.7	65.4	128.1	*1.5*	1.59	87	*6.4*	*12.2*	*62.2*	*19.2*
South Norfolk	908	114	51.1	52.6	103.7	*8.9*	1.76	86	*5.4*	*13.2*	*60.1*	*21.3*
Suffolk	3,798	170	317.4	328.7	646.2	*7.4*	1.81	91	*6.6*	*13.9*	*59.2*	*20.3*
Babergh	595	134	39.5	40.1	79.6	*7.5*	1.87	91	*5.6*	*14.3*	*60.1*	*20.1*
Forest Heath	374	167	31.1	31.5	62.5	*18.7*	1.43	94	*9.0*	*15.1*	*61.5*	*14.5*
Ipswich	39	2,913	56.2	58.6	114.8	*-4.4*	1.96	92	*7.2*	*14.1*	*58.8*	*20.0*
Mid Suffolk	871	90	38.9	39.5	78.4	*10.8*	2.02	90	*6.2*	*14.2*	*59.7*	*19.9*
St Edmundsbury	657	141	46.0	46.7	92.7	*6.3*	1.80	94	*6.3*	*13.2*	*62.2*	*18.3*
Suffolk Coastal	892	124	53.9	56.6	110.5	*14.0*	1.66	89	*6.6*	*13.9*	*57.3*	*22.2*
Waveney	370	291	51.9	55.8	107.7	*7.7*	1.90	91	*6.1*	*13.0*	*56.4*	*24.5*
SOUTH EAST	27,224	653	8,698.9	9,070.5	17,769.4	*4.5*	1.75	95	*6.8*	*13.4*	*62.3*	*17.5*
Bedfordshire	1,236	437	269.4	270.0	539.4	*5.8*	1.94	96	*7.4*	*15.0*	*62.9*	*14.7*
Bedford	477	288	68.0	69.3	137.3	*2.9*	1.83	94	*6.4*	*14.3*	*62.3*	*16.9*
Luton	43	4,121	89.5	89.1	178.6	*8.4*	2.16	102	*8.6*	*15.9*	*62.4*	*13.1*
Mid Bedfordshire	503	226	56.9	56.5	113.5	*8.6*	1.80	90	*7.0*	*14.3*	*64.0*	*14.6*
South Bedfordshire	213	517	54.9	55.1	110.0	*2.5*	1.83	96	*7.2*	*14.9*	*63.4*	*14.5*
Berkshire	1,259	607	382.2	381.5	763.7	*9.9*	1.74	93	*7.0*	*14.3*	*64.2*	*14.5*
Bracknell Forest	109	932	51.5	50.4	101.9	*20.3*	1.73	102	*7.5*	*15.0*	*64.9*	*12.6*
Newbury	704	200	70.3	70.6	141.0	*14.9*	1.72	88	*6.8*	*14.8*	*63.7*	*14.6*
Reading	40	3,410	69.3	68.4	137.7	*0.2*	1.60	94	*7.0*	*13.0*	*64.5*	*15.5*
Slough	27	3,772	51.4	52.1	103.5	*6.0*	2.03	102	*8.1*	*15.2*	*62.2*	*14.4*
Windsor and Maidenhead	198	689	67.8	68.9	136.7	*0.9*	1.68	96	*6.0*	*13.5*	*63.4*	*17.1*
Wokingham	179	798	71.8	71.1	142.9	*22.2*	1.72	81	*6.8*	*14.9*	*66.0*	*12.3*
Buckinghamshire	1,877	347	322.6	329.0	651.7	*14.3*	1.81	93	*7.0*	*15.0*	*63.4*	*14.6*
Aylesbury Vale	903	168	75.3	76.2	151.6	*13.0*	1.75	99	*7.1*	*14.6*	*64.0*	*14.3*
Chiltern	196	462	44.1	46.7	90.8	*0.2*	1.74	78	*5.8*	*14.3*	*62.1*	*17.8*
Milton Keynes	309	598	91.6	92.9	184.4	*46.4*	1.90	103	*8.0*	*16.9*	*63.5*	*11.6*
South Buckinghamshire	145	439	31.2	32.2	63.4	*1.7*	1.75	95	*6.1*	*13.1*	*62.0*	*18.8*
Wycombe	325	497	80.4	81.0	161.4	*2.7*	1.80	88	*6.9*	*14.4*	*64.1*	*14.7*
East Sussex	1,795	402	341.0	381.2	722.2	*8.6*	1.68	92	*5.8*	*12.1*	*56.8*	*25.2*
Brighton	58	2,646	75.5	78.9	154.4	*3.3*	1.47	95	*5.8*	*11.0*	*63.0*	*20.1*
Eastbourne	44	1,966	39.5	47.3	86.8	*12.0*	1.70	88	*5.6*	*11.4*	*53.0*	*30.1*
Hastings	30	2,790	39.1	43.8	82.9	*9.6*	1.96	101	*6.8*	*13.7*	*57.1*	*22.5*
Hove	24	3,809	42.7	48.3	91.0	*3.6*	1.61	103	*5.6*	*10.2*	*59.3*	*24.9*
Lewes	292	303	41.9	46.7	88.6	*12.1*	1.80	87	*5.9*	*13.2*	*55.0*	*25.9*
Rother	511	166	38.9	46.0	84.8	*10.9*	1.82	88	*5.1*	*12.0*	*49.6*	*33.3*
Wealden	836	160	63.5	70.2	133.7	*12.0*	1.80	84	*5.9*	*13.7*	*56.3*	*24.2*

15.1 *(continued)*

	Persons Area (sq km)	per sq km	Population (thousands)			Total population percentage change 1981-1993	Total Period Fertility Rate (TPFR)[1]	Stand-ardised Mortality Ratio (SMR)[2]	Percentage of population aged			
			Males	Females	Total				Under 5	5-15	16 up to pension age[3]	Pension age[3] or over
Essex	3,675	425	764.1	796.2	1,560.3	5.2	1.82	94	6.5	13.6	61.1	18.7
Basildon	110	1,470	79.2	82.5	161.7	6.0	1.94	94	7.2	14.9	62.0	16.0
Braintree	612	199	60.1	61.7	121.8	8.2	1.83	93	6.9	14.2	61.6	17.3
Brentwood	149	479	34.8	36.4	71.2	-1.6	1.55	92	5.9	12.5	62.4	19.2
Castle Point	45	1,910	42.3	43.7	86.0	-1.0	1.74	88	6.0	14.1	62.7	17.2
Chelmsford	342	455	77.1	78.6	155.7	11.5	1.69	83	6.6	14.2	63.5	15.7
Colchester	334	447	74.0	75.0	149.1	7.8	1.76	92	6.6	13.4	63.2	16.8
Epping Forest	340	348	57.7	60.5	118.2	1.2	1.82	95	6.1	12.4	61.9	19.6
Harlow	30	2,440	36.2	37.3	73.5	-7.6	1.91	95	7.2	14.6	61.4	16.8
Maldon	360	148	26.5	26.6	53.1	9.9	2.20	97	6.2	14.5	61.3	18.0
Rochford	169	448	37.2	38.8	75.9	3.1	1.73	96	6.1	14.1	61.0	18.9
Southend-on-Sea	42	4,012	80.1	87.4	167.5	6.3	1.76	100	6.5	12.5	58.3	22.6
Tendring	337	382	60.9	67.9	128.7	12.2	1.90	94	5.7	11.7	52.3	30.3
Thurrock	164	801	64.9	66.3	131.2	3.0	2.00	102	7.5	14.2	63.0	15.3
Uttlesford	641	104	33.2	33.5	66.6	6.2	1.76	91	6.2	14.3	62.8	16.7
Greater London	1,578	4,393	3,383.2	3,549.8	6,933.0	1.9	1.72	98	7.1	12.9	64.0	16.0
Barking and Dagenham	34	4,264	70.7	74.8	145.5	-4.0	2.12	107	7.9	14.2	58.2	19.7
Barnet	89	3,406	147.1	157.7	304.7	3.2	1.67	89	6.7	13.3	62.3	17.7
Bexley	61	3,626	107.4	112.4	219.9	1.3	1.76	92	7.0	13.6	62.0	17.4
Brent *	44	5,604	122.3	125.4	247.6	-2.6	1.86	97	7.3	13.9	64.9	13.9
Bromley	152	1,923	140.7	151.1	291.8	-2.2	1.74	87	6.2	12.4	61.6	19.8
Camden	22	8,354	87.5	93.9	181.4	1.3	1.41	102	5.9	10.5	67.7	15.9
City of London	3	1,434	2.2	1.3	3.9	-27.4	1.09	102	3.3	4.3	73.8	18.6
City of Westminster	22	8,770	92.8	96.2	189.0	0.4	1.33	95	5.2	8.7	69.5	16.5
Croydon	87	3,733	157.8	165.5	323.3	0.7	1.74	97	7.3	13.6	63.6	15.5
Ealing	55	5,151	140.7	144.9	285.6	1.2	1.76	98	7.2	13.4	64.8	14.6
Enfield	81	3,227	127.8	134.0	261.8	0.3	1.86	90	7.3	13.4	62.2	17.1
Greenwich *	48	4,506	103.8	111.0	214.8	-0.3	1.87	108	7.9	14.7	60.8	16.6
Hackney *	20	9,787	93.6	97.3	190.9	3.1	2.04	110	8.6	14.8	63.5	13.0
Hammersmith and Fulham *	16	9,627	74.4	81.1	155.5	2.8	1.38	101	6.4	9.8	69.7	14.1
Haringey	30	6,996	104.7	107.2	211.9	2.3	1.75	108	7.5	12.6	67.0	12.9
Harrow	51	4,067	100.8	105.9	206.6	3.8	1.65	84	6.6	13.9	62.8	16.6
Havering	118	1,972	113.5	118.6	232.2	-4.2	1.64	97	6.1	13.6	61.4	18.9
Hillingdon	110	2,172	118.4	121.2	239.6	2.7	1.75	89	7.1	13.2	63.2	16.6
Hounslow	58	3,582	102.4	104.1	206.5	1.3	1.82	96	7.2	13.7	64.0	15.0
Islington *	15	11,790	84.9	90.6	175.5	5.7	1.67	110	7.2	12.1	66.2	14.5
Kensington and Chelsea *	12	12,467	72.2	76.7	148.8	6.2	1.25	95	5.4	8.7	71.6	14.3
Kingston upon Thames	38	3,678	67.7	70.4	138.1	2.8	1.47	88	6.3	12.1	63.9	17.7
Lambeth *	27	9,503	126.4	132.8	259.2	2.5	1.68	111	7.7	12.4	66.5	13.4
Lewisham *	35	6,920	115.7	124.6	240.4	1.7	1.68	106	7.7	12.9	63.7	15.7
Merton	38	4,617	85.3	89.8	175.1	4.5	1.71	95	7.0	12.2	63.9	16.9
Newham *	36	6,224	112.9	113.4	226.3	6.3	2.33	116	9.4	16.2	61.6	12.8
Redbridge	56	4,121	113.5	119.3	232.7	1.5	1.81	92	6.8	13.8	61.8	17.6
Richmond-upon-Thames	55	3,015	80.0	86.5	166.6	2.9	1.58	90	6.2	11.4	64.1	18.3
Southwark *	29	7,976	111.9	117.4	229.4	5.1	1.88	107	8.1	13.1	63.7	15.1
Sutton	43	3,995	83.9	89.4	173.3	1.9	1.76	95	7.0	13.0	62.0	18.0
Tower Hamlets *	20	8,593	85.0	84.6	169.6	16.8	2.32	113	8.8	16.9	59.9	14.3
Waltham Forest	40	5,544	107.2	112.6	219.8	1.0	1.96	99	8.1	13.3	63.0	15.7
Wandsworth *	35	7,617	128.1	137.5	265.7	1.4	1.48	110	6.6	9.8	68.9	14.7
Hampshire	3,779	422	788.5	805.2	1,593.7	7.0	1.77	93	6.6	13.7	61.9	17.8
Basingstoke and Deane	634	231	72.8	73.7	146.5	11.0	1.79	93	7.1	14.4	64.7	13.8
East Hampshire	515	207	52.1	54.4	106.4	16.2	1.82	94	6.5	14.8	61.6	17.1
Eastleigh	80	1,374	54.2	55.3	109.6	17.9	1.73	90	6.9	14.4	62.8	15.9
Fareham	74	1,360	49.3	51.6	101.0	13.5	1.35	90	6.1	13.6	61.7	18.6
Gosport	25	3,006	36.8	39.1	75.9	-2.5	1.31	95	7.2	14.4	61.2	17.2
Hart	215	385	41.9	41.0	82.9	18.6	1.67	81	6.3	14.6	66.0	13.0
Havant	55	2,123	56.9	60.6	117.5	1.6	1.88	93	6.5	14.8	59.0	19.8
New Forest	753	218	79.4	85.1	164.5	13.1	1.76	86	5.7	12.8	56.8	24.7
Portsmouth	40	4,696	95.2	93.8	189.1	-1.2	1.72	100	6.7	12.2	62.4	18.7
Rushmoor	39	2,191	43.8	41.8	85.6	-1.7	1.92	102	7.8	13.3	65.9	13.0
Southampton	50	4,197	104.7	104.5	209.2	-0.3	1.72	97	6.9	13.0	61.9	18.2
Test Valley	637	165	52.6	52.3	105.0	12.0	1.80	92	6.4	14.3	63.1	16.1
Winchester	661	152	48.7	51.8	100.5	8.1	1.62	89	5.6	13.6	61.1	19.7

15.1 *(continued)*

	Area (sq km)	Persons per sq km	Population (thousands)			Total population percentage change 1981-1993	Total Period Fertility Rate (TPFR)[1]	Stand- ardised Mortality Ratio (SMR)[2]	Percentage of population aged			
			Males	Females	Total				Under 5	5-15	16 up to pension age[3]	Pension age[3] or over
Hertfordshire	**1,639**	**610**	**493.4**	**506.3**	**999.7**	*3.4*	**1.80**	**91**	*6.8*	*13.8*	*62.3*	*17.1*
Broxbourne	52	1,581	40.9	41.7	82.5	*3.4*	1.73	88	*6.7*	*13.7*	*63.9*	*15.8*
Dacorum	212	632	66.3	68.0	134.3	*2.6*	1.86	88	*6.9*	*14.4*	*61.9*	*16.9*
East Hertfordshire	477	251	59.8	59.9	119.6	*9.2*	1.72	94	*6.6*	*13.6*	*64.5*	*15.4*
Hertsmere	98	947	45.1	47.6	92.7	*4.6*	1.69	98	*6.9*	*13.5*	*60.0*	*19.5*
North Hertfordshire	375	303	56.1	57.6	113.7	*4.6*	1.80	95	*6.5*	*13.9*	*61.6*	*18.0*
St Albans	161	792	63.0	64.6	127.7	*1.9*	1.79	94	*6.3*	*13.5*	*63.2*	*17.0*
Stevenage	26	2,917	37.5	38.2	75.7	*1.4*	1.99	86	*8.2*	*15.3*	*61.4*	*15.0*
Three Rivers	89	930	40.4	42.2	82.6	*1.9*	1.63	85	*6.2*	*13.4*	*61.4*	*19.0*
Watford	21	3,530	37.5	38.2	75.6	*1.4*	1.93	93	*7.8*	*13.5*	*63.3*	*15.4*
Welwyn Hatfield	127	747	46.9	48.3	95.3	*1.2*	1.80	84	*6.6*	*13.4*	*60.9*	*19.1*
Isle of Wight	**380**	**328**	**59.6**	**65.1**	**124.8**	*5.7*	**1.90**	**96**	*5.3*	*13.0*	*55.2*	*26.5*
Medina	117	613	34.8	37.0	71.8	*5.7*	1.82	93	*5.9*	*13.1*	*57.2*	*23.8*
South Wight	263	202	24.9	28.1	53.0	*5.6*	2.02	99	*4.5*	*12.9*	*52.5*	*30.1*
Kent	**3,735**	**412**	**751.4**	**788.3**	**1,539.7**	*3.7*	**1.87**	**97**	*6.6*	*13.9*	*60.4*	*19.1*
Ashford	581	162	45.6	48.2	93.9	*8.0*	1.95	95	*6.8*	*14.0*	*60.4*	*18.8*
Canterbury	309	429	63.7	68.7	132.4	*8.4*	1.65	93	*5.6*	*12.9*	*57.8*	*23.6*
Dartford	73	1,134	40.9	41.7	82.6	*1.7*	1.73	105	*6.8*	*13.0*	*63.5*	*16.7*
Dover	315	337	52.0	54.1	106.1	*2.5*	1.99	94	*6.5*	*13.6*	*58.3*	*21.6*
Gillingham	32	2,958	47.6	48.4	96.0	*-0.6*	1.87	100	*7.3*	*15.7*	*62.3*	*14.6*
Gravesham	99	939	45.5	47.5	93.0	*-2.6*	1.94	103	*7.0*	*14.2*	*61.7*	*17.1*
Maidstone	393	352	68.0	70.6	138.5	*5.9*	1.78	95	*6.5*	*13.9*	*62.4*	*17.2*
Rochester-upon-Medway	160	916	72.5	73.7	146.2	*1.7*	2.01	108	*7.7*	*14.6*	*63.4*	*14.3*
Sevenoaks	368	297	53.4	56.0	109.4	*-0.3*	1.84	87	*6.3*	*14.2*	*60.8*	*18.6*
Shepway	357	267	45.3	49.8	95.1	*10.5*	1.79	97	*6.4*	*12.8*	*56.9*	*23.9*
Swale	373	314	58.2	59.0	117.2	*6.4*	2.00	100	*6.8*	*14.9*	*61.0*	*17.3*
Thanet	103	1,215	59.4	66.1	125.5	*3.1*	1.89	99	*6.1*	*13.3*	*53.8*	*26.8*
Tonbridge and Malling	240	425	50.6	51.5	102.1	*4.3*	1.97	94	*6.9*	*13.9*	*62.8*	*16.4*
Tunbridge Wells	332	307	48.8	53.0	101.8	*3.4*	1.73	99	*6.1*	*13.8*	*60.6*	*19.5*
Oxfordshire	**2,606**	**225**	**293.1**	**292.7**	**585.8**	*8.1*	**1.70**	**88**	*6.9*	*13.5*	*63.5*	*16.1*
Cherwell	589	213	62.0	63.2	125.1	*14.6*	1.86	90	*8.2*	*14.7*	*62.5*	*14.6*
Oxford	46	2,894	66.3	65.7	132.0	*1.2*	1.37	90	*5.8*	*11.9*	*66.5*	*15.8*
South Oxfordshire	679	179	60.5	61.3	121.8	*4.0*	1.84	89	*6.8*	*13.8*	*62.5*	*16.9*
Vale of White Horse	579	196	57.1	56.1	113.2	*9.4*	1.75	84	*6.5*	*14.4*	*62.7*	*16.5*
West Oxfordshire	714	131	47.2	46.5	93.7	*14.7*	1.87	87	*7.2*	*13.0*	*62.8*	*17.0*
Surrey	**1,677**	**619**	**507.6**	**530.3**	**1,037.9**	*2.3*	**1.69**	**88**	*6.2*	*13.1*	*61.9*	*18.7*
Elmbridge	97	1,213	56.6	60.7	117.3	*4.2*	1.71	84	*6.4*	*13.4*	*61.0*	*19.2*
Epsom and Ewell	34	2,019	33.6	35.2	68.8	*-0.8*	1.62	86	*5.8*	*12.9*	*61.1*	*20.2*
Guildford	271	466	62.2	64.0	126.2	*1.0*	1.61	80	*6.2*	*12.7*	*63.1*	*18.0*
Mole Valley	258	306	38.4	40.7	79.1	*2.1*	1.88	90	*5.6*	*12.2*	*60.3*	*21.9*
Reigate and Banstead	129	920	57.9	60.9	118.8	*1.5*	1.72	97	*6.3*	*13.1*	*60.9*	*19.7*
Runnymede	78	963	36.9	38.2	75.1	*3.1*	1.63	92	*6.2*	*11.7*	*63.5*	*18.7*
Spelthorne	57	1,621	45.4	46.2	91.6	*-1.3*	1.63	86	*6.2*	*11.6*	*63.8*	*18.3*
Surrey Heath	95	855	40.5	40.8	81.3	*6.9*	1.74	90	*6.8*	*14.6*	*65.2*	*13.4*
Tandridge	250	307	37.0	39.6	76.6	*-1.8*	1.64	92	*5.9*	*13.8*	*60.6*	*19.7*
Waverley	345	333	55.6	59.5	115.1	*2.6*	1.71	84	*5.9*	*14.2*	*59.6*	*20.4*
Woking	64	1,387	43.6	44.6	88.2	*7.6*	1.78	93	*7.0*	*13.9*	*62.8*	*16.3*
West Sussex	**1,988**	**361**	**342.9**	**374.8**	**717.7**	*7.7*	**1.73**	**92**	*5.9*	*13.0*	*57.4*	*23.7*
Adur	42	1,382	27.6	30.2	57.8	*-1.4*	1.88	91	*5.8*	*12.6*	*55.8*	*25.8*
Arun	221	605	62.6	70.8	133.4	*12.5*	1.70	93	*5.4*	*11.4*	*52.8*	*30.4*
Chichester	786	130	47.8	54.6	102.5	*3.6*	1.59	89	*5.5*	*12.4*	*55.6*	*26.5*
Crawley	44	2,025	44.0	45.3	89.3	*8.9*	1.83	87	*7.3*	*14.5*	*61.9*	*16.3*
Horsham	530	212	54.9	57.4	112.3	*11.9*	1.77	87	*6.3*	*14.2*	*60.2*	*19.3*
Mid Sussex	333	375	61.2	63.8	125.0	*8.3*	1.62	90	*5.9*	*14.3*	*61.5*	*18.3*
Worthing	32	3,002	44.9	52.6	97.5	*5.4*	1.77	99	*5.7*	*11.6*	*53.7*	*29.0*

15.1 *(continued)*

	Persons Area (sq km)	per sq km	Population (thousands)			Total population percentage change 1981-1993	Total Period Fertility Rate (TPFR)[1]	Stand-ardised Mortality Ratio (SMR)[2]	Percentage of population aged			
			Males	Females	Total				Under 5	5-15	16 up to pension age[3]	Pension age[3] or over
SOUTH WEST	**23,829**	**200**	**2,324.4**	**2,443.6**	**4,768.0**	*8.8*	**1.74**	**91**	*6.1*	*13.2*	*59.4*	*21.3*
Avon	**1,332**	**730**	**478.3**	**495.0**	**973.3**	*4.8*	**1.68**	**93**	*6.4*	*13.0*	*61.7*	*18.9*
Bath	29	2,898	40.0	43.1	83.1	*-1.4*	1.43	92	*5.4*	*11.6*	*60.7*	*22.3*
Bristol *	110	3,628	196.1	201.4	397.6	*-0.9*	1.66	98	*6.7*	*12.8*	*62.1*	*18.4*
Kingswood	48	1,922	45.2	46.3	92.0	*8.7*	1.72	83	*6.6*	*13.6*	*62.0*	*17.7*
Northavon	449	308	69.3	68.8	138.1	*16.5*	1.84	84	*7.0*	*13.5*	*65.4*	*14.1*
Wansdyke	322	249	39.4	41.0	80.4	*4.1*	1.81	94	*6.0*	*13.4*	*60.3*	*20.3*
Woodspring	375	486	88.3	93.8	182.1	*11.8*	1.69	91	*5.8*	*13.4*	*58.9*	*21.9*
Cornwall and the Isles of Scilly	**3,559**	**134**	**230.4**	**246.6**	**477.0**	*11.8*	**1.83**	**95**	*5.8*	*13.5*	*57.9*	*22.8*
Caradon	664	117	38.0	39.8	77.8	*14.8*	1.95	89	*5.8*	*14.2*	*58.8*	*21.2*
Carrick	461	183	40.3	44.2	84.5	*11.6*	1.80	90	*5.6*	*13.0*	*56.8*	*24.6*
Kerrier	473	188	43.3	45.8	89.1	*6.6*	1.78	96	*6.2*	*13.5*	*58.7*	*21.6*
North Cornwall	1,190	64	36.5	39.1	75.6	*16.7*	1.71	96	*6.0*	*13.7*	*57.1*	*23.2*
Penwith	304	197	28.6	31.1	59.7	*10.4*	2.03	96	*5.3*	*12.9*	*57.0*	*24.8*
Restormel	452	195	42.8	45.5	88.3	*12.4*	1.80	100	*5.9*	*13.6*	*58.5*	*22.1*
Isles of Scilly	15	133	1.0	1.0	2.1	*4.6*	1.58	123	*6.2*	*14.8*	*59.0*	*20.0*
Devon	**6,703**	**157**	**508.6**	**540.6**	**1,049.2**	*8.7*	**1.70**	**90**	*5.9*	*12.9*	*58.4*	*22.8*
East Devon	814	148	56.1	64.2	120.3	*11.6*	1.66	79	*5.0*	*11.5*	*52.6*	*30.9*
Exeter	47	2,235	51.2	53.8	105.1	*4.4*	1.48	92	*6.0*	*12.5*	*62.5*	*19.0*
Mid Devon	915	72	31.8	33.8	65.6	*11.7*	1.92	83	*6.1*	*14.2*	*58.8*	*20.9*
North Devon	1,086	80	42.2	44.5	86.7	*10.8*	1.90	92	*5.9*	*13.1*	*58.2*	*22.8*
Plymouth *	80	3,250	130.1	128.9	259.0	*2.3*	1.62	103	*6.5*	*13.3*	*62.5*	*17.6*
South Hams	887	88	37.8	40.6	78.5	*17.6*	1.32	80	*5.7*	*13.3*	*57.6*	*23.4*
Teignbridge	674	166	53.7	58.4	112.1	*17.0*	1.76	87	*5.7*	*12.6*	*56.2*	*25.5*
Torbay	63	1,926	56.5	64.6	121.1	*7.1*	1.72	90	*5.5*	*12.1*	*55.0*	*27.4*
Torridge	979	55	26.4	27.8	54.1	*11.3*	1.78	91	*6.0*	*13.9*	*57.3*	*22.9*
West Devon	1,160	40	22.7	24.0	46.7	*9.2*	1.90	95	*5.6*	*13.7*	*58.0*	*22.7*
Dorset	**2,653**	**252**	**320.9**	**346.6**	**667.5**	*11.5*	**1.71**	**85**	*5.5*	*12.3*	*56.8*	*25.4*
Bournemouth	46	3,462	75.3	84.5	159.9	*11.5*	1.49	91	*5.4*	*10.7*	*57.4*	*26.5*
Christchurch	50	834	19.7	22.4	42.0	*9.8*	1.89	75	*4.6*	*10.5*	*50.8*	*34.1*
East Dorset	354	225	38.6	41.2	79.8	*15.5*	1.66	73	*4.7*	*12.5*	*55.1*	*27.7*
North Dorset	609	90	26.6	28.1	54.7	*11.5*	1.88	77	*5.8*	*14.4*	*56.3*	*23.4*
Poole	65	2,118	66.3	70.8	137.2	*14.0*	1.76	85	*6.2*	*12.7*	*58.5*	*22.5*
Purbeck	404	108	21.6	22.3	43.8	*8.3*	1.85	83	*5.5*	*13.1*	*58.3*	*23.2*
West Dorset	1,082	81	42.0	45.7	87.7	*9.5*	1.75	84	*5.3*	*12.9*	*54.5*	*27.3*
Weymouth and Portland	42	1,495	30.8	31.6	62.4	*7.6*	1.90	100	*6.3*	*13.2*	*59.7*	*20.8*
Gloucestershire	**2,653**	**205**	**266.4**	**277.5**	**543.9**	*7.4*	**1.78**	**92**	*6.4*	*13.5*	*60.3*	*19.8*
Cheltenham	47	2,288	51.9	54.9	106.7	*3.8*	1.53	94	*6.1*	*12.6*	*61.0*	*20.4*
Cotswold	1,165	68	38.5	40.8	79.2	*12.6*	1.68	81	*6.0*	*13.0*	*58.8*	*22.2*
Forest of Dean	526	144	37.3	38.3	75.6	*3.2*	1.84	100	*5.9*	*13.6*	*60.6*	*20.0*
Gloucester	41	2,586	51.8	53.0	104.8	*4.5*	1.97	102	*7.6*	*14.2*	*61.1*	*17.2*
Stroud	461	229	51.7	53.8	105.4	*9.7*	1.93	90	*6.2*	*14.0*	*59.8*	*20.0*
Tewkesbury	414	174	35.3	36.8	72.2	*13.6*	1.74	87	*6.4*	*13.6*	*60.1*	*19.9*
Somerset	**3,452**	**137**	**231.3**	**242.8**	**474.1**	*10.1*	**1.86**	**89**	*6.2*	*13.7*	*58.2*	*21.9*
Mendip	739	133	48.1	50.0	98.1	*9.2*	1.93	89	*6.4*	*14.9*	*59.2*	*19.4*
Sedgemoor	564	178	49.4	51.2	100.7	*11.9*	1.91	91	*6.1*	*13.6*	*58.5*	*21.8*
Taunton Deane	462	211	47.5	50.0	97.5	*10.4*	1.79	91	*6.0*	*13.7*	*58.5*	*21.7*
South Somerset	727	201	71.4	74.9	146.3	*9.9*	1.77	89	*6.3*	*13.5*	*58.3*	*21.9*
West Somerset	959	33	14.8	16.6	31.5	*6.7*	2.13	85	*5.3*	*11.2*	*52.3*	*31.1*
Wiltshire	**3,476**	**168**	**288.5**	**294.5**	**583.0**	*11.0*	**1.80**	**94**	*6.7*	*13.9*	*61.7*	*17.7*
Kennet	957	76	35.7	36.7	72.4	*10.2*	1.95	82	*6.9*	*14.3*	*60.8*	*18.0*
North Wiltshire	768	152	58.1	58.6	116.7	*11.3*	1.86	94	*7.0*	*13.8*	*62.3*	*16.8*
Salisbury	1,004	109	53.7	56.1	109.8	*7.0*	1.66	91	*6.0*	*13.5*	*60.3*	*20.2*
Thamesdown	230	755	86.6	87.1	173.8	*14.6*	1.77	100	*7.2*	*14.1*	*63.1*	*15.6*
West Wiltshire	517	213	54.3	56.0	110.3	*10.0*	1.84	98	*6.4*	*13.8*	*60.5*	*19.3*

15.1 *(continued)*

	Persons Area (sq km)	per sq km	Population (thousands)			Total population percentage change 1981-1993	Total Period Fertility Rate (TPFR)[1]	Stand-ardised Mortality Ratio (SMR)[2]	Percentage of population aged			
			Males	Females	Total				Under 5	5-15	16 up to pension age[3]	Pension age[3] or over
WEST MIDLANDS	13,004	407	2,610.1	2,679.6	5,289.7	*2.0*	1.83	103	*6.8*	*14.2*	*61.0*	*17.9*
Hereford and Worcester	3,923	177	341.4	353.5	694.8	*9.2*	1.78	95	*6.3*	*14.0*	*60.7*	*19.0*
Bromsgrove	220	423	45.3	47.5	92.8	*5.3*	1.63	100	*6.0*	*14.0*	*61.7*	*18.2*
Hereford	20	2,495	24.6	26.1	50.7	*5.7*	1.91	98	*7.2*	*13.6*	*59.5*	*19.7*
Leominster	933	43	20.0	20.5	40.5	*7.6*	1.98	99	*5.8*	*13.1*	*58.1*	*23.1*
Malvern Hills	899	99	43.4	45.8	89.3	*4.8*	1.75	94	*5.3*	*13.6*	*57.8*	*23.2*
Redditch	54	1,449	39.0	39.5	78.5	*16.1*	1.93	95	*7.5*	*16.6*	*62.6*	*13.3*
South Herefordshire	904	59	26.5	27.0	53.6	*14.7*	1.79	90	*6.3*	*13.6*	*59.1*	*21.0*
Worcester	33	2,633	43.2	44.5	87.6	*13.6*	1.83	89	*7.0*	*13.5*	*62.4*	*17.2*
Wychavon	664	158	51.4	53.5	104.9	*11.4*	1.72	97	*6.0*	*13.4*	*60.7*	*19.9*
Wyre Forest	195	495	47.9	49.0	96.8	*5.6*	1.69	98	*6.2*	*13.8*	*62.1*	*17.8*
Shropshire	3,488	119	204.3	209.6	413.9	*8.7*	1.84	96	*6.5*	*14.2*	*61.1*	*18.3*
Bridgnorth	633	79	25.0	25.1	50.0	*-0.9*	1.67	99	*5.4*	*13.3*	*62.4*	*18.8*
North Shropshire	679	79	26.9	27.0	53.9	*5.2*	1.92	92	*6.1*	*13.4*	*60.1*	*20.5*
Oswestry	256	133	16.5	17.7	34.2	*8.3*	1.73	104	*6.0*	*14.2*	*58.9*	*20.8*
Shrewsbury and Atcham	602	156	45.7	47.9	93.7	*6.7*	1.72	94	*6.4*	*13.6*	*60.4*	*19.6*
South Shropshire	1,027	38	19.5	19.9	39.4	*15.3*	1.74	83	*5.7*	*12.5*	*58.2*	*23.6*
The Wrekin *	290	492	70.7	72.1	142.7	*13.8*	1.98	103	*7.4*	*15.5*	*62.7*	*14.4*
Staffordshire	2,715	388	522.3	531.3	1,053.6	*3.4*	1.72	107	*6.5*	*14.0*	*62.2*	*17.3*
Cannock Chase	79	1,150	45.3	45.4	90.7	*6.5*	1.81	113	*7.0*	*14.5*	*63.4*	*15.0*
East Staffordshire	390	252	48.5	49.8	98.3	*2.0*	1.94	106	*7.0*	*14.1*	*60.6*	*18.2*
Lichfield	329	286	46.7	47.2	94.0	*5.6*	1.71	103	*6.2*	*13.7*	*64.3*	*15.8*
Newcastle-under-Lyme	211	583	60.4	62.6	123.0	*2.0*	1.53	101	*6.0*	*13.6*	*61.2*	*19.2*
South Staffordshire	408	259	52.5	53.4	105.9	*8.7*	1.60	97	*6.0*	*14.0*	*64.2*	*15.8*
Stafford	599	203	60.2	61.3	121.5	*3.6*	1.67	106	*6.1*	*13.4*	*62.4*	*18.1*
Staffordshire Moorlands	576	166	47.5	48.2	95.7	*-0.1*	1.58	106	*5.6*	*13.6*	*62.1*	*18.8*
Stoke-on-Trent	93	2,727	125.3	127.6	252.9	*0.2*	1.76	118	*7.0*	*13.6*	*61.0*	*18.5*
Tamworth	31	2,321	35.8	35.8	71.6	*9.8*	1.87	103	*7.7*	*16.9*	*63.6*	*11.8*
Warwickshire	1,979	249	243.8	249.9	493.6	*3.4*	1.69	100	*6.3*	*13.6*	*61.9*	*18.2*
North Warwickshire	285	217	30.7	31.0	61.8	*3.0*	1.56	109	*6.8*	*13.7*	*63.0*	*16.5*
Nuneaton and Bedworth	79	1,500	58.8	59.6	118.5	*4.0*	1.81	110	*7.0*	*14.6*	*62.2*	*16.2*
Rugby	356	242	43.0	43.2	86.2	*-1.5*	1.82	102	*6.3*	*14.1*	*61.4*	*18.2*
Stratford-on-Avon	977	111	53.0	55.6	108.6	*7.8*	1.56	94	*5.4*	*12.6*	*61.8*	*20.2*
Warwick	282	420	58.1	60.5	118.6	*3.0*	1.66	94	*6.0*	*13.1*	*61.6*	*19.3*
West Midlands (Met. County)	899	2,930	1,298.4	1,335.3	2,633.7	*-1.5*	1.91	105	*7.3*	*14.5*	*60.4*	*17.8*
Birmingham *	265	3,813	499.5	512.8	1,012.4	*-0.8*	1.98	106	*7.7*	*15.1*	*60.0*	*17.2*
Coventry *	97	3,151	150.2	153.9	304.1	*-4.8*	1.88	102	*7.2*	*14.4*	*60.3*	*18.1*
Dudley *	98	3,180	154.1	157.4	311.5	*3.5*	1.78	101	*6.5*	*13.4*	*62.0*	*18.1*
Sandwell *	86	3,436	144.3	149.9	294.2	*-5.0*	1.93	114	*7.2*	*14.2*	*59.6*	*19.1*
Solihull	179	1,122	98.0	102.4	200.4	*1.1*	1.75	87	*6.4*	*14.1*	*61.7*	*17.8*
Walsall*	106	2,503	130.9	133.8	264.7	*-1.1*	1.91	111	*7.1*	*14.6*	*61.0*	*17.4*
Wolverhampton *	69	3,582	121.2	125.2	246.4	*-4.0*	1.94	104	*7.3*	*14.4*	*59.7*	*18.6*

15.1 *(continued)*

	Persons Area (sq km)	per sq km	Population (thousands)			Total population percentage change 1981-1993	Total Period Fertility Rate (TPFR)[1]	Stand-ardised Mortality Ratio (SMR)[2]	Percentage of population aged			
			Males	Females	Total				Under 5	5-15	16 up to pension age[3]	Pension age[3] or over
NORTH WEST	7,342	873	3,127.0	3,285.4	6,412.4	-0.7	1.81	111	6.9	14.4	60.5	18.2
Cheshire	2,331	417	476.8	495.2	971.9	4.2	1.76	102	6.6	14.3	61.6	17.5
Chester	448	270	58.6	62.2	120.8	3.4	1.59	97	6.2	13.2	61.4	19.1
Congleton	211	403	41.7	43.3	85.0	6.2	1.64	98	5.8	14.3	62.1	17.9
Crewe and Nantwich	430	254	54.2	55.3	109.5	11.1	1.74	99	7.0	13.5	61.6	17.9
Ellesmere Port and Neston	87	939	39.9	41.5	81.5	-1.3	1.76	97	7.0	14.7	61.4	16.9
Halton *	74	1,681	60.8	63.3	124.1	0.7	1.90	117	7.4	16.7	61.1	14.7
Macclesfield	525	288	73.7	77.7	151.4	1.0	1.67	99	5.9	13.2	61.3	19.6
Vale Royal	380	301	56.3	58.2	114.6	2.7	1.86	99	6.6	14.4	61.1	17.9
Warrington	176	1,051	91.5	93.5	185.0	8.9	1.82	110	6.9	14.3	62.5	16.3
Greater Manchester	1,286	2,006	1,264.5	1,314.4	2,578.9	-1.5	1.85	114	7.2	14.5	60.9	17.4
Bolton *	140	1,896	130.0	134.8	264.9	1.0	1.85	111	7.2	14.8	60.7	17.4
Bury	99	1,830	89.1	92.3	181.4	2.7	1.81	105	6.9	14.3	61.7	17.1
Manchester *	116	3,721	212.5	219.5	432.0	-6.6	1.86	123	8.0	14.8	60.5	16.7
Oldham *	141	1,563	107.6	112.9	220.5	-0.4	2.02	122	7.5	15.5	60.1	16.9
Rochdale *	160	1,296	100.9	105.9	206.8	-0.7	2.03	125	7.7	15.7	59.9	16.7
Salford *	97	2,369	113.0	116.2	229.3	-7.2	1.86	121	7.2	13.7	60.1	19.0
Stockport	126	2,314	141.9	149.6	291.4	0.4	1.68	102	6.4	13.9	61.2	18.5
Tameside	103	2,149	108.6	113.1	221.6	1.4	1.88	112	7.3	14.4	60.8	17.5
Trafford	106	2,063	106.1	111.6	217.8	-1.8	1.78	103	6.6	14.1	60.8	18.5
Wigan *	199	1,575	154.7	158.5	313.2	0.9	1.75	115	6.9	14.2	62.7	16.3
Lancashire	3,070	463	691.4	729.2	1,420.7	2.5	1.86	109	6.7	14.2	59.7	19.4
Blackburn *	137	1,018	68.3	71.2	139.5	-2.1	2.29	119	8.2	16.6	58.8	16.5
Blackpool	35	4,399	73.5	80.1	153.6	3.0	1.70	112	6.1	11.6	59.2	23.2
Burnley *	111	826	44.6	46.9	91.4	-1.4	2.10	119	7.7	15.6	58.7	18.0
Chorley	203	479	47.9	49.2	97.1	5.4	1.78	113	6.5	14.6	62.6	16.3
Fylde	166	445	35.4	38.3	73.7	6.8	1.67	94	5.2	11.7	57.0	26.1
Hyndburn	73	1,082	38.7	40.3	79.0	-0.6	2.16	114	7.5	15.0	59.1	18.4
Lancaster	576	232	64.4	69.2	133.6	6.7	1.57	101	6.1	13.2	59.5	21.3
Pendle	169	507	41.8	44.0	85.9	-0.6	2.07	105	7.2	15.9	58.3	18.6
Preston *	142	929	65.4	66.3	132.2	4.6	1.84	117	7.4	14.3	61.0	17.2
Ribble Valley	584	89	25.7	26.1	51.8	-4.0	1.87	104	5.3	13.9	60.8	20.0
Rossendale	138	477	32.2	33.5	65.8	1.3	2.03	120	7.1	14.9	60.7	17.3
South Ribble	113	916	50.6	52.3	103.5	6.9	1.68	103	6.6	14.6	62.0	16.8
West Lancashire	338	324	53.4	56.3	109.7	2.1	1.77	107	6.5	14.9	62.0	16.6
Wyre	284	366	49.6	54.3	103.9	4.6	1.68	101	5.7	12.9	56.3	25.1
Merseyside	655	2,199	694.3	746.5	1,440.9	-5.3	1.75	113	6.8	14.5	59.9	18.7
Knowsley *	97	1,596	75.2	80.1	155.3	-10.7	1.91	129	7.9	16.6	59.9	15.6
Liverpool *	113	4,228	231.2	245.8	477.0	-7.7	1.66	120	7.0	14.3	60.9	17.8
Sefton *	153	1,925	140.1	154.1	294.3	-2.0	1.69	107	6.4	13.9	58.6	21.1
St Helens *	133	1,351	88.4	91.9	180.2	-5.3	1.77	112	6.5	14.1	62.0	17.5
Wirral *	159	2,105	159.4	174.7	334.1	-1.9	1.86	103	6.6	14.6	58.7	20.1
ENGLAND	130,423	372	23,781.7	24,751.0	48,532.7	3.7	1.76	99	6.7	13.7	61.2	18.3

15.1 *(continued)*

	Area (sq km)	per sq km	Population (thousands) Males	Females	Total	Total population percentage change 1981-1993	Total Period Fertility Rate (TPFR)[1]	Standardised Mortality Ratio (SMR)[2]	Under 5	5-15	16 up to pension age[3]	Pension age[3] or over
WALES	20,766	140	1,416.6	1,489.8	2,906.5	3.3	1.84	104	6.5	14.2	59.3	20.0
Clwyd	2,430	171	200.9	215.0	415.9	5.7	1.84	102	6.3	14.0	59.0	20.7
Alyn and Deeside	154	484	36.8	37.8	74.7	2.9	1.81	108	7.0	14.1	62.4	16.5
Colwyn	552	103	26.5	30.3	56.8	15.6	1.81	100	5.6	12.9	54.0	27.5
Delyn	281	249	34.3	35.7	70.1	6.1	1.81	96	6.1	14.6	61.6	17.7
Glyndwr	968	44	20.6	21.6	42.2	4.9	1.97	93	6.2	13.4	57.5	22.9
Rhuddlan	109	507	25.8	29.1	55.0	4.9	1.95	99	6.4	13.1	55.1	25.5
Wrexham Maelor	367	320	56.8	60.4	117.1	3.4	1.79	109	6.4	14.7	60.2	18.7
Dyfed	5,766	61	170.8	180.7	351.5	5.4	1.76	100	5.9	13.9	58.3	22.0
Carmarthen	1,180	48	27.2	29.2	56.4	8.4	1.73	103	5.4	13.9	58.5	22.3
Ceredigion	1,794	38	33.7	35.2	68.9	12.6	1.46	97	5.5	12.7	60.2	21.6
Dinefwr	972	40	18.9	19.6	38.5	3.3	1.79	100	5.6	13.4	57.5	23.5
Llanelli	233	317	35.9	38.1	74.0	-2.4	1.85	104	5.9	13.8	56.7	23.6
Preseli Pembrokeshire	1,151	62	34.5	36.4	70.9	2.5	1.91	100	6.3	15.0	58.6	20.1
South Pembrokeshire	436	98	20.7	22.2	42.9	12.2	2.06	95	6.5	14.3	57.7	21.5
Gwent	1,377	327	220.7	229.6	450.3	2.0	1.96	104	6.9	14.5	59.8	18.9
Blaenau Gwent	127	606	37.8	39.2	77.0	-3.5	2.04	108	7.0	14.2	59.0	19.8
Islwyn	102	660	33.1	34.1	67.2	1.3	1.93	106	6.8	14.2	60.7	18.2
Monmouth	831	94	38.4	40.0	78.4	8.1	1.70	87	6.0	14.1	60.0	19.8
Newport	190	720	67.0	70.1	137.0	3.5	2.01	107	7.2	14.7	59.6	18.4
Torfaen	126	721	44.4	46.3	90.7	0.1	2.06	110	6.9	14.8	59.8	18.5
Gwynedd	3,863	62	116.1	124.0	240.2	3.9	1.88	98	6.1	13.5	57.5	23.0
Aberconwy	601	90	25.9	28.5	54.4	6.0	1.80	94	5.7	12.1	55.2	27.0
Arfon	410	138	27.4	29.2	56.6	3.7	1.75	102	6.7	14.1	60.5	18.8
Dwyfor	620	44	13.2	14.0	27.1	4.7	1.96	101	5.3	12.6	55.6	26.5
Meirionnydd	1,517	22	15.8	16.9	32.8	4.4	2.10	93	5.7	13.0	56.3	24.9
Ynys Mon-Isle of Anglesey	715	97	33.9	35.5	69.3	1.9	1.98	102	6.3	14.5	58.2	20.9
Mid Glamorgan	1,017	535	266.2	278.1	544.3	0.6	1.90	116	6.9	14.9	60.1	18.2
Cynon Valley	176	371	32.0	33.5	65.5	-3.5	1.99	125	7.0	14.8	58.6	19.6
Merthyr Tydfil	111	540	28.9	30.8	59.7	-1.4	2.03	127	7.4	15.5	58.5	18.6
Ogwr	286	472	65.6	69.4	134.9	3.5	1.84	110	6.7	14.1	60.1	19.2
Rhondda	101	780	38.3	40.2	78.5	-4.7	1.96	121	6.7	14.6	58.0	20.7
Rhymney Valley	177	588	51.0	53.3	104.3	-1.1	2.04	115	7.3	16.0	60.5	16.3
Taff Ely	167	608	50.4	51.0	101.4	7.5	1.66	111	6.6	14.8	63.0	15.6
Powys	5,077	24	59.4	60.4	119.9	8.3	1.92	94	5.8	13.7	58.5	22.0
Brecknock	1,791	23	20.5	21.1	41.5	1.4	1.91	100	5.3	14.0	58.0	22.7
Montgomeryshire	2,059	26	27.0	27.2	54.1	11.8	1.95	91	6.3	13.5	59.4	20.9
Radnorshire	1,228	20	12.0	12.2	24.2	13.9	1.87	91	5.9	13.5	57.3	23.4
South Glamorgan	416	993	201.6	211.7	413.2	6.0	1.79	100	7.1	14.3	60.5	18.2
Cardiff	120	2,486	145.8	152.9	298.7	6.4	1.74	100	7.2	14.0	60.9	17.9
Vale of Glamorgan	296	387	55.8	58.7	114.5	4.9	1.99	97	6.7	15.0	59.5	18.8
West Glamorgan	820	453	180.9	190.3	371.2	-0.2	1.78	107	6.2	14.0	59.3	20.6
Lliw Valley	218	297	31.4	33.2	64.6	7.8	1.87	106	6.5	14.6	58.8	20.1
Neath	204	323	31.9	33.9	65.9	-1.9	1.74	118	6.2	14.0	58.9	20.9
Port Talbot	152	338	25.0	26.3	51.4	-6.3	2.02	113	6.2	14.3	58.2	21.2
Swansea	246	770	92.5	96.8	189.3	-0.4	1.72	102	6.1	13.7	59.8	20.4

15.1 *(continued)*

	Persons Area (sq km)	per sq km	Population (thousands)			Total population percentage change 1981-1993	Total Period Fertility Rate (TPFR)[1]	Stand-ardised Mortality Ratio (SMR)[2]	Percentage of population aged			
			Males	Females	Total				Under 5	5-15	16 up to pension age[3]	Pension age[3] or over
SCOTLAND	77,080	66	2,478.5	2,641.7	5,120.2	*-1.2*	1.62	100	*6.3*	*13.8*	*62.0*	*17.8*
Borders	4,670	23	50.6	54.7	105.3	*4.0*	..	84	*5.9*	*13.1*	*59.3*	*21.8*
Berwickshire	876	22	9.3	10.0	19.4	*5.5*	..	71	*6.1*	*13.4*	*57.9*	*22.6*
Ettrick and Lauderdale	1,355	26	16.9	18.2	35.0	*5.2*	..	88	*5.8*	*13.2*	*60.5*	*20.6*
Roxburgh	1,540	23	17.0	18.4	35.4	*0.1*	..	91	*5.8*	*12.7*	*59.2*	*22.3*
Tweeddale	899	17	7.4	8.2	15.6	*9.0*	..	79	*6.0*	*13.4*	*58.3*	*22.4*
Central	2,627	104	132.2	140.7	272.9	*-0.2*	..	99	*6.2*	*13.9*	*62.6*	*17.3*
Clackmannan	160	304	23.8	24.9	48.7	*0.9*	..	91	*6.6*	*14.8*	*62.2*	*16.3*
Falkirk	291	489	69.1	73.5	142.6	*-1.7*	..	107	*6.3*	*13.6*	*62.6*	*17.4*
Stirling	2,176	38	39.3	42.3	81.6	*1.7*	..	89	*5.8*	*13.8*	*62.6*	*17.8*
Dumfries and Galloway	6,370	23	71.8	76.1	147.9	*1.6*	..	92	*6.0*	*13.7*	*59.6*	*20.7*
Annandale and Eskdale	1,553	24	18.1	19.0	37.1	*4.2*	..	90	*5.9*	*13.4*	*59.9*	*20.8*
Nithsdale	1,433	40	27.7	29.5	57.2	*0.9*	..	92	*6.4*	*13.8*	*60.8*	*19.0*
Stewartry	1,671	14	11.4	12.2	23.7	*3.5*	..	91	*5.4*	*13.5*	*56.3*	*24.8*
Wigtown	1,713	17	14.5	15.4	29.9	*-1.3*	..	98	*6.1*	*13.9*	*59.3*	*20.7*
Fife	1,308	269	171.3	179.9	351.2	*2.8*	..	93	*6.3*	*14.2*	*61.5*	*18.0*
Dunfermline	302	432	64.5	65.3	130.2	*2.9*	.	95	*6.7*	*14.7*	*62.5*	*16.2*
Kirkcaldy	248	599	71.8	76.3	148.6	*-0.6*	..	95	*6.4*	*14.5*	*60.8*	*18.4*
North East Fife	758	96	34.9	37.5	72.4	*10.5*	..	86	*5.4*	*12.8*	*61.3*	*20.5*
Grampian	8,707	61	260.6	267.5	528.1	*8.9*	..	93	*6.4*	*13.9*	*63.3*	*16.4*
Aberdeen City	184	1,183	106.4	111.8	218.2	*2.7*	..	95	*5.9*	*11.9*	*65.1*	*17.1*
Banff and Buchan	1,528	58	43.6	44.4	88.0	*6.3*	.	95	*6.7*	*15.0*	*61.7*	*16.6*
Gordon	2,214	36	39.8	39.9	79.7	*24.9*	.	85	*7.0*	*16.2*	*63.0*	*13.8*
Kincardine and Deeside	2,550	22	27.9	28.1	56.0	*32.0*	.	87	*6.9*	*15.7*	*62.3*	*15.0*
Moray	2,231	39	42.9	43.3	86.3	*3.3*	..	95	*6.7*	*14.3*	*61.4*	*17.6*
Highland	25,304	8	101.6	105.3	206.9	*6.2*	..	91	*6.4*	*14.9*	*61.0*	*17.7*
Badenoch and Strathspey	2,317	5	5.5	5.6	11.1	*12.6*	..	93	*5.3*	*13.4*	*61.0*	*20.3*
Caithness	1,776	15	13.1	13.3	26.4	*-4.6*	..	106	*6.2*	*15.5*	*60.6*	*17.6*
Inverness	2,789	23	31.0	32.9	63.9	*11.8*	..	92	*6.7*	*14.2*	*62.6*	*16.5*
Lochaber	4,468	4	9.5	9.9	19.4	*-0.4*	..	96	*6.6*	*15.3*	*62.2*	*16.0*
Nairn	422	26	5.3	5.5	10.9	*9.0*	..	84	*5.7*	*14.9*	*58.1*	*21.4*
Ross and Cromarty	4,976	10	25.0	25.3	50.3	*7.1*	..	83	*6.6*	*15.9*	*60.8*	*16.7*
Skye and Lochalsh	2,691	4	5.8	6.0	11.9	*11.8*	..	80	*6.3*	*14.8*	*58.8*	*20.1*
Sutherland	5,865	2	6.4	6.8	13.2	*-0.9*	..	96	*5.6*	*14.2*	*57.2*	*23.0*
Lothian	1,756	429	364.9	389.0	753.9	*0.6*	..	96	*6.2*	*12.5*	*63.9*	*17.4*
East Lothian	713	120	41.5	44.1	85.6	*6.1*	..	92	*6.5*	*13.2*	*60.3*	*20.0*
Edinburgh City	261	1,691	212.1	229.5	441.6	*-1.0*	..	94	*5.9*	*11.2*	*64.5*	*18.5*
Midlothian	358	223	39.1	40.8	79.9	*-4.2*	..	98	*6.6*	*14.4*	*63.0*	*16.1*
West Lothian	423	347	72.1	74.6	146.7	*5.3*	..	104	*7.0*	*15.2*	*64.7*	*13.1*
Strathclyde	13,529	169	1,099.5	1,187.3	2,286.8	*-5.3*	..	107	*6.4*	*14.1*	*61.9*	*17.6*
Argyll and Bute	6,497	10	30.3	32.9	63.3	*-2.7*	..	101	*5.8*	*13.7*	*58.2*	*22.4*
Bearsden and Milngavie	36	1,127	19.8	21.3	41.1	*4.7*	..	75	*5.5*	*14.7*	*62.0*	*17.8*
Clydebank	35	1,314	21.8	24.7	46.6	*-11.8*	..	102	*6.3*	*14.6*	*59.4*	*19.7*
Clydesdale	1,322	44	28.4	29.9	58.3	*1.8*	..	103	*6.2*	*14.6*	*62.2*	*17.0*
Cumbernauld and Kilsyth	103	621	31.4	32.6	63.9	*2.7*	..	102	*6.7*	*15.6*	*65.7*	*11.9*
Cumnock and Doon Valley	800	54	20.8	22.1	42.8	*-4.6*	..	106	*7.1*	*14.6*	*60.7*	*17.6*
Cunninghame	878	158	66.8	72.2	139.0	*1.2*	..	105	*6.5*	*15.0*	*61.0*	*17.5*
Dumbarton	472	166	38.5	40.0	78.5	*-0.5*	..	98	*6.8*	*14.9*	*61.9*	*16.4*
East Kilbride	285	299	41.7	43.7	85.4	*2.6*	..	99	*6.7*	*14.3*	*63.7*	*15.3*
Eastwood	115	529	29.3	31.6	60.9	*13.2*	..	75	*6.6*	*14.5*	*61.6*	*17.3*
Glasgow City	198	3,446	324.3	357.2	681.5	*-12.0*	..	117	*6.5*	*13.1*	*61.7*	*18.7*
Hamilton	131	821	52.0	55.5	107.5	*-1.7*	..	107	*6.3*	*14.9*	*63.4*	*15.3*
Inverclyde	158	571	43.1	46.9	90.0	*-11.1*	..	117	*6.4*	*14.5*	*60.6*	*18.6*
Kilmarnock and Loudoun	373	217	39.0	42.0	81.0	*-1.8*	..	99	*6.5*	*14.0*	*61.5*	*18.1*
Kyle and Carrick	1,317	87	54.4	59.6	114.0	*0.7*	..	99	*5.7*	*13.6*	*59.8*	*20.9*
Monklands	164	626	49.5	53.1	102.6	*-7.8*	..	117	*6.6*	*15.3*	*62.3*	*15.8*
Motherwell	172	836	69.8	73.9	143.7	*-5.0*	..	112	*6.5*	*14.8*	*61.8*	*16.9*
Renfrew	307	654	96.8	104.3	201.2	*-4.2*	..	106	*6.5*	*14.1*	*62.7*	*16.6*
Strathkelvin	164	522	41.7	43.9	85.7	*-2.0*	..	98	*6.4*	*14.9*	*64.0*	*14.7*

15.1 *(continued)*

	Persons Area (sq km)	per sq km	Population (thousands)			Total population percentage change 1981-1993	Total Period Fertility Rate (TPFR)[1]	Stand-ardised Mortality Ratio (SMR)[2]	Percentage of population aged			
			Males	Females	Total				Under 5	5-15	16 up to pension age[3]	Pension age[3] or over
Tayside	7,502	53	190.2	205.0	395.2	*-0.5*	..	96	*6.1*	*13.5*	*60.5*	*19.9*
Angus	2,031	48	47.5	50.0	97.4	*4.7*	..	91	*6.2*	*14.1*	*60.3*	*19.4*
Dundee City	235	723	81.3	88.8	170.1	*-7.9*	..	101	*6.1*	*12.8*	*61.6*	*19.4*
Perth and Kinross	5,236	24	61.5	66.2	127.7	*7.0*	..	95	*5.9*	*13.8*	*59.3*	*21.0*
Orkney	976	20	9.8	10.0	19.8	*3.0*	..	96	*6.6*	*15.0*	*60.0*	*18.4*
Shetland	1,433	16	11.6	11.3	22.8	*-13.3*	..	105	*7.2*	*16.0*	*61.5*	*15.2*
Western Isles	2,898	10	14.6	14.8	29.4	*-6.8*	..	98	*6.1*	*15.0*	*58.1*	*20.8*
Northern Ireland	13,483	121	797.0	835.0	1,631.8	*6.1*	2.01	..	*8.0*	*17.7*	*59.3*	*15.1*
Antrim	405	117	..	..	47.5	*3.5*	..	..	..	..	..	..
Ards	368	180	..	..	66.2	*14.5*	..	..	..	..	..	..
Armagh	667	79	..	..	52.4	*6.5*	..	..	..	..	..	..
Ballymena	634	90	..	..	57.0	*4.0*	..	..	..	..	..	..
Ballymoney	417	59	..	..	24.4	*6.6*	..	..	..	..	..	..
Banbridge	441	83	..	..	34.4	*22.0*	..	..	..	..	..	..
Belfast	130	2,282	..	..	296.7	*-5.9*	..	..	..	..	..	..
Carrickfergus	85	406	..	..	34.5	*20.6*	..	..	..	..	..	..
Castlereagh	84	750	..	..	63.0	*3.8*	..	..	..	..	..	..
Coleraine	478	112	..	..	53.6	*14.8*	..	..	..	..	..	..
Cookstown	512	60	..	..	30.9	*9.2*	..	..	..	..	..	..
Craigavon	280	274	..	..	76.8	*4.8*	..	..	..	..	..	..
Derry	373	269	..	..	101.0	*11.9*	..	..	..	..	..	..
Down	638	95	..	..	60.5	*12.9*	..	..	..	..	..	..
Dungannon	763	61	..	..	46.2	*5.5*	..	..	..	..	..	..
Fermanagh	1,700	32	..	..	54.8	*5.6*	..	..	..	..	..	..
Larne	337	88	..	..	29.8	*2.8*	..	..	..	..	..	..
Limavady	585	52	..	..	30.3	*11.4*	..	..	..	..	..	..
Lisburn	436	239	..	..	104.1	*22.6*	..	..	..	..	..	..
Magherafelt	562	65	..	..	36.3	*11.4*	..	..	..	..	..	..
Moyle	494	30	..	..	14.7	*2.1*	..	..	..	..	..	..
Newry and Mourne	886	92	..	..	83.9	*5.7*	..	..	..	..	..	..
Newtownabbey	151	515	..	..	77.7	*7.6*	..	..	..	..	..	..
North Down	72	1,022	..	..	73.6	*10.3*	..	..	..	..	..	..
Omagh	1,124	41	..	..	46.2	*5.5*	..	..	..	..	..	..
Strabane	861	41	..	..	35.7	*-1.4*	..	..	..	..	..	..

* Urban Programme authorities.

1 The Total Period Fertility Rate (TPFR) measures the average number of children which would be born if women were to experience the age-specific fertility rates of the year in question throughout their child-bearing life.

2 Adjusted for the age structure of the population. See Appendix notes to the population chapter.

3 Pension age is 60 for women and 65 for men.

Source: *Office of Population Censuses and Surveys; General Register Offices for Scotland and Northern Ireland*

15.2 Housing and households

	Housing starts 1993 (numbers)			Households 1993				Local authority tenants average weekly unrebated rent per dwelling (£) April 1994[2]	Council tax (£) April 1994[3]
	Private enterprise	Housing associations, local authorities etc	Stock of dwellings 1993 (thousands)	All households (thousands)	Average household size (numbers)	Lone parents[1] as a percentage of all households	One person households as a percentage of all households		
UNITED KINGDOM	144,576	44,688	24,053	23,430.1	2.48	..	27.5	..	.
NORTH	5,761	1,839	1,301	1,265.0	2.42	5.9	28.1	30.23	441
Cleveland	1,059	514	226	221.1	2.51	7.2	26.4	34.04	487
Hartlepool *	162	162	37	36.4	2.50	6.6	26.4	32.71	483
Langbaurgh *	134	100	59	57.7	2.47	6.5	26.4	33.72	494
Middlesbrough *	296	151	58	56.9	2.53	9.6	27.0	37.57	504
Stockton-on-Tees *	467	101	71	70.1	2.52	6.2	25.8	31.64	468
Cumbria	1,093	339	213	200.3	2.41	3.9	27.8	32.56	475
Allerdale	166	80	41	38.9	2.43	3.7	28.1	31.29	451
Barrow-in-Furness	67	18	31	30.3	2.40	4.9	27.5	37.35	464
Carlisle	227	108	43	42.3	2.40	4.3	28.1	30.50	454
Copeland	171	27	30	28.3	2.49	4.9	26.1	30.33	416
Eden	161	29	21	19.0	2.42	2.8	25.6	40.47	499
South Lakeland	301	77	47	41.6	2.33	2.7	29.8	32.63	552
Durham	1,341	195	252	246.0	2.44	5.4	26.8	32.48	395
Chester-le-Street	395	18	23	22.2	2.41	4.3	25.7	30.06	376
Darlington	69	47	42	41.0	2.40	5.3	29.0	28.96	413
Derwentside	147	24	37	35.4	2.42	5.8	26.8	36.34	379
Durham	243	21	34	34.7	2.50	5.0	26.0	30.64	369
Easington	131	0	41	39.5	2.47	6.2	27.0	35.63	388
Sedgefield	184	55	38	37.0	2.44	6.0	25.3	30.00	418
Teesdale	75	20	11	9.9	2.41	2.5	28.1	27.32	452
Wear Valley	97	10	27	26.3	2.40	5.7	26.5	33.93	391
Northumberland	498	92	132	124.0	2.43	4.2	26.5	27.67	434
Alnwick	76	43	14	12.5	2.39	4.0	25.6	28.43	431
Berwick-upon-Tweed	75	9	13	11.5	2.29	3.2	32.5	23.21	366
Blyth Valley	31	0	34	32.5	2.46	5.1	25.7	25.56	398
Castle Morpeth	79	0	20	19.4	2.46	3.4	24.9	31.24	548
Tynedale	75	40	24	23.0	2.44	3.7	27.4	31.76	487
Wansbeck	162	0	27	25.2	2.44	4.8	25.4	26.79	381
Tyne and Wear	1,770	699	479	473.6	2.38	6.7	30.2	28.06	429
Gateshead *	374	41	87	84.9	2.37	5.9	30.2	30.09	431
Newcastle-upon-Tyne *	326	234	121	121.2	2.32	7.6	33.4	32.46	499
North Tyneside *	387	165	86	82.9	2.33	5.8	30.0	24.24	462
South Tyneside *	244	74	67	65.6	2.37	7.2	30.6	24.41	403
Sunderland *	439	185	119	119.0	2.48	6.9	26.8	26.84	350
YORKSHIRE & HUMBERSIDE	11,142	3,303	2,058	2,032.9	2.43	5.4	27.6	27.63	434
Humberside	2,549	667	364	355.3	2.46	5.5	26.5	28.24	469
Beverley	651	35	48	46.9	2.44	3.1	25.3	28.58	542
Boothferry	165	13	27	26.0	2.49	4.1	22.6	27.16	505
Cleethorpes	233	0	28	27.9	2.50	4.7	24.0	29.43	508
East Yorkshire	354	62	38	36.1	2.39	3.7	26.3	30.02	468
Glanford	306	38	29	28.7	2.49	3.9	21.9	25.86	502
Great Grimsby	78	62	38	36.4	2.48	7.7	27.0	27.72	449
Holderness	179	12	21	20.4	2.51	3.5	22.3	27.81	499
Kingston upon Hull *	546	445	111	108.9	2.43	7.3	30.4	28.33	417
Scunthorpe	37	0	25	24.1	2.49	6.7	26.2	28.30	439
North Yorkshire	2,610	505	308	293.0	2.40	3.9	27.2	33.86	459
Craven	74	91	23	20.8	2.39	3.9	28.5	34.63	470
Hambleton	512	8	33	31.6	2.53	3.1	23.4	.	430
Harrogate	567	166	62	59.9	2.37	3.6	27.9	38.29	533
Richmondshire	114	0	19	17.5	2.48	3.6	24.1	34.76	513
Ryedale	456	28	40	37.5	2.43	2.6	24.3	.	470
Scarborough	173	49	50	45.9	2.30	4.6	30.1	33.49	410
Selby	505	4	37	36.0	2.51	3.4	23.1	31.53	452
York	209	159	44	43.9	2.32	5.6	32.1	32.44	404

15.2 *(continued)*

	Housing starts 1993 (numbers)			Households 1993				Local authority tenants: average weekly unrebated rent per dwelling (£) April 1994[2]	Council tax (£) April 1994[3]
	Private enterprise	Housing associations, local authorities etc	Stock of dwellings 1993 (thousands)	All households (thousands)	Average household size (numbers)	Lone parents[1] as a percentage of all households	One person households as a percentage of all households		
South Yorkshire	2,172	991	534	533.6	2.42	5.3	27.2	25.24	402
Barnsley *	515	76	92	89.9	2.48	5.1	24.5	25.23	364
Doncaster *	650	152	118	116.7	2.47	5.7	24.8	23.99	373
Rotherham *	413	193	102	102.0	2.49	5.3	24.7	21.19	417
Sheffield *	594	570	223	224.9	2.34	5.3	30.7	27.47	427
West Yorkshire	3,811	1,140	851	850.9	2.44	5.9	28.5	28.38	431
Bradford *	677	204	185	185.5	2.55	6.6	27.9	31.24	399
Calderdale	211	118	82	79.6	2.41	5.4	28.8	29.72	472
Kirklees *	892	48	158	155.6	2.46	5.7	28.1	33.05	504
Leeds *	1,540	562	297	302.3	2.37	6.0	30.2	26.32	425
Wakefield	491	208	129	128.0	2.46	4.8	25.6	26.34	374
EAST MIDLANDS	13,361	2,361	1,676	1,636.5	2.46	4.7	25.5	29.98	449
Derbyshire	2,823	538	395	385.0	2.44	4.3	25.8	27.62	453
Amber Valley	421	3	48	46.2	2.44	3.2	24.6	24.66	466
Bolsover	227	90	30	28.5	2.48	3.6	23.3	26.49	391
Chesterfield	306	23	44	42.7	2.35	3.8	29.2	25.44	421
Derby *	708	185	94	92.8	2.43	5.9	28.3	30.02	399
Derbyshire Dales	131	6	29	27.5	2.45	2.7	25.2	29.77	578
Erewash	224	107	45	43.6	2.43	4.6	25.3	27.19	446
High Peak	198	54	35	34.6	2.48	4.2	25.6	30.25	511
North East Derbyshire	234	0	40	40.2	2.45	3.9	23.3	25.88	487
South Derbyshire	374	70	30	28.8	2.54	3.4	22.3	30.52	481
Leicestershire	2,827	343	358	354.7	2.54	4.8	25.2	30.33	458
Blaby	475	42	34	32.6	2.58	3.2	19.8	25.45	450
Charnwood	560	77	58	59.8	2.52	3.9	24.8	27.71	483
Harborough	349	62	28	27.3	2.53	2.8	23.1	37.12	522
Hinckley and Bosworth	419	0	40	39.0	2.49	3.1	23.5	31.33	413
Leicester *	166	106	112	111.7	2.56	7.7	29.7	30.90	435
Melton	185	0	19	18.4	2.49	3.5	23.3	28.88	478
North West Leicestershire	421	12	33	32.6	2.52	3.6	23.7	28.08	442
Oadby and Wigston	111	34	21	20.8	2.55	3.7	21.3	27.19	476
Rutland	141	10	13	12.5	2.57	4.3	22.8	38.33	551
Lincolnshire	2,876	412	258	246.1	2.40	3.9	25.1	30.27	408
Boston	172	36	23	22.4	2.39	3.7	25.9	30.90	388
East Lindsey	510	71	54	50.1	2.36	3.2	25.6	32.17	398
Lincoln	106	91	36	36.3	2.32	6.0	30.8	27.37	360
North Kesteven	585	83	35	32.7	2.42	3.5	21.5	31.51	443
South Holland	403	0	30	28.7	2.39	2.8	23.6	31.18	408
South Kesteven	868	85	48	45.1	2.48	4.3	24.1	31.16	429
West Lindsey	232	46	32	30.8	2.48	3.9	23.7	29.49	426
Northamptonshire	2,219	338	242	233.3	2.51	4.9	24.3	32.72	421
Corby	161	132	21	20.1	2.61	8.5	21.1	28.92	387
Daventry	291	4	26	24.8	2.54	3.3	22.0	30.66	468
East Northamptonshire	263	18	29	27.3	2.51	3.3	23.5	34.96	460
Kettering	324	80	33	31.5	2.47	4.3	25.1	33.52	400
Northampton	743	37	77	74.7	2.47	5.6	26.4	34.48	445
South Northamptonshire	273	57	28	27.7	2.56	2.9	21.8	36.59	526
Wellingborough	164	10	28	27.2	2.49	6.0	25.1	29.61	221
Nottinghamshire	2,616	730	421	417.6	2.43	5.5	26.3	30.11	479
Ashfield	329	57	45	43.8	2.49	4.3	24.2	24.86	435
Bassetlaw	279	51	44	42.1	2.46	3.9	23.9	28.32	477
Broxtowe	641	0	45	45.4	2.41	4.4	25.2	28.89	505
Gedling	214	55	46	45.5	2.44	3.6	24.7	27.38	503
Mansfield	225	156	42	41.1	2.47	5.4	24.7	31.10	445
Newark and Sherwood	224	0	42	41.5	2.48	4.4	23.9	29.42	524
Nottingham *	434	389	116	117.1	2.37	8.8	30.8	32.08	439
Rushcliffe	270	22	41	41.0	2.43	3.7	25.6	31.73	564

15.2 *(continued)*

	Housing starts 1993 (numbers)			Households 1993				Local authority tenants: average weekly unrebated rent per dwelling (£) April 1994[2]	Council tax (£) April 1994[3]
	Private enterprise	Housing associations, local authorities etc	Stock of dwellings 1993 (thousands)	All households (thousands)	Average household size (numbers)	Lone parents[1] as a percentage of all households	One person households as a percentage of all households		
EAST ANGLIA	8,191	1,592	890	849.5	2.42	*4.1*	*25.9*	34 27	422
Cambridgeshire	2,472	580	275	272.0	2.47	*4.4*	*25.5*	35.90	415
Cambridge	333	142	42	47.2	2.35	*5.8*	*34.1*	37.53	472
East Cambridgeshire	253	47	26	25.0	2.46	*2.3*	*23.4*	.	404
Fenland	517	129	34	32.1	2.41	*3.0*	*25.1*	36.02	372
Huntingdonshire	664	120	59	57.4	2.55	*4.3*	*21.3*	35.77	404
Peterborough	370	40	65	62.6	2.47	*6.3*	*26.3*	35.10	384
South Cambridgeshire	335	102	48	47.7	2.55	*2.8*	*22.3*	35.23	459
Norfolk	3,607	521	337	316.6	2.38	*4.1*	*26.4*	32.52	404
Breckland	393	44	47	45.0	2.43	*3.7*	*24.2*	.	399
Broadland	791	108	46	43.1	2.47	*2.8*	*21.6*	.	436
Great Yarmouth	267	10	39	36.7	2.38	*4.7*	*27.8*	28.76	348
Kings Lynn and West Norfolk	1,035	115	59	53.9	2.40	*3.4*	*25.4*	32.23	397
North Norfolk	569	60	46	39.2	2.32	*3.3*	*27.9*	33.59	404
Norwich	85	150	55	56.5	2.23	*6.9*	*33.4*	32.79	400
South Norfolk	467	34	45	42.2	2.43	*3.4*	*23.3*	36.01	443
Suffolk	2,112	491	276	260.9	2.43	*3.9*	*25.7*	34.69	449
Babergh	209	28	34	31.9	2.46	*3.5*	*23.6*	39.44	451
Forest Heath	188	41	23	23.9	2.54	*4.9*	*23.3*	35.92	387
Ipswich	77	120	50	47.5	2.39	*5.6*	*28.8*	31.82	485
Mid Suffolk	343	70	34	31.0	2.50	*2.6*	*23.2*	37.70	475
St Edmundsbury	430	20	39	36.9	2.45	*3.4*	*23.6*	35.14	456
Suffolk Coastal	496	127	49	44.5	2.43	*2.7*	*26.5*	36.52	460
Waveney	369	85	49	45.1	2.35	*4.2*	*27.5*	32.33	404
SOUTH EAST	35,756	14,876	7,391	7,244.4	2.41	*5.3*	*28.4*	44.38	494
Bedfordshire	2,094	361	215	210.9	2.53	*4.7*	*24.9*	37.80	454
Bedford	545	187	56	55.1	2.46	*4.5*	*27.4*	31 58	442
Luton	419	87	70	68.7	2.58	*6.2*	*25.4*	37.25	410
Mid Bedfordshire	539	87	45	44.0	2.54	*2.9*	*23.1*	36.10	485
South Bedfordshire	591	0	44	43.2	2.53	*4.5*	*23.1*	40.47	507
Berkshire	1,778	111	296	297.7	2.53	*4.3*	*24.5*	44.95	528
Bracknell Forest	831	5	39	39.2	2.56	*4.7*	*22.7*	37.91	510
Newbury	99	0	54	53.9	2.58	*3.6*	*22.6*	36.20	535
Reading	14	0	54	56.9	2.39	*5.8*	*29.4*	47.39	498
Slough	238	69	41	39.7	2.58	*6.2*	*26.3*	45.41	396
Windsor and Maidenhead	237	37	54	54.3	2.47	*3.0*	*25.9*	49.90	585
Wokingham	359	0	54	53.7	2.62	*3.0*	*19.8*	44.41	607
Buckinghamshire	2,169	895	260	252.3	2.55	*4.2*	*23.6*	39.05	526
Aylesbury Vale	644	31	59	58.1	2.55	*3.3*	*22.9*	40.28	497
Chiltern	72	41	35	35.4	2.53	*3.2*	*23.7*	.	633
Milton Keynes	1,107	469	78	72.1	2.54	*6.5*	*24.8*	35.58	451
South Buckinghamshire	112	117	26	25.0	2.49	*3.5*	*23.2*	32.71	586
Wycombe	234	237	62	61.7	2.60	*3.3*	*23.1*	44.59	561
East Sussex	1,137	429	326	315.1	2.23	*4.5*	*32.9*	39.78	481
Brighton	193	130	70	69.5	2.17	*5.5*	*35.6*	41.83	429
Eastbourne	113	4	40	38.9	2.15	*5.0*	*35.1*	37.07	476
Hastings	103	151	38	35.5	2.26	*6.1*	*33.5*	37.56	408
Hove	35	63	42	42.4	2.07	*4.6*	*39.0*	39.69	440
Lewes	73	6	39	37.6	2.30	*3.7*	*29.5*	41.44	510
Rother	235	62	40	36.6	2.25	*3.2*	*30.8*	44.50	523
Wealden	385	13	57	54.5	2.41	*3.0*	*26.5*	34.27	579

15.2 *(continued)*

	Housing starts 1993 (numbers)			Households 1993				Local authority tenants: average weekly unrebated rent per dwelling (£) April 1994[2]	Council tax (£) April 1994[3]
	Private enterprise	Housing associations, local authorities etc	Stock of dwellings 1993 (thousands)	All households (thousands)	Average household size (numbers)	Lone parents[1] as a percentage of all households	One person households as a percentage of all households		
Essex	**4,095**	**1,712**	**645**	**626.2**	**2.46**	*4.3*	*25.4*	**40.50**	**478**
Basildon	757	382	66	63.9	2.52	*5.5*	*24.0*	38.56	518
Braintree	253	11	50	48.6	2.48	*4.0*	*25.0*	40.31	459
Brentwood	101	136	29	28.3	2.47	*3.0*	*25.1*	44.23	545
Castle Point	5	0	34	33.3	2.57	*3.4*	*21.2*	49.87	496
Chelmsford	337	182	62	61.7	2.50	*3.6*	*24.1*	41.18	514
Colchester	478	232	61	59.0	2.47	*4.9*	*24.7*	39.77	467
Epping Forest	313	155	48	47.8	2.45	*3.5*	*25.1*	42.52	505
Harlow	367	46	30	29.4	2.48	*5.9*	*25.4*	36.02	550
Maldon	143	31	22	20.8	2.53	*3.0*	*23.6*	46.19	469
Rochford	174	76	30	29.5	2.54	*3.4*	*22.4*	38.83	487
Southend-on-Sea	265	170	73	71.7	2.29	*5.2*	*31.3*	36.04	413
Tendring	201	153	60	55.4	2.27	*3.1*	*30.8*	37.72	407
Thurrock	502	78	53	50.8	2.56	*5.4*	*22.2*	40.56	435
Uttlesford	199	60	27	26.0	2.54	*3.1*	*23.2*	42.54	558
Greater London	**7,352**	**6,836**	**2959**	**2,906.0**	**2.35**	*7.1*	*32.1*	**47.09**	**484**
Barking and Dagenham	147	112	61	58.3	2.48	*6.4*	*28.0*	34.77	398
Barnet	365	548	123	120.9	2.48	*5.1*	*29.0*	50.10	590
Bexley	459	144	90	88.2	2.48	*4.5*	*24.4*	45.41	470
Brent *	284	166	101	97.5	2.51	*8.7*	*29.6*	50.18	443
Bromley	269	239	126	122.0	2.36	*4.3*	*28.4*	40.47	484
Camden	44	462	87	84.5	2.05	*7.5*	*43.5*	51.35	594
City of London	0	0	3	2.1	1.63	*2.6*	*55.3*	51.60	370
City of Westminster	354	154	102	91.2	1.95	*5.2*	*47.4*	61.44	257
Croydon	291	691	132	130.7	2.44	*6.3*	*27.6*	51.87	479
Ealing	206	344	114	114.2	2.47	*6.4*	*31.0*	59.16	433
Enfield	849	362	108	104.8	2.48	*5.5*	*27.1*	49.65	537
Greenwich *	185	206	90	88.2	2.41	*9.0*	*30.5*	44.60	495
Hackney *	137	501	81	80.7	2.34	*12.0*	*35.6*	46.42	504
Hammersmith and Fulham *	137	43	74	73.9	2.07	*7.9*	*40.1*	48.20	506
Haringey	96	260	90	91.3	2.30	*9.5*	*34.6*	53.99	598
Harrow	151	69	80	79.4	2.58	*4.3*	*25.5*	63.04	547
Havering	270	110	93	91.4	2.52	*4.2*	*23.9*	36.91	453
Hillingdon	344	254	96	96.1	2.46	*4.6*	*26.6*	59.48	534
Hounslow	363	60	84	82.3	2.48	*5.7*	*28.3*	39.99	557
Islington *	11	115	78	78.8	2.18	*10.4*	*38.0*	49.97	560
Kensington and Chelsea *	132	107	80	75.3	1.90	*6.3*	*47.2*	60.47	554
Kingston upon Thames	136	94	58	57.8	2.36	*3.9*	*30.9*	60.27	541
Lambeth *	100	202	115	117.4	2.18	*12.1*	*36.7*	42.12	507
Lewisham *	147	144	105	104.4	2.28	*10.3*	*32.0*	42.59	441
Merton	76	90	75	73.2	2.37	*5.2*	*29.0*	49.95	480
Newham *[4]	-37	183	86	84.9	2.65	*9.9*	*28.6*	39.90	439
Redbridge	327	228	93	91.5	2.52	*4.3*	*27.7*	63.77	465
Richmond-upon-Thames	101	17	74	74.1	2.22	*3.8*	*34.9*	48.24	658
Southwark *	313	135	108	101.8	2.23	*11.7*	*36.7*	44.36	414
Sutton	440	142	73	72.2	2.37	*4.6*	*28.9*	43.03	506
Tower Hamlets *	235	292	71	67.7	2.47	*10.2*	*35.7*	37.73	408
Waltham Forest	142	163	92	91.2	2.39	*7.3*	*31.5*	42.42	449
Wandsworth *	278	199	117	117.8	2.22	*7.4*	*34.6*	55.64	323
Hampshire	**4,199**	**1,050**	**642**	**635.4**	**2.46**	*4.5*	*25.1*	**40.62**	**448**
Basingstoke and Deane	322	157	57	56.7	2.56	*4.1*	*21.9*	47.94	451
East Hampshire	260	0	42	41.4	2.52	*3.6*	*22.9*	41.21	525
Eastleigh	611	82	44	43.3	2.51	*3.8*	*21.7*	45.03	418
Fareham	324	175	41	40.0	2.48	*3.2*	*21.5*	37.58	458
Gosport	101	42	32	30.6	2.44	*5.9*	*24.7*	42.56	426
Hart	255	10	31	31.1	2.61	*3.3*	*20.2*	50.15	542
Havant	85	60	48	46.4	2.50	*5.0*	*23.7*	31.03	454
New Forest	514	122	71	68.2	2.37	*3.3*	*26.2*	42.34	480
Portsmouth	120	148	77	78.1	2.36	*6.2*	*30.0*	36.50	364
Rushmoor	255	53	32	32.6	2.52	*4.4*	*22.9*	42.61	464
Southampton	670	68	86	86.8	2.38	*6.0*	*30.2*	37.08	379
Test Valley	281	33	41	40.7	2.53	*3.7*	*22.7*	43.03	494
Winchester	401	100	40	39.6	2.47	*3.1*	*26.0*	43.64	508

15.2 *(continued)*

	Housing starts 1993 (numbers)			Households 1993				Local authority tenants average weekly unrebated rent per dwelling (£) April 1994[2]	Council tax (£) April 1994[3]
	Private enterprise	Housing associations, local authorities etc	Stock of dwellings 1993 (thousands)	All households (thousands)	Average household size (numbers)	Lone parents[1] as a percentage of all households	One person households as a percentage of all households		
Hertfordshire	**3,498**	**390**	**401**	**396.6**	**2.49**	**4.1**	**25.2**	**39.80**	**528**
Broxbourne	191	63	33	32.0	2.57	3.5	21.6	49.15	511
Dacorum	342	5	55	54.1	2.46	4.4	26.2	37.03	495
East Hertfordshire	615	93	48	47.1	2.52	3.0	23.6	42.80	522
Hertsmere	369	17	36	36.1	2.51	4.1	24.1	45.00	575
North Hertfordshire	321	31	46	46.0	2.44	3.7	26.6	33.40	480
St Albans	270	61	51	50.3	2.48	3.7	25.7	41.23	559
Stevenage	464	48	31	29.8	2.53	6.3	23.5	39.48	479
Three Rivers	134	0	31	32.1	2.52	3.6	24.3	41.26	598
Watford	558	60	31	30.4	2.46	5.3	28.8	38.20	551
Welwyn Hatfield	234	12	39	38.8	2.43	4.3	27.1	37.58	533
Isle of Wight	**188**	**97**	**57**	**51.8**	**2.33**	**4.1**	**28.6**	**33.44**	**452**
Medina	103	42	32	29.5	2.36	4.5	28.8	33.55	438
South Wight	85	55	25	22.2	2.29	3.5	28.4	32.98	471
Kent	**2,282**	**1,316**	**635**	**613.6**	**2.47**	**4.3**	**25.6**	**44.01**	**468**
Ashford	142	72	39	37.5	2.47	4.2	24.6	47.38	479
Canterbury	132	78	54	53.4	2.42	4.3	28.2	44.45	471
Dartford	266	34	33	32.4	2.50	3.8	23.9	44.27	474
Dover	134	133	45	43.3	2.39	4.6	28.2	47.93	461
Gillingham	77	164	38	37.2	2.55	5.0	23.6	38.15	443
Gravesham[4]	-6	35	38	36.2	2.56	4.8	23.8	43.29	444
Maidstone	219	68	55	54.1	2.52	3.8	23.4	44.95	540
Rochester-upon-Medway	209	174	60	56.9	2.54	4.7	22.9	.	350
Sevenoaks	129	105	44	42.8	2.53	3.4	24.0	.	567
Shepway	108	19	43	40.4	2.30	5.0	30.4	38.62	476
Swale	195	152	43	45.7	2.54	4.3	22.6	34.96	414
Thanet	231	86	57	53.2	2.29	5.1	31.2	42.46	432
Tonbridge and Malling	309	45	41	39.6	2.55	3.6	22.2	.	533
Tunbridge Wells	137	151	42	41.1	2.42	3.2	28.4	59.60	515
Oxfordshire	**2,551**	**710**	**224**	**226.1**	**2.54**	**4.3**	**24.5**	**38.88**	**499**
Cherwell	629	82	48	47.9	2.58	4.6	22.3	41.65	425
Oxford	588	425	46	51.0	2.51	6.4	31.5	35.52	544
South Oxfordshire	592	100	49	47.2	2.54	3.7	23.2	46.56	546
Vale of White Horse	281	12	44	43.4	2.58	2.7	21.7	35.18	497
West Oxfordshire	461	91	37	36.6	2.51	3.6	22.8	36.51	478
Surrey	**2,513**	**440**	**419**	**413.6**	**2.46**	**3.2**	**25.8**	**46.10**	**581**
Elmbridge	583	67	49	47.3	2.45	3.6	26.7	43.57	662
Epsom and Ewell	56	50	27	26.5	2.47	3.1	26.7	87.94	562
Guildford	104	10	50	50.2	2.45	3.7	25.9	45.51	572
Mole Valley	152	2	33	32.6	2.38	2.2	26.9	38.87	585
Reigate and Banstead	393	81	49	47.7	2.43	2.9	26.4	47.18	569
Runnymede	137	88	29	30.2	2.42	3.0	26.5	49.94	506
Spelthorne	77	87	38	37.8	2.40	2.9	25.7	50.43	545
Surrey Heath	266	9	31	30.9	2.59	3.8	20.6	.	605
Tandridge	280	1	31	29.7	2.50	2.6	25.4	39.27	618
Waverley	232	14	47	45.6	2.47	3.5	26.6	45.94	599
Woking	233	31	35	35.2	2.47	3.8	25.2	50.20	535
West Sussex	**1,900**	**529**	**310**	**299.1**	**2.35**	**3.6**	**28.7**	**41.91**	**498**
Adur	24	66	26	24.3	2.34	3.6	28.7	40.48	480
Arun	246	121	61	58.5	2.21	3.2	31.0	48.20	491
Chichester	263	82	46	42.9	2.32	3.2	28.6	40.28	503
Crawley	341	36	36	35.1	2.53	5.5	23.7	37.33	466
Horsham	660	87	47	45.4	2.44	3.0	25.9	48.65	529
Mid Sussex	292	137	50	49.4	2.47	3.3	25.5	.	545
Worthing	74	0	45	43.5	2.17	3.7	36.1	42.09	452

15.2 *(continued)*

	Housing starts 1993 (numbers)			Households 1993				Local authority tenants: average weekly unrebated rent per dwelling (£) April 1994[2]	Council tax (£) April 1994[3]
	Private enterprise	Housing associations, local authorities etc	Stock of dwellings 1993 (thousands)	All households (thousands)	Average household size (numbers)	Lone parents[1] as a percentage of all households	One person households as a percentage of all households		
SOUTH WEST	12,591	2,294	2,015	1,947.3	2.40	*4.2*	*26.9*	37.19	484
Avon	1,769	196	398	397.6	2.41	*4.8*	*27.2*	36.72	539
Bath	24	0	36	36.0	2.25	*4.8*	*32.2*	37.28	481
Bristol *	248	63	164	166.6	2.35	*6.2*	*30.6*	34.66	537
Kingswood	275	54	37	36.1	2.52	*3.9*	*22.6*	33.40	507
Northavon	590	57	54	54.0	2.53	*3.6*	*21.8*	43.82	565
Wansdyke	179	0	33	31.6	2.52	*2.7*	*22.3*	35.78	593
Woodspring	453	22	74	73.3	2.42	*3.7*	*25.5*	43.75	545
Cornwall and the Isles of Scilly	1,147	175	211	194.0	2.40	*4.3*	*26.2*	35.36	447
Caradon	299	0	35	31.5	2.43	*4.3*	*23.7*	35.31	456
Carrick	94	68	37	35.0	2.36	*3.9*	*27.8*	32.81	488
Kerrier	250	5	38	35.7	2.44	*4.8*	*25.1*	34.69	412
North Cornwall	195	36	35	30.7	2.41	*4.1*	*26.1*	37.17	457
Penwith	53	11	29	25.0	2.33	*5.0*	*28.3*	36.41	430
Restormel	255	55	37	35.4	2.42	*4.1*	*26.9*	36.06	438
Isles of Scilly	1	0	1	0.8	2.53	*6.7*	*22.5*	40.73	435
Devon	2,243	498	448	431.2	2.37	*4.5*	*27.7*	34.65	461
East Devon	386	22	55	51.9	2.25	*3.5*	*29.5*	33.47	513
Exeter	228	0	42	43.6	2.35	*5.2*	*30.6*	32.42	449
Mid Devon	151	54	37	26.2	2.47	*3.4*	*25.2*	35.08	497
North Devon	40	0	28	35.4	2.38	*4.2*	*26.7*	44.86	474
Plymouth *	216	15	102	104.3	2.42	*5.9*	*26.5*	30.84	412
South Hams	267	77	38	32.0	2.39	*3.1*	*25.8*	43.76	502
Teignbridge	495	101	49	46.2	2.35	*3.3*	*27.2*	36.93	498
Torbay	207	179	55	51.3	2.27	*5.2*	*31.2*	41.00	421
Torridge	144	50	23	21.5	2.47	*3.6*	*24.8*	31.52	407
West Devon	109	0	20	18.8	2.42	*3.4*	*25.8*	33.81	518
Dorset	2,172	412	294	281.1	2.31	*3.7*	*28.9*	39.11	468
Bournemouth	327	136	71	69.5	2.20	*4.8*	*33.1*	42.27	429
Christchurch	256	24	20	19.1	2.17	*3.3*	*31.1*	.	477
East Dorset	221	58	34	33.3	2.37	*2.7*	*23.9*	45.98	553
North Dorset	273	31	24	22.2	2.42	*3.7*	*26.9*	36.55	453
Poole	443	48	59	56.5	2.39	*3.8*	*27.5*	39.72	473
Purbeck	138	46	19	17.8	2.41	*2.4*	*25.7*	43.47	488
West Dorset	389	5	40	37.2	2.31	*2.6*	*29.6*	.	475
Weymouth and Portland	125	64	27	25.5	2.34	*5.2*	*28.1*	32.62	434
Gloucestershire	1,874	314	227	221.1	2.42	*4.0*	*26.7*	39.83	478
Cheltenham	177	29	46	45.9	2.28	*5.1*	*32.9*	42.05	460
Cotswold	359	96	34	32.4	2.42	*2.8*	*26.6*	43.62	510
Forest of Dean	247	83	31	29.7	2.51	*2.9*	*23.6*	37.13	527
Gloucester	489	64	43	42.0	2.46	*5.6*	*26.1*	40.10	407
Stroud	258	27	44	42.0	2.47	*3.6*	*24.8*	39.02	558
Tewkesbury	344	15	30	29.2	2.44	*3.5*	*23.6*	35.31	401
Somerset	978	427	198	191.8	2.43	*3.8*	*26.4*	37.74	477
Mendip	242	47	40	38.7	2.50	*3.7*	*26.5*	37.93	500
Sedgemoor	142	44	41	40.7	2.43	*4.1*	*25.4*	39.47	467
South Somerset	302	110	61	59.2	2.44	*3.2*	*25.6*	39.45	494
Taunton Deane	191	157	40	39.7	2.40	*4.7*	*27.8*	33.24	436
West Somerset	101	69	15	13.4	2.25	*2.7*	*28.7*	40.47	491
Wiltshire	2,408	272	237	230.5	2.48	*4.0*	*23.7*	39.14	502
Kennet	298	52	29	27.6	2.56	*3.5*	*22.9*	43.95	525
North Wiltshire	730	26	47	45.2	2.53	*4.0*	*21.5*	37.57	560
Salisbury	450	144	44	43.6	2.45	*3.5*	*24.9*	44.41	497
Thamesdown	523	0	71	69.7	2.47	*4.9*	*23.9*	32.99	464
West Wiltshire	407	50	46	44.4	2.45	*3.4*	*25.2*	43.44	493

15.2 *(continued)*

	Housing starts 1993 (numbers)			Households 1993				Local authority tenants: average weekly unrebated rent per dwelling (£) April 1994[2]	Council tax (£) April 1994[3]
	Private enterprise	Housing associations, local authorities etc	Stock of dwellings 1993 (thousands)	All households (thousands)	Average household size (numbers)	Lone parents[1] as a percentage of all households	One person households as a percentage of all households		
WEST MIDLANDS	**12,142**	**2,846**	**2,117**	**2,081.2**	**2.51**	**5.3**	**25.9**	**32.78**	**452**
Hereford and Worcester	**2,685**	**218**	**282**	**274.5**	**2.49**	**4.3**	**23.9**	**33.41**	**463**
Bromsgrove	364	15	37	35.9	2.55	3.9	20.9	29.53	485
Hereford	56	28	21	20.5	2.44	6.3	27.1	30.47	398
Leominster	122	20	17	16.0	2.49	2.7	23.4	.	496
Malvern Hills	233	32	36	35.9	2.44	3.1	25.2	38.80	474
Redditch	155	0	30	29.7	2.63	6.4	21.2	33.95	454
South Herefordshire	323	2	22	21.0	2.49	2.9	23.4	34.90	491
Worcester	756	48	33	35.5	2.43	5.1	26.4	32.35	424
Wychavon	475	7	43	41.8	2.48	3.4	23.6	34.99	499
Wyre Forest	201	66	39	38.3	2.49	4.4	24.7	32.05	438
Shropshire	**1,719**	**303**	**170**	**162.7**	**2.51**	**4.4**	**24.6**	**33.62**	**470**
Bridgnorth	59	48	21	19.7	2.48	3.7	23.8	32.35	509
North Shropshire	181	16	22	20.9	2.53	2.4	23.7	29.75	512
Oswestry	117	59	15	13.8	2.44	3.6	27.1	28.02	412
Shrewsbury and Atcham	363	31	39	37.7	2.44	4.5	27.8	29.31	448
South Shropshire	149	35	17	16.0	2.43	2.9	23.9	.	482
The Wrekin *	850	114	57	54.7	2.59	5.9	22.5	37.61	467
Staffordshire	**2,679**	**536**	**420**	**412.1**	**2.53**	**4.2**	**23.6**	**30.29**	**428**
Cannock Chase	217	41	35	34.6	2.61	4.7	20.9	31.88	443
East Staffordshire	305	41	41	38.6	2.52	3.3	24.3	29.03	431
Lichfield	208	57	36	35.5	2.60	3.6	20.2	27.00	490
Newcastle-under-Lyme	263	54	50	49.4	2.47	3.7	26.4	23.81	419
South Staffordshire	231	42	41	41.0	2.56	3.4	20.5	33.29	432
Stafford	554	23	48	46.8	2.54	3.6	23.0	28.51	456
Staffordshire Moorlands	294	4	39	37.3	2.54	3.0	22.1	29.50	468
Stoke-on-Trent	330	226	103	102.0	2.46	5.4	27.0	31.85	381
Tamworth	277	48	27	26.9	2.65	5.8	20.4	36.66	396
Warwickshire	**1,724**	**155**	**202**	**197.6**	**2.47**	**4.1**	**25.0**	**31.96**	**527**
North Warwickshire	321	14	25	24.2	2.54	3.9	23.6	28.43	542
Nuneaton and Bedworth	330	101	47	46.3	2.55	4.8	22.9	27.72	481
Rugby	285	21	35	34.7	2.46	4.6	25.1	32.62	494
Stratford-on-Avon	493	19	45	44.1	2.44	2.9	25.8	34.04	580
Warwick	295	0	50	48.4	2.41	4.3	27.0	36.49	541
West Midlands (Met. County)	**3,335**	**1,634**	**1,045**	**1,034.2**	**2.52**	**6.4**	**27.8**	**33.38**	**441**
Birmingham *	924	779	394	396.4	2.52	7.8	30.5	35.02	442
Coventry *	209	74	123	122.2	2.46	7.3	28.8	32.18	528
Dudley *	677	62	124	123.8	2.50	4.0	24.6	31.08	438
Sandwell *	645	168	121	115.7	2.53	5.3	27.5	36.14	419
Solihull	360	108	80	78.4	2.54	4.9	23.3	35.59	498
Walsall*	232	281	103	101.0	2.60	5.1	23.9	28.88	388
Wolverhampton *	288	162	100	96.8	2.52	6.9	27.6	31.02	377

15.2 (continued)

	Housing starts 1993 (numbers)			Households 1993				Local authority tenants:	
	Private enterprise	Housing associations, local authorities etc	Stock of dwellings 1993 (thousands)	All households (thousands)	Average household size (numbers)	Lone parents[1] as a percentage of all households	One person households as a percentage of all households	average weekly unrebated rent per dwelling (£) April 1994[2]	Council tax (£) April 1994[3]
NORTH WEST	14,272	4,696	2,622	2,563.3	2.47	*6.6*	*27.9*	31.59	491
Cheshire	2,579	385	394	386.2	2.49	*5.0*	*25.3*	27.87	509
Chester	336	84	50	49.6	2.40	*5.1*	*28.5*	26.87	524
Congleton	491	16	35	33.2	2.53	*3.2*	*23.4*	28.50	545
Crewe and Nantwich	268	19	44	44.2	2.46	*4.3*	*25.5*	29.25	483
Ellesmere Port and Neston[4]	173	-1	33	31.8	2.54	*5.6*	*22.8*	20.68	485
Halton *	110	62	47	47.0	2.62	*8.0*	*23.7*	28.41	420
Macclesfield	302	21	65	61.9	2.40	*4.0*	*26.4*	32.30	592
Vale Royal	345	84	46	44.8	2.54	*4.1*	*23.6*	30.30	541
Warrington	554	100	75	73.7	2.48	*5.1*	*26.0*	27.34	477
Greater Manchester	5,323	1,839	1,067	1,039.7	2.45	*6.9*	*28.8*	32.08	475
Bolton *	415	135	108	105.6	2.49	*5.7*	*27.7*	28.67	459
Bury	429	120	74	72.2	2.47	*5.2*	*26.7*	30.27	429
Manchester *	898	645	186	178.5	2.38	*12.0*	*34.2*	36.13	492
Oldham *	389	113	90	88.2	2.48	*6.8*	*28.1*	29.80	473
Rochdale *	554	167	85	81.8	2.50	*7.2*	*27.9*	32.74	462
Salford *	740	130	100	94.7	2.39	*7.5*	*32.0*	32.52	496
Stockport	203	220	119	118.4	2.44	*4.8*	*27.6*	28.00	568
Tameside	366	163	92	89.1	2.47	*5.8*	*26.6*	30.96	474
Trafford	466	98	88	87.6	2.46	*5.5*	*28.1*	31.30	449
Wigan *	863	48	125	123.6	2.52	*5.0*	*25.3*	27.31	414
Lancashire	3,159	594	583	567.6	2.45	*5.6*	*27.6*	32.49	491
Blackburn *	434	21	56	53.4	2.57	*7.4*	*27.4*	37.24	448
Blackpool	162	87	66	64.6	2.28	*5.3*	*31.7*	30.35	452
Burnley *	173	135	39	36.5	2.47	*7.5*	*27.3*	34.76	444
Chorley	48	0	39	37.6	2.54	*4.9*	*23.0*	25.15	502
Fylde	337	12	32	31.0	2.29	*3.2*	*29.9*	27.89	558
Hyndburn	202	41	34	31.6	2.47	*6.2*	*27.4*	35.82	469
Lancaster	324	14	54	54.6	2.38	*6.0*	*29.0*	30.93	480
Pendle	78	71	37	34.7	2.46	*5.8*	*29.0*	32.42	471
Preston *	397	104	53	52.3	2.47	*6.7*	*30.2*	34.20	482
Ribble Valley	261	16	21	19.8	2.52	*3.1*	*26.0*	26.10	594
Rossendale	75	35	28	26.2	2.48	*5.6*	*26.5*	32.12	512
South Ribble	221	0	41	40.0	2.57	*4.7*	*22.2*	.	524
West Lancashire	169	0	42	42.2	2.57	*6.3*	*23.7*	30.64	521
Wyre	278	58	44	43.4	2.36	*3.7*	*28.3*	28.67	522
Merseyside	3,211	1,878	582	569.8	2.49	*8.1*	*28.4*	31.92	508
Knowsley *	536	145	58	57.6	2.68	*12.4*	*23.4*	37.49	436
Liverpool *	1,316	1,172	198	191.2	2.46	*9.9*	*31.7*	28.29	552
Sefton *	253	125	117	115.6	2.48	*5.9*	*28.0*	33.31	503
St Helens *	501	258	72	71.0	2.52	*5.9*	*24.6*	31.46	467
Wirral *	605	178	138	134.5	2.45	*6.9*	*28.3*	34.04	504
ENGLAND	113,216	33,807	20,070	19,620.2	2.47	*5.3*	*27.5*	35.68	470

15.2   *(continued)*

	Housing starts 1993 (numbers)			Households 1993				Local authority tenants: average weekly unrebated rent per dwelling (£) April 1994[2]	Council tax (£) April 1994[3]
	Private enterprise	Housing associations, local authorities etc	Stock of dwellings 1993 (thousands)	All households (thousands)	Average household size (numbers)	Lone parents[1] as a percentage of all households	One person households as a percentage of all households		
WALES	7,303	3,287	1,203	1,148.2	2.53	5.4	25.9	34.04	350
Clwyd	1,145	481	172	164.9	2.48	4.9	26.1	28.66	373
Alyn and Deeside	300	64	30	28.5	2.60	4.4	21.6	28.83	385
Colwyn	174	14	25	23.6	2.33	3.9	31.4	30.50	363
Delyn	162	55	27	26.8	2.58	5.0	22.2	32.55	369
Glyndwr	96	22	18	16.6	2.49	4.1	26.2	26.30	358
Rhuddlan	104	162	24	23.1	2.32	6.2	30.3	29.90	376
Wrexham Maelor	309	164	47	46.3	2.50	5.4	26.3	27.76	380
Dyfed	1,302	388	150	139.7	2.48	4.6	26.2	33.30	390
Carmarthen	196	89	23	21.9	2.53	3.6	25.3	33.12	381
Ceredigion	181	27	29	28.0	2.43	5.0	28.6	34.04	395
Dinefwr	98	54	17	15.3	2.48	4.2	25.9	26.93	386
Llanelli	346	67	32	29.8	2.46	4.7	26.8	35.78	438
Preseli Pembrokeshire	199	74	30	27.8	2.52	5.1	24.5	31.00	373
South Pembrokeshire	282	77	19	16.9	2.49	4.7	25.8	34.19	360
Gwent	910	381	183	176.8	2.52	5.5	24.4	37.55	317
Blaenau Gwent	107	34	32	30.0	2.54	6.1	24.4	34.01	312
Islwyn	28	32	27	26.0	2.57	4.9	23.9	34.34	301
Monmouth	404	128	32	30.8	2.50	3.7	22.7	38.75	323
Newport	222	0	55	54.4	2.49	6.5	25.7	37.90	321
Torfaen	149	187	37	35.7	2.51	5.5	24.1	41.00	319
Gwynedd	498	257	111	97.1	2.42	4.8	28.7	31.37	354
Aberconwy	165	123	25	22.6	2.32	5.2	30.2	31.09	353
Arfon	126	66	24	22.2	2.51	5.3	29.2	32.05	357
Dwyfor	59	9	14	11.1	2.38	4.5	28.5	30.42	339
Meirionnydd	25	39	17	13.5	2.38	3.9	29.4	30.52	348
Ynys Mon-Isle of Anglesey	123	20	31	27.7	2.47	4.8	26.9	31.43	362
Mid Glamorgan	1,133	516	219	211.6	2.55	5.7	24.6	34.28	349
Cynon Valley	143	62	28	26.1	2.50	6.8	26.6	31.50	348
Merthyr Tydfil	111	67	25	23.3	2.54	7.4	26.4	32.69	341
Ogwr	357	219	54	52.5	2.53	4.8	24.0	33.88	350
Rhondda	81	39	33	31.1	2.51	5.6	27.0	33.95	346
Rhymney Valley	87	97	41	40.0	2.59	6.1	23.7	37.14	349
Taff Ely	354	32	38	38.7	2.61	5.1	21.9	34.62	357
Powys	455	215	52	47.9	2.46	4.0	26.1	32.48	338
Brecknock	80	54	18	16.2	2.49	3.9	24.9	30.61	348
Montgomeryshire	253	106	23	21.7	2.47	4.3	26.2	32.36	333
Radnorshire	122	55	10	10.0	2.38	3.5	28.1	37.01	333
South Glamorgan	1,060	411	165	162.5	2.50	6.5	27.0	38.30	296
Cardiff	582	392	118	118.4	2.49	7.0	28.6	38.28	292
Vale of Glamorgan	478	19	46	44.1	2.55	5.1	22.6	38.35	306
West Glamorgan	800	638	152	147.7	2.48	5.8	26.0	33.09	389
Lliw Valley	220	5	26	25.4	2.52	4.9	23.5	28.89	376
Neath	111	123	27	26.1	2.50	4.8	25.2	33.24	413
Port Talbot	91	55	21	20.4	2.49	5.7	24.0	34.19	376
Swansea	378	455	77	75.8	2.46	6.4	27.6	33.97	388

15.2 *(continued)*

	Housing starts 1993 (numbers)			Households 1993				Local authority tenants: average weekly unrebated rent per dwelling (£) April 1994[2]	Council tax (£) April 1994[3]
	Private enterprise	Housing associations, local authorities etc	Stock of dwellings 1993 (thousands)	All households (thousands)	Average household size (numbers)	Lone parents[1] as a percentage of all households	One person households as a percentage of all households		
SCOTLAND	16,987	5,973	2,193	2,089.1	2.42	..	29.3	27.79	492
Borders	188	134	48	44.5	2.32	..	31.5	24.89	395
Berwickshire	17	32	9	8.1	2.37	..	29.9	24.76	377
Ettrick and Lauderdale	74	50	16	14.7	2.34	..	32.4	22.77	403
Roxburgh	42	22	16	15.2	2.29	..	31.5	28.77	377
Tweedale	55	30	7	6.6	2.32	..	31.8	23.25	441
Central	1,132	155	114	109.0	2.46	..	26.9	26.40	474
Clackmannan	236	26	20	19.3	2.48	..	25.4	26.15	497
Falkirk	529	62	60	57.8	2.43	..	27.1	23.80	418
Stirling	367	67	34	31.8	2.51	..	27.5	29.26	559
Dumfries and Galloway	480	197	64	60.5	2.40	..	28.1	28.14	430
Annandale and Eskdale	64	22	16	15.1	2.42	..	27.6	28.66	439
Nithsdale	289	61	24	23.4	2.40	..	28.0	25.72	439
Stewartry	72	78	11	9.8	2.37	..	28.6	28.39	415
Wigtown	55	36	13	12.2	2.42	..	28.7	29.77	416
Fife	1,239	442	148	141.5	2.45	..	27.2	25.88	506
Dunfermline	536	115	53	51.4	2.50	..	25.7	25.95	484
Kirkcaldy	379	280	64	62.0	2.38	..	27.5	26.69	481
North East Fife	324	47	31	28.1	2.52	..	29.3	25.00	599
Grampian	3,231	593	223	211.7	2.45	..	28.2	26.20	456
Aberdeen City	1,502	284	98	94.1	2.28	..	32.2	22.58	491
Banff and Buchan	472	115	36	33.8	2.57	..	25.9	23.65	379
Gordon	432	104	31	29.6	2.66	..	22.4	31.07	480
Kincardine and Deeside	355	23	22	20.7	2.65	..	23.8	27.87	472
Moray	470	67	36	33.6	2.52	..	27.0	25.81	403
Highland	948	414	91	82.4	2.45	..	28.4	31.02	437
Badenoch and Strathspey	49	0	6	4.5	2.32	..	30.2	28.49	448
Caithness	49	2	12	10.7	2.44	..	29.5	29.86	347
Inverness	387	152	27	25.5	2.43	..	28.6	30.19	454
Lochaber	46	105	9	7.5	2.53	..	26.5	32.10	471
Nairn	46	15	5	4.3	2.45	..	26.7	30.71	471
Ross and Cromarty	242	79	21	19.3	2.56	..	25.9	31.90	465
Skye and Lochalsh	72	45	6	4.8	2.42	..	31.0	32.44	425
Sutherland	57	16	7	5.8	2.25	..	33.4	32.46	377
Lothian	2,335	802	330	316.9	2.34	..	30.6	25.52	612
East Lothian	268	62	37	35.3	2.39	..	27.7	23.58	571
Edinburgh City	1,188	535	203	194.0	2.24	..	34.5	35.40	674
Midlothian	174	48	31	30.2	2.61	..	22.6	19.22	560
West Lothian	705	157	59	57.4	2.54	..	23.5	23.88	455
Strathclyde	5,837	2,528	967	929.3	2.43	..	29.3	27.29	481
Argyll and Bute	306	53	31	26.6	2.32	..	33.2	31.95	483
Bearsden and Milngavie	158	0	15	15.1	2.71	..	22.1	28.45	654
Clydebank	128	121	20	19.1	2.42	..	28.8	29.07	439
Clydesdale	202	83	23	22.5	2.49	..	25.5	24.79	471
Cumbernauld and Kilsyth	203	0	24	23.9	2.63	..	21.3	25.76	453
Cumnock and Doon Valley	58	11	17	16.7	2.55	..	25.2	25.31	402
Cunninghame	550	252	59	56.1	2.48	..	27.3	26.47	435
Dumbarton	163	42	32	30.4	2.53	..	27.3	32.18	551
East Kilbride	410	103	33	33.3	2.52	..	24.6	30.98	501
Eastwood	122	0	24	23.1	2.61	..	23.3	22.39	595
Glasgow City	1,064	990	311	297.4	2.29	..	35.2	31.49	474
Hamilton	82	37	42	41.5	2.37	..	25.6	27.00	482
Inverclyde	87	35	38	36.7	2.42	..	30.1	26.94	419
Kilmarnock and Loudoun	162	82	34	32.8	2.42	..	27.3	21.42	428
Kyle and Carrick	339	88	48	46.3	2.45	..	28.8	28.18	561
Monklands	186	80	39	38.8	2.63	..	25.1	27.37	466
Motherwell	626	222	57	56.0	2.54	..	26.3	25.51	411
Renfrew	575	322	86	82.1	2.42	..	28.1	25.88	487
Strathkelvin	416	7	32	31.0	2.71	..	21.8	27.41	603

Regional Trends 30, © Crown copyright 1995

15.2 *(continued)*

	Housing starts 1993 (numbers)			Households 1993				Local authority tenants: average weekly unrebated rent per dwelling (£) April 1994[2]	Council tax (£) April 1994[3]
	Private enterprise	Housing associations, local authorities etc	Stock of dwellings 1993 (thousands)	All households (thousands)	Average household size (numbers)	Lone parents[1] as a percentage of all households	One person households as a percentage of all households		
Tayside	1,317	595	176	165.3	2.35	..	*31.2*	*65.49*	481
Angus	209	189	42	39.6	2.42	..	*29.2*	*19.81*	430
Dundee City	419	193	78	73.8	2.27	..	*33.4*	*32.71*	493
Perth and Kinross	689	213	56	51.9	2.40	..	*29.6*	*23.94*	603
Orkney	75	71	9	8.0	2.44	..	*29.7*	*29.53*	336
Shetland	82	12	9	8.7	2.57	..	*26.7*	*31.06*	317
Western Isles	123	30	13	11.3	2.57	..	*31.2*	*34.19*	338
NORTHERN IRELAND	7,070	1,621	590	572.6	2.85	*7.0*	*25.0*	*27.60*	.
Antrim	274	26	.	..	..	..	..	..	.
Ards	436	106	.	..	..	..	..	..	.
Armagh	235	0	.	..	..	..	..	..	.
Ballymena	326	113	.	..	..	..	..	..	.
Ballymoney	135	0	..	..	..	..	..	..	.
Banbridge	274	22	..	..	..	..	..	..	.
Belfast	172	278	..	..	..	..	..	..	.
Carrickfergus	302	0	..	..	..	..	..	..	.
Castlereagh	390	70	..	..	..	..	..	..	.
Coleraine	458	43	..	..	..	..	..	..	.
Cookstown	130	0	..	..	..	..	..	..	.
Craigavon	427	52	..	..	..	..	..	..	.
Derry	492	327	..	..	..	..	..	..	.
Down	259	68	..	..	..	..	..	..	.
Dungannon	50	29	..	..	..	..	..	..	.
Fermanagh	316	71	..	..	..	..	..	..	.
Larne	106	53	..	..	..	..	..	..	.
Limavady	181	13	..	..	..	..	..	..	.
Lisburn	494	41	..	..	..	..	..	..	.
Magherafelt	159	62	..	..	..	..	..	..	.
Moyle	67	27	..	..	..	..	..	..	.
Newry and Mourne	574	64	..	..	..	..	..	..	.
Newtownabbey	376	77	..	..	..	..	..	..	.
North Down	209	24	..	..	..	..	..	..	.
Omagh	142	9	..	..	..	..	..	..	.
Strabane	86	46	..	..	..	..	..	..	.

* Urban programme authorities.
1 Lone parents with dependent children. These figures are not comparable with those in previous editions of *Regional Trends* which related to lone parents with children of any age.
2 Some local authorities in England have nil housing stock following large scale voluntary transfers to Housing Associations.
3 September 1994 for Scotland.
4 Negative figure for Housing starts is a result of dwellings originally reported as started but subsequently withdrawn.

Source: Department of the Environment; Welsh Office; The Scottish Office Environment Department; Department of the Environment, Northern Ireland

15.3 Employment and economic statistics

| | Economically active[1] Spring 1994 (percentages) | Claimant unemployed January 1995 | | | Income Support bene-ficiaries[3] Nov. 1993 (percentages) | Gross value added in manufac-turing 1992 (£ million) | Net capital expenditure in manufac-turing 1992 (£ million) |
		Total (thousands)	Of which females (percentages)	Of which long-term unemployed[2] (percentages)			
UNITED KINGDOM	*62.2*	**2,503.4**	*23.4*	*37.0*	..	108,144	12,094
NORTH	*58.8*	**159.7**	*19.8*	*36.3*	17	6,329	837
Cleveland	*55.7*	**36.7**	*18.4*	*38.1*	21	1,175	110
Hartlepool *	*41.7*	6.0	*17.5*	*36.8*	22	224	30
Langbaurgh *	*59.5*	9.1	*18.6*	*38.5*	19	318	24
Middlesbrough *	*55.6*	10.8	*17.8*	*39.5*	24	111	9
Stockton-on-Tees *	*59.5*	10.8	*19.4*	*36.9*	18	522	47
Cumbria	*65.4*	**19.5**	*22.9*	*30.0*	11	1,079	103
Allerdale	*64.9*	4.5	*24.3*	*35.7*	13	213	23
Barrow-in-Furness	*67.5*	3.8	*17.9*	*27.0*	15	238	11
Carlisle	*63.6*	3.7	*25.0*	*30.4*	12	244	21
Copeland	*65.0*	4.1	*19.8*	*36.4*	13	83	16
Eden	*65.9*	1.0	*32.2*	*17.6*	8	86	9
South Lakeland	*66.3*	2.4	*26.9*	*17.9*	7	215	22
Durham	*58.8*	**24.4**	*19.0*	*29.8*	15	1,413	175
Chester-le-Street	*66.4*	2.2	*19.6*	*31.9*	12	25	2
Darlington	*65.1*	4.6	*19.6*	*30.1*	16	171	18
Derwentside	*62.5*	3.9	*18.1*	*33.3*	17	109	9
Durham	*55.4*	3.0	*20.8*	*30.5*	11	124	8
Easington	*47.8*	4.0	*17.4*	*26.0*	19	161	16
Sedgefield	*64.5*	3.2	*20.2*	*25.5*	15	407	93
Teesdale	*63.5*	0.7	*23.7*	*25.7*	7	315	21
Wear Valley	*48.3*	2.9	*16.9*	*33.4*	20	101	6
Northumberland	*59.5*	**13.5**	*22.2*	*32.4*	12	411	59
Alnwick	*59.7*	1.3	*24.4*	*32.4*	10	16	2
Berwick-upon-Tweed	*51.5*	1.1	*24.3*	*21.6*	12	47	3
Blyth Valley	*58.8*	4.0	*21.1*	*33.9*	14	135	32
Castle Morpeth	*51.9*	1.8	*22.3*	*31.5*	8	71	7
Tynedale	*69.1*	1.6	*27.8*	*28.5*	9	74	8
Wansbeck	*61.0*	3.7	*19.5*	*36.1*	14	68	7
Tyne and Wear	*57.3*	**65.6**	*19.4*	*40.5*	19	2,252	391
Gateshead *	*59.4*	10.6	*19.2*	*41.0*	19	473	47
Newcastle-upon-Tyne *	*54.0*	17.6	*20.0*	*45.1*	21	537	38
North Tyneside *	*57.6*	10.6	*21.1*	*34.8*	17	383	47
South Tyneside *	*54.6*	10.2	*17.9*	*39.8*	19	213	19
Sunderland *	*60.4*	16.7	*18.9*	*39.1*	20	646	239
YORKSHIRE & HUMBERSIDE	*61.3*	**222.5**	*22.1*	*34.7*	15	9,636	1,244
Humberside	*62.2*	**44.2**	*21.8*	*33.9*	17	2,208	400
Beverley	*58.8*	3.1	*26.7*	*28.4*	7	243	36
Boothferry	*63.2*	2.7	*24.7*	*28.2*	13	114	13
Cleethorpes	*63.2*	3.4	*21.3*	*26.5*	13	102	10
East Yorkshire	*59.4*	3.6	*26.0*	*30.9*	13	103	13
Glanford	*64.4*	2.5	*23.6*	*28.6*	10	101	66
Great Grimsby	*65.0*	5.8	*18.3*	*33.9*	21	365	135
Holderness	*71.3*	1.9	*25.0*	*29.6*	9	126	25
Kingston upon Hull *	*58.5*	17.8	*20.7*	*39.9*	26	652	59
Scunthorpe	*72.4*	3.3	*19.8*	*29.3*	19	402	44
North Yorkshire	*62.9*	**21.8**	*27.0*	*27.6*	9	1,010	150
Craven	*60.9*	1.1	*26.0*	*29.0*	8	88	8
Hambleton	*60.3*	2.0	*29.2*	*25.8*	7	63	10
Harrogate	*63.1*	3.3	*29.7*	*26.0*	8	135	10
Richmondshire	*59.5*	1.1	*38.9*	*18.7*	6	18	2
Ryedale	*68.1*	2.0	*28.1*	*26.8*	6	136	17
Scarborough	*62.6*	4.9	*26.2*	*29.2*	15	149	7
Selby	*68.7*	2.8	*26.1*	*26.7*	8	149	28
York	*57.3*	4.6	*22.5*	*30.6*	13	273	68

15.3 *(continued)*

| | Economically active[1] Spring 1994 (percentages) | Claimant unemployed January 1995 | | | Income Support beneficiaries[3] Nov. 1993 (percentages) | Gross value added in manufacturing 1992 (£ million) | Net capital expenditure in manufacturing 1992 (£ million) |
		Total (thousands)	Of which females (percentages)	Of which long-term unemployed[2] (percentages)			
South Yorkshire	*55.7*	**69.7**	*20.6*	*37.5*	*18*	2,075	231
Barnsley *	*51.2*	10.9	*18.8*	*32.2*	17	294	28
Doncaster *	*56.0*	16.5	*19.6*	*35.6*	17	397	49
Rotherham *	*58.7*	13.6	*20.1*	*37.7*	17	465	63
Sheffield *	*55.9*	28.7	*22.1*	*40.4*	18	920	91
West Yorkshire	*64.0*	**86.8**	*22.3*	*34.7*	*15*	4,342	462
Bradford *	*62.9*	21.3	*21.5*	*35.9*	18	990	116
Calderdale	*69.9*	7.2	*24.1*	*31.8*	15	510	32
Kirklees *	*63.3*	14.3	*23.8*	*31.7*	15	938	107
Leeds *	*64.4*	30.3	*22.1*	*37.4*	14	1,320	142
Wakefield	*61.9*	13.7	*21.5*	*31.4*	14	585	64
EAST MIDLANDS	*62.8*	**162.1**	*23.5*	*35.4*	*13*	9,684	1,284
Derbyshire	*63.7*	**39.2**	*22.1*	*35.3*	*12*	2,493	574
Amber Valley	*59.4*	3.8	*24.5*	*30.2*	10	400	37
Bolsover	*65.2*	3.8	*17.7*	*36.9*	14	100	6
Chesterfield	*62.5*	5.2	*21.1*	*39.4*	15	249	27
Derby *	*64.0*	12.1	*21.5*	*38.7*	17	856	406
Derbyshire Dales	*66.6*	1.5	*27.2*	*28.1*	6	142	16
Erewash	*58.7*	4.1	*22.2*	*33.8*	13	224	24
High Peak	*66.7*	2.6	*25.6*	*28.2*	9	276	27
North East Derbyshire	*63.1*	4.0	*21.9*	*35.0*	10	117	12
South Derbyshire	*66.4*	2.1	*23.7*	*29.6*	9	130	20
Leicestershire	*62.7*	**30.8**	*24.9*	*35.6*	*13*	2,659	248
Blaby	*66.0*	2.0	*27.6*	*28.2*	6	157	13
Charnwood	*63.5*	4.2	*27.0*	*30.6*	3	464	59
Harborough	*59.2*	1.3	*26.8*	*26.7*	11	120	14
Hinckley and Bosworth	*70.0*	2.3	*30.1*	*28.8*	14	245	23
Leicester *	*58.3*	15.6	*22.9*	*41.2*	23	877	70
Melton	*69.6*	1.0	*27.4*	*23.9*	7	121	21
North West Leicestershire	*65.9*	2.6	*23.2*	*36.6*	9	457	37
Oadby and Wigston	*62.3*	1.1	*26.2*	*28.7*	7	151	9
Rutland	*57.5*	0.6	*30.2*	*24.3*	6	66	4
Lincolnshire	*60.0*	**22.6**	*26.2*	*28.1*	*13*	862	84
Boston	*60.5*	2.2	*23.5*	*25.2*	14	54	3
East Lindsey	*57.4*	5.5	*25.9*	*21.6*	15	105	12
Lincoln	*56.7*	4.9	*22.6*	*40.6*	19	171	13
North Kesteven	*61.0*	2.4	*30.0*	*27.3*	9	91	8
South Holland	*56.3*	1.8	*29.5*	*21.0*	10	121	12
South Kesteven	*59.2*	3.0	*29.8*	*24.1*	10	218	25
West Lindsey	*71.3*	2.9	*25.8*	*31.1*	12	101	10
Northamptonshire	*69.2*	**19.0**	*25.9*	*32.3*	*12*	1,532	164
Corby	*59.1*	2.5	*24.1*	*34.3*	15	285	44
Daventry	*71.1*	1.5	*30.9*	*22.5*	7	181	13
East Northamptonshire	*72.4*	1.7	*25.8*	*27.2*	9	112	11
Kettering	*66.4*	2.4	*24.8*	*32.0*	11	176	18
Northampton	*68.6*	7.0	*25.4*	*36.4*	14	473	52
South Northamptonshire	*68.5*	1.5	*28.4*	*27.3*	8	97	7
Wellingborough	*77.2*	2.4	*25.5*	*31.9*	13	207	19
Nottinghamshire	*60.0*	**50.5**	*21.7*	*39.7*	*15*	2,137	214
Ashfield	*61.8*	5.3	*20.1*	*37.4*	13	337	27
Bassetlaw	*66.7*	5.2	*21.9*	*32.6*	12	216	23
Broxtowe	*64.9*	3.7	*26.7*	*33.5*	10	345	45
Gedling	*59.7*	4.0	*24.8*	*36.2*	9	126	9
Mansfield	*57.5*	5.4	*19.9*	*36.4*	15	150	27
Newark and Sherwood	*57.2*	4.6	*20.9*	*34.6*	12	139	13
Nottingham *	*55.9*	19.1	*20.5*	*47.2*	23	742	61
Rushcliffe	*62.4*	3.3	*25.8*	*35.2*	9	82	7

15.3 (continued)

	Economically active[1] Spring 1994 (percentages)	Claimant unemployed January 1995			Income Support bene-ficiaries[3] Nov. 1993 (percentages)	Gross value added in manufac-turing 1992 (£ million)	Net capital expenditure in manufac-turing 1992 (£ million)
		Total (thousands)	Of which females (percentages)	Of which long-term unemployed[2] (percentages)			
EAST ANGLIA	*64.8*	**71.9**	*25.5*	*31.1*	*12*	3,921	421
Cambridgeshire	*68.8*	**20.6**	*26.2*	*32.5*	*11*	1,529	147
Cambridge	*75.0*	3.6	*26.3*	*33.8*	*10*	245	20
East Cambridgeshire	*59.7*	1.4	*27.7*	*30.5*	*9*	57	5
Fenland	*66.4*	3.1	*27.3*	*32.3*	*14*	145	13
Huntingdonshire	*72.5*	3.6	*29.7*	*29.9*	*9*	297	32
Peterborough	*65.6*	6.8	*22.7*	*34.9*	*17*	471	44
South Cambridgeshire	*68.9*	2.2	*28.2*	*29.1*	*6*	313	33
Norfolk	*60.6*	**29.9**	*25.0*	*30.5*	*13*	1,247	139
Breckland	*59.5*	3.4	*25.9*	*28.0*	*11*	178	19
Broadland	*62.1*	2.8	*26.8*	*26.4*	*9*	130	12
Great Yarmouth	*66.0*	6.0	*25.3*	*30.8*	*17*	79	6
Kings Lynn and West Norfolk	*59.5*	4.6	*24.6*	*30.1*	*13*	329	49
North Norfolk	*56.2*	3.0	*24.6*	*25.1*	*25*	77	6
Norwich	*61.7*	7.2	*22.5*	*35.9*	*9*	332	35
South Norfolk	*59.5*	3.0	*28.6*	*29.4*	*9*	122	11
Suffolk	*65.6*	**21.3**	*25.7*	*30.5*	*11*	1,144	136
Babergh	*67.9*	2.3	*26.0*	*31.1*	*10*	145	15
Forest Heath	*75.6*	1.2	*27.7*	*34.0*	*8*	92	10
Ipswich	*67.5*	4.6	*21.5*	*33.9*	*15*	170	16
Mid Suffolk	*60.6*	1.8	*28.8*	*24.9*	*8*	137	11
St Edmundsbury	*70.1*	2.7	*28.9*	*29.5*	*10*	266	39
Suffolk Coastal	*59.2*	3.2	*26.5*	*26.8*	*9*	83	10
Waveney	*63.0*	5.6	*25.6*	*31.2*	*14*	253	35
SOUTH EAST	*65.3*	**768.5**	*24.8*	*38.3*	*15*	28,381	2,550
Bedfordshire	*67.2*	**19.6**	*24.0*	*35.5*	*12*	1,384	105
Bedford	*65.7*	5.3	*24.3*	*34.6*	*12*	278	23
Luton	*64.2*	8.3	*22.1*	*38.6*	*17*	656	39
Mid Bedfordshire	*71.7*	2.7	*28.0*	*30.9*	*8*	171	20
South Bedfordshire	*69.3*	3.3	*25.0*	*32.9*	*10*	279	24
Berkshire	*67.5*	**21.9**	*23.1*	*32.0*	*10*	1,564	121
Bracknell Forest	*78.0*	2.5	*23.3*	*29.5*	*9*	86	7
Newbury	*71.8*	3.1	*24.5*	*28.1*	*7*	208	14
Reading	*64.4*	5.8	*20.5*	*34.2*	*16*	301	20
Slough	*56.9*	4.9	*22.7*	*37.8*	*17*	575	43
Windsor and Maidenhead	*62.0*	3.0	*25.5*	*28.7*	*7*	238	23
Wokingham	*71.7*	2.6	*25.3*	*26.8*	*5*	156	13
Buckinghamshire	*69.4*	**18.4**	*24.1*	*31.4*	*9*	1,387	115
Aylesbury Vale	*73.3*	4.1	*24.6*	*32.1*	*9*	275	18
Chiltern	*68.4*	1.8	*24.3*	*28.9*	*6*	147	16
Milton Keynes	*71.4*	6.9	*24.3*	*30.2*	*13*	423	39
South Buckinghamshire	*61.9*	1.3	*23.4*	*35.6*	*6*	161	18
Wycombe	*67.1*	4.3	*23.4*	*32.4*	*9*	381	24
East Sussex	*60.6*	**33.1**	*24.0*	*41.2*	*15*	567	53
Brighton	*67.0*	11.3	*24.6*	*45.2*	*21*	65	14
Eastbourne	*51.7*	3.1	*23.4*	*31.6*	*14*	81	5
Hastings	*67.3*	4.9	*20.4*	*41.4*	*22*	90	6
Hove	*58.9*	5.2	*26.7*	*44.0*	*19*	54	4
Lewes	*59.4*	2.9	*22.6*	*42.6*	*12*	114	7
Rother	*54.0*	2.9	*23.7*	*37.8*	*11*	63	4
Wealden	*61.4*	2.7	*25.3*	*31.5*	*8*	102	12

15.3 *(continued)*

| | Economically active[1] Spring 1994 (percentages) | Claimant unemployed January 1995 | | | Income Support bene-ficiaries[3] Nov. 1993 (percentages) | Gross value added in manufac-turing 1992 (£ million) | Net capital expenditure in manufac-turing 1992 (£ million) |
		Total (thousands)	Of which females (percentages)	Of which long-term unemployed[2] (percentages)			
Essex	*63.1*	**60.5**	*24.4*	*35.2*	*13*	**2,150**	196
Basildon	*62.7*	7.5	*25.3*	*34.1*	*16*	429	47
Braintree	*71.0*	4.4	*26.6*	*32.9*	*12*	176	-4
Brentwood	*57.6*	1.8	*25.0*	*27.2*	*8*	127	25
Castle Point	*65.2*	3.3	*22.0*	*34.4*	*14*	53	8
Chelmsford	*72.1*	4.4	*25.1*	*32.4*	*8*	261	20
Colchester	*62.6*	5.5	*24.5*	*31.4*	*12*	169	15
Epping Forest	*61.4*	4.3	*27.1*	*41.0*	*9*	117	18
Harlow	*72.6*	3.5	*25.9*	*35.8*	*18*	188	20
Maldon	*58.5*	1.8	*24.7*	*37.7*	*11*	71	5
Rochford	*60.0*	2.4	*24.5*	*30.8*	*9*	74	6
Southend-on-Sea	*59.1*	9.0	*23.6*	*41.7*	*18*	102	10
Tendring	*54.6*	5.5	*21.6*	*34.7*	*15*	66	6
Thurrock	*59.0*	5.5	*22.7*	*34.9*	*16*	221	12
Uttlesford	*67.2*	1.6	*27.0*	*30.1*	*8*	93	7
Greater London	*63.1*	**407.5**	*25.5*	*41.9*	*20*	**9,856**	843
Barking and Dagenham	*59.2*	7.5	*21.3*	*40.1*	*21*	475	92
Barnet	*61.1*	12.2	*28.7*	*36.4*	*14*	149	11
Bexley	*68.1*	8.7	*25.2*	*36.3*	*12*	321	46
Brent *	*61.5*	19.8	*25.9*	*42.8*	*26*	542	44
Bromley	*64.7*	10.2	*24.6*	*35.7*	*10*	251	28
Camden	*65.8*	13.5	*29.5*	*41.6*	*24*	352	24
City of London	*..*	0.2	*32.9*	*32.3*	*..*	97	2
City of Westminster	*59.0*	10.5	*29.0*	*33.6*	*19*	802	37
Croydon	*65.9*	15.6	*24.2*	*41.7*	*16*	276	16
Ealing	*63.5*	14.5	*25.2*	*37.2*	*18*	385	38
Enfield	*61.2*	13.6	*24.6*	*42.5*	*17*	361	37
Greenwich *	*62.5*	13.9	*24.8*	*44.6*	*25*	206	22
Hackney *	*57.5*	20.0	*25.1*	*49.4*	*37*	262	18
Hammersmith and Fulham *	*64.8*	11.0	*28.2*	*42.1*	*21*	250	6
Haringey	*58.2*	19.8	*25.9*	*45.7*	*32*	144	10
Harrow	*68.0*	7.0	*27.3*	*33.8*	*12*	200	27
Havering	*59.2*	7.8	*22.9*	*33.5*	*12*	163	8
Hillingdon	*68.9*	7.7	*25.1*	*36.3*	*12*	603	42
Hounslow	*63.7*	9.4	*26.0*	*35.2*	*16*	389	36
Islington *	*63.8*	15.5	*27.5*	*46.0*	*27*	418	26
Kensington and Chelsea *	*62.0*	8.1	*32.5*	*41.5*	*17*	169	11
Kingston upon Thames	*66.5*	4.4	*25.1*	*34.8*	*11*	233	16
Lambeth *	*64.7*	24.0	*26.1*	*45.6*	*28*	177	7
Lewisham *	*62.7*	18.9	*24.7*	*46.3*	*24*	67	5
Merton	*70.7*	7.7	*25.8*	*38.7*	*14*	263	49
Newham *	*54.5*	18.4	*22.2*	*44.3*	*33*	247	27
Redbridge	*61.6*	10.0	*24.7*	*39.2*	*16*	133	8
Richmond-upon-Thames	*66.5*	5.0	*28.3*	*33.8*	*9*	135	6
Southwark *	*64.4*	20.6	*25.2*	*46.1*	*29*	549	39
Sutton	*66.0*	5.8	*23.2*	*35.4*	*11*	142	8
Tower Hamlets *	*51.9*	15.4	*20.4*	*46.0*	*35*	697	66
Waltham Forest	*61.8*	14.8	*24.5*	*42.7*	*24*	199	13
Wandsworth *	*66.3*	16.0	*26.9*	*43.7*	*17*	200	17
Hampshire	*66.0*	**51.5**	*23.0*	*33.6*	*11*	**2,934**	333
Basingstoke and Deane	*70.5*	4.0	*24.5*	*32.2*	*9*	487	65
East Hampshire	*58.9*	2.5	*25.6*	*29.3*	*14*	142	16
Eastleigh	*69.5*	2.5	*22.8*	*28.0*	*9*	253	35
Fareham	*69.2*	2.5	*25.4*	*27.5*	*8*	135	16
Gosport	*70.0*	2.8	*24.8*	*28.6*	*11*	147	17
Hart	*75.7*	1.5	*24.7*	*27.3*	*14*	72	4
Havant	*56.3*	4.9	*22.0*	*35.9*	*4*	132	44
New Forest	*62.0*	4.1	*23.1*	*29.6*	*8*	278	23
Portsmouth	*66.5*	9.5	*22.6*	*39.2*	*19*	409	38
Rushmoor	*74.8*	2.1	*23.5*	*27.3*	*10*	110	7
Southampton	*63.9*	10.7	*20.4*	*38.7*	*18*	505	48
Test Valley	*63.4*	2.0	*26.0*	*25.8*	*9*	194	17
Winchester	*66.9*	2.3	*23.9*	*29.9*	*7*	71	5

15.3 *(continued)*

| | Economically active[1] Spring 1994 (percentages) | Claimant unemployed January 1995 | | | Income Support bene-ficiaries[3] Nov. 1993 (percentages) | Gross value added in manufac-turing 1992 (£ million) | Net capital expenditure in manufac-turing 1992 (£ million) |
		Total (thousands)	Of which females (percentages)	Of which long-term unemployed[2] (percentages)			
Hertfordshire	**68.2**	**30.1**	**24.8**	**33.5**	**10**	**2,357**	**153**
Broxbourne	72.4	3.5	27.6	44.0	12	125	14
Dacorum	70.4	3.8	22.7	30.5	9	249	9
East Hertfordshire	70.3	3.3	28.9	34.4	8	368	34
Hertsmere	62.9	2.5	24.3	34.7	11	120	9
North Hertfordshire	72.4	3.6	24.7	34.6	10	223	22
St Albans	63.9	2.8	25.9	23.9	8	134	12
Stevenage	64.5	3.4	24.3	33.1	15	548	18
Three Rivers	65.9	1.9	21.3	33.2	8	100	9
Watford	70.2	2.8	22.8	34.6	15	175	9
Welwyn Hatfield	67.3	2.5	23.1	29.9	10	315	15
Isle of Wight	**58.3**	**6.9**	**26.5**	**32.6**	**16**	**133**	**16**
Medina	62.9	3.8	25.9	33.3	15	113	15
South Wight	52.6	3.1	27.2	31.8	17	20	1
Kent	**65.0**	**62.6**	**22.6**	**34.5**	**13**	**2,463**	**281**
Ashford	67.1	3.2	20.9	29.6	12	147	17
Canterbury	52.6	5.0	21.2	35.7	12	80	5
Dartford	69.8	3.0	23.3	37.0	12	241	45
Dover	58.7	4.9	21.3	33.5	14	209	56
Gillingham	69.5	4.3	25.2	35.4	15	92	4
Gravesham	72.2	4.6	23.4	36.3	15	151	25
Maidstone	68.1	4.2	23.5	32.5	12	444	29
Rochester-upon-Medway	72.3	7.3	23.9	32.9	15	214	14
Sevenoaks	63.3	3.0	22.9	33.8	9	98	6
Shepway	57.7	4.8	19.7	34.3	16	86	5
Swale	62.6	5.7	23.3	36.9	16	252	37
Thanet	60.9	7.0	20.8	38.9	20	93	8
Tonbridge and Malling	70.8	2.8	25.5	28.9	9	268	29
Tunbridge Wells	67.2	2.7	22.9	31.0	10	87	1
Oxfordshire	**65.9**	**14.4**	**25.7**	**30.1**	**8**	**1,111**	**121**
Cherwell	72.1	3.4	27.9	27.0	8	296	34
Oxford	57.9	4.3	23.8	35.4	13	434	56
South Oxfordshire	60.6	3.1	24.6	29.9	6	102	8
Vale of White Horse	70.2	1.9	25.5	26.4	7	187	16
West Oxfordshire	71.0	1.7	28.5	27.2	7	91	8
Surrey	**66.5**	**22.4**	**25.1**	**30.7**	**7**	**1,279**	**117**
Elmbridge	66.5	2.7	26.3	34.1	7	184	18
Epsom and Ewell	63.3	1.4	24.5	30.3	7	17	1
Guildford	61.1	2.6	23.9	30.3	8	144	17
Mole Valley	63.8	1.5	24.0	28.0	7	82	10
Reigate and Banstead	68.8	2.8	24.8	30.6	7	83	4
Runnymede	68.1	1.8	26.4	32.6	8	92	12
Spelthorne	67.4	2.4	25.6	33.2	8	129	28
Surrey Heath	67.1	1.6	26.6	24.9	6	233	10
Tandridge	69.9	1.7	25.0	32.7	8	39	7
Waverley	67.2	2.1	25.8	29.5	7	104	5
Woking	69.8	1.7	22.7	28.8	9	173	4
West Sussex	**61.2**	**19.5**	**23.9**	**33.1**	**10**	**1,197**	**97**
Adur	53.2	1.8	23.9	37.0	13	103	8
Arun	54.6	4.3	22.7	32.4	12	133	11
Chichester	60.0	2.6	23.1	31.1	9	95	10
Crawley	66.7	2.6	24.7	34.3	13	310	27
Horsham	64.9	2.4	25.0	28.7	7	155	12
Mid Sussex	66.4	2.7	26.2	30.4	8	156	10
Worthing	61.3	3.1	22.6	38.3	14	245	20

15.3 *(continued)*

| | Economically active[1] Spring 1994 (percentages) | Claimant unemployed January 1995 | | | Income Support bene- ficiaries[3] Nov. 1993 (percentages) | Gross value added in manufac- turing 1992 (£ million) | Net capital expenditure in manufac- turing 1992 (£ million) |
		Total (thousands)	Of which females (percentages)	Of which long-term unemployed[2] (percentages)			
SOUTH WEST	*62.1*	**184.2**	*25.3*	*32.4*	*13*	**7,379**	**745**
Avon	*64.0*	**41.3**	*24.8*	*37.2*	*13*	**1,582**	**175**
Bath	*61.6*	4.2	*27.3*	*38.0*	*15*	96	7
Bristol *	*61.1*	22.0	*23.6*	*41.1*	*17*	668	87
Kingswood	*68.4*	3.0	*24.7*	*30.7*	*10*	143	12
Northavon	*69.7*	3.8	*27.0*	*27.7*	*8*	329	19
Wansdyke	*65.6*	2.2	*27.6*	*33.0*	*9*	189	25
Woodspring	*64.1*	6.2	*25.3*	*33.5*	*11*	157	23
Cornwall and the Isles of Scilly	*59.0*	**24.0**	*27.7*	*26.4*	*16*	**491**	**35**
Caradon	*60.2*	3.3	*27.2*	*24.6*	*12*	45	7
Carrick	*61.3*	4.0	*26.4*	*25.9*	*15*	64	3
Kerrier	*57.9*	4.7	*26.7*	*30.6*	*17*	68	6
North Cornwall	*58.1*	3.2	*28.4*	*27.3*	*15*	85	12
Penwith	*55.5*	3.7	*28.6*	*26.4*	*19*	40	3
Restormel	*60.4*	5.1	*28.4*	*23.8*	*17*	188	4
Isles of Scilly	*..*	0.1	*50.8*	*12.7*	*..*	-	-
Devon	*58.8*	**44.4**	*24.8*	*30.8*	*14*	**1,293**	**141**
East Devon	*51.2*	3.1	*27.2*	*24.1*	*9*	100	15
Exeter	*60.5*	4.2	*22.8*	*32.8*	*15*	79	3
Mid Devon	*65.8*	1.8	*26.9*	*29.0*	*9*	118	15
North Devon	*61.4*	3.9	*26.4*	*29.4*	*17*	124	12
Plymouth *	*61.3*	13.9	*23.5*	*33.2*	*16*	386	40
South Hams	*60.6*	2.7	*29.8*	*23.9*	*10*	129	17
Teignbridge	*55.1*	3.8	*24.3*	*25.8*	*13*	103	9
Torbay	*52.7*	7.1	*24.5*	*31.1*	*20*	153	16
Torridge	*56.7*	2.4	*24.8*	*37.7*	*13*	53	7
West Devon	*70.0*	1.5	*26.3*	*33.1*	*10*	47	6
Dorset	*59.2*	**24.3**	*23.5*	*32.2*	*12*	**798**	**65**
Bournemouth	*58.2*	8.8	*22.3*	*37.8*	*18*	82	5
Christchurch	*61.8*	1.3	*23.3*	*32.8*	*9*	111	9
East Dorset	*62.8*	1.7	*25.8*	*27.1*	*9*	101	8
North Dorset	*70.0*	0.9	*25.2*	*17.4*	*9*	58	6
Poole	*56.7*	4.9	*22.0*	*34.2*	*12*	290	27
Purbeck	*51.7*	1.3	*26.2*	*28.8*	*9*	45	3
West Dorset	*59.6*	2.3	*26.4*	*26.8*	*9*	89	6
Weymouth and Portland	*55.8*	3.0	*24.2*	*25.6*	*14*	22	1
Gloucestershire	*65.9*	**18.0**	*24.8*	*34.9*	*11*	**1,162**	**98**
Cheltenham	*67.6*	3.8	*23.0*	*41.2*	*12*	179	4
Cotswold	*56.8*	1.6	*28.8*	*29.4*	*7*	77	5
Forest of Dean	*70.6*	2.6	*25.9*	*31.3*	*11*	183	17
Gloucester	*66.7*	4.5	*21.9*	*38.5*	*15*	163	16
Stroud	*65.9*	3.2	*26.6*	*29.0*	*11*	202	15
Tewkesbury	*66.8*	2.3	*27.2*	*33.1*	*9*	358	41
Somerset	*59.8*	**15.8**	*25.6*	*32.7*	*11*	**914**	**74**
Mendip	*58.0*	3.4	*27.8*	*33.3*	*11*	223	21
Sedgemoor	*52.2*	3.8	*24.1*	*32.0*	*12*	151	17
South Somerset	*69.4*	3.9	*26.1*	*32.9*	*12*	395	20
Taunton Deane	*59.0*	3.2	*23.0*	*34.0*	*11*	127	13
West Somerset	*47.3*	1.4	*28.4*	*30.1*	*12*	17	3
Wiltshire	*69.1*	**16.5**	*27.0*	*30.8*	*10*	**1,138**	**157**
Kennet	*64.5*	1.8	*29.7*	*30.2*	*7*	64	8
North Wiltshire	*70.0*	3.2	*28.4*	*32.2*	*3*	177	24
Salisbury	*64.2*	2.8	*26.7*	*29.6*	*9*	93	10
Thamesdown	*69.2*	5.5	*25.6*	*32.5*	*12*	540	81
West Wiltshire	*75.6*	3.2	*26.9*	*27.8*	*10*	259	35

15.3 *(continued)*

	Economically active[1] Spring 1994 (percentages)	Claimant unemployed January 1995			Income Support bene- ficiaries[3] Nov. 1993 (percentages)	Gross value added in manufac- turing 1992 (£ million)	Net capital expenditure in manufac- turing 1992 (£ million)
		Total (thousands)	Of which females (percentages)	Of which long-term unemployed[2] (percentages)			
WEST MIDLANDS	*62.9*	**227.1**	*23.9*	*40.8*	*16*	**12,727**	**1,232**
Hereford and Worcester	*67.2*	22.6	*26.0*	*32.4*	*10*	1,256	126
Bromsgrove	*69.4*	2.9	*25.7*	*35.7*	*7*	63	5
Hereford	*60.7*	2.2	*25.8*	*29.0*	*14*	157	26
Leominster	*56.5*	1.2	*25.0*	*29.7*	*9*	47	4
Malvern Hills	*67.6*	2.4	*26.2*	*32.2*	*10*	96	10
Redcitch	*67.9*	3.0	*27.1*	*36.2*	*13*	231	22
South Herefordshire	*64.2*	1.5	*28.1*	*26.5*	*9*	61	5
Worcester	*71.5*	3.1	*24.2*	*33.2*	*13*	169	5
Wychavon	*63.2*	2.7	*27.2*	*25.2*	*8*	212	32
Wyre Forest	*75.2*	3.6	*25.6*	*36.5*	*13*	221	18
Shropshire	*66.8*	13.1	*25.4*	*31.0*	*12*	825	122
Bridgnorth	*76.1*	1.4	*28.6*	*31.2*	*10*	71	8
North Shropshire	*57.3*	1.4	*26.6*	*27.8*	*10*	77	6
Oswestry	*70.1*	1.2	*28.5*	*32.0*	*13*	46	2
Shrewsbury and Atcham	*63.6*	2.8	*24.4*	*30.0*	*12*	110	9
South Shropshire	*62.0*	1.1	*27.6*	*30.1*	*10*	48	8
The Wrekin *	*69.8*	5.3	*23.7*	*32.2*	*15*	473	89
Staffordshire	*63.0*	34.9	*24.4*	*32.5*	*12*	2,593	257
Cannock Chase	*65.0*	3.5	*23.3*	*33.3*	*12*	153	14
East Staffordshire	*68.0*	3.6	*23.5*	*30.9*	*11*	422	50
Lichfield	*71.4*	2.6	*26.4*	*29.7*	*10*	150	13
Newcastle-under-Lyme	*61.7*	3.5	*23.8*	*32.7*	*10*	314	52
South Staffordshire	*67.1*	3.4	*27.5*	*36.2*	*9*	126	9
Stafford	*63.6*	3.5	*25.8*	*30.9*	*9*	330	23
Staffordshire Moorlands	*68.9*	2.2	*28.8*	*27.6*	*8*	178	17
Stoke-on-Trent	*52.4*	9.4	*20.9*	*33.3*	*17*	769	69
Tamworth	*66.7*	3.2	*27.7*	*33.8*	*17*	151	11
Warwickshire	*63.8*	15.2	*26.4*	*32.8*	*11*	1,201	117
North Warwickshire	*70.2*	1.9	*26.6*	*31.9*	*9*	115	7
Nuneaton and Bedworth	*59.6*	4.5	*25.2*	*37.7*	*15*	189	25
Rugby	*72.3*	2.8	*28.0*	*28.3*	*11*	512	51
Stratford-on-Avon	*65.3*	2.6	*27.7*	*30.2*	*8*	139	16
Warwick	*57.4*	3.4	*25.7*	*32.3*	*12*	246	18
West Midlands (Met. County)	*60.9*	141.3	*23.0*	*46.0*	*21*	6,851	609
Birmingham *	*59.3*	63.3	*22.8*	*49.0*	*24*	2,139	165
Coventry *	*62.6*	14.8	*22.7*	*43.6*	*20*	1,432	166
Dudley *	*63.8*	12.6	*24.8*	*41.8*	*15*	575	42
Sandwell *	*57.9*	16.8	*22.7*	*47.0*	*22*	953	85
Solihull	*62.8*	7.2	*25.4*	*41.5*	*11*	344	45
Walsall*	*63.5*	12.7	*22.4*	*43.6*	*19*	697	58
Wolverhampton *	*60.7*	13.9	*22.8*	*42.4*	*22*	711	48

15.3 *(continued)*

| | Economically active[1] Spring 1994 (percentages) | Claimant unemployed January 1995 | | | Income Support bene-ficiaries[3] Nov. 1993 (percentages) | Gross value added in manufac-turing 1992 (£ million) | Net capital expenditure in manufac-turing 1992 (£ million) |
		Total (thousands)	Of which females (percentages)	Of which long-term unemployed[2] (percentages)			
NORTH WEST	*60.1*	*276.0*	*22.1*	*36.0*	*17*	*13,585*	*1,663*
Cheshire	*64.6*	*32.6*	*24.1*	*30.0*	*12*	*2,978*	*548*
Chester	55.8	4.1	22.4	32.1	11	102	38
Congleton	71.7	2.1	31.4	25.7	8	257	39
Crewe and Nantwich	66.2	3.9	26.1	30.1	12	214	14
Ellesmere Port and Neston	60.6	3.2	22.9	27.3	13	567	127
Halton *	57.6	6.5	21.6	35.2	20	499	176
Macclesfield	65.6	3.3	25.3	25.3	8	775	89
Vale Royal	69.0	3.5	25.1	30.7	10	246	32
Warrington	69.4	5.9	23.7	28.2	12	317	35
Greater Manchester	*61.5*	*111.6*	*21.9*	*35.0*	*18*	*5,370*	*586*
Bolton *	61.8	9.4	19.5	30.2	17	502	73
Bury	66.1	5.2	25.5	24.6	13	337	22
Manchester *	50.8	31.2	21.2	41.5	32	805	73
Oldham *	69.2	9.5	22.6	34.7	17	492	35
Rochdale *	63.4	8.7	21.5	30.2	16	437	49
Salford *	54.2	10.9	20.2	40.7	20	440	50
Stockport	63.6	8.6	23.5	29.8	11	511	37
Tameside	65.6	8.5	22.3	30.4	15	707	45
Trafford	64.0	8.1	23.2	34.1	12	645	146
Wigan *	64.5	11.5	23.4	32.2	15	495	57
Lancashire	*60.5*	*47.0*	*21.8*	*27.5*	*14*	*3,104*	*244*
Blackburn *	59.9	5.3	17.7	27.6	20	436	48
Blackpool	50.8	7.8	21.1	24.9	19	101	10
Burnley *	65.8	2.6	18.9	27.0	16	239	22
Chorley	65.9	2.8	24.0	27.0	11	101	2
Fylde	51.8	1.3	25.3	15.9	10	509	14
Hyndburn	62.6	2.1	20.1	18.5	14	200	17
Lancaster	60.6	5.3	23.2	30.2	14	111	11
Pendle	54.5	2.5	22.7	27.6	16	311	18
Preston *	62.8	5.7	20.8	34.1	19	232	16
Ribble Valley	68.7	0.7	25.9	18.4	5	79	7
Rossendale	74.3	1.4	20.4	17.8	14	187	12
South Ribble	67.2	2.6	24.0	26.9	9	295	31
West Lancashire	58.5	4.2	25.5	35.5	15	209	27
Wyre	56.4	2.7	22.3	24.4	10	95	9
Merseyside	*54.0*	*84.8*	*21.8*	*44.4*	*23*	*2,134*	*284*
Knowsley *	57.0	10.4	20.8	46.1	31	523	94
Liverpool *	48.9	34.4	21.2	48.6	30	647	70
Sefton *	57.8	13.8	22.2	41.3	18	207	14
St Helens *	58.1	8.4	23.1	38.6	16	347	54
Wirral *	54.3	17.9	22.4	40.5	19	410	52
ENGLAND	*62.7*	*2,071.9*	*23.6*	*36.7*	*15*	*91,642*	*9,976*

15.3 (continued)

	Economically active[1] Spring 1994 (percentages)	Claimant unemployed January 1995			Income Support bene- ficiaries[3] Nov. 1993 (percentages)	Gross value added in manufac- turing 1992 (£ million)	Net capital expenditure in manufac- turing 1992 (£ million)
		Total (thousands)	Of which females (percentages)	Of which long-term unemployed[2] (percentages)			
WALES	*56.9*	115.8	*22.2*	*34.3*	*16*	5,359	730
Clwyd	*56.6*	14.2	*23.3*	*31.1*	*14*	1,127	154
Alyn and Deeside	*67.2*	2.4	*23.8*	*30.0*	*12*	425	41
Colwyn	*48.7*	2.0	*23.4*	*34.3*	*16*	47	5
Delyn	*56.2*	2.1	*22.6*	*29.3*	*12*	159	26
Glyndwr	*50.5*	1.4	*26.9*	*33.0*	*10*	64	6
Rhuddlan	*53.1*	2.4	*22.5*	*27.7*	*17*	37	3
Wrexham Maelor	*58.1*	4.0	*22.4*	*32.4*	*16*	395	73
Dyfed	*57.5*	13.5	*25.2*	*29.2*	*14*	258	52
Carmarthen	*61.6*	1.7	*24.9*	*29.4*	*13*	29	4
Ceredigion	*60.8*	2.2	*28.4*	*24.5*	*10*	27	3
Dinefwr	*64.0*	1.2	*25.4*	*32.2*	*14*	25	5
Llanelli	*52.9*	2.6	*25.4*	*31.2*	*17*	119	34
Preseli Pembrokeshire	*58.2*	3.3	*22.7*	*32.5*	*16*	42	5
South Pembrokeshire	*47.8*	2.5	*25.9*	*25.6*	*16*	15	1
Gwent	*58.2*	18.2	*22.8*	*37.1*	*17*	1,261	143
Blaenau Gwent	*49.9*	3.2	*20.7*	*38.9*	*19*	209	13
Islwyn	*50.7*	2.1	*22.9*	*28.5*	*15*	122	23
Monmouth	*61.5*	2.4	*27.8*	*35.1*	*11*	155	10
Newport	*61.5*	6.9	*22.8*	*41.1*	*19*	512	59
Torfaen	*63.7*	3.6	*21.0*	*34.3*	*17*	263	37
Gwynedd	*55.2*	11.8	*24.9*	*34.0*	*15*	139	16
Aberconwy	*57.9*	2.3	*25.6*	*26.5*	*13*	26	2
Arfon	*58.8*	3.1	*22.3*	*37.2*	*18*	39	6
Dwyfor	*45.7*	1.4	*29.4*	*27.4*	*13*	8	-
Meirionnydd	*55.3*	1.6	*29.4*	*27.0*	*13*	18	3
Ynys Mon-Isle of Anglesey	*54.1*	3.4	*22.9*	*41.9*	*15*	47	5
Mid Glamorgan	*54.4*	22.0	*19.7*	*35.8*	*18*	1,082	131
Cynon Valley	*51.5*	3.0	*18.8*	*35.2*	*20*	72	7
Merthyr Tydfil	*66.9*	2.6	*19.6*	*44.0*	*22*	68	11
Ogwr	*51.7*	4.8	*21.0*	*31.5*	*14*	396	58
Rhondda	*49.7*	3.3	*18.3*	*32.9*	*20*	61	4
Rhymney Valley	*56.7*	4.7	*19.0*	*38.2*	*20*	190	23
Taff Ely	*54.1*	3.6	*21.0*	*35.8*	*13*	295	29
Powys	*69.8*	3.0	*28.7*	*29.2*	*10*	161	12
Brecknock	*68.4*	1.3	*26.8*	*32.6*	*11*	32	2
Montgomeryshire	*74.1*	1.1	*28.9*	*24.1*	*10*	91	7
Radnorshire	*63.0*	0.7	*32.3*	*31.0*	*10*	38	3
South Glamorgan	*60.6*	19.3	*21.0*	*37.7*	*17*	541	75
Cardiff	*60.6*	14.4	*20.6*	*39.9*	*18*	437	45
Vale of Glamorgan	*60.8*	4.8	*22.1*	*31.3*	*14*	105	30
West Glamorgan	*51.7*	13.9	*19.7*	*32.8*	*17*	789	147
Lliw Valley	*65.6*	2.1	*20.5*	*30.0*	*14*	102	21
Neath	*49.8*	2.3	*19.8*	*30.8*	*15*	73	12
Port Talbot	*46.6*	1.7	*20.0*	*28.6*	*19*	376	74
Swansea	*49.4*	7.8	*19.4*	*35.1*	*18*	239	41

Regional Trends 30, © Crown copyright 1995

15.3 *(continued)*

| | Economically active[1] Spring 1994 (percentages) | Claimant unemployed January 1995 | | | Income Support bene- ficiaries[3] Nov. 1993 (percentages) | Gross value added in manufac- turing 1992 (£ million) | Net capital expenditure in manufac- turing 1992 (£ million) |
		Total (thousands)	Of which females (percentages)	Of which long-term unemployed[2] (percentages)			
SCOTLAND	*62.3*	**223.7**	*22.5*	*33.2*	*11*	8,799	1,074
Borders	*59.8*	**2.7**	*26.3*	*21.1*	..	189	18
Berwickshire	..	0.6	*25.5*	*16.8*	..	27	3
Ettrick and Lauderdale	*56.2*	0.8	*26.7*	*20.7*	..	55	6
Roxburgh	*68.0*	0.9	*26.8*	*22.2*	..	88	8
Tweedale	..	0.4	*25.5*	*26.3*	..	19	1
Central	*64.3*	**11.6**	*22.9*	*32.7*	..	568	206
Clackmannan	*62.0*	2.3	*22.3*	*33.6*	..	137	30
Falkirk	*63.0*	6.3	*21.8*	*34.6*	..	331	166
Stirling	*68.2*	3.1	*25.4*	*28.2*	..	100	10
Dumfries and Galloway	*60.9*	**6.4**	*26.7*	*27.7*	..	267	18
Annandale and Eskdale	*59.3*	1.2	*31.2*	*20.7*	..	83	6
Nithsdale	*61.9*	2.6	*23.1*	*30.8*	..	136	10
Stewartry	*67.0*	0.9	*33.8*	*21.7*	..	31	1
Wigtown	*57.3*	1.7	*25.3*	*31.3*	..	17	1
Fife	*64.0*	**16.2**	*22.4*	*33.0*	..	676	62
Dunfermline	*67.9*	6.1	*21.5*	*33.1*	..	289	15
Kirkcaldy	*58.1*	8.0	*21.8*	*34.9*	..	344	42
North East Fife	*69.1*	2.1	*27.7*	*25.5*	..	43	6
Grampian	*68.4*	**15.3**	*25.8*	*22.2*	..	822	86
Aberdeen City	*69.9*	7.0	*22.9*	*22.9*	..	419	38
Banff and Buchan	*71.2*	2.5	*25.0*	*21.0*	..	129	8
Gordon	*64.2*	1.5	*29.4*	*22.0*	..	84	16
Kincardine and Deeside	*70.5*	1.1	*28.5*	*20.0*	..	33	4
Moray	*63.7*	3.2	*30.0*	*22.5*	..	157	21
Highland	*68.3*	**11.1**	*26.5*	*28.4*	..	253	24
Badenoch and Strathspey	..	0.6	*33.4*	*21.9*	..	10	1
Caithness	*75.1*	1.4	*21.5*	*33.7*	..	18	2
Inverness	*66.9*	3.1	*21.1*	*30.2*	..	80	5
Lochaber	*78.5*	1.1	*38.3*	*19.5*	..	14	1
Nairn	..	0.6	*24.1*	*28.0*	..	6	1
Ross and Cromarty	*68.7*	2.8	*24.5*	*29.3*	..	116	12
Skye and Lochalsh	..	0.7	*34.6*	*25.6*	..	4	1
Sutherland	..	0.8	*35.7*	*29.2*	..	6	1
Lothian	*65.2*	**30.4**	*22.1*	*30.9*	..	1,282	144
East Lothian	*60.5*	3.1	*22.1*	*32.2*	..	57	6
Edinburgh City	*64.6*	18.9	*22.1*	*32.4*	..	752	73
Midlothian	*60.4*	2.8	*21.3*	*31.3*	..	101	6
West Lothian	*72.6*	5.6	*22.3*	*25.0*	..	371	59
Strathclyde	*58.8*	**110.8**	*21.2*	*36.7*	..	4,053	402
Argyll and Bute	*54.6*	3.1	*29.7*	*31.4*	..	34	4
Bearsden and Milngavie	*62.3*	0.9	*23.9*	*25.7*	..	10	1
Clydebank	*55.3*	2.7	*18.2*	*42.0*	..	106	7
Clydesdale	*66.7*	2.3	*23.0*	*33.2*	..	45	5
Cumbernauld and Kilsyth	*73.3*	2.4	*23.5*	*21.7*	..	383	58
Cumnock and Doon Valley	*52.7*	2.4	*18.4*	*41.9*	..	28	1
Cunninghame	*62.1*	7.2	*23.4*	*31.4*	..	88	8
Dumbarton	*57.3*	3.8	*23.2*	*35.9*	..	160	6
East Kilbride	*67.3*	3.2	*23.8*	*29.9*	..	514	46
Eastwood	*61.9*	1.2	*28.0*	*22.2*	..	13	2
Glasgow City	*52.3*	41.3	*19.9*	*40.8*	..	1,215	96
Hamilton	*61.4*	4.3	*18.0*	*40.4*	..	115	8
Inverclyde	*55.6*	3.9	*18.6*	*28.4*	..	-7	29
Kilmarnock and Loudoun	*66.6*	3.9	*23.6*	*38.9*	..	149	10
Kyle and Carrick	*56.0*	4.9	*26.2*	*31.5*	..	163	15
Monklands	*64.2*	4.6	*18.5*	*40.9*	..	154	18
Motherwell	*55.1*	6.7	*17.9*	*37.7*	..	232	30
Renfrew	*67.6*	9.2	*22.0*	*34.5*	.	584	52
Strathkelvin	*63.0*	2.8	*23.5*	*29.0*	.	65	4

15.3 *(continued)*

	Economically active[1] Spring 1994 (percentages)	Claimant unemployed January 1995			Income Support bene-ficiaries[3] Nov. 1993 (percentages)	Gross value added in manufac-turing 1992 (£ million)	Net capital expenditure in manufac-turing 1992 (£ million)
		Total (thousands)	Of which females (percentages)	Of which long-term unemployed[2] (percentages)			
Tayside	*63.9*	16.5	*24.4*	*32.4*	..	645	109
Angus	*64.8*	3.8	*28.1*	*30.4*	..	174	72
Dundee City	*59.1*	8.7	*22.3*	*37.1*	..	356	29
Perth and Kinross	*69.8*	3.9	*25.5*	*24.1*	..	115	9
Orkney	*67.7*	0.5	*27.6*	*23.2*	..	12	1
Shetland	*76.6*	0.4	*22.3*	*17.2*	..	17	2
Western Isles	*61.0*	1.7	*18.3*	*34.8*	..	14	2
NORTHERN IRELAND	*57.5*	91.9	*21.3*	*56.4*	..	2,344	314
Antrim	..	2.0	*25.1*	*45.8*	..	..	..
Ards	..	2.5	*24.4*	*45.9*	..	..	..
Armagh	..	2.7	*21.6*	*58.2*	..	..	..
Ballymena	..	2.5	*26.2*	*49.8*	..	..	..
Ballymoney	..	1.3	*21.1*	*56.3*	..	..	..
Banbridge	..	1.2	*26.3*	*50.3*	..	..	..
Belfast	..	22.8	*20.2*	*59.6*	..	..	..
Carrickfergus	..	1.5	*26.5*	*49.0*	..	..	..
Castlereagh	..	2.2	*25.1*	*47.0*	..	..	..
Coleraine	..	3.2	*22.3*	*53.2*	..	..	..
Cookstown	..	1.8	*22.6*	*60.2*	..	..	..
Craigavon	..	3.3	*20.7*	*54.7*	..	..	..
Derry	..	7.4	*16.1*	*60.5*	..	..	..
Down	..	3.0	*25.4*	*47.8*	..	..	..
Dungannon	..	2.8	*19.6*	*62.1*	..	..	..
Fermanagh	..	3.4	*18.5*	*62.5*	..	..	..
Larne	..	1.5	*23.1*	*46.9*	..	..	..
Limavady	..	2.0	*17.9*	*58.0*	..	..	..
Lisburn	..	4.5	*23.9*	*53.8*	..	..	..
Magherafelt	..	2.1	*20.8*	*59.7*	..	..	..
Moyle	..	1.1	*19.2*	*56.9*	..	..	..
Newry and Mourne	..	5.9	*19.1*	*61.4*	..	..	..
Newtownabbey	..	3.1	*25.2*	*48.8*	..	..	..
North Down	..	2.7	*29.9*	*43.9*	..	..	..
Omagh	..	2.8	*21.0*	*62.2*	..	..	..
Strabane	..	2.7	*15.5*	*65.0*	..	..	..

* Urban programme authorities.
1 Economic activity rate of persons aged 16 or over. Data are from the Labour Force Survey.
2 Persons who have been unemployed for 12 months or more as a percentage of all claimants.
3 Claimants and their partners aged 16 or over as a percentage of the population aged 16 and over. Data are from the Income Support Quarterly Statistical Enquiry.

Source: Employment Department; Department of Social Security; Central Statistical Office

Appendix

REGIONAL CLASSIFICATION

Standard Regions

Most of the statistics in *Regional Trends* are for the 11 standard regions of the United Kingdom. These are illustrated on pages 9, 188 and 189.

Counties of England and Wales

The 46 counties of England and the 8 counties of Wales are listed in the selected sub-regional statistics in Chapter 14 on pages 190-197. Their relationship to the standard regions is shown in the map on page 188.

Metropolitan Counties and Districts

Selected statistics are given for the six former metropolitan counties in Chapters 14 and 15 and a few maps in other chapters.

Greater London

Greater London is not a standard region (nor was it a metropolitan county), but statistics for Greater London are given wherever possible throughout this edition of *Regional Trends*.

Local Authority Regions of Scotland

The 10 LA regions of Scotland are listed in the selected statistics in Chapter 14 and illustrated on page 189. The Islands area comprises Orkney, Shetland and the Western Isles.

Northern Ireland

In Chapter 14, the 26 districts of Northern Ireland (illustrated on page 6 of *Regional Trends 17*) have been grouped into five Education and Library Boards. Some data are, however, available only for Health and Social Services Boards or for travel-to-work areas. In the latter case, data are shown only for the Belfast travel-to-work area. The districts comprising the Education and Library Boards are as follows:

Board	Districts
Belfast	Belfast
South Eastern	Ards, Castlereagh, Down, Lisburn, North Down.
Southern	Armagh, Banbridge, Cookstown, Craigavon, Dungannon, Newry and Mourne.
North Eastern	Antrim, Ballymena, Ballymoney, Carrickfergus, Coleraine, Larne, Magherafelt, Moyle, Newtownabbey.
Western	Derry, Fermanagh, Limavady, Omagh, Strabane.

Health and Social Services Boards are as follows:

Northern	as North Eastern Education and Library Board but including Cookstown.
Eastern	as South Eastern Education and Library Board but including Belfast.
Southern	as Southern Education and Library Board but excluding Cookstown.
Western	as Western Education and Library Board.

Education and Library Boards are illustrated on page 189.

All travel-to-work areas in the United Kingdom were revised in September 1984.

Other Regional Classifications

Maps of non-standard regions used in *Regional Trends* are shown on pages 232 and 233.

Regional figures for unemployment up to 1983 are built up by aggregating the appropriate local employment office areas. The boundaries, however, do not in all cases agree precisely with county or regional boundaries. From 1984, the data are based on electoral wards - see supplement to the September 1984 edition of *Employment Gazette*.

The UK Continental Shelf (see notes to Tables 12.1-12.3 on GDP) is treated as a separate region in Tables 12.1-12.3.

Regional Health Authority Areas*

ENGLAND

—— Health Authority boundary*

1. MERSEYSIDE
2. NORTH WEST THAMES
3. SOUTH WEST THAMES
4. NORTH EAST THAMES
5. SOUTH EAST THAMES

NORTHERN
YORKSHIRE
NORTH WESTERN
TRENT
WEST MIDLANDS
EAST ANGLIA
OXFORD
WESSEX
SOUTH WESTERN

* Pre 1 April 1994

NHS Executive Regional Offices*

ENGLAND

—— NHS Regional Office boundary*

NORTHERN & YORKSHIRE
NORTH WEST
TRENT
WEST MIDLANDS
ANGLIA & OXFORD
NORTH THAMES
SOUTH THAMES
SOUTH WEST

* Post 1 April 1994

Training, Enterprise and Education Directorate regions

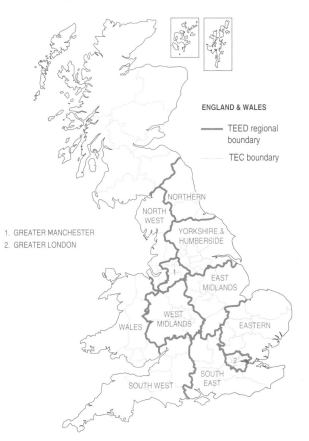

ENGLAND & WALES

—— TEED regional boundary
—— TEC boundary

1. GREATER MANCHESTER
2. GREATER LONDON

NORTHERN
NORTH WEST
YORKSHIRE & HUMBERSIDE
EAST MIDLANDS
WEST MIDLANDS
EASTERN
WALES
SOUTH WEST
SOUTH EAST

Police Force areas

—— Police Force area boundary

Northern
Grampian
Tayside
Fife
Central
Strathclyde
Lothian & Borders
Dumfries & Galloway
Northumbria
RUC
Cumbria
Durham
Cleveland
N. Yorks
Lancs
W. Yorks
Humberside
Mersey
G.M.P.
S. Yorks
Lincolnshire
Cheshire
Derbys
Notts
N. Wales
Staffs
Leicester
Norfolk
West Mercia
W. Mids
Northants
Cambs
Suffolk
Warwicks
Dyfed-Powys
Beds
Herts
Essex
S. Gwent
Gloucs
Thames Valley
Met
City
S. Wales
Met
Surrey
Kent
Avon & Somerset
Wilts
Hampshire
Sussex
Devon & Cornwall
Dorset

Department of Trade and Industry regions

ENGLAND

—— DTI regional boundary

NORTH EAST

NORTH WEST

YORKSHIRE & HUMBERSIDE

EAST MIDLANDS

WEST MIDLANDS

EAST

SOUTH WEST

SOUTH EAST

National Rivers Authority areas

ENGLAND & WALES

—— NRA regional boundary

NORTHUMBRIA & YORKSHIRE

NORTH WEST

CENTRAL

EASTERN

WELSH

THAMES

SOUTH WESTERN

SOUTHERN

Gas regions

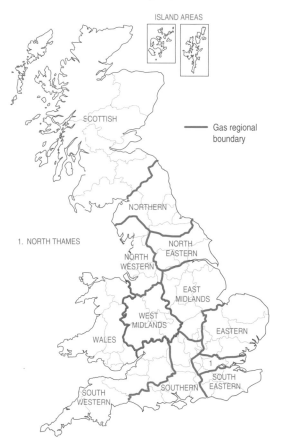

ISLAND AREAS

SCOTTISH

—— Gas regional boundary

1. NORTH THAMES

NORTHERN

NORTH EASTERN

NORTH WESTERN

EAST MIDLANDS

WEST MIDLANDS

WALES

EASTERN

1

SOUTHERN

SOUTH EASTERN

SOUTH WESTERN

Regional Electricity Companies

NORTH OF SCOTLAND

SOUTH OF SCOTLAND

—— Electricity regional boundary

1. LONDON

NORTH WESTERN (NORWEB)

NORTH EASTERN

YORKSHIRE

MERSEYSIDE & NORTH WALES (MANWEB)

EAST MIDLANDS

EASTERN

SOUTH WALES (SWALEC)

MIDLANDS

SOUTHERN

1 SOUTH EASTERN (SEEBOARD)

SOUTH WESTERN

CHAPTER 1:
REGIONAL PROFILES

The Regional Profiles do not highlight much information from Chapter 7: Health due to the boundary differences between the standard planning regions and the Regional Health Authority areas.

CHAPTER 2:
EUROPEAN COMMUNITIES
REGIONAL STATISTICS
Table 2.1 European Community comparisons

The data appearing in this section are based on information in the statistical yearbook *Regions* produced by the Statistical Office of the European Communities (EUROSTAT).

The average total population of a country consists of all persons, national or foreign, who are permanently settled in that country, even if temporarily absent from it.

Dependency rates are calculated as the number of non-active persons (total population *less* labour force) expressed as a percentage of those active.

Employment statistics are derived from the annual Community Labour Force Survey (CLFS), which closely resembles national labour force surveys. Since the survey is conducted on a sample basis, results relating to small regions should be treated with caution. The main statistical objectives of the LFS are to divide the population of working age into three groups: persons in employment, unemployed persons and inactive persons (those not classified as employed or unemployed).

The above groups are used to derive the following measures: Activity rates - the labour force as a percentage of the population of working age); Employment/population ratios - persons in employment as a percentage of the population of working age; Unemployment rates - unemployed persons as a percentage of the labour force.

The definitions of employment and unemployment used in the CLFS closely follow those adopted by the 13th International Conference of Labour Statisticians (ILO) and are as follows (further detail is available in the EUROSTAT publication *Labour Force Survey, Methods and Definitions*, 1992):
Employment: the employed comprise all persons above a specified age who during a specified brief period either one week or one day were in the following categories:
a) paid employment - at work or with a job but not at work ie temporarily absent but in receipt of a wage or salary;
b) self-employment - at work ie persons who during the reference period performed some work for profit or family gain, in cash or kind, or with an enterprise but not at work ie temporarily absent. (An 'enterprise' may be a business enterprise, a farm or a service undertaking.)

Unemployment: the unemployed comprise all persons above a specified age who, during the reference period, were:
a) without work - ie were not in paid employment or self-employment;
b) currently available for work - ie were available for paid employment or self-employment during the reference period;
c) seeking work - ie had taken specific steps in a specified recent period to seek paid employment or self-employment.

The type of employment is classified by *Economic activity* in accordance with the General Classification of Economic Activities in the European Communities (NACE): Agriculture (NACE code O), Industry (NACE codes 1 to 5) and Services (NACE codes 6 to 9).

Long-term unemployment: persons who have been unemployed for 12 or more consecutive months.

Agricultural holdings/enterprise economic value: the 'gross margin' of an agricultural enterprise is defined as the monetary value of gross production from which corresponding specific costs are deducted. The 'Standard Gross Margin' (SGM) is the value of gross margin corresponding to the average situation in a given region for each agricultural characteristic eg crop production, livestock production. 'Gross production' is the sum of the value of the principal product(s) and of any secondary product(s). The values are calculated by multiplying production per unit (less any losses) by the farm-gate price, excluding VAT. Gross production also includes subsidies linked to products, to area and/or to livestock.

Basic data are collected in Member States from farm accounts, specific surveys or compiled from appropriate calculations for a reference period which covers three successive years or agricultural production years. The reference period is the same for all Member States. SGMs are first calculated in Member States national currencies and then converted into European currency units (ECUs) using the average exchange rates for the reference period.

Footnotes to the tables in Chapter 2

1 Definitions of population, employment and unemployment differ from those used in UK tables, see above.
2 All data refer to the unified German state. Data for Berlin refer to the 'New' Berlin (East+West).
3 Including 'centraal persoons register'.
4 Participation rates are calculated by dividing the number of pupils enrolled in a region by the resident population in that region. As some young people may be resident in one region and in education in another, this inter-regional movement may influence the results.
5 Unadjusted death rates using 1992 population estimates. For Belgium figures relate to 1989; for Denmark, Germany, France and Italy they relate to 1991.

6 For EUR12, Belgium, Greece, Spain, France, Italy and Portugal figures relate to 1991.

7 For Italy figures relate to 1990; for Greece, Spain and France relate to 1991.

8 Figures for Luxembourg and the Netherlands relate to 1991.

9 The economic value of farms is measured in Standard gross margins (SGM); see above.

CHAPTER 3: POPULATION AND HOUSEHOLDS

Tables 3.1 and 3.3 and Chart 3.2 Resident population

The estimated population of an area includes all those usually resident in the area, whatever their nationality. HM Forces stationed outside the United Kingdom are excluded but foreign forces stationed here are included. Students are taken to be resident at their term-time address.

The population estimates for mid-1993 are based on the 1991 Census results (with allowance for Census under-enumeration) and take account of births, deaths and migration between 1991 and mid-1993. In Table 3.1 and Chart 3.2 annual growth rates are shown as geometric averages.

Table 3.8 Standardised mortality ratios

The standardised mortality ratio compares overall mortality in a region with that for the UK. The ratio expresses the number of deaths in a region as a percentage of the hypothetical number that would have occurred f the region's population had experienced the sex/age-specific rates of the UK in that year.

Table 3.9 Live births, deaths and natural increase in population

Numbers shown are registrations during a calendar year, except for births in England and Wales which are numbers occurring in a calendar year. Crude birth/death rates and natural increase are affected by the age and sex structure of the population. For example, for any given levels of fertility and mortality, a population with a relatively high proportion of persons in the younger age-groups will have a higher crude birth-rate and a lower crude death-rate, and consequently a higher rate of natural increase, than a population with a higher proportion of elderly people.

Tables 3.10 Inter-regional movements

Estimates for internal population movements are counts of the transfers of NHS doctors' patients between Family Health Services Authorities (FHSAs) in England and Wales and Area Health Boards (AHBs) in Scotland and Northern Ireland. These transfers are recorded at the NHS Central Registers (NHSCRs) in Southport and Edinburgh and at the Central Services Agency in Belfast. The figures shown here have been adjusted to take account of differences in recorded cross-border flows between England and Wales, Scotland, and Northern Ireland.

These figures provide a detailed indicator of population movement within the United Kingdom. However, they should not be regarded as a perfect measure of migration as there is variation in the delay between a person moving and registering with a new doctor. Additionally, some moves may not result in a re-registration, ie individuals may migrate again before registering with a doctor. Conversely, there may be others who move and re-register several times in a year.

The NHSCR at Southport was computerised in 1990. Before 1990, the time lag was assumed to be three months between moving and the processing of data. (It was estimated that processing at NHSCR took two months.) Since computerisation, estimates of internal migration derived from the NHSCR are based on the date of acceptance of the new patient by the FHSA (not previously available), and a one-month time lag assumed.

Table 3.11 International migration

The data are derived from the International Passenger Survey (IPS), a continuous voluntary sample survey covering the principal air and sea routes between the United Kingdom and overseas. Routes between the United Kingdom and the Irish Republic, and those between the Channel Islands, Isle of Man and the rest of the world are excluded. It also does not count as migrants those seeking asylum after entering the United Kingdom, and others who enter as visitors but subsequently are granted an extension of stay for a year or longer ('visitor switchers'). The effect of this latter group is partly balanced by visitor switchers leaving the country. IPS results shown in Table 3.11 appear to indicate a net outflow from the United Kingdom in 1993. However if allowance is made for asylum seekers, visitor switchers, and movements to and from the Irish Republic, there was a net civilian inward migration of about 87 thousand.

The proportion of passengers sampled in the IPS varies between 0.1 and 5 per cent according to route and time of year. In view of the small number of migrants in the sample, it should be noted that the estimates of migration, in particular the differences between inflow and outflow, are subject to large sampling errors. As a rough guide, the standard error for an estimate of one thousand migrants is around 40 per cent, whilst that for an estimate of 40 thousand migrants reduces to about 10 per cent, but on occasions these standard errors can be higher. However, the structure of the sample is such that estimates based on the sampling of passengers on certain routes have much larger standard errors associated with them.

For demographic purposes a migrant into the UK is defined as a person who has resided abroad for a year or more and states the intention to stay in the UK for a year or more, and vice versa for a migrant from the UK. Migrants, defined in this way were asked an additional group of questions which form the basis of these statistics.

Based on the Labour Force Survey (see Appendix notes to the Labour market chapter), the table gives percentages of economically active people aged 16 and over in each social class based on occupations. The method used is designed to group together as far as possible people with similar levels of occupational skills. The basis of the groupings is given in Volume 3, *Standard Occupational Classification*, HMSO, 1991.

Table 3.13 Social class

The six occupational social classes in the classification are as follows:

I		Professional occupations (including doctors, solicitors, chemists, university professors and clergymen)
II		Managerial and technical occupations (including school teachers, computer programmers, personnel managers, nurses, actors and laboratory technicians)
III		Skilled occupations
	(N)	Non-manual (including typists, clerical workers, photographers, sales representatives and shop assistants)
	(M)	Manual (including cooks, bus drivers, railway guards, plasterers, bricklayers, hairdressers and carpenters)
IV		Partly skilled occupations (including bar staff, waitresses, gardeners and caretakers)
V		Unskilled occupations (including refuse collectors, messengers, lift attendants, cleaners and labourers).

For those in employment in the reference week of the survey, the occupation was that of their main job, and for the unemployed, (on the ILO definition), their last occupation if they had done any paid work in the previous eight years.

Table 3.14 Ethnic group

The information about the ethnic origins of all people is collected by the Labour Force Survey using the classification first used in the 1991 Census of Population. Those classified as 'other' includes Chinese, some other Asians and those of mixed origin.

The question about ethnic origin is not included in the Northern Ireland survey. The estimates relate to the quarterly survey carried out in Great Britain, Summer 1994.

Table 3.18 Household size

The source of data for this table is the Family Resources Survey (FRS), conducted by the Department of Social Security. See Appendix notes for Tables 8.3 and 8.6. The FRS defines a household as a single person or group of people living at the same address as their only or main residence, who either share one meal a day together or share the living accommodation.

CHAPTER 4:
EDUCATION AND TRAINING

School classifications

Schools are generally classified according to the ages for which they cater, or the type of education they provide. Nursery schools are for children below compulsory age; primary schools consist of infants' schools (for children up to age 7) and junior schools (for children aged 8-11). The norm in Scotland and Ireland is 7 years of primary education as against 6 years in England and Wales. Special schools provide education for children with special education needs who cannot be educated satisfactorily in an ordinary school.

United Kingdom educational establishments are administered and financed in one of three ways:

a. by local education authorities which form part of the structure of local government partly through funds provided by central government;

b. by governing bodies which have a substantial degree of autonomy from public authorities but which receive grants from centrally financed funding bodies and from central government sources directly;

c. by the private sector, including individuals, companies and charitable institutions.

Types of school establishment falling within the categories typically have different names in England, Wales, Scotland and Northern Ireland. Therefore, to avoid confusion, standardised terms are used for the purposes of United Kingdom statistics:

a.	Public sector or maintained	-	LEA maintained and grant-maintained (England and Wales)
		-	assisted and grant-aided establishments of further education (England and Wales) until 1993
		-	education authority (Scotland)

	-	controlled, maintained, voluntary and grant-maintained integrated (Northern Ireland)
b. Part-maintained	-	grant-aided (Scotland) until 1985/86
	-	direct grant (England and Wales) until 1980
c. Non-maintained	-	independent including City Technology Colleges (England)

In the tables in this chapter the non-maintained sector generally includes the part-maintained establishments.

Sixth form colleges

Sixth form colleges in England and Wales became part of the further education sector from 1 April 1993. They are generally included with FE colleges in the tables in this chapter (even where time series have been shown).

Academic years

Count dates for the various surveys of educational institutions on which most of the statistics are based differ between countries. The information collected on a particular date is taken as a proxy for the academic year as a whole.

Table 4.1 Pupils and teachers by type of school

In England and Wales qualified teachers only are included for public sector, nursery and special schools. In Scotland and Northern Ireland all teachers employed in schools, other than in independent schools, are required to be qualified. Part-time pupils counted as halves except in Scotland where full-time equivalence is recorded.

Pupils and teachers in non-maintained (or part-maintained) special schools in Scotland and Wales are excluded from the table.

Table 4.2 Average class sizes

The 'all classes' figures include classes where more than one teacher may be present.

Table 4.3 Primary and secondary schools

Schools in Scotland and Northern Ireland with separate primary and secondary departments have been counted once for each department.

Table 4.5 Day care

The total number of day care places in day nurseries, playgroups and with childminders is expressed as a total rate, without subdivision for local authority and registered provision. The different kinds of provision offer quite different kinds of care, for different periods of the day. Day nurseries and childminders will generally offer coverage for the whole adult working day throughout the week. The coverage of playgroup places varies considerably, from just one or two sessions (of four hours or less) a week in some cases to a full ten sessions a week in others.

As a result of the implementation of the *Children Act 1989*, childminders are now required to register places for children under the age of eight; thus data relating to places for those under the age of five are no longer available. However, the majority of places registered are available for use by under fives as only a small proportion are with childminders registered solely for after-school care of five to seven year olds. The England total shown in Table 4.5 comprises 53.4 thousand places with childminders registered for under fives only, 19.7 thousand with those registered for school age children only and 229.6 thousand with those registered for both age groups. In Wales the comparable figures are 1.9 thousand, 0.9 thousand and 8.8 thousand respectively. A breakdown is not available for Scotland. In Northern Ireland, childminders are required to register places for children who have not attained the upper limit of compulsory school age under the *Children and Young Persons (NI) Act 1968*.

Table 4.6 16 year olds participating at school or in further education

Ages and census count dates for the countries refer to the academic years 1985/86 and 1993/94 except for Scotland which is 1984/85 and 1993/94. From 1 April 1993 sixth form colleges transferred from the schools sector to the further education sector. In order that comparisons can be made, for England sixth form colleges have been included with further education for both 1985/86 and 1993/94.

Tables 4.7 and 4.8 Examination achievements

GCSE and equivalent figures relate to achievements by 16 year olds (year 4 in Scotland) at the end of the 1992/93 academic year and are shown as percentages of 16 year olds in school (year 4 in Scotland). GCE 'A' level and equivalent figures for 17-19 year olds are based on the 18 year old population.

In Table 4.8 Mathematics figures exclude computing science (England) and computer studies and statistics (Wales) while 'Any science' includes biology, chemistry and physics which are also shown as separate subjects. Scotland also include science Standard Grades.

In Wales, the Certificate of Education examination is also available and is widely used by schools. In all countries pupils may sit non-GCE/GCSE examinations such as BTEC (SCOTVEC in Scotland), City and Guilds, RSA and Pitman. Inevitably, a proportion of pupils who are recorded as achieving no GCSE, AS or 'A' level qualification will have with passes in one or more of these other examinations. Many pupils in Wales take Welsh as their first language at GCSE, with English as a second language

Standard Grade is, in Scotland, the replacement for 'O' grade. The courses begin in third year and continue to the end of fourth year. Each subject has a number of elements, some of which are internally assessed in school. The award for the subject as a whole is given on a 7 point scale at three levels: Credit (1 and 2), General (3 and 4) and Foundation (5 and 6). An award of 7 means that the course has been completed. Pupils who do not complete the course or do not sit all parts of the examination get 'no award'. Standard Grades 1-3 are broadly the equivalent of the old 'O' Grade pass. The Higher Grade usually requires a further year of study.

Table 4.9 Enrolments on adult education in LEA maintained centres

Some LEAs contract all or part of their adult education provision to further education colleges whilst others have free standing adult education centres. Only those enrolments in the free standing centres are recorded in this table.

Table 4.10 New student awards made by LEAs/ SAAS

First degrees exclude teacher training for England, Wales and Scotland, but include it for Northern Ireland. Discretionary awards can be made by LEAs in England and Wales under Section 2 of the Education Act 1962 in respect of any course which is not 'designated' for mandatory or certain postgraduate awards, including courses of FE and certain courses of HE. Awards made under Section 1(6) of the Act may be made at the LEA's discretion to students on designated courses who are personally ineligible to receive a mandatory award. In Scotland, student awards are administered by the Student Awards Agency for Scotland (SAAS).

Table 4.13 Further education

This item includes all students on courses of further education. Students in England and Wales are counted once only, irrespective of the number of courses for which a student has enrolled. In Scotland and Northern Ireland, students enrolled in more than one course in unrelated subjects are counted for each of these courses with the exception of those on SCE and/or GCE courses, who are counted once only irrespective of the number of levels/grades.

Sandwich courses are those where periods of full-time study are broken by a period (or periods) of associated industrial training or experience, and where the total period (or periods) of full-time study over the whole course averages more than 18 weeks per year.

Part-time day courses are mainly those organised for students released by their employers either for one or two days a week, or for a period (or periods) of block release.

Chart 4.14 and Table 4.15 Education expenditure by local government

Figures for both items are total net recurrent and capital expenditure on, or related to, education including expenditure by local education authorities on grant maintained schools.

In Table 4.15 transport of pupils for England and Wales is allocated across the schools sectors. Continuing education includes expenditure on adult education centres, teacher and curriculum centres and on awards (fees and maintenance exclusive of parental contributions) to students normally resident within the local authority area prior to going to colleges. 'Other educational services' includes school welfare, youth service and other facilities such as sports, outdoor activity and residential study centres, and educational research. For Scotland and Northern Ireland it also includes transport of pupils. Loan charges are excluded.

Table 4.16 National Targets for Education and Training

Initial attention has been focused on measuring the three main quantifiable targets:
Foundation Target 1- by the year 1997, 80 per cent of young people should be qualified to at least NVQ level 2, equivalent to 5 GCSE passes at grades A-C.
Foundation Target 3 - by the year 2000, 50 per cent of young people should be qualified to at least NVQ level 3, equivalent to 2 'A' levels, 3 Scottish Highers or an Advanced Diploma.
Lifetime Target 3 - by the year 2000, 50 per cent of the employed workforce should be qualified to at least NVQ level 3.

Tables 4.16 and 4.19 Labour Force Survey

Please see Appendix notes to Chapter 5 below.

Chart 4.17 and Table 4.18 Training For Work (TfW) and Youth Training (YT)

TfW replaced Employment Training (ET) on 1 April 1993. It is a programme for the long-term unemployed, locally planned and delivered to help people find and stay in employment. Training and Enterprise Councils (TECs) in England and Wales and Local Enterprise Companies (LECs) in Scotland are responsible for the planning and delivery of TfW.

YT aims to provide broad-based training mainly for 16 and 17 year olds and to provide better qualified young entrants into the labour market. Training and Enterprise Councils (TECs) in England and Wales and Local Enterprise Companies (LECs) in Scotland are responsible for the planning and delivery of YT.

Leavers were followed up six months after they left TfW/YT. Response to the survey was generally low. Figures for both programme participants and leavers are by TEED regions; see map on page 233.

CHAPTER 5: LABOUR MARKET

Tables and Charts 5.1-5.3, 5.6-5.12, 5.16, 5.18, 5.19 and 5.26 Labour Force Survey

The Labour Force Survey (LFS) is a sample survey of about 65,000 private households in the United Kingdom, with questions also being asked about students living away from home in halls of residence; a sample of people living in NHS accommodation is also interviewed. It was conducted biennially from 1973, and annually from 1983. In Great Britain the survey has been conducted quarterly since Spring 1992, but in Northern Ireland the survey was carried out annually until the Winter of 1994/95, when a quarterly survey was introduced. The latest estimates for all regions are therefore from the Spring 1994 survey. The survey results are grossed up to give the correct population total and reflect the distributions by sex, age and region shown by the population figures.

All LFS estimates have been rounded to the nearest thousand, and those of less than 10,000 are not given because they are likely to be subject to high sampling error and are therefore considered unreliable.

Table 5.1 Labour Force

Estimates from the LFS relating to employees and self-employed cover those aged 16 or over and are based upon the respondents' own assessment of their employment status, and the Standard Industrial Classification 1992. Those on Government employment and training programmes comprise all people aged 16 or over who were at the time of interview participating in Youth Training, Community Industry, Training for Work or Employment Action, together with those on similar programmes administered by the Training and Enterprise Councils (TECs) in England and Wales or Local Enterprise Companies (LECs) in Scotland or the Training & Employment Agency (T&EA) in Northern Ireland. Other similar programmes such as the Youth Training Scheme were included when they were in operation. Unpaid family workers were only identified separately in the survey from Spring 1992.

Tables 5.1-5.3 and 5.8 The labour force and activity rates

The *civilian labour force* includes people aged 16 or over who are either in employment (whether employed, self-employed or on work-related Government employment and training programmes, but excluding those in the armed forces) or unemployed.

Estimates up to 1984 are on the former 'Great Britain Labour Force definition', which counted as unemployed people without a job and seeking work in a reference week (or prevented from seeking work by temporary sickness or holiday, or waiting for the results of a job application, or waiting to start a job they had already obtained), whether or not they were available to start (except students not able to start because they must complete their education).

From 1984, estimates and projections are based on definitions which follow the guidelines of the International Labour Office (ILO) and are used by the Organisation for Economic Co-operation and Development (OECD).

The 'ILO definition' of unemployment counts as unemployed people without a job who were available to start work within two weeks and had either looked for work in the past four weeks or were waiting to start a job they had already obtained. Estimates on the ILO definition are not available before 1984, as the Labour Force Survey did not then collect information on job search over a four-week period.

The *civilian activity rate* in a given age/sex category is the civilian labour force expressed as a percentage of the population in that category.

The most recent national (Great Britain) labour force projections were published in the April 1995 edition of *Employment Gazette*. However, the regional projections presented are consistent with an earlier round of national projections published in the June 1992 edition of *Employment Gazette*.

Estimates of the civilian labour force and activity rates for 1971 are based mainly on data from the Census of Population. Estimates for later years incorporate survey estimates from the Labour Force Survey (see note below) supplemented by data from the Census of Population on the economic activity of those not in private households. Further details of sources and methods appear in *Employment Gazette*, June 1992.

Table 5.4 The civilian workforce

The civilian workforce (Table 5.4) is broadly similar in concept to the civilian labour force (Tables 5.2 and 5.3). There are, however, numerous differences in definition and coverage between the two series. For example, employees in employment with two jobs will be counted twice in the workforce but once in the labour force; while persons seeking work but not claiming benefits are in the labour force but are not covered by the workforce. This can lead the two series to exhibit different short-term movements; over the longer term the paths followed are similar.

Tables 5.4 and 5.5 Employees

A count of civilian jobs of employees paid by employers who run a Pay-As-You-Earn scheme. Participants in Government employment and training schemes are included if they have a contract of employment. HM Forces, homeworkers and private domestic servants are excluded.

Numbers of employees in employment are based on the Census of Employment which is held periodically. Between census dates, quarterly estimates are derived from sample surveys benchmarked on the latest census and 100 per cent coverage of government and certain trade organisations. In total this covers 50 per cent of all employee jobs.

Table 5.5 Industrial distribution of employees

See notes to Tables 13.4 and 13.5 on the Standard Industrial Classification 1980.

Table 5.7 Self-employment

The data are based on the respondents' own classification of their economic status, and the Standard Industrial Classification 1992.

Table 5.9 Head of Household

The head of household is defined as the member of the household who was, in order of precedence, the husband of the person, or the person who either owned the household accommodation or was legally responsible for the rent or had the responsibility for the occupation of the accommodation. For accommodation jointly owned by a man and a women the head of household was taken as the man, and if jointly owned by people of the same gender the head of household was taken as the elder.

Table 5.10 Educational qualifications

Covers all people of working age (16-64 for men, 16-59 for women) who were economically active, either in employment or unemployed in accordance with the ILO definition. See notes to Tables 4.7 and 4.8.

Degree or equivalent includes graduate membership of a professional institute.

Higher education below degree includes: Diploma in Higher Education and Higher HND-HNC BTEC.

GCE 'A' level or equivalent includes: National OND-ONC BTEC, and SCE Higher Grade in Scotland.

GCE 'O' level equivalent includes: all GCSE qualifications and CSE grade 1, and SCE Standard Grade in Scotland.

Table 5.11 Occupational grouping

The occupation groupings used are based on major groups in the *Standard Occupational Classification* (HMSO), first published February 1990.

Tables 5.13-5.15 New Earnings Survey

These contain some of the regional results of the New Earnings Survey 1994, fuller details of which are given in part E of the report *New Earnings Survey 1994* (HMSO), published in November 1994. Results for Northern Ireland are published separately by the Department of Economic Development, Northern Ireland. The survey measured gross earnings of a 1 per cent sample of employees, most of whom were members of Pay-As-You-Earn (PAYE) schemes for a pay-period which included 13 April 1994. The earnings information collected was converted to a weekly basis where necessary, and to an hourly basis where normal basic hours were reported.

Figures for Great Britain regions are given only where the number of employees reporting in the survey was 50 or more and the standard error of average weekly earnings was 5 per cent or less. Figures for Northern Ireland are only given where the number of employees reporting in the survey was ten or more. Gross earnings are measured before tax, National Insurance or other deductions. They include overtime pay, bonuses and other additions to basic pay but exclude any payments for earlier periods (eg back pay), most income in kind, tips and gratuities. All the results in this volume relate to full-time male and female employees on adult rates whose pay for the survey pay-period was not affected by absence. Employees were classified to the region in which they worked (or were based if mobile), and to manual or non-manual occupations on the basis of the Standard Occupational Classification (SOC). Part A of the report for Great Britain gives full details of definitions used in the survey.

Full-time employees are defined as those normally expected to work more than 30 hours per week, excluding overtime and main meal breaks (but 25 hours or more in the case of teachers) or, if their normal hours were not specified, as those regarded as full-time by the employer.

Table 5.15 Average weekly earnings

See notes to Tables 13.4 and 13.5 on the Standard Industrial Classification 1980.

Table 5.17 Labour disputes

The table shows rates per 1,000 employees of working days lost for various years by standard region for all industries and services. The statistics relate only to disputes connected with terms and conditions of employment. Stoppages involving fewer than ten workers or lasting less than one day are excluded except where the aggregate of working days lost exceeded 100. When interpreting the figures the following points should be borne in mind:

    i.   geographical variations in industrial structure affect overall regional comparisons;

    ii.   a few large stoppages affecting a small number of firms may have a significant effect;

iii.   the number of working days lost and workers involved relate to persons both directly and indirectly involved at the establishments where the disputes occurred;

iv.   the regional figures involve a greater degree of estimation than the national figures as some large national stoppages cannot be disaggregated to a regional level and are only shown in the national figure.

Table 5.19 Redundancies

Estimates cover those people who reported that they had been made redundant during the three calendar months prior to the week in which the LFS interview was conducted.

Tables and Charts 5.20-5.24 Unemployment statistics

Figures in Tables and Charts 5.20-5.21 and 5.23-5.24 relate to persons claiming unemployment-related benefits (that is, Unemployment Benefit, Income Support or National Insurance credits) at an Employment Service Office on the day of the monthly count, who on that day were unemployed and satisfied the conditions for claiming benefit. The unemployment figures include disabled people, so long as they meet the eligibility criteria and are claiming unemployment-related benefits, but exclude students seeking vacation work and temporarily stopped workers. A full description of the system of compiling the figures appeared in the September 1982 *Employment Gazette*. Figures for the claimant basis for Great Britain prior to May 1982 and for Northern Ireland prior to November 1982 are estimates - see the article in *Employment Gazette*, December 1982.

National and regional unemployment rates are calculated by expressing the number of unemployed as a percentage of the estimated total workforce (the sum of the unemployed claimants, employees in employment, self-employed, HM Forces and participants on work-related Government training programmes). These rates are shown in Table 5.21, while rates for ILO unemployment are shown in Table 5.22. For the ILO definition of unemployment, see the notes to Tables 5.1-5.3 and 5.8.

Table 5.26 Trade Union membership

The question on trade union membership was first included in the 1989 annual LFS. With the introduction of the quarterly survey in Great Britain the question was moved to the Autumn survey, although still only asked each Spring in the Northern Ireland annual survey. For technical reasons, Spring 1994 data for Northern Ireland were not obtainable and were estimated.

CHAPTER 6: HOUSING

Tables 6.1-6.3 Dwellings

In the 1981 Census, a dwelling was defined as: structurally separate accommodation whose rooms, excluding bathrooms and WCs, are self-contained. In the 1991 Census the definition changed to: structurally separate accommodation whose rooms, including bath or shower, WC, and kitchen facilities, are self-contained. The figures in Table 6.1 include vacant dwellings and temporary dwellings occupied as a normal place of residence. Estimates of the stock in England are based on data from the 1981 and 1991 Censuses. Northern Ireland stock figures are based on rating lists, Northern Ireland Housing Executive and Housing Association figures. Estimates of the tenure distribution in Table 6.2 are based on the above estimates and certain assumptions regarding the tenure distribution of gains and losses in the housing stock. Estimates for Table 6.3 of the age distribution of the dwelling stock use data from the census reports from 1851 to 1991 together with assumed rates of new construction and demolition (for periods before these were recorded) and further assumptions about the ages of dwellings lost from the housing stock.

Table 6.5 Renovations

The current system of grants to private owners, landlords and tenants came into operation in England and Wales in 1990. They are provided under the *Local Government and Housing Act 1989*; the previous system was provided under the *Housing Act 1985* and, while approvals from this system have ceased, some payments continue.

Table 6.6 New dwellings completed

A dwelling is defined for the purposes of this table as a building or any part of a building which forms a separate and self-contained set of premises designed to be occupied by a single family. The figures relate to new permanent dwellings only, ie dwellings with a life expectancy of 60 years or more. A dwelling is counted as completed when it becomes ready for occupation, whether actually occupied or not.

Table 6.7 Private sector 'Fair' Rents

Figures relate to average fair rents registered by Rent Officers during the first six months of 1994, virtually all of which were for unfurnished tenancies. A fair rent is normally fixed for two years, after which an application for reregistration can be made. Unlike rents quoted for local authorities and housing associations, fair rent figures **include** any service charge, which, on average, adds 3 per cent to basic rents.

Prior to 1989, most lettings by private landlords were classified as Regulated; such tenancies provided full security of tenure and were eligible to have a fair rent registered. The *Housing Act 1988* deregulated new lettings from 15 January 1989. Existing regulated tenancies continued to be covered by *Rent Act* legislation, as amended, but new tenancies after that date are generally Assured tenancies, with the rent freely negotiated by the landlord and the tenant.

Table 6.8 Sales of local authority dwellings	The figures for the stock at the end of 1993 are estimates obtained by adding sales during the period January to March 1994 to stock figures for 31 March 1994.

The percentages are calculated as the sales in the period April 1979 to December 1993 expressed as a percentage of the stock at 31 December 1993 plus sales in the period April 1979 to December 1993.

Tables 6.9 and 6.10 Building societies

Figures in these tables are taken from The Five per cent Sample Survey of Building Society Mortgages at completion stage. Full details of the survey are given in *The Five per cent Sample Survey of Building Society Mortgages*, CSO Studies in Official Statistics No. 26 1975 (HMSO).

The income of borrowers is the total recorded income taken into account when the mortgage is granted, but it should be noted that societies' practices vary. Some record the basic income of the main applicant; others record total income from all sources including that of spouse or other joint applicant(s).

Table 6.11 Council Tax bandings

For Council Tax purposes, dwellings were banded according to their valuation at 1 April 1991. The bands are:

	England	*Wales*	*Scotland*
Band A	up to £40,000	up to £30,000	up to £27,000
Band B	£40,001-£52,000	£30,001-£39,000	£27,001-£35,000
Band C	£52,001-£68,000	£39,001-£51,000	£35,001-£45,000
Band D	£68,001-£88,000	£51,001-£66,000	£45,001-£58,000
Band E	£88,001-£120,000	£66,001-£90,000	£58,001-£80,000
Band F	£120,001-£160,000	£90,001-£120,000	£80,001-£106,000
Band G	£160,001-£320,000	£120,001-£240,000	£106,001-£212,000
Band H	£320,001 or over	£240,001 or over	£212,001 or over

Table 6.12 County Court actions for mortgage possessions

The figures do not indicate how many houses have been repossessed through the courts; not all the orders will have resulted in the issue and execution of warrants of possession.

Actions entered: a plaintiff begins an action for an order for possession of residential property by way of a summons in a county court.

Orders made: the court, following a judicial hearing, may grant an order for possession immediately. This entitles the plaintiff to apply for a warrant to have the defendant evicted. However, even where a warrant for possession is issued, the parties can still negotiate a compromise to prevent eviction.

Suspended orders: frequently, the court grants the mortgage lender possession but suspends the operation of the order. Provided the defendant complies with the terms of the suspension, which usually require them to pay the current mortgage instalments plus some of the accrued arrears, the possession order cannot be enforced.

Table 6.13 Homeless households by reason

In England and Wales the basis for these figures is households accepted for permanent re-housing by local authorities under the homelessness provisions of Part III of the *Housing Act 1985*. The Welsh figures, however, also include:

i.   non-priority cases, given advice and assistance;
ii. intentionally homeless, priority accepted; and
iii. intentionally homeless, non-priority accepted.

For Scotland, the closest possible approximation to the English definition has been used. In Northern Ireland, the *Housing (Northern Ireland) Order 1988* (Part II) defines the basis under which households (including one-person households) are classified as homeless.

CHAPTER 7: HEALTH

For many of the tables in this section, figures for the Regional Health Authority (RHA) areas of England, as opposed to standard regions, are given. Prior to 1 April 1994 there were 14 RHAs; on that date they were reorganised to form eight new NHS Executive regions. Most of the statistics in this edition relate to periods before the reorganisation. However maps of both the old and the new structures are given on page 232.

In Scotland and Northern Ireland procedures may differ slightly from those used in England and Wales; reference is made to these differences in footnotes to the tables.

Tables 7.1 and 7.2 Still births

On 1 October 1992 the legal definition of a still birth was altered from a baby born dead after 28 completed weeks gestation or more to one born dead after 24 completed weeks gestation or more.

Figures for 1971 and 1981 in Table 7.2 for are based on still births of 28 weeks completed gestation or more. The still birth and perinatal mortality rates for 1993 are provided on both the old and the new definitions of a still birth to assist comparison with the earlier years.

Table 7.3 Limiting long-standing illness

'Long-standing illness' is measured by asking respondents if they have any long-standing illness, disability or infirmity. Long standing means anything that has troubled the respondent over a period of time or that is likely to affect the respondent over a period of time. A limiting long-standing illness/disability/ infirmity is one which limits the respondent's activities in any way.

Table 7.5 Blood pressure

The source of the data in Table 7.5 is the Health Survey for England 1993. Fieldwork for the survey was conducted throughout 1993 and yielded more than 16,500 interviews.

For the purposes of the survey, blood pressure was measured using an automatic machine and only valid blood pressure readings were included in the analyses. A summary measure to describe blood pressure which takes into account both systolic and diastolic pressure and also whether any medication was being taken for the treatment of raised blood pressure is used in Table7.5. The categories to which people were classified are:

Normotensive - systolic less than 160 mmHg and diastolic untreated less than 95 mmHg, not currently taking drug(s) prescribed for high blood pressure

Normotensive - systolic less than 160 mmHg and diastolic treated less than 95 mmHg, currently taking drug(s) prescribed for high blood pressure

Hypertensive - systolic greater than 159 mmHg and/or treated diastolic greater than 94 mmHg, currently taking drug(s) prescribed for high blood pressure

Hypertensive - systolic greater than 159 mmHg and/or untreated diastolic greater than 94 mmHg, not currently taking drug(s) prescribed for high blood pressure.

Where people are described as having high blood pressure, this means that they were in any of the three categories normotensive treated, hypertensive treated or hypertensive untreated. The blood pressure level classification excludes respondents who were taking prescribed medicines, for reasons other than high blood pressure, which may nevertheless affect blood pressure because it is not known what their blood pressure would have been if they were not taking them.

Table 7.6 Body mass index

In order to measure obesity, the use of weight alone is clearly not appropriate as there is a strong relationship between height and weight. The body mass index (BMI) measures weight corrected for height and is calculated as weight(kg)/height(m)2. BMI has the disadvantage that it can be misleading as a measure of fatness of people with certain types of physique. For example, those who have muscular physiques, who are heavy but lean, will have a high BMI even though they are not fat. Nevertheless, BMI is currently the most widely used index of obesity.

BMI is classified according to the following internationally recognised categories:

Level of index	Description
20 or less	Underweight
Over 20, up to 25	Desirable
Over 25, up to 30	Overweight
Over 30	Obese.

Chart 7.7 Standardised registration ratio (SRR)

The incidence of cancer varies greatly with age. The SRR is an index which enables ready comparison of incidence rates in populations with different age structures. It is calculated by denoting one set of age-specific rates as the standard. These are then applied to each of several index populations of known age structure to show how many registrations would have been expected in these index populations had they, at each age, experienced the cancer incidence of the standard population. The 'expected' incidence so found is then compared with the observed, their ratio being multiplied by 100 to give an index in which 100 is the value for the standard population.

Chart 7.7 shows the 1989 SRRs in RHAs of residence. For each cancer, the 1989 registration rates in England and Wales are taken as the standards (with males and females considered separately).

Table 7.8 Reports of HIV infections

The cumulative number of reports in the 'undetermined' category may be lower at the end of one year than that recorded in the preceding year since all cases of infection where exposure category is unreported are routinely followed up. The exposure category of cases may therefore be reassigned as a result of further information becoming available.

Tables 7.10 and 7.16 Age adjusted mortality rates

The mortality rates are derived from the product of the UK rate and the Standardised Mortality Ratio (SMR) for each region/cause. In turn, each SMR is the ratio of observed deaths to those expected by applying standard death rates to the regional population.

The causes of death included in Table 7.10 correspond to International Classification of Diseases (9th Revision) codes as follows: all circulatory diseases - 390-459; ischaemic heart disease - 410-414; cerebrovascular disease - 430-438; all respiratory diseases - 460-519; bronchitis et. al. - 490-493; cancers - 140-208; all injuries and poisonings - 800-999; road traffic accidents - E810-E819; suicides and open verdicts -E950-E959 and E980-E989.

Table 7.14 Alcohol consumption

A unit of alcohol is 8 grammes of pure alcohol, approximately equivalent to half a pint of ordinary strength beer, a glass of wine, or a pub measure of spirits.

The consumption levels shown in Table 7.14 are amalgamations of a wider range available from the General Household Survey (Great Britain) and the Continuous Household Survey (Northern Ireland). The full range is as follows:

Non-drinker	- zero alcohol consumption per week
Very low	- less than 1 unit of alcohol per week
Low	- between 1 and 10 units per week for men and between 1 and 7 for women
Moderate	- between 11 and 21 units per week for men and between 8 and 14 for women
Fairly high	- between 22 and 35 units per week for men and between 15 and 25 for women
High	- between 36 and 50 units per week for men and between 26 and 35 for women
Very high	- 51 units or more per week for men and 36 units or more for women.

Recommended sensible levels are 21 units per week for men and 14 for women; maximum safe levels are 50 units per week for men and 35 for women.

Table 7.17 National Food Survey

This is a continuous sample survey of about 7-8,000 households per year in Great Britain, where a record is kept of the type, quantity and cost of foods entering the home during one week. Nutritional values are also calculated from the information collected. Confectionery, soft drinks and alcoholic drinks brought home have been included in the survey since 1992, but these are excluded from certain analyses (including Table 7.17) for consistency. Each household member over the age of 11 is given a separate diary for their personal expenditure and consumption. Detailed survey results, including the results of this extension, will be published in the 1994 annual report National Food Survey published by HMSO.

Tables 7.19 Hospital activity

Data for England are based on Finished Consultant Episodes (FCEs). An FCE is a completed period of care of a patient using an NHS hospital bed, under one consultant within one health care provider (an NHS Trust or a Directly Managed Unit). If a patient is transferred from one consultant to another, even if this is within the same provider, the episode ends and another one begins. The transfer of a patient from one hospital to another with the same consultant and within the same provider does not end the episode. Healthy live born babies are included. Data for Wales, Scotland and Northern Ireland are based on a system which counts a patient transferring from one hospital to another, with the same consultant, as a discharge and excludes new born babies. Additionally, data for Scotland include patients transferred from one consultant to another within the same hospital, provided there is a change of specialty. Deaths are included in all four countries.

A day case is a person who comes for investigation, treatment or operation under clinical supervision on a planned non-resident basis and who occupies a bed for part or all of that day.

An out-patient is defined as a person attending an out-patients' department for treatment or advice. A new out-patient is one whose first attendance of a continuous series (or single attendance where relevant) at a clinical out-patient department for the same course of treatment falls within the period under review. Each out-patient attendance of a course or series is included in the year in which the attendance occurred. Persons attending more than one department are counted in each department.

Table 7.24 Health Authority expenditure

The functional analysis is derived from the Authorities' annual accounts. Brief details of the expenditure covered by the headings are as follows:

Purchase of health care: includes all expenditure on patient care and related services including ambulance services, research and development, undergraduate medical facilities and other training costs.

Other services: includes the Emergency Bed service, planning and set-up costs of shadow NHS Trusts, registration and inspection of nursing homes, grants not related to the purchase of contracted health care and related services, resource management, Regional Health Authorities' expenditure on education and training, and Community Health Councils which were introduced on 1 April 1974 as part of the reorganised NHS.

Headquarters administration: the expenditure incurred in administering the health service at regional and district levels including office accommodation costs, etc.

Capital additions: shows the cost of new buildings and improvements to health service properties, the initial equipment of these new buildings and the purchase of additional sites. It also includes certain other additional items of equipment.

Table 7.25 Health Authority Staff

Whole-time equivalents are the number of whole-time staff plus the total hours or sessions per week contracted by part-time staff divided by the number of hours or sessions in the appropriate standard working week.

The main NHS staff groups are nursing and midwifery, professional and technical, professions allied to medicine, scientific and professional, maintenance and works, ancillary, administrative and clerical, general and senior managers, ambulance, medical and dental and other practitioners.

The number of staff employed by the NHS is affected by the phased transfer of basic nursing training to the higher education sector. To give a consistent time series, the figures for NHS staff in Wales and Scotland have been revised to exclude all nurses in training from the totals and consequently they are not comparable with figures published in earlier editions. Nor are they comparable with the figures for England and Northern Ireland which have not been revised to take account of this change in classification

England totals include staff in Special Health Authorities for London post graduate teaching hospitals, Dental Estimates Board, Prescription Pricing Authority and Family Practitioner Committees (directly employed staff only). From 1987 other statutory Authorities are included, eg Public Health Laboratory Service.

Medical and dental staff included are those holding permanent paid (whole-time, part-time and part-time sessional) and/or honorary appointments in NHS hospitals and Community Health Services. Figures now include clinical assistants and hospital practitioners; these were excluded in the overall figure in previous years. Pharmacists in General Pharmaceutical Services are excluded. Occasional sessional staff in Community Health Medical and Dental Services for whom no whole-time equivalent is collected are not included. The whole-time equivalent of staff holding appointments with more than one region is included in the appropriate region.

Table 7.27 General Practitioners

An unrestricted principal is a medical practitioner who provides the full range of general medical services and whose list is not limited to any particular group or persons. Doctors may also practise in the general medical services as restricted principals, assistants, associates or trainees.

CHAPTER 8: LIVING STANDARDS

Comparability of earnings statistics

Earnings statistics shown in this and the labour market sections are not comparable owing to differences in the coverage of the surveys, differences in classifying individuals to regions and different levels of reliability of the regional data. The basis of the surveys differ, in that the Survey of Personal Incomes is a sample of administrative records, the Family Expenditure Survey is a sample of households and the New Earnings Survey is a sample of employees. The administrative and household surveys are classified according to regions of residence while the surveys of employees and firms are classified according to the region of work place. The reliability depends partly upon the size of the sample and response rates. Different surveys will have their own sources of bias which will affect the reliability of their results.

Tables 8.1 and 8.2 Household income

The 1980-1981 and 1993 figures for income (Table 8.1) cannot be directly compared, following the introduction in 1982 of the Housing Benefit Scheme. From 1984, housing expenditure is shown on a strictly net basis; the element of housing benefit is eliminated from the figures in addition to the exclusion of other rent and rates rebates and rent allowances. The housing benefit component has also been excluded from total recorded household income.

These tables contain results from the Family Expenditure Survey. The survey covers all types of private households in the United Kingdom. It is a continuous sample survey of about 10,000 households per year, of which around 70 per cent co-operate. The available evidence suggests that co-operation is less likely in older households, households where the head is self-employed, those without children and higher income households. In Greater London response is noticeably lower than in other areas. Data for Northern Ireland for 1993 are calculated from an enhanced sample which enables detailed analyses within the region and to reduce the possibility of sampling errors; however, for consolidation into UK figures the standard sample is used.

Results of this survey are published annually in the FES report *Family Spending* (HMSO), together with a full list of definitions and items on which information is collected.

A household comprises one person living alone or a group of people living at the same address having common housekeeping. The members of a household are not necessarily related by blood or marriage. As the survey covers only private households, people living in hostels, hotels, boarding houses or institutions are excluded.

Gross household income is the aggregate of the gross incomes of the individual members of the household before deduction of income tax, national insurance contributions and any other deductions at source. Income thus defined excludes housing benefit; money received by one member from another member of the household; withdrawals of savings, receipts from maturing insurance policies, proceeds from the sale of financial and other assets (eg cars, furniture, houses, etc.); winnings from betting, lump sum gratuities and windfalls such as legacies; the value of income in kind, including the value of goods received free, of meal vouchers, and of bills paid by someone who is not a member of the household.

Tables 8.3 and 8.6 Family Resources Survey (FRS)

The Family Resources Survey (FRS) is a new continuous survey of over 26,000 private households in Great Britain. As with any survey, results are subject to sampling errors. In addition, there is the possibility of bias, firstly because not everyone approached agreed to take part, and secondly because some information may be incorrectly reported. The survey has been weighted to compensate for regional differences in response rates. Results from the first full year of the survey are published in the report *Family Resources Survey Great Britain 1993/94*, available from the Department of Social Security. Available evidence suggests particular problems of misreporting certain types of benefit, such as the under-reporting of income support, where respondents have stated that all money received comes from a single benefit, eg retirement pension, unemployment benefit, sickness benefit.

A household comprises a single person or a group of people who have the address as their only main residence and who either share one meal a day or share the living accommodation.

Tables 8.4 and 8.5 Survey of Personal Incomes

The Survey of Personal Incomes uses a sample of around 80 thousand cases drawn from all individuals for whom income tax records are held by the Inland Revenue: not all are taxpayers -about 7 per cent do not pay tax because the operation of personal reliefs and allowances removes them from liability. The data in Table 8.4 relate to individuals whose income over the year amounted to the threshold for operation of Pay-As-You-Earn (£3,445 in 1992-93) or more. Below this threshold, coverage of incomes is incomplete in tax records. A more complete description of the survey appears in *Inland Revenue Statistics*.

Table 8.4 Distribution of income liable to assessment for tax

The income shown is that liable to assessment in the tax year. For most incomes this is the amount earned or receivable in that year, but for business profits and professional earnings the assessments are normally based on the amount of income arising in the trading account ending in the previous year. Those types of income that were specifically exempt from tax eg certain social security benefits are excluded.

Incomes are allocated to regions according to the place of residence of the recipient, except for the self-employed, where allocation is according to the business address. For many self-employed people home address and business address are the same, and for the majority the region will correspond.

The table classifies incomes by range of total income. This is defined as gross income, whether earned or unearned, including estimates of employees' superannuation contributions, but after deducting employment expenses, losses, capital allowances, and any expenses allowable as a deduction from gross income from lettings or overseas investment income. Superannuation contributions have been estimated and distributed among earners in the Survey of Personal Incomes consistently with information about numbers contracted in or out of the State Earnings Related Pension Scheme and the proportion of their earnings contribution. The coverage of unearned income also includes estimates of that part of the investment income (whose liability to tax at basic rate has been satisfied at source) not known to tax offices.

Sampling errors need to be borne in mind when interpreting small differences in income distributions between regions.

Table 8.5 Income tax payable

Income tax is calculated as the liability for the income tax year, regardless of when the tax may have been paid or how it was collected.

The income tax liability shown here is calculated from the individual's total income, including tax credits on dividends, and interest received after the deduction of tax grossed up at the basic rate. From total income is deducted allowable reliefs etc, and personal allowances in order to calculate the tax liability, but not relief given at source on mortgage interest, which cannot be estimated with sufficient reliability at regional level.

A lower rate of tax of 20 per cent was introduced in 1992-93. The estimate of the total number of individuals liable to tax is shown under the 'Lower rate' heading as all taxpayers pay some tax at this rate. The amount of tax shown is the tax paid at the 20 per cent rate by all taxpayers.

The numbers shown under the 'Basic rate' heading include taxpayers liable at higher rate and the amount of tax includes the component of tax paid at basic rate for higher rate taxpayers' taxable income above the basic rate threshold. The amount of tax shown under the 'Tax in excess of basic rate' heading is the amount of tax paid above the basic rate (corresponding to the 15 per cent excess over the basic rate for 1992-93) for higher rate taxpayers' taxable income above the basic rate tax threshold.

Table 8.6 Households in receipt of benefits

See notes on Family Resources Survey above.

Income Support replaced Supplementary Benefit in April 1988. It is a non-contributory benefit payable to people working less than 16 hours a week, whose incomes are below the levels (called 'applicable amounts') laid down by Parliament. The applicable amounts generally consist of personal allowances for members of the family and premiums for families, lone parents, pensioners, the disabled and carers. Amounts for certain housing costs (mainly mortgage interest) are also included.

Housing benefit is administered by local authorities. People are eligible only if they are liable to pay rent in respect of the dwelling they occupy as their home. Couples are treated as a single benefit unit. The amount of benefit depends on eligible rent, income, deductions in respect of any non-dependants and the applicable amount. 'Eligible rent' is the amount of a tenant's rental liability which can be met by Housing Benefit. Payments made by owner-occupiers do not count. Deductions are made for service charges in rent which relate to personal needs.

Council tax benefit is also administered by local authorities. Generally, it mirrors the Housing Benefit scheme in the calculation of the claimants' applicable amount, resources and deductions in respect of any non-dependants.

Unemployment benefit (UB) is payable to those who are unemployed, available for, and actively seeking employment, satisfy conditions for the receipt of UB and are free from certain grounds for disallowance or disqualification; for example, disqualification for up to 26 weeks may be imposed if any former employment was left voluntarily without just cause, or employment has been refused without good reason. In National Insurance contribution conditions are satisfied in full, UB is normally payable at a standard rate with additional components for dependants.

Retirement pensions are paid to men aged 65 or over and women aged 60 or over who have paid sufficient National Insurance contributions over their working life. A wife who cannot claim a pension in her own right may qualify on the basis of her husband's contributions. The table excludes non-contributory pensions which are paid to people aged 80 or over who did not qualify for the standard retirement pension, or whose pension was lower than the non-contributory rate.

Sickness and Invalidity Benefit: these benefits are generally paid to claimants who are certified incapable of work and satisfy the contribution conditions for the benefits. The figures do not include expenditure for Statutory Sick Pay (SSP). Invalidity Benefit is generally payable after there has been an entitlement to SSP or Sickness Benefit for 28 weeks in a period of interruption of employment.

Industrial injuries includes pensions, gratuities and sundry allowances for disablement and specified deaths arising from industrial causes.

Child Benefit is normally paid for children up to the age of 16. Benefit may continue up to age 19 for children in full-time education up to 'A' level standard. 16 and 17 year olds are also eligible for a short period after leaving school.

A brief description of the main features of the various benefits paid in Great Britain is set out in *Social Security Statistics* (published annually by HMSO). Detailed information on benefits paid in Northern Ireland is contained in *Northern Ireland Annual Abstract of Statistics* and *Northern Ireland Social Security Statistics*.

Table 8.11 Family Expenditure Surveys

This table contains results from the Family Expenditure Survey for 1993. Some details of the survey are given in the notes to Tables 8.1 and 8.2.

Expenditure excludes savings or investments (eg life assurance premiums), income tax payments, National Insurance contributions, housing benefit and mortgage and other payments for the purchase of, or major additions to, dwellings.

Housing expenditure of households living in owner-occupied dwellings consists of the payments by these households for rates/community charge (council tax from April 1993), water, ground rent, etc., insurance of the structure and mortgage interest payments. Mortgage capital repayments and amounts paid for the outright purchase of the dwelling or for major structural alterations are not included as housing expenditure.

Estimates of household expenditure on a few items are below those which might be expected by comparison with other sources eg alcoholic drink, tobacco and, to a lesser extent, confectionery and ice cream.

Tables 8.12 and 8.13 National Food Survey

This is a continuous sample survey of about 7-8,000 households per year in Great Britain, where a record is kept of the type, quantity and amount spent on foods entering the home during one week. Nutritional values are also calculated from the information collected.

Detailed survey results and definitions are published by HMSO in an annual report *National Food Survey* (previously *Household Food Consumption and Expenditure*).

Tables 8.14 and 8.17 General Household Survey

Figures for Great Britain are taken from the General Household Survey (GHS), which is a continuous survey of about 13,000 addresses per year. An effective sample of some 12,000 private households is obtained, of which 83 per cent co-operated for 1992 and 82 per cent for 1993.

Results for Northern Ireland for 1980-1981 are taken from the expanded sample of households taken for the Family Expenditure Survey (FES). Data for 1992-1993 are derived from the Continuous Household Survey (CHS).

Until 1981 the GHS and FES used the same definition of a household (see notes to Tables 8.1 and 8.2). In 1981 a new definition was adopted in the GHS in order to improve comparability with the Census of Population. From 1981 a household is 'a single person or a group of people who have the address as their only or main residence and who either share one meal a day or share the living accommodation' (not just a kitchen or bathroom). This is also the definition used in the Continuous Household Survey.

CHAPTER 9: CRIME AND JUSTICE

There are three main reasons why the recorded crime figures for Scotland and the notifiable offences figures for England and Wales and for Northern Ireland cannot be compared. They are as follows:

i. Differences in the *legal systems*. The legal system operating in Scotland differs from that in England and Wales and in Northern Ireland.

ii. Differences in *classification*. The offences included within the recorded crime category and the notifiable offence category vary significantly. For example, simple possession of a controlled drug is included in the Scottish figures but excluded from notifiable offences figures in England and Wales and Northern Ireland.

iii. *Counting rules*. In Scotland each individual offence occurring within an incident is recorded whereas in England and Wales and in Northern Ireland a principal offence rule is applied (in general) ie only the main offence is counted.

Table 9.1, Chart 9.3 - Table 9.9

The figures are compiled from police returns to the Home Office and The Scottish Office Home and Health Department and from statistics supplied by the Royal Ulster Constabulary in Northern Ireland. Figures for notifiable offences recorded by the police in England and Wales and Northern Ireland for 1980 onward are not comparable with those for earlier years given in earlier volumes because of new counting rules introduced at the beginning of 1980. Similarly figures for recorded crimes in Scotland for 1980 are not comparable with earlier data due to changes in both classification and counting rules.

In England and Wales and in Northern Ireland, indictable offences cover those offences which must or may be tried by jury in the Crown Court and include the more serious offences. Summary offences are those for which a defendant would normally be tried at a magistrates' court and are generally less serious - the majority of motoring offences fall into this category. In general in Northern Ireland non-indictable offences are dealt with at a magistrate's court. Some indictable offences can also be dealt with there.

In Scotland the term 'crimes' is generally used for the more serious criminal acts (roughly equivalent to indictable offences); the less serious are termed 'offences', although the term 'offence' is also used in relation to serious breaches of criminal law. The majority of cases are tried summarily (without a jury) in the Sheriff or District Court, while the more serious cases are tried in the Sheriff Court under solemn procedure (with a jury), or in the High Court.

Cautions - if a person admits to committing an offence he may be given a formal police caution by, or on the instruction of, a senior police officer as an alternative to court proceedings. The figures exclude informal warnings given by the police, written warnings issued for motoring offences and warnings given by non-police bodies eg a department store in the case of shoplifting. Cautions by the police are not available in Scotland, but warnings may be given by the Procurator Fiscal.

Tables 9.2 and 9.15 British Crime Survey and Scottish Crime Survey

The British Crime Survey (BCS) has been conducted by the Home Office Research and Planning Unit in 1982, 1984, 1988, 1992 and 1994, each survey measuring experience of crimes in the previous year, whether or not reported to the police. The 1994 survey was based on a nationally representative sample of about 14,500 people aged 16 or over in England and Wales. They were sampled from the Postcode Address File - a listing of all postal delivery points. The response rate was 77 per cent.

Scotland was included in the sweeps of the British Crime Survey carried out in 1982 and 1988, but not in 1984 or 1992. The Scottish Office ran a separate Scottish Crime Survey in 1993 which was based on a representative sample of 5,000 respondents. The addresses for the sample were drawn at random from the Postcode Address File and, for the first time the 1993 SCS covered the whole of mainland Scotland and the larger islands. In previous years only southern and central Scotland were sampled. The response rate in 1993 was 77 per cent.

In each of the surveys, respondents answered questions about offences against their household (such as theft or damage of household property) and about offences against them personally (such as assault or robbery). However, none of the surveys provides a complete count of crime. Many offence types cannot be covered in a household survey (eg shoplifting, fraud or drug offences). Crime surveys are also prone to various forms of error, mainly to do with the difficulty of ensuring that samples are representative, the frailty of respondents' memories, their reticence to talk about their experiences as victims, and their failure to realise an incident is relevant to the survey.

Chart 9.3 and Table 9.4 Clear-up rates

In England and Wales and in Northern Ireland offences recorded by the police as having been cleared up include offences for which persons have been charged, summonsed or cautioned, those admitted and taken into consideration when persons are tried for other offences, and those admitted by prisoners who have been sentenced for other offences (except in Northern Ireland). In Scotland a crime or offence is regarded as cleared-up if one or more offenders is apprehended, cited, warned or traced for it.

The clear-up rate is the ratio of offences cleared up in the year to offences recorded in the year. Some offences cleared up may relate to offences recorded in previous years. There is considerable variation between police forces in the way in which these different categories of clear-up are used. The Metropolitan Police District and the City of London have lower rates than other forces due to their high use of the primary categories of clear-up (charge, summons and caution). As a measure of police performance the clear-up rate has its limitations and it is not necessarily well correlated with other measures.

Tables 9.8 and 9.9 Persons found guilty/against whom a charge proved

The power to partly suspend certain sentences of imprisonment in England and Wales was abolished on 1 October 1992 following the implementation of Section 5 of the *Criminal Justice Act 1991*. As a result, the term 'suspended sentence' is known as 'fully suspended sentence' and 'immediate custody' includes unsuspended sentences of imprisonment and sentence to detention in a young offender institution. Fully and partly suspended sentences are not available to Scottish courts; partly suspended sentences are not available to courts in Northern Ireland.

Table 9.10 Seizure of controlled drugs

The figures in this table, which are compiled from returns to the Home Office, relate to seizures made by the police, officials of HM Customs and Excise and other bodies such as the Port of London Authority, and to drugs controlled under the *Misuse of Drugs Act 1971*. The act divides drugs into three categories according to their harmfulness. A full list of drugs in each category is given in Schedule 2 to the *Misuse of Drugs Act 1971* as amended by Orders in council.

Table 9.12 Driving etc after consuming alcohol or drugs

Driving etc includes all drink/drug related driving offences ie driving, attempting, in charge of, failing to provide a specimen etc.

CHAPTER 10: TRANSPORT

Tables 10.3 and 10.4 Road accidents/casualties

An accident is one involving personal injury occurring on the public highway (including footways) in which a road vehicle is involved and which becomes known to the police within 30 days. The vehicle need not be moving and it need not be in collision with anything.

Persons killed are those who sustained injuries which caused death less than 30 days after the accident.

A serious injury is one for which a person is detained in hospital as an in-patient, or any of the following injuries whether or not they are detained in hospital: fractures, concussion, internal injuries, crushing, severe cuts and lacerations, severe general shock requiring medical treatment, injuries causing death 30 or more days after the accident.

There are many reasons why accident rates per head and per vehicle vary between regions. They will be influenced by the mix of pedestrian and vehicle traffic within each region. High accident rates per vehicle may reflect a relatively low vehicle ownership rate and a high level of pedestrian activity and vice versa.

In addition, an area that 'imports' large numbers of visitors or commuters will have a relatively high proportion of accidents related to vehicles or drivers from outside the area. A rural area with low population density but high road mileage can be expected, other things being equal, to have lower than average accident rates.

Tables 10.5, 10.7, 10.8 and Chart 10.6 National Travel Survey

The National Travel Survey (NTS) is the only comprehensive national source of travel information for Great Britain which links different kinds of travel with the characteristics of travellers and their families. Since July 1988, the NTS has been conducted on a small scale continuous basis. The last of the previous ad hoc surveys was carried out in 1985/86.

From about 3,500 households in Great Britain each year, every member provides personal information (eg age, gender, working status, driving licence, season ticket) and details of journeys carried out in a sample week, including purpose of journey, method of travel, time of day, length, duration, and cost of any tickets bought.

Travel included in the NTS covers all journeys by GB residents within Great Britain for personal reasons, including travel in the course of work, which involves a person moving from one place to another in order to reach a destination. Travel information is recorded at two levels for multi-stage journeys: journey and stage.

A *journey* is defined as a one-way course of travel having a single main purpose. It is the basic unit of personal travel in the survey. A round trip is split into two journeys, with the first ending at a convenient point about half way round as a notional stopping point for the outward destination and return origin.

A *stage* is that portion of a journey defined by the use of a specific method of transport or of a specific ticket (a new stage being defined if either the mode or ticket changes).

CHAPTER 11: ENVIRONMENT

Table 11.2 Rivers and canals: by quality

In England and Wales river quality has most recently been assessed using a new system of classification, the General Quality Assessment (GQA) Scheme, which has been developed and introduced by the National Rivers Authority (NRA). This provides a more rigorous and objective method, than was used in the past, for assessing the basic chemical quality of rivers and canals based on three determinants - dissolved oxygen, biochemical oxygen demand (BOD), and ammoniacal nitrogen. The GQA and the previously used National Water Council (NWC) classification system are not directly comparable for a number of reasons. The main reasons are that the 90 percentile standards of the GQA are not a direct mathematical translation of the 95 percentile standards of the NWC, and the subjective criteria of the NWC do not appear in the GQA. The GQA consistently uses three years of data rather than data for a single year, but some regions in the past also used three years' data for NWC. The changes provided by the GQA result in an estimated 35 per cent improvement in precision of classification over the NWC system.

The new GQA Scheme has been used to assess chemical quality of rivers and canals across England and Wales where sufficient data are available for the years 1988-1990 and 1991-1993. The GQA grades river stretches into six categories (A-F) of chemical quality and these in turn have been grouped into four broader groups - good (classes A and B), fair (classes C and D), poor (class E), and bad (class F). While these groups bear the same names as the categories used in the NWC system, they are not comparable.

Water quality in Northern Ireland is assessed using the four categories of the NWC classification system. In Scotland the chemical quality is also assessed into four classes, unpolluted, fairly good, poor, and grossly polluted. Both these systems are not directly comparable with each other nor are they comparable with the GQA system now used in England and Wales.

Table 11.3 Water pollution incidents

The National Rivers Authority defines three categories of pollution incidents:

Category 1

A 'major' incident involving one or more of the following:
a) potential or actual persistent effect on water quality or aquatic life;
b) closure of potable water, industrial or agricultural abstraction necessary;
c) extensive fish kill;
d) excessive breaches of consent conditions;
e) extensive remedial measures necessary;
f) major effect on amenity value.

Category 2

A 'significant' pollution which involves one or more of the following:

a) notification to abstractors necessary;
b) significant fish kill;
c) measurable effect on invertebrate life;
d) water unfit for stock;
e) bed of watercourse contaminated;
f) amenity value to the public, owners or users reduced by odour or appearance.

Category 3

'Minor suspected or probable' pollution which, on investigation, proves unlikely to be capable of substantiation or to have no notable effect.

Chart 11.6 Emissions of sulphur dioxide and nitrogen oxide

The source of the data in Chart 11.6 is the Chemical Release Inventory (CRI). The CRI contains details of releases of polluting substances from industrial processes subject to integrated pollution control by Her Majesty's Inspectorate of Pollution under Part I of the *Environmental Protection Act 1990*. These processes are detailed in the *Environmental Protection (Prescribed Processes and Substances) Regulations 1991* as amended. Integrated pollution control does not cover all polluting processes in the United Kingdom. It is intended to apply to the most potentially polluting or technologically complex industrial and other processes throughout England and Wales, which involve significant releases to one or more environmental medium, or which make a significant contribution to cross-media pollution. The inventory is still evolving and hence data are not yet available for all counties. It will be 1996 before all scheduled processes are brought within integrated pollution control and contribute to the CRI.

The CRI does not cover information relating to the local authority air pollution control system under Part I of the *Environmental Protection Act 1990*. Nor does it estimate the impact of other sources of pollution, for example transport, agriculture and domestic sources.

Chart 11.10 Protected areas

'Ramsar sites': wetland sites of international importance, particularly for water fowl, designated under the Ramsar Convention in 1971. Sites in the United Kingdom are protected by Sites of Special Scientific Interest (SSSI) status.

CHAPTER 12: REGIONAL ACCOUNTS

The sources and methodology used to compile the regional accounts are given in a booklet in the *Studies in Official Statistics series* (HMSO), No 31, *Regional Accounts*, and more recently in the Eurostat publication *Methods used to compile regional accounts*.

Tables 12.1-12.3 and Chart 12.4 Gross Domestic Product (GDP)

Regional estimates of GDP are compiled as the sum of factor incomes, ie incomes earned by residents, whether corporate or individual, from the production of goods and services. This approach breaks the total down into four components: income from employment; income from self-employment; profits and surpluses; and rent (including the imputed charge for consumption of non-trading capital). Stock appreciation is deducted from the sum of total domestic income to give GDP. The figures for all regions are adjusted to sum to the national totals as published in *United Kingdom National Accounts 1994* (HMSO).

In order to accommodate the offshore oil and gas extraction industry in the regional accounts, a region known as the Continental Shelf is included. GDP for this region includes only profits and stock appreciation related to the offshore activities of UK and foreign contractors. The allocation of income from employment is not altered by the Continental Shelf region since throughout the regional accounts this is allocated according to the region of residence of the employee.

Chart 12.6 and Tables 12.10 and 12.11 Consumers' expenditure

Consumers' expenditure measures expenditure by households and private non-profit-making bodies resident in a region. Estimates are based mainly on the Family Expenditure Survey and are subject to sampling error and should be used with caution.

Up-to-date information on the data can be obtained from *Economic Trends*, No. 494, December 1994 and 499, May 1995 (HMSO).

Tables 12.8 and 12.9 Personal incomes

Total personal income is an estimate of the income of the personal sector including households, other individuals and non-profit-making bodies serving persons. Total personal incomes include the wages and salaries of employees plus employers' contributions; self-employment income; rent, dividends, and net interest received by the personal sector; National Insurance benefits and other current grants from general government; and the imputed charge for consumption of private non-profit-making bodies. Figures are also shown of personal disposable income, which is the income remaining

Central Statistical Office

KEEPING TRACK OF THE ECONOMY

.....is easier with Economic Trends, the Central Statistical Office flagship monthly which brings together all the key economic indicators.

At £19.95 it is an essential reference guide for anyone who needs to keep abreast of economic statistics.

- stocks
- employment
- prices
- government finance
- investment
- earnings
- trade
- bank lending

Statistics and graphs cover these and many other areas for the last 5 years or more.

There is also a monthly analysis of indicators and the business cycle over the last 20 years, surveys of international and regional economic indicators and regular articles offering in-depth commentary on important areas of economic statistics.

A companion quarterly publication, *UK Economic Accounts*, price £18.00 net, offers up-to-date analysis of the national and financial accounts and the balance of payments.

From HMSO and through good booksellers.

Economic Trends

Published for the Central Statistical Office by HMSO.
Price £19.95 net
ISSN 0013 0400
(Annual subscription including the Annual Supplement,
UK Economic Accounts and postage £320)